SELF CONDEMNED

WYNDHAM LEWIS

SELF
CONDEMNED

HENRY REGNERY COMPANY
CHICAGO, 1955

Printed and Bound in Great Britain by Butler & Tanner Ltd., Frome and London

CONTENTS

Part One—THE RESIGNATION

CHAPTER   PAGE

I THAT OTHER MAN AGAIN   3

II 'YOU ARE NOT BY ANY CHANCE A FOOL, MY SON?'   15

III A TAXI-RIDE AND A DINNER AT 'LA TOULOUSAINE'   27

IV HESTER HEARS THE NEWS   33

V IDEALISM RECOGNIZED   45

VI HOW VICTOR SAW THE MATTER   64

VII ROTTER   76

VIII AN AGREEABLE DINNER-PARTY   106

IX HOW MUCH CAN WE AFFORD TO JETTISON?   133

X THE PASSENGER WHO WORE THE RIBBON OF THE LEGION OF HONOUR   146

Part Two—THE ROOM

XI TWENTY-FIVE FEET BY TWELVE   169

XII THE HOTEL AND WHAT CONTAINS THE HOTEL   189

XIII AFFIE AND THE 'ROACHES   197

XIV THE PATRONESS OF ROTTEN JANITORS   203

XV THE MARVELS OF MOMACO   210

XVI THE WORD 'BRUTE' IS NOT LIKED IN THE BEVERAGE ROOM   224

XVII VOWS OF HARDSHIP   236

XVIII MR. FURBER   247

XIX THE JANITORS   263

XX THE PRIVATE LIFE OF BILL MURDOCH   271

XXI THE MICROCOSM BECOMES AN ICEBERG   277

XXII HAD I THE WINGS OF THE MORNING   293

83334

Part Three—AFTER THE FIRE

CHAPTER		PAGE
XXIII	MOMACO OR LONDON?	307
XXIV	THE PARTY OF SUPERMAN	312
XXV	DINNER AT THE MCKENZIES	328
XXVI	RENÉ BECOMES A COLUMNIST	339
XXVII	THE BLACK FLY	343
XXVIII	A NEW BOOK ON THE STOCKS	349
XXIX	A CHAIR AT MOMACO	359
XXX	POLICE HEADQUARTERS	365
XXXI	THE WHITE SILENCE	372
XXXII	THE COLLEGE OF THE SACRED HEART	379
XXXIII	RETURN TO THE NORMAL	389
XXXIV	THE CEMETERY OF SHELLS	398

Part One

THE RESIGNATION

CHAPTER I

That Other Man Again

'IF you call five *six*, you embarrass five, seeing that people then are going to expect of him the refulgence of six.' He looked up, coughed and continued. 'If you rename six *seven*, far more bustle is expected of him. I have been speaking, naturally, of the ante-meridian. In the post-meridian it is the reverse. Put your clock on, call five-thirty six-thirty, and people will exclaim how much more light six-thirty has. You push back the night. If you call Clara Stella, people would say how dull Stella has become, or how bright Clara has become. Five and six, post-meridian, are like Stella and Clara. See?'

'The little girl sees,' Essie Harding said.

From the other side of the breakfast table Essie had stared at her husband under a wide clear brow, with blankly bold, large, wide-open eyes. It was a mature face, the natural wide-openness not disagreeably exploited: the remains of the child-mind were encouraged to appear in the clear depths of the grey-blue. But as he spoke of five and six, she thought, rather, of forty-seven and of thirty-seven (but not of thirty-four and twenty-four). She renamed ages: as her husband spoke of renaming the hours of daybreak and the sunset, she shuffled about the years of life, calling thirty forty and vice versa. As to the explanation of what occurred when you put the clock forward or backward, Essie did not follow or would not follow. Allergic to learning, as are many children, for her the teacher was a life-long enemy. As she had stared, wide-eyed and with her mind a wilful blank, at her mistress as a child, her eyes hung open like a gaping mouth; and the fact that her husband was a professional teacher, a trained imparter of knowledge, caused Essie all the more readily to drop back into the mulish trance of childhood; expertly unreceptive she stripped her large defiant eyes of all intelligence, and left them there staring

A* 3

at his face, while her moist red lips were parted as she slowly raised a fresh spoonful of sugared porridge.

'Have I made it clear what it means to put the clock on?' he enquired, with no expectancy that the reply would be that he had.

'No.' She shook her head.

He laughed.

'You are lazy,' he told her. 'Had you been a boy, and had you lived a few decades ago, your bottom would have been furrowed up by the cane; *fessée* after *fessée* would have been your lot.'

She slowly sucked the spoon, and there was substituted in her eyes for the aggressive blank, an amorous and inviting light, as he had expected.

Deliberately he had referred to the caned posterior, as if it were a bait the other way round in order to provoke the re-action in question. He looked at her curiously. For a moment he almost embarked upon a didactic account of the periodic nature of sexual desire in the animal kingdom. Instead he enquired, 'Why this sudden interest in daylight saving?'

'Rosemary . . .'

'Ah. I see. Just repeat what I said about calling five six. She is a bright child, you will not have to interpret.'

Essie laughed. 'Any more questions of that sort and I shall explain that I am dumb, and that she must wait until Gladys gets well. She has one of those enquiring minds. I think she is an awful little brat, between ourselves.'

'Her mama has an enquiring mind, too. It's a beastly thing to have, I agree.'

He lighted a cigarette and watched her almost furtively for a few seconds. Then he placed his hand upon an open letter at the side of his plate.

'What shall we do about Richard?'

'When does he want us to go?'

'About the tenth, I think, of next month. How do you feel about it?'

She sat with her hands behind her head, staring silently at the wall behind his head. Neither spoke for some minutes.

'I do not feel terribly like the idyllic landscape of England just at present,' he observed. 'Do you feel like going down yourself for a week-end? It would do you good.'

'Not by myself; because I look countryfied, they would want me to milk their cow and draw water from their well. I came back last time from their place thoroughly worn out.'

'Right. Anything would be better than bucolic England just at present, for me. I must write him.'

A bell in the little hallway exploded into hysterical life. A door, from behind which the hum of a vacuum cleaner had for some time been heard, opened, and one of London's Dickensian charladies stood there without moving for a moment, a small bird-like figure with a white crest, which bobbed backwards and forwards, and an irascible eye. This eye was directed across the breakfast table towards the front door. The charlady propelled herself around the room, head shooting in and out, and darted at the front door, ready for battle. Her small raucous challenge was heard, 'What is it? Ooder ye want?' The landing was extremely dark, and Mrs. Harradson never could see who her enemy was. In the present case a telegram appeared out of the shadows impolitely near her little beak. She seized it, and, with considerable suspicion, holding it between thumb and forefinger, she re-entered the breakfast room.

'It's for you Professor Harding, sir.'

'Thank you, Mrs. Harradson.'

'Shall I tell 'im there's an answer, sir?'

Harding opened the telegram, and shook his head. 'No, thank you, no reply.'

Having banged the front door upon the uniformed intruder, Mrs. Harradson with her violent gait re-entered the bedroom, from whence she had come, and almost on the instant there came the angry hum of the indignant vacuum.

It was a large, gaunt and very dark room in which they sat. It was lighted only by one window in the extreme corner, opening on to the central air-hole. Between the window and the front door was a shadowy dresser, and a minute water-closet nestled indelicately in the small hall, the first thing to confront the visitor. The room in which the Hardings sat was eccentrically withdrawn from the light of day, as though London had been Cadiz: had it not been for the electric light they could not have seen to eat. For more than half the year no more than a token daylight found its way through the corner window. 'The house was designed by an imbecile or an Eskimo,' Harding would say. 'Why do we stop here?' To which Essie would reply, 'That I have often wondered myself.' It was an incomplete cylinder, for its central air-hole was little more than a semi-circle, the back yard of another house completing it on one side. Opening off this cavernous chamber (dining-room, kitchen, 'store-room', all in one) were a bedroom and sitting-room. Both of these were, in the ordinary way, day-lit: but because of the tower-like design of the building, they had a somewhat eccentric shape.

Rainfall was occurring, a thunderstorm threatening London, and the immured Hardings felt the need of more light. René Harding sprang up to switch on a standing lamp.

'Another beastly day,' he said absentmindedly.

'From whom is the telegram?' Essie enquired.

'From Canada. It is from a colleague of mine with some information I required.'

Essie was looking at him, as if expecting the answer about the telegram to complete itself. Professor René Harding was tall, about five foot eleven with broad shoulders and such markedly narrow hips that the lower part of his jacket was inclined to flap. His beard did not crudely blot out his face, nesting his eyes in a blue-black bush or surrounding them with a disturbing red vegetation. It merely lengthened the face, and stylistically grained and striped it with a soft material not differing greatly from it in tone, reminiscent of the elegant stone hair which leaved, curled upon, and grooved the long French faces upon the west façade at Chartres. His eyes were of a brown to match the somewhat sallow skin. When he laughed, rather than bisecting his face laterally, he thrust forward his bristling mouth in what might be called the ho-ho-ho position, employed by the actor if he wishes to give the idea of something stiltedly primitive. Should it be one of an archaically masculine, bearded chorus of uncouth warriors that he has to represent, that is when he ho-ho-ho's (not ha-ha-ha's). René's eyes were at the cat-like angle, glittering out of a slit rather than, as with his wife, showing the eye in its full circular expansion. He was one of those men it is difficult to imagine without a beard: and who one felt was very handsome bearded, but did not feel sure about its being so becoming were he to be beardless.

Speaking generally, he was inclined to furrow up his forehead à la Descartes, and to assume half-recumbent attitudes by choice, rather than to sit erect.

These physical idiosyncrasies corresponded to an innate preference for the dressed rather than the undressed, even if the costume or the disguise was nothing more than hair. His wife was of course a born nudist; and he had recently, it is true, come to feel, especially at breakfast time, that he was in a nudist camp.

But this was a very abstracted man. He seldom saw his wife in full focus, but behind, or through, something else. He did not often *completely* withdraw himself from the intellectual problem he had in hand, when conversing with an intimate or even with a stranger. Inside him, he left simmering as it were, in the background of his mind, the dominant problem, in the way that a housewife reduces to a simmer something she has in hand, to leave her free for a short while for action elsewhere, in response to a sudden summons.

As he sat down he placed the telegram in his pocket and picked up the *Daily Express*. Filling himself a fresh cup of coffee he drank this in a long gulp. Replacing the cup in the saucer with *fracas* he continued to stare dully and angrily at the *Daily Express* headlines.

Monday, 15th May, 1939.

THE KING WILL BE TWO DAYS LATE
IT'S THAT OTHER MAN AGAIN
DUCE SAYS PEACE
'Nothing to Justify a War.'

Essie was still looking at him, and now she asked, 'What is in your paper, René?'

'It's that "Other Man Again",' he replied, almost mechanically, echoing the headlines. He looked up at her, his face wrinkled, with a dismally roguish smile. 'The German Chancellor, you know.'

'So I gathered,' Essie said, and slowly lowered her head to look at her own paper, the *Daily Telegraph*.

For about ten minutes, husband and wife read their papers without speaking. Rather abruptly Harding rose, wiped his moustache, and exclaimed, 'Are you going out to the shops, my dear?'

Hester Harding rose too.

'A little later, yes.'

'See if you can get me *The Times*, will you? Also the *Manchester Guardian*. I am going in to work now. If anyone should telephone, do not put them through.'

'No one?'

'No one at all!'

'All right,' said Essie. 'You look preoccupied. Is there anything in the papers you don't like?'

'A damn lot, but not more so than usual! I shall be through with what I have to do about one o'clock!'

They had rented the next-door flat, a one-room affair, the front doors facing one another across the dark landing. He was inserting his key in the opposite door, that of No. 7, as he was closing his own. This other flat, which he used as a study, was walled with books. There was a small desk at which he now seated himself hurriedly and drew the telegram out of his pocket.

For her part, Hester went into the room where Mrs. Harradson was still at work with the vacuum cleaner, a novelty she greatly appreciated.

'Oo, ma'am, Mrs. Harding, I didn't hear you, m'am,' said Mrs. Harradson jumping up and down, an excitable marionette, as she heard Essie's voice. She turned off the vacuum.

'What do you think that old wretch Hitler has done now, Mrs. Harradson?'

'Oo! I'm sure I don't know, m'am. What is it, m'am, the nasty ole man?'

'Yes, he's a horrid old beast. He says woman's place is in the kitchen. What do you say to that, Mrs. Harradson?'.

'Oo, 'e do do 'e, ma'am! What does that dirty ole German want to be givin' us orders for, where we oughter be, nasty ole man.'

'I don't know what their wives are doing. That is a man's country where women seem to have no rights at all. The men shave their heads in the most disgusting way; they don't mind *what* they look like. If my husband shaved his head I would sue for divorce on the spot!'

'Nasty ole man!' Mrs. Harradson barked: and it was not clear whether she was referring to Professor Harding or to 'That Other Man', except that her employer did not belong to that evil category, which she classified invariably as 'nasty ole men'.

After a little more desultory conversation about the political scene, the lot of women, and the arbitrary behaviour of men generally, especially those that rang the front-door bell, Essie strolled away into the sitting-room, the *Daily Telegraph* and an illustrated tabloid in her hand. She propped herself upon cushions on the settee and plunged into the tabloid. It was not long before she heard Mrs. Harradson at work in the large 'cooking' and 'eating' room; there was also a piano there and she could hear her dusting the keys. Essie read in the tabloid how a woman had gone into a neighbour's house about ten in the morning for a nice chat and had not returned till the afternoon. She discovered her two children both dead: they had swallowed all her aspirin tablets, which she had left by the side of her bed. Essie reflected how careless the lower classes were, and yawned. Mrs. Harradson's voice was heard in the next room, furiously apostrophizing someone as she scrubbed the sink.

'Nasty ole man—nasty ole *maaan*.' She heard 'maaan' repeated several times: it could be none other than Hitler, and Essie, smiling, got up and moved, with a smile still on her face, into the next room.

'Who are you talking about, Mrs. Harradson, Herr Hitler?'

'Not Hitler, not him!' Mrs. Harradson replied, after a
violent start at the sound of her employer's voice. 'It's that
Lucifer, nasty ole man. Walking the earth, nasty ole man!'
She scrubbed harder, as if to scrub him away.

Lucifer was a new one on Essie. *She* thought in terms of
Hitler and such minor devils. But Mrs. Harradson was a
devout catholic and she of course saw that the Führer was
nothing but a minion of Lucifer's.

Mrs. Harradson was a perpetual Punch and Judy show for
Essie. But also, in her way, she had become attached to this
little being as she would to a small disgruntled squirrel, had
she received so eccentric a gift. One of Essie's morning amuse-
ments, for instance, was to ask Mrs. Harradson to TIM it for
her on the telephone, to check the exact time. Mrs. Harradson
was always very diffident, polite and nervous while speaking
on the telephone. It was a piece of pagan music to which she
never grew used. The deference she exhibited on these occasions was quite unlike her usual behaviour. She would dial
TIM, in obedience to Essie's request, but when the voice began
saying, 'At the third stroke, it will be e-l-e-v-e-n forty-three
and ten seconds,' she began nodding, bowing and smiling into
the telephone, 'Yes, Miss, thank you, Miss. Yes, Miss, twenty
seconds. No, Miss, *thirty* seconds. Yes, Miss, thank you, Miss,
forty seconds—thank you, Miss,' a little confused and nervous
at the last at the continued affability of this young woman,
whose habit it was to say a different time whenever she spoke.
Essie was obliged literally to drag her away from the telephone. She became positively mesmerised and without this
intervention of her employer, might have stood there all day
bowing and smiling.

The house was run on a principle of extreme parsimony:
should the ball-valve in a lavatory cease to do its work a
shrivelled and diminutive plumber would, sooner or later,
appear, a certain Mr. Shotstone. Since the ball-valve was constantly in need of attention, the Hardings were very familiar
with Mr. Shotstone, and it was seldom that he failed to
diversify his professional visits in the following manner.
Indeed, with this difficulty of Mr. Shotstone's Essie was so
familiar that she took it as a matter of course when the

summons arrived. A hoarse whispered call would reach her
from the little lavatory in the hall. ' 'Ere, Missis, come 'ere.'
When she approached, finding him standing on the lavatory
seat, she would distinguish the words hissed hoarsely over
his shoulder—'Me truss is slipping—ask 'er to come'—Essie
would signal Mrs. Harradson and repeat the message. 'His
truss is slipping,' she would say. Mrs. Harradson would be
transfixed with indignation, her head would shoot in and out,
her white crest weirdly flashing. In a high-pitched staccato
grunt came the usual sounds, 'Oo . . . disgusting . . . what,
Madam? . . . What? . . . Did 'ee? . . . Did 'ee say that? . . .
nasty ole man. . . .' Shooting her head in and out, she hurtled
across to the water closet. There her sharp liquid grunts could
be heard as she adjusted the truss. In a few minutes she
returned. Mr. Shotstone was a prostatic elder and at times
literally stank the lavatory out. Herself slightly impregnated
with this disagreeable odour, Mrs. Harradson shot angry
glances over her shoulder in the direction of the hall and
continued to snarl, 'Dirty ole man—dirty ole man.'

Harding showed what can only be described as apprehension where the charlady was concerned. It was as though he
had been called upon to enjoy the antics of a demented
person. He would join Essie in explosions of mirth, sometimes
in spite of himself, but on the whole he was uneasy.

If Mrs. Harradson was a source of cheap amusement for
Hester, she had been born, as it were, with the house in which
they lived: the House that Jack Built, as René called it. She
was as if she had been one of its bricks, cemented into it.
And if she was absurd, so was the house and its cast. Essie
watched it, mainly through the rapportage of Mrs. Harradson,
through which medium its events were magnified and distorted. Her husband, too, was entertained by the continuation
of Mrs. Harradson, namely the house. But, as with her, this
building, so replete with absurdity, produced in him a *malaise*,
which he endeavoured to conceal, although he would say to
Essie, 'Is it not *unusually* absurd? Or is it just the average
human mean? What do you think?' But she would answer, 'As
you know, darling, the philosophy of the absurd is not in
my line. But if you really want to know what I think. . . .'

—'Yes? You mean that *we* are part of the house. That *is* the
difficulty.'

It might be argued that all the absurdity flowed from the
owner of the house. This large, circular, red-brick building,
containing some twenty flats standing back a little pretentiously from the other houses in the street, was the property of
a strong-minded, disagreeable moustachioed old lady, named
Mrs. Abbott. She was one of several sisters who had inherited
various properties. This house had been her share, and the
least desirable legacy. She heartily disliked the house and all
her tenants. Her refusal to spend a penny on it had a number
of comic consequences. One of the climaxes was when slates
began raining on the heads of those leaving or entering it.
It needed badly 'pointing': the cement was distintegrating
between the bricks. Any day it might begin to collapse. Then
half a dozen of the tenants appealed to the local Town Hall.
Eventually one morning a notice was found posted inside the
front doors, 'To whom it may concern'—and a statement
declaring that 'This building is not safe.' Mrs. Abbott immediately served a week's notice on the six rebellious tenants,
but some repairs were thereupon undertaken.

Mrs. Harradson was the caretaker, at a salary of four and
sixpence a week. For this she was needed to wash all the stairs
and all the windows that lighted them. She was forbidden to
accept any other employment, her charing for the Hardings
being a breach of trust. But she was also provided with a small
flat. So, legally, she had a roof over her head and four and
sixpence a week.

The tenants were a typical set of tenants. 'All houses have
the same tenants, however much they may be disguised, just
as all worlds have congenial inhabitants,' René Harding com-
mented. On the street floor a flat had, much against the grain,
been sacrificed by Mrs. Abbott, a three-pound-a-week flat;
a family obligation. Her brother, Mr. Buckland, and his
wife occupied their flat rent-free, until Mr. Buckland lost his
reason. The first notice that the neighbours had had of his
approaching derangement were certain violent noises which
could be heard within the flat. The next thing they knew was
that Mr. Buckland would rush out, and thunder on their doors

crying, 'Let him out!' Then one day a coal-man with a sack of coals on his back was climbing the stairs when Mr. Buckland pursued him, and seized the bag of coals shouting, 'Let him out! Let him out!' The coal and the coal-man fell on top of Mr. Buckland, who was madly convulsed in the midst of a torrent of glistening carbon, and ended by nearly murdering the amazed coal-man. At this point Mr. Buckland left for Colney Hatch. For some years Mrs. Buckland had occupied the flat alone. She was a barmaid-like woman, amiably blonde and somewhat fat.

Now upon the floor immediately above the Hardings dwelt a certain Mr. Whitaker. He was a bank-manager of a most morose and reticent type and not very neighbourly. But he was noticed descending the stairs a little furtively, about nine-thirty in the evening, and on these occasions he would be admitted to Mrs. Buckland's flat, which he would leave about midnight; and it was said that he was at times intoxicated. But in the flat facing that of Mr. Whitaker dwelt a Mr. Ambrose Dewes. Mr. Dewes was an actor of some thirty-six summers, much addicted to gallantry. If any good-looking girl happened, for whatever reason, to ascend the stairs, and if Mr. Dewes chanced to see her, he would undoubtedly say, 'What a fine day it is, and yet how awfully dark on the staircase'; and then, all smiling charm, would produce an electric torch and render her every assistance in his power. And if she were the kind of girl who seemed to suffer from the heat—or from the cold—she might follow him into his flat to have a snort and a little friendly chat, before proceeding on her way. Nor did Mr. Dewes by any means rely upon such girls as might happen to ascend the stairs of this particular house. For great numbers of women were seen to enter his flat by his neighbours. These facts attracted the censorious comment of his immediate neighbour, Mr. Whitaker. But Mr. Dewes retorted by pointedly alluding to the bank manager's habit of nightly visiting the flat of the blonde downstairs. The actor was a very jovial young Casanova, an old Etonian, not disagreeably impressing Mrs. Hester Harding.

Upon the same landing as the Hardings was an elderly spinster-lady of great respectability who would especially enjoin Mrs. Harding to put a new bulb of somewhat superior power upon the landing when the Marchioness of Shewburyness came to visit her once a month. There were many other tenants of great typicality: in a word, the house was properly stocked, in all its little compartments, in such a way as emotionally to equip it for its passage through time. The Hardings were shortly to leave it. A certain percentage of its tenants were to leave it, too, when London was blitzed. The Blitz, indeed, changed it a great deal: it shook the decaying cement between its bricks, it shook the slates from its roof. Indeed, in the depths of the war-years it became somewhat a wild place. Mrs. Abbott had refused to spend any money on blacking-out the stair-windows, and consequently there was no illumination at night. It was not, however, at night that Mrs. Harradson plunged down the stairs and was killed. A pail of water and a brush made it plain what she had been doing. Those familiar with her repertoire of enemies spoke of foul play, and whispered that it was the postman, who had stopped her tongue with his boot. The actor still dwelt there, but he was a changed man, greying at the temples, it was said. By forty-five Mr. Dewes had lost the sight of both eyes. A woman-friend of the Hardings, who saw him not long after the Blitz, recalled how he had told her that the cellar was full of dead leaves and a wild cat had established its home there, a brood of wild kittens springing about among the leaves. This wild cat so terrorized the tenants that they dared not go down to their trash bins just outside the cellar-door. And then this same woman narrated how she had passed him down the street while a rain of incendiaries was falling in the district, and the roof of the building where the Hardings had dwelt was on fire and the tenants of the upper flats were flinging blazing cushions and other articles into the street. Professor Harding's comment was that the House that Jack Built was always built in the same way. And its destiny was in accordance with its architecture. Some houses built by Jack attracted incendiaries, some did not. But it did not matter whether they did or whether they did not. All in the end had wild cats in their cellars, for civilization never continued long enough to keep the wild cats out—if you call it civilization, René Harding would shout.

CHAPTER II

'You are not by any Chance a Fool, My Son?'

THE sun of St. John's Wood reddened the walls of a substantial sitting-room, and warmed the distracted faces of a family group, sitting in a rather huddled knot, deep in conversation. The birds in the trees outside the open windows sang the sparrow-songs which give the rows of private gardens in this north-west district their rustic sweetness. The shadow of 'That Other Man' lay across the ugly lethargic city, but in the beautiful recesses of St. John's Wood you could believe yourself in the Victorian middleclass paradise, where Mr. Gladstone, big-nosed and big-collared, chopped down trees for longevity, or where the towers of the Crystal Palace looked down upon crinolined throngs moving between the rhododendrons, and stopping to admire the swans upon the glassy lakes.

Could anyone have entered this apartment unperceived, and have stood there observing this agitated group, he would have heard from time to time, phrases in French escaping it, such as *à la bonne heure*, or *par exemple*, or *mon pauvre petit, mon pauvre petit*. This latter phrase in a faint voice fell from the lips of the dominant figure, a very old lady, reminiscent of an ancestral miniature, in her faded dignity. A period costume, of the severest black with the inevitable cameo, was too severe to be English. The *pauvre petit* of the above-mentioned exclamation was René Harding, who, crouching upon a low boat-like stool at the feet of the aged woman, looked unusually the reverse of *petit*. But she was his mother: and the intrusion of french phrases in the talk of these three people, of mother, son, and daughter, had a simple explanation. Mrs. Harding senior was French, which accounted also for the gallic Christian name of her son, as it did for many other things about Professor René Harding. René's sister Mary sat close up against Mrs. Harding, on the right-hand side. She was in her early forties, and more obviously *handsome*, with her well-cut nose and broad forehead, than her brother with his hair-sculptured, gothic mask.

Biologically incomplete, the missing male principle of this group was to be found in effigy upon the wall behind René. A large photograph hanging there, displayed the massive nordic handsomeness, the solid brow, the clear germanic of Mr. Harding senior, plainly related to the particular good looks of Mary Harding. On the other hand, the dark eyes and hair testified to the latin strain, and a certain carriage of the head, and noble severity in Mary's glance, belonged to the older civilizations, which her mother represented.

At his mother's feet, René, like a suppliant, crouched gazing bleakly up into her face. His fingers entangled themselves in hers, and sometimes with both hands he would crush her small brown fists. His sister was pressed so close against their mother, that she seemed to share the prerogatives of motherhood, and it was usually four eyes which gazed back at his, and Mary visibly shared the distress of the greatly shocked parent.

'I have shut the door behind me,' he said. 'There is no going back upon what I have said. I have been specific. The Council have been informed with a brutal clarity what my mind has become like. It is no longer an instrument which can be used in the way that my position requires that it should be. I am no longer able to teach a story of the world which they would find acceptable: they would not let me teach my students the things which I now know, so I have had to tell them that there is no longer anything that I can teach. To take one instance only, my position in the matter of economics would alone be more than sufficient to disqualify me. No, the die, I fear, is cast, I have to find other employment. That would be very difficult in England. So . . .'

There was a long silence, during which a few tears ran down the cheeks of René's mother, who was sitting in a motionless rigor, staring into the distance as though she saw another

René over the shoulder of her son; and Mary's head was turned away with a grimace of despair.

René broke the silence shrilly, as if it frightened him; as though it had been a prophetess and not a mother that he had come to consult, and the processes of whose vaticination he was no longer able to bear.

'Please do not condemn me before you have heard me. I know that with my professorship and my budding notoriety as an author I am someone to whom my family looks . . . looks . . . for honour and not dishonour. I know that I have to give up part of myself to Mother, to sisters, to wife. I am a responsible man. There has been no levity in the action I have taken. I took it secretly because there can be no consultation with others in a matter of conscience. But I did nevertheless consult everyone of you in my private mind. I heard what you had to say, for I knew what your feelings must be: I did not consult only my own ego, and take my orders from that.'

'I know you would not do that, my poor René.' His mother's voice quavered hoarsely.

'I know that, too, René,' his sister echoed falteringly.

'My distress has been as great as anyone else's can be. It has been terrible for me. I do not drop my career down the drain with as light a heart as it would seem, to see me do it. Of course not. Men are not made that way. They say Good-bye to common ambition with horror. They become nobodies as if they were dying.'

'Do not speak like that,' his mother said.

'No, I feel just like you about myself. I consider myself mad, as you do. I am in two halves, one half of which is *you*.'

Mary began to sob, wiping her eyes quickly.

'I have had a first-rate job, as good as a man of my mental habits can have; my position in the world has been excellent; I shall never have as good a one again. These things have to be built up from early years, they cannot be re-made once lost. I see with remarkable clarity what going to a colony must mean. When I get to Canada I may have to teach Algebra or . . . oh yes, or History in an elementary school. Or of course I may prefer to earn my living as a waiter in some large hotel.'

He produced the cable he had received that morning.

'Here is a message from a colleague in Winnipeg. He is an Englishman who went out there recently. He is honest and reliable. The chances of my obtaining any satisfactory work in Canada are extremely slender.'

'Surely then . . .'

But René stopped his sister, saying, 'Let me finish, Mary. Just a few words more. Let me finish the painting of my black picture. Because of the success of my book I am fairly widely known. It was reviewed, for instance, everywhere in Canada and the States. Over there it would be quite obvious to all its readers why I had resigned my post. As far as an academic appointment is concerned this is fatal. Colleges are very conventional places. It is no part of the educator's equipment to have "ideas". But such ideas as *mine* are naturally anathema. Nowhere is unorthodoxy in politics and economics respectable: my kind of unorthodoxy, however, is especially revolting, to all those in a "position of trust". You see, I think in a manner in which one is not allowed to think. So I become an outsider, almost a pariah.'

He strained his arms up into the air above his head, and rotated upon his hips as if about to perform some eccentric dance. Then he continued, 'You may ask, cannot I think differently? Why can I not purge myself of this order of thinking? Well, of course there are some things that everyone thinks which hot irons could not burn out of them. It is the circumstances of the time in which we live which have made it impossible for me to mistake my road: there have been signposts or rather lurid beacons all the way along it, leading to only one end, to one conclusion. How anyone, as historically informed as I am, can come to any very different conclusions from my own I find it hard to understand. They must have blind eyes for all the flaming signs. But really there is no more to say, I have resigned my professorship. On Monday I am going to the offices of the steamship company.'

'The picture you have painted certainly is black,' said Mary.

'En effet, il est bien noir,' the mother assented.

'The worst of it is'—and a smile it had had vanished from

Mary's face—'that it does not seem to be blacker than life. That is the worst of it.'

'Ma foi, oui. On ne pourrait pas le depeindre autrement que noir.'

The two women looked at one another. Then Mary spoke.

'What does Hester think about it?'

René felt the four eyes bracketed upon him and squinted a little as he answered,

'She knows nothing. I have told her nothing, so far.'

There was a sudden relaxation. Mary smiled as she said,

'Your wife is in ignorance. Was it your idea to leave Hester out of your calculations?'

René laughed very softly, his ho-ho laugh. 'Hardly that,' he told her. 'One cannot leave a wife out of one's calculations.'

The mother smiled, and as she did so the furrows and bony accents of her face arranged themselves almost with a click in what was a miniature of his own characteristic mask.

'Les femmes, ça se trouve quelquepart, n'est-ce pas, avec les valises et les parapluies.'

René ho-ho-ho'ed placidly. 'Mais écoute, ma femme à moi n'est pas si commode.' When René and his mother spoke to one another in French their resemblance was accentuated.

'You think Hester may disagree with what you propose to do?' Mary asked him.

'Could be,' he rapped, looking away.

The relaxation was affirmed. Mary drew away a little from her mother.

'Naturally'—René then proceeded with great firmness—'I shall tell Essie what I propose to do before I go to the offices of the steamship company. I have no doubt that she will reproach me. But nothing that Essie says will cause me to change my plans. In a case of this kind there is only one thing to do.'

The easier atmosphere was at an end. Mary looked anxiously towards her mother and drew closer to her again.

'I know I shall be distressing Hester a great deal. I realize all that side of it fully. She is a very conventional woman. She may even leave me.'

'René, will you not think this over, for our sake,' the old lady said in a trembling voice.

'I'm going to say something that will annoy you I'm afraid.' Mary leant towards him. 'You know, René, that Mother and I will back you up if it comes to a showdown. It is because you know that, that I hope you will allow me to say what has been passing through my mind. As you were speaking it occurred to me that you might have allowed yourself to be influenced by the success of your book. Perhaps—and I only make this suggestion at the risk of seeming tiresome—but were you not perhaps *ébloui*, dazzled, by all the praise of what you have written. I'm not accusing you of vanity; please do not think that I mean that. But public applause *might*—excuse me if I am talking nonsense—even in the case of the strongest mind, and yours is a very firm mind, René, I know that, might play tricks with the firmest judgement. There is an intoxication . . .'

'No.' René shook his head.

'I noticed,' she went on quickly, 'in what you said just now that there was no mention of the possibility of making money by writing books. You spoke of being a waiter in a hotel, of doing all kinds of degrading things, but never of doing the obvious thing: that is, writing for your living.'

'No, but I should have mentioned that, of course. I was not concealing that possibility.' And he smiled at her obliquely.

'No, but there *is* always that. You could, I suppose, to judge by the success of your book, always make a living of some sort by writing. There is always that, so do not let us talk about hotel waiters and teaching Algebra in a secondary school. That obscures the issue. Surely the two ways of life which confront one another are, first, your being a professor, and secondly, your writing books. Those are the two alternatives, are they not? Don't be cross with me, I only want to make clear in my own mind what is occurring. I have been very shocked by what you have said. We all admire you very much, and followed your academic career with great pride, mother and I. And all of us, of course. We don't want you to make a mistake, a great mistake.'

'Because I have been intoxicated by the reception of my

book?' René enquired gravely. 'You mean that? That is what you mean, is it not?'

'Not quite that,' she protested. 'That would be suggesting that you were vain indeed. No, I do not mean that you are chucking up your professorship for that reason, I can see that you are very distressed about something. All I mean is that if it were not for that other possibility of making a living in some other way, tempting you in the background, would you take this step with all that it signifies of . . . of, well, of ruin?'

There was a sofa at René's back and he transferred himself to that, sitting with his elbows upon his knees with his fingers stuck into his thick hair.

'You are quite wrong, Mary, about the part the author's vanity plays in this business. That is not your fault and I know in working it out the way you have, it was in all kindness. It was because you wanted to help me that you did your bit of psychoanalysis on me. What you have not been able to allow for has been something that you could not be expected to understand. You see, I have been *driven* into this situation, I have not pushed myself into it or allowed myself to be led into it, lured there by ambition. Ambition plays no part in it at all.' He jumped down into the low boat-like seat before his mother's knees.

'I am sorry to have turned out such a "problem child" after all.'

There was silence. A great discouragement had set in; it was almost as if the two women had played their last card. They shrank together into a collective huddle again, and Mary looked away out of the farther window where the night was setting in, a redness upon the walls having turned into a livid grey, and Mr. Harding senior seeming to have become a little forbidding in his faded brown frame.

The old lady evidently experienced great difficulty in finding any words at all. But at last she said, tremulous and slow, 'There is nothing I can say. You know all the hopes we had placed in you; but what is the use of saying that. It is of course a reproach, and the last thing I wish to do is to reproach you. We will do all we can, your sisters and I, to make things a little easier, to the extent of our ability.' |

'I know you will,' he muttered.

'What you said about a loan is a very difficult matter, René. In fact, I have hardly any available funds. Outside of my annuity, what have I? Let me see, I might be able to scrape together, oh, a matter of five hundred pounds. Of what use would that be to you?'

Mary at this point burst into tears,. René sprang up and walked quickly about hither and thither exclaiming,

'This is a nice way of behaving. I propose to rob my mother of her last savings. I grieve my sister.'

'Don't, please, René.' His sister practically shouted through her tears.

'Next it will be Hester. Next it will be Hester!'

The telephone rang; he snatched it up and shouted, .

'What is it, what is it?'

'Taxi! Taxi!'

He banged the receiver down and came back to the higher of the two seats. There he sat with his legs stuck out, looking upwards in a typical lecturer's position, arranging what he wanted to say. The two women watched him sorrowfully. Then he looked down at them.

'When-one thinks these things out for oneself,' he began, 'that is one thing. It is quite another thing when one begins to share one's thoughts with other people. Complexities make their appearance immediately. I thought this all out for myself without consultation with anybody.'

'You certainly did,' Mary agreed. 'There is no doubt about that.'

'Just as it would be impossible to write *Paradise Lost* or *Hamlet*, collectively, so it is impossible to plan some major change in the individual life, collectively.'

'Most people,' Mary objected, 'do not lock themselves up at such a juncture. They talk it over with others, don't they?'

'Most people think collectively, I agree. But they do not usually think very clearly. They have no pretensions to being individuals. They are a collective individual, a group of some sort.'

'Are you not a group?' his sister asked, smiling.

'I was a group, a university. But when I wished, or when I

felt compelled to cease to be that, I had to isolate myself, of course, and think the matter out by myself.'

'But . . .'

'But there was the domestic group, that is what you were about to say, Mary. I know. But I had to think the matter out in isolation from that. For *that* group would merely have pushed me back into the other group. The morals of all groups are the same. If you wish to act upon a heroic moral plane . . .'

'Oh, *là là*!' Mary broke in with an unexpected boisterousness.

The Professor smiled at the sisterly heckle.

'I was not using the word "heroic" with any sentimental accent. Only to define. The same applies to the word moral. You cannot help choosing the moral, rather than its opposite. I am afraid that I derive none of the average satisfactions from heroic moral action. I am a hero *malgré moi*.'

He ho-ho-ho'ed faintly, and mother and sister smiled.

'Anyhow, there it is. It is stupid of us to take this tragically. Probably I shall get along well enough outside the academic fold. For the world I am leaving, I am a finished man. But do not let us take that too seriously. I know at my age I should have grown up: of course I should. But you do not have to worry about this situation so much as you are preparing to do.'

Mary began to cry again. But her mother said to her, 'René is right. We do not help matters by taking this so tragically.'

'Or anything so tragically as is usually the case,' he smiled.

'Perhaps you are right,' his mother sighed.

'What a philosophy!' protested Mary, with lifted eyebrows and ironic smile.

'But, but, he has not committed murder or robbed a bank!' The mother answered her almost testily.

Mary laughed up at her mother, and exclaimed,

'All right, I have been behaving like an idiot. All René has done is to throw a Chair of History out of the window. What is there in that?'

They all laughed, almost merrily.

'Ah, *voila*!' René cried. 'You see, we are emerging from the mist that we ourselves have created!'

'Not quite that.' His mother shook her head sombrely. 'But still, there are always several ways of looking at anything.'

'Let us not pass so precipitately from the black picture to the very rosy one we are approaching now,' said Mary, standing up. Her brother rose, standing with his hands in his jacket pockets. She gazed at him, and as he raised his head, for he had been staring at the floor, they looked at one another for a moment. She did not answer his smile with another smile, but began speaking instead. 'I want to hear more about this, René,' she said. 'I am not at all sure I have understood. Will you and Hester come to dinner? I think next Tuesday would be all right, but I will telephone.'

'I am free on Tuesday.'

'I would like you to have a talk with Percy.'

René bowed his head. Mary returned to her mother's side and thrust her face down and kissed her where the aged cheek was hollow, patting her clenched hands as they rested upon the margin of the hollow lap. As Mary moved away René accompanied her, opening the door as they reached it.

'Are you sure I can't give you a lift? Where are you dining?'

'That would get me there a little before my time,' he answered.

Mary looked back towards her mother as she left the room, fluttering a farewell towards the stationary figure, more immobile than usual. Closing the door, René went to a tray and poured himself a glass of sherry.

Alone with one another, mother and son drew closer together, like two confederates. Mary, though the nearest to them, far nearer than the other two sisters, belonged to the outside world when it came to these two, who were allied in a very special union. À deux, this extraordinary identity became apparent. To commune with one another, everyone else, even Mary, had to be excluded. René drew up a chair, talking to her softly in the language she still liked best to speak, the tongue she had spoken when she was young but which she had found it quite impossible to induce Mr. Harding senior to learn. She patted and caressed his hand, and he almost danced in his chair with pleasure, like a big dog that is caressed. He arched his legs in a rampant attitude, his toes beating for a moment a quick tattoo. Afterwards, he drank his sherry *d'un trait*, as though it had been a cocktail. Both their faces were broken up into deeply engraved masks of civilized irony. What he loved best about this old woman was her robust refusal to be too serious, her gnome-like raillery, her frail gaiety: the something of Voltaire, the something of Fénélon, which is secreted in all those of her race, the grimace of amusement she would wear upon her deathbed, for the same grimace would serve at need for pain. Really they had nothing to say to one another. All they required to do when they were alone was to gaze into one another's faces and smile an ancestral smile.

However, René began idly to gossip, to enquire about the tiresome new priest, and the even more tiresome physician.

'Et le prêtre, il t'embête toujours?' he smiled.

'Mais non, je l'ai chassé.'

'Il est grotesque ce prêtre. Les prêtres anglais sont une race à eux. Ça doit être difficule d'être catholique chez nous.'

'Bien sur. Et puis leur liturgie!'

'Pauvre chérie.'

The newly arrived priest who had complicated his mother's religious life was discussed for a little and they then turned to the vexations attendant upon the housekeeper's menopause. After that René enquired about the asthma of the family physician, which made the ascent of the stairs for that poor man a cruel ordeal. This imposed upon Mrs. Harding a less sick doctor. The ailments of the cat were not forgotten: and as their indolent chat moved along, gently playing with absurdity after absurdity, at last the subject of the recent interview was referred to by his mother, but in an almost negligent tone, as if it were floating about in the background of her mind, but were a matter of no great importance.

'One must not take such things *au grand sérieux*.' She seemed to be dismissing the subject. She stopped, turned to him and observed, 'We have always been such great friends, René, have we not? I do not know why. You are so like my brother Jacques, whom you never saw. You look at life the same way that he did.' Then suddenly her mind appeared to be traversed by a new thought. She shook her head violently, and exclaimed, 'Il ne faut pas trop plaisanter, quand même. La vie est dur pour ceux qui la traitent avec trop de mépris.'

René ceased to smile. But then a terrible look of surprised enquiry was shot up at him which made him quail.

'You are not by any chance *a fool*, my son?'

Enormously disconcerted René sprang up and gazed down at his mother as though without warning she had slapped his face. She sat peering up at him out of her grimace, her head bent forwards.

'Of course I am a fool, my little mother. But calm your fears, I am not too utter a fool to live.'

He bent down and kissed her, then stood in front of her, looking abstractedly over her head.

'I must be going. Hester will be angry if I keep her waiting. We must not make Hester angry.'

He bent down again and kissed his mother on the forehead. Neither said any more: he turned and walked rapidly across the floor to the door, erect as though stiffened against some parting shot.

'René,' the old woman cried, as he was passing through the door. 'Ne te fâche pas, n'est-ce pas?'

'Tu veux dire avec toi? Quel idée, ma petite mère!'

He blew a kiss, all the ornamental curves of his beard seeming to centre in his lips, the heavy cheek-bones impending upon the jutting mouth. But the eyes were still distracted.

CHAPTER III

A Taxi-Ride and a Dinner at 'La Toulousaine'

HE sprang into the taxi and crouched with his hands cupped around his face as it shook and rattled preparatory to starting. Then he straightened himself, and sat bolt upright, in the centre of the seat. Nature had given its answer. The judgement of his mother uprooted him, as it were. He had to accept detachment from all that his family had meant for him. Or at least this must be so in the deepest sense. She was an ignorant, worldly old woman, it was true. But he remained shaken.

He realized, as he drew very near to himself, in the dark of the obstreperous old vehicle, how his personality must strike other people; his sister, or his mother, for instance. He was *un exalté*, a fanatic, a man apt to become possessed of some irrational idea, which would blind him to everything, as if it were in a delirium. No: he was quite the opposite, or so it would seem. He was a man whose bearded mask was haunted by an ironic smile at all times, as much as was his mother's, a man inclined to meet with a sceptical eye the enthusiast, every variety of *emportement*. Yet he was now declaring it as his intention to behave in so eccentric a manner that an explanation—a *theory*—seemed to be demanded. It must have been some such mental process, this, which had brought his mother to ask herself whether this 'brilliant' and amusing son of hers were not, at bottom, *stupid*. To be so level-headed, so *'realist'*, qualifying so little for the term 'dreamer', and yet suddenly to act in a way reminiscent of romantic adolescence, could only be explained by some sudden alteration, some disturbance of the personality, or else, it must signify the presence of some streak which had never been suspected even by those nearest to him. There were only these two explanations available. He forced his face into a bitter travesty of a smile. To be so realistic that you came to appear a dreamer, to be so sceptical that you acted like a man possessed of some violent belief, this was an irony indeed! So to be sitting as he had been just now in a room with his nearest and dearest, calmly and matter-of-factly announcing his line of action, watching dismay and embarrassment deepening upon their faces, he had had the sensation of being demented. He might just as well have been explaining to them that he was really Napoleon Bonaparte, or an isosceles triangle. They could not have been more amazed and shocked.

The taxi crossed the canal bridge and entered the circular road within the precincts of Regent's Park. René in his cab began to circle around the slumbering Zoo animals, the lions, the elephants, the anthropoid apes, all dreaming of Africa, Siberia, and Malaya, Bengal and the Polar Sea. What was in fact their dream-life was in the cages and pools, on the imitation rocks, and in the miniature savannahs of the Zoological Gardens. But *their* real life of course was where lions live under the blazing suns, or where the Polar bear prowls upon the ice caps. They step back, when they close their eyes in sleep, into the reality, out of the squalid nightmare of Regent's Park. Oh, where was *his* real life! For it certainly was not in the restaurant towards which he was speeding. But he soon left behind the sleeping snakes and snoring tigers, and the reflections that their proximity provoked. He began to think that, after all, his lecture-room might be his habitat, as the river-side was the water-rat's, and the prairie was the buffalo's. As he creaked and banged along in this deliberately archaic London 'hackney' vehicle, his mind darted from one absurdity to another. It was human stupidity he was reacting against. Yet he was now obliged to justify himself to a number of persons typically stupid. His darling mother, and dear old Mary as loyal as she was obstinate, were fundamentally as unenlightened as Mrs. Harradson, at least as that concerned the matter in hand/ He would not dream of describing himself to Mrs. Harradson as a 'hero', would he? No, but he had just committed that absurdity with his sister, the best woman in the world, but completely deluded. The delusion under which the majority sleepwalked its way from decade to decade, from disaster to disaster, had numbed her mind as much as that of any other Mrs. Everyman. His mother, too, was numbed, was part of the same somnambulism, and age now was super-added. No means of enlightening *her*. She was the dearest person in the world, but, to come down to brass tacks, it was *she* who was the fool, not he. This he agreed sounded very conceited, and he had not the least idea how it was that he came to be awake, while all these others slept. It was an explicable accident, it signified no superiority. He just had suddenly woken up.

However, faced with this overwhelming difficulty, he had made use of the term hero, as a stimulus to the imagination. His sister, of course, would regard what he was doing as heroic —that would be her way of thinking of it if she could understand; if her intelligence were not numbed and doped groupishly by mass hypnotism. And her intelligence was quite a good one, as a matter of fact.

So he picked his way among people who could not see: dealing in this way with the blind produced in him sometimes the sensation of being an Invisible Man; at others, of being brutally concrete in an unsubstantial universe. During this period he began to acquire a consciousness of his physical presence which was extremely disagreeable. He thought of himself as an animal among delicate and vapourish humans. Even his hairiness embarrassed him. At times his acute self-consciousness would take the form of feeling that he was on view, an exhibit. He had thought once or twice that Essie had been looking at him in an odd kind of way. And in fact so she had. But the reason for that was not what he supposed, but was merely that she had seen that he was concealing something. Anyone who is inexpertly engaged in covering something up is bound to attract attention, and also to appear absurd. There was nothing he dreaded so much as the absurd, in himself, a part of his French idiosyncratic legacy, exaggerated if anything in the course of its grafting to a British stock. But his growing sense of the absurd in everything was painful and to suspect its presence in himself supremely uncomfortable. Once or twice he had observed Mrs. Harradson and asked himself if he was a male Mrs. Harradson. What was the rational, after all? Where was one to look for the *norm*? The nervous impetuousness of his movements, of which he was perfectly aware, he had once compared with the charlady's. However, he had concluded, with a laugh, if it is a question of the human kind and its essential absurdity, then of course all right, why should I care? In so absurd a place it was hardly likely that he himself could be otherwise than absurd.

As the car inserted its decrepit bulk into the Albany Street traffic and crawled noisily past Great Portland Street Station into Great Portland Street, hot on the scent of the absurd, he recognized that his mother had behaved with absurdity in conspiring with Mr. Harding to beget him, in an embrace that is not objectively edifying and is accompanied by pants and grunts and expressions of ridiculous and unmerited approval of the dull solicitor whose name he bore. Dignified as she was in the antechamber of death, lying exhausted by life in that chair to which she seemed glued, in that, her present form, his mother had little connection with the young Frenchwoman who passed almost half her life in a bed with Mr. Harding, for the sole purpose of bringing into life René and his three sisters. All the values were wrong in that bed. Neither of the excited couple considered what they were doing or they would have quitted the bed immediately. Of course his mother now, with a great big bearded monster like himself in front of her, must dimly realize how frivolous she had been (for she was not such a brute as Essie); and today she had, with disgust, even believed that she had given birth to a fool, into the bargain, *pauvre chérie*!

His mind now shifted to that boldly-bland-eyed lady, probably awaiting him not far from Piccadilly—the absurdly *mesquin* and petty centre of this jellyfish of a city. As his taxi propelled itself into the broad street ending in Broadcasting House, his face wrinkled up as though he had been confronted with a peculiarly involved historical problem.

As he drew nearer to Essie her figure began to loom more insistently in his mind: at the same time his mind flashed back to the figures of Mr. and Mrs. Harding, père and mère, as life-long inhabitants of a handsome four-poster; for the nocturnal half of life Essie and he at night had beds that were twins. Same thing, same idea, but less oppressively barbarous. Why did he and Essie live together? Same idea. Nothing would have induced him to live with a man of Essie's disposition and mediocre intellect. For though smart enough, she had not a fraction of Mary's or of his mother's judgement. Their marriage had been a bus-accident. No offspring had resulted. A good thing. The male offspring would have resembled Essie more or less. Sex would have been unpleasantly prominent. Big staring eyes and all that. This was absurd. Human dignity would have been sacrificed to an exaggerated idea of size of population required. The piling up of huge populations immoral. Cannon-fodder. What nations wanted was smaller and smaller populations, not bigger and bigger. Quality not quantity. He gave a ghost of a ho-ho-ho. Here he was legislating for Overman. In the Yahooesque mass the nightly tête-à-tête between the sheets was one of the sole compensations for a life-sentence of hard labour. '*Je divague*,' he muttered, as the cab stopped at the door of the 'Toulousaine'.

Hester was sitting, demure and wide-eyed, near the vestiaire. He led her into the restaurant, mentally prescribing for himself some tonic *consommation* in view of the unpleasant task which lay before him. Also, a quiet corner—*surtout* somewhere really quiet with no eavesdroppers. He did in fact find, in the upstairs rear of the 'Toulousaine', a table, which answered to his requirements.

Next came the meal. He discovered that he felt hungry. He had enough of the Frenchman in him to succumb very quickly to the attractions of a well-arranged menu. Hester, although never losing sight of the problem of the waistline, was nevertheless rather fond of food. They ordered what would have seemed a somewhat elaborate meal to the average Englishman. The *sommelier*, who knew René, took matters a step farther: and before he had left, they had decided, after the cocktails, on a wine decidedly on the heavy side, and, in a word, his plan for a somewhat austere meal, with some brandy to brace him up, had been forgotten. Or it would be more true to say that good reasons had been found, under the pressure of hunger, to *feed*, even to overfeed, rather than merely to *stimulate* as had originally been intended.

Essie watched the proceedings with a certain surprise.

What, she asked herself, was the cause of this lavish repast? She enquired if anything serious had taken him up to St. John's Wood; for he had not explained why he was going and she considered that it might be that something up there had produced this appetite and unusual conviviality. His melancholy response convinced her that it was nothing to do with that visit: so she thought she would wait and watch, and when the wine began to have its effect something doubtless would emerge.

As if escaping from something, he gave himself up almost childishly to the delights of the table. The wine of the Rhône rolled down his throat, the brandies of Normandy attacked his membranes and caused his animal fires to blaze. By the time he was through with this meal he gave up all idea of explaining to Hester that he had planned a change of life. His well-being was such that the charms of Essie assumed great prominence: he ho-ho-ho'd as he lifted his glass and nothing in the world could have been more different from what he had foreseen. He tripped brilliantly out of the restaurant and Essie was actually a little tipsy. In the taxi he behaved like an amorous student. And once or twice, when the sterner side of his nature had attempted to intervene, he pushed it away with a ho-ho-ho. When, some time later, his glands emptied and his head as clear as a bell, this hairy faun in a jack-knife jump sprang into his own pillowless bed, it was without a shadow upon his conscience.

CHAPTER IV

Hester Hears the News

NEXT morning it was a different matter. Hester and Mrs. Harradson put in their appearance, but more than anything else it was Essie's exultant freshness, her speaking orbs hung over the breakfast table, her very bare arms although it was a very chilly day, and the significant glances she cast at Mrs. Harradson, which caused a deep reaction. It was all very well giving spectacular proof that he was a fool, but his conversation with Essie was now going to be considerably more difficult. However, after breakfast, he decided he would at once ask her to come into his study and come to the point immediately. Meantime, he must steer her mind into severer channels. He had noticed *Princess Casamassima* upon her table: he asked her if she had been reading it. As he had expected, a studious look was the result. Her brow was slightly knitted, she looked a very serious girl. Yes, she told him, she had always wanted to read this particular book of James and had at last started doing so a week or so before. Did she like it? he asked. She *thought* she did, she said, but James' London slums appeared to her a little theatrical, as if copied from some sentimental victorian bookplate.

René knew that she must have heard or read this somewhere, but he looked suitably impressed.

'Don't you think that Lady Aurora is very good?' he enquired.

'Oh yes, and the bed-ridden girl is terribly sweet,' she answered.

'Ah, that bed-ridden girl! James intended, with her, to serve up one of Dickens' most tear-compelling creatures. But she nauseated him so much half-way, that he changed her into the disagreeable character she all along, in spite of him, had been.'

This gave Essie a shock: for she saw that she had got

somehow into deep waters. This was not an easy book to talk about, as she had supposed.

'I see what you mean, I think. The bed-ridden are always bores anyway, aren't they? But I did think . . .'

'No, there are no extenuating circumstances,' he told her. 'All his Dickens personæ, in any case, are terrible failures. Hyacinth—what a little hero to have! Could anyone be interested in such an unreal, comic little figure? His suicide is the duddest climax to a long, long yarn that it is possible to imagine.'

'Ah, I have not come to that. So that is the end of Hyacinth, is it?'

René could see that she was carefully storing away these criticisms of the book, to be used, along with the victorian bookplate, to impress some intellectual friend. Meanwhile, he had got her toned down in the problems of a James' novel. Having finished his eggs and bacon, he turned to his mail.

Had Hester received convincing evidence that René had deliberately led her into a high-brow discussion from strategical purposes she would have been as astonished as mortified. She regarded herself as well-endowed with 'low-cunning'; but she was accustomed to think of him as ingenuous as a child, and as easy to see through as plate-glass. If he was ever opaque, that was his learning blurring the glass a little in her view. It was this acceptance by Hester of the Victorian convention of the strong but stupid masculine in contrast to the weak but wily feminine, which made it the simplest thing in the world for René to deceive her if he wanted to, though it is true that so far he had never availed himself of this, except for bagatelles, for pulling her leg.

As soon as she saw that he was occupied with his correspondence (and she was not detained by her own, which had been nothing but a few bills), she shook off the contretemps of the *Princess Casamassima* discussion—such a highbrow feature for their breakfast-table talk was almost without precedent—and returned to the setting of her own little traps. The terrific success of the night before, and René had been in perfect honeymoon form, must really be put to some good use. The moment had come, it seemed to her, to seize time by the forelock while his eyes were still gooey and his brain still drugged with the fumes of the Venusberg. Her eyes shining, her waist arched in and hips thrust out, she held up a page of her newspaper, on which were displayed a bunch of late-spring coats, a bait for those who were so silly as to imagine that in the warm weather fur coats grew cheaper.

'Now *that*,' she exclaimed, arching her eyebrows, 'is what, if you ever had a really *lavish* fit—*that* is the sort of thing I should get you to buy.'

René looked up from his correspondence, momentarily stung almost to fury by the brazen naïvely mercenary calculations of the good Hester, with her garishly stock notion of what was a propitious moment.

'Oh, that would be it? I'm glad to know that. I shall bear that in mind.' He pushed his correspondence away. 'Hester. Apropos.'

'Yes, René.' She had sunk back in her chair and stared at him apprehensively.

'Yes, very much, I am afraid, apropos. There is something I have to talk to you about, and this seems a good moment. I have just sent in my resignation to the University. I had not obtained special leave of absence. I fear that I deceived you; I said that in order to delay giving you the news of my resignation. There is going to be another of these crazy and extremely wicked wars. As I no longer have my job, I propose to go to Canada. That, in the crudest outline, is what had to be imparted.'

He fastened a hard stare upon her, as though he had dropped something into Essie and were waiting to see it emerge. But at the moment she appeared incapable of any reaction at all. Her face had gone a little grey, her eyes still stared, but very blankly, even a shade piteously. Among other things she had the sensation of having been unmasked, or (the same thing) seen through. As Essie did not possess a very tough core, she was unprepared and a little abashed. And he went on staring at her so coldly that her uppermost impulse was to cry. But she did not do so. Instead she said, 'I knew that something was the matter. I saw you were . . . I saw you were trying very hard to hide something.' To see her

2*

pathetically clinging, even at this juncture, to what she regarded as her superior insight, in her capacity of female of
the species, faintly amused her husband. He smiled, almost
contemptuously.

'Your penetration is admittedly extraordinary. But there
was no Gunpowder Plot. I just thought it better to wait a little
until things were settled.'

'It did not occur to you to consult me?'

'No. Nothing would have been gained. What was involved
could only be settled by myself, not in discussion with others.
Talking would only have blurred the issue.'

'I suppose you mean,' she drawled coldly, 'that I should
have protested. Have you told the others, have you told your
mother? Oh yes, of course, that was what you were doing
yesterday evening. Well, really! You behave in a very high-
handed way, don't you, Professor Harding?'

'Mr. Harding, please.'

She blinked at him slowly, as if interrupting herself to
absorb this bleak item.

'A debating society is all right for some things, not for such
as this. I'm sorry.'

She stood up. 'There are things which I am not prepared to
debate about also.'

'Of course,' he answered, so visibly uninterested that Essie
flushed.

'All this is settled, then?' she demanded.

'Absolutely.' He lay back and scratched his head.

She resumed her seat, nervously lighting a cigarette, rapidly
inhaling the smoke. They were silent for a few moments, as
she gazed speculatively at him, as though at some not very
attractive problem-child.

'Am I allowed to know why you have left the University?
Were you dismissed?'

He shook his head. 'No. I have dismissed myself.'

'Are you displeased with . . . annoyed at anything?'

He laughed. 'Displeased? Yes, highly displeased. But not
specifically with the University. It is what I am obliged to
teach that displeases me.'

'What they have asked you to teach! What is it?'

'No, you have misunderstood me. It is history itself I
am displeased with. I have no authority to teach the truth.
We now arrive at something which involves a great deal of
explanation of a technical order . . .'

'Something entirely over my head. Bird-brain could not
hope to grapple. . . . I see.'

René had sunk back in his chair, till his shoulders were level
with his ears, watchfully checking the course being taken by
Hester. Her reactions, however, had been very much what he
had expected. From his lazy huddle in the Windsor chair, he
straightened himself almost violently, banging his elbows upon
the table with force, and clasping his hands at right angles
with one another as though he had caught a fly.

'There are three facts regarding which I am afraid there is
no possible argument. You are now married to an unemployed
man. That is number one. There are no jobs for this out-of-
work in this country. That is number two. Number three is the
said man will in about two months sail for Canada. You may
add to these facts if you like, a fourth: another world war is
about to break out—as they say.'

'As to that last fact, René, I have something to say.'

'Yes.'

'It does not happen to be a *fact*, I think.'

'No? Evidently I must be mistaken.'

'I think you are. Most people do not think there will be a
war. Stephen, for instance, was telling me the other day that
Hitler's aeroplanes are all made of Ersatz—is that the right
word? They often drop to pieces in mid-air.'

'Indeed? How very interesting.'

'It is, isn't it. Stephen also told me that the uniforms of the
German soldiers are Ersatz, too. They have no raw materials,
so practically everything is Ersatz. Actually, the cloth of their
tunics is a sort of paper. Stephen said a friend of his had seen
them marching along the street and suddenly it came on to
rain. They all got under cover in an archway. Had they
not done so their uniforms would have dropped to pieces
once the rain had soaked into them. You laugh, but I really
think you ought to listen to what is said by eye-witnesses,
René.'

René, who had been laughing, rubbed his face, and came out of the rub purged of mirth.

'Now listen, Hester, you old goose. When the Englishman hears all these stories, specimens of which you have been retailing, what does the simple fellow think? Well, the answer is pretty obvious. He says to himself: "Oh well, if it does come to a war, it's going to be a walk-over for us. All their planes will drop to pieces, their uniforms will melt, their rifles will explode and kill them as soon as they pull the trigger, the Ersatz shells will never leave the Ersatz cannon and the war will be over in no time. Old Hitler will be hanged, and Germany cut up and shared among the Allies." That is what the Englishman will say to himself, is it not: that is what he *is intended* to say to himself. You see, these stories are what is called propaganda. That means, they are reports invented to influence people, to guide opinion in a specific direction.'

'I know what propaganda means.'

'You know the word,' he corrected her, 'but evidently you do not understand it very well. You do not know propaganda when you see it.'

'Oh no?'

'No, otherwise you would not repeat to me what Stephen .. has told you. Your trustfulness is limitless.'

'But my *dear* René! Why should Stephen of all people be engaged in such propaganda?'

René shrugged his shoulders.

'Stephen is a parlour pink! It is just as simple as that.'

Hester silently demurred with her mouth, conveying in dumb show that 'yes she knew but . . .'

'Hang it all, Stephen makes no secret of his Party-alignment, does he?'

'Stephen of course is not a Tory, René! But you describe so many people as communists, darling!'

'But so they *are*. Whether they are officially members of the Party is unimportant. We are passing through a period in which, in England, communist sympathy is fashionable among the young, the educated young. This is not a novel view of mine. It is generally accepted as being the case.'

Hester's face was that of a person who had just discovered

in her hand a good card which she had overlooked, and which she meant to make the most of.

'Very well,' she answered, with what she intended should be an irritating indolence, 'but it is still quite ridiculous to say that Stephen·Vickers spends his time disseminating propaganda, in favour of war. Stephen is the last person to fancy himself as a soldier.'

'I agree with you there. But it would not be Stephen who would do the fighting.'

'But I don't see that, Stephen is young, he knows he would be called up. He would hardly be likely therefore to stir up wars, would he? No. I am afraid you have a·bee in your bonnet. . . .'

From being coldly watchful and aloof, he had begun to show signs of a mounting choler. The card she had discovered in her hand was not a new one, it was one which had often been there before. But she had never used it at a moment so liable to enrage him. He now sprang to his feet, glaring down at her. 'It is not in the marriage contract that wives should hold the same political·views as their husbands,' he told her harshly. 'Nor is it necessary for them to display more intelligence than a domestic cat. But they *do* have, on certain occasions, to keep their big silly mouths closed. It is required to develop sufficient intelligence to know when to do that. And for Heaven's sake give your eyes a rest, no one wants to see your eyeballs.'

The bedroom door opened. 'Oo, Miss,' croaked Mrs. Harradson, balancing backwards and forwards in the gap, as with the limited mobility of a mechanical toy; her frosty crest, the independent strand of hair which tented up over her occiput, rising and falling, giving her a startled expression· when it was most erect. So she advanced, only to fall back, and then advanced again once more to be checked and to retreat holding a witch's broom. 'Ooo, Miss, was you going to harsk Mrs. Beddin'ton 'oos cat 'ad kittens time I was took sick . . .' ·

'Mrs. Harradson!' René shot his arm out towards her, his finger pointing at her pale, narrow, now eerily jeering face.

'Please—shut—that—door!'

Mrs. Harradson fell back as if she had received a blow, the closing of the door coinciding with her eclipse.

Hester, her lips drawn tight over her teeth, rose to her feet, but not with an unladylike abruptness.

'I am afraid you are misbehaving,' she remarked.

René sat down, crossed his legs and looked at her with undiminished hostility. For him, she had been quite aware what she was doing, in her references to Stephen: it was *she* who had misbehaved—in her persistently ladylike way.

'You provoke misbehaviour,' he said after he resumed his seat.

Hester moved over to the bedroom and pushed the door open; for Mrs. Harradson had apparently set it ajar in order to miss nothing of the ensuing dialogue.

'Mrs. Harradson,' she said in a voice of particular politeness. 'Thank you for reminding me about Mrs. Beddington. It was very kind of you. We shall not be wanting a kitten, thank you. Yes, a good cat is a nice thing to have. . . . Thank Mrs. Beddington very much for keeping the kitten for us. . . . I am so sorry it is now too large to drown. It is a great pity. But I am sure she will have no difficulty in disposing of a fine young cat. . . . A good mouser was she? Yes, that of course will count. Everyone wants a mouser.'

Hester pulled the door to. René, who was standing, looked up and said, 'I am in no mood to listen to any more idiotic conversations about cats. Unless you have anything you want to say to me, I shall now go to my study.'

Without taking any notice of these remarks, Hester walked with a dignified composure along the wall to the sitting-room door, turned the handle (and this is an action which, in such a case, is a trap for those not dignified by nature, for it is impossible to avoid slightly protruding the posterior—but which she accomplished with quiet mastery), entered the room beyond, closing the door behind her neither too gently nor too loudly. This act was entirely lost upon René who was collecting the one or two opened letters and other mail, which he thrust inside the newspapers; this done, he turned and passed out through the front door to his work-room across the landing.

. The room was only vacant for a few moments; then the bedroom door opened and the charlady was exposed to view. Irony holding her eyebrows high up on her shallow forehead, and her eyes, which first had seen the light in County Mayo, derisively illuminated, she surveyed the empty breakfast table. As if exaggerating her own rachitic mode of locomotion, shooting her head in and out, she rattled over noisily to the sink.

When, crossing the landing, René entered his study, he was trembling slightly. But the tension soon relaxed, out of direct contact with his wife. This was the first occasion on which disagreements between them had taken the form of a 'row'. His training had led to his locking up any irascibility in a frigid silence. On this occasion it had taken a violent form with great unexpectedness; what had enabled it to do so called for an immediate investigation. Why had the control, by now second nature, been found wanting? If his attitude to Hester had hardened into a critical analysis, he was still very attached to her upon the sexual level. Being a man of great natural severity, an eroticism which did not live very easily with it was instinctively resented: and the mate who automatically classified under the heading 'Erotics' was in danger, from the start, of being regarded as a frivolous interloper by his dominant intellectuality.

It was thus at the breakfast table that he tended to be harshest with his Hester. The latter unquestionably had not the talent to leave 'Erotics' in the bedroom, and to create a neutral climate for herself among the bacon and eggs, the mail, and the morning papers. She had the knack, during the first hour of day, of reminding her husband of what he regarded as an undesirable excess. Her 'big baby' eyes, as he described them in his private thoughts, had at this period of great strain tended to irritate him more than usual. It had become almost a parlour-game with him of late to set little traps for her and to watch her rush into them.

He now sat staring at his 'blotter', on which, as was his habit. he fiercely 'doodled'. He censured himself in the

severest manner, more especially for the 'eyeballs' part. For
at least ten minutes he thus sat, analysing his behaviour with
great care. The conclusion he reached was that this row must
be regarded as a danger-signal of the first order. Ex-professors
had just as much need of discipline as had professors. Was he
by any chance afraid that Essie might leave him and was
he reacting against such a feeling by rudeness, as it were to
scorn the thing he feared? He rejected that at once, for he
experienced no pang at the thought of Hester's departure. The
response he received to further testing was that the great crisis
in his affairs dwarfed into insignificance any merely domestic
crisis. He would keep Hester at his side, if Hester would stop.
But that was all. That settled, with a sigh he turned to the
newspaper. But this interlude of self-examination did not proceed in the mechanical way in which, deprived of its density,
it must seem to have done. Other matters intruded and were
expelled. At one point he gave himself up to a fascinating
doodle, and so forth. But academic life had compelled him
to be methodic; and if it would be untidy to leave some
unorthodox happening unexplained he would force himself to
sit down and attempt to reduce it to logical proportions. It was
not at all his nature to be methodical: as a consequence his life
was a little over-full of the apparatus of method.

But the paper lay there, and the headlines barred the way
for a while.

CITRINE BEATS A.R.P. WALK-OUT
Unions draw up war-work plans

Everyone was in every way preparing for war. The British
Government was aware that war was inevitable. Their secret
service provided them with information of the progress of
Herr Hitler's tremendous air-armament: their figures were
no doubt just as accurate as those obtained by Mr. Churchill,
and published with such a clatter, or those found in the newspapers, and in no way less alarming. But it was most improbable that the Government were building an air-fleet even
half the size of the Nazis'. They would see to it, according to
plan, that a war should occur, but they would also see to it
that England was in a condition of glaring inferiority. It was

'the English way': provoke an enemy, but never be ready to meet him on equal terms. This was intended as an alibi. 'It was not England who started it, was it?' If it had been she would be better prepared. A hypocrite's device—which cost England a great deal of money, and many quite unnecessary dead and maimed in the war that would ensue.

He stared with stony hatred at the picture which he knew so well. It was quite impossible to make anyone understand, except a very few like Rotter, the significance of the events about to occur, the international pressures which made it impossible to avoid them, the mountain of debt which would be standing there at the end of the chapter and what part this mountain played in the transaction. It made him feel a little sick as he read a few paragraphs of the bland automatic discussion regarding preparations for war, as if it were an international football match which was being staged in an unusually elaborate manner. But he closed the newspapers, and turned to his more obviously personal affairs.

It was nearly an hour later when he heard Mrs. Harradson make her exit from their flat, and convulsively descend to her own quarters. He had been writing, but he now put down his pen, stood up, and made his way across the landing.

Hester had not left, or he certainly would have heard her. He found her, as he had expected, in their miniature sitting-room. She was writing a letter. As he entered the room she rose from her seat. They faced one another rather starkly, for the space for manœuvre being so limited there was nothing else to do. With the best will in the world, he could not refrain from noting the ludicrousness of her expression. She stood lady-likely at bay, exposing reproachfully her 'eyeballs' and holding her 'big silly mouth' ostentatiously sealed; to laugh was the only rational action, and he came very near to surrendering to the dictates of common sense.

If this woman would only forget the ladylike shrouding of her hips, if this mermaid would be oblivious of her well-tailored tail! Aloud his words were,

'Hester, are you sure I am not disturbing you?'

Hester answered clearly and even sharply,

'No.'

'I say, you must have thought I had taken leave of my senses. Well, that is exactly what did happen. I am most frightfully sorry. Please do forgive me, Hester!'

'I suppose I must,' she said. 'I did not at all like the form your madness took.'

'I know! They say that under an anæsthetic people say the most awful things.'

'You were not under an anæsthetic,' she retorted.

'True. But the fact is I probably need an anæsthetic. Then people sometimes say worse things without them.'

He took one step forward, all that was needed for complete contact, and placed both his arms around her. She turned, of course, the big silly mouth away. But very soon the mutual warmth and marital pressures converted her from an indignant icicle into a mass of melting flesh. A similar transformation occurred in the masterful analyst. This was not at all, at the conference in the neighbouring flat, as it had been planned to proceed. Eros was a factor he always left out of his calculations and when he first remarked that the above pressures were resulting in the same warmth on his side as he had intended them to induce on hers, he was traversed by what almost amounted to a shudder. The absurd was happening. He was unable to escape from the absurd; that absurd which was for him an analogous enormity to *l'infâme*. It was with mortification that he arrived a quarter of an hour late at the restaurant where he was meeting for lunch an ex-colleague, a man whose friendship he greatly prized.

CHAPTER V

Idealism Recognized

THE house and garage of Percy Lamport was hemmed in by high walls and laurel bushes. In the most 'desirable' part of Hampstead, above which were once the wastes of the Heath, an unusual degree of privacy had been contrived by the original 'homemaker'. What was at present to be found at the core of this seclusion, within the massive Edwardian walls of the many-roomed palatial site? An individual, but not exactly the kind of human being around whom high walls must be raised.

Percy Lamport was a heavy doe-like creature. He had dwelt for a long time in Welwyn, the original 'garden-city': one of a group of families who had collectively evolved a strongly-marked mannerism, suggestive of the coy shyness of a retiring herbivore. If one can imagine a phenomenally smart, forever quietly-amused yak, standing quite still, slyly self-conscious, its big knowing eye shining with quiet, self-satisfied humour, standing almost as if it expected to be stroked or hugged, for being so entirely *understanding* an animal, if you can summon to stand there in your fancy such a curious beast, always *sideways*, always one-eyed, not looking at you, but at some mesmerically absurd thought which bemused and transfixed it, *then* you would, by the same token, be in the presence of Percy Lamport Esq.

In a street in Welwyn, to this day, a herd of these animals may be encountered: a whole tribe of people, neighbours and friends, who stand quietly like obedient ponies, or like Yaks on a secluded hillside; or in the cages of a zoo, presenting you with a profile in which is a big, amused, contemplative eye. One of these Welwynites was known to René, a colleague, a lecturer in physics. This strange professor would stand there, before his academic audience, as if thunderstruck with quiet fun, in front of a chart of the astral universe, making the

45

entire galaxies and starry clusters seem delightfully ridiculous. René had watched him with uneasiness, almost with alarm, and with his brother-in-law Percy Lamport, most true to type and capable of remaining in profile with the 'Welwyn eye' as René called it for minutes at a time, he was never quite at his ease.

This great retiring mansion situated near the crest of Hampstead Hill, far from the built-over bog-lands of the Thames-side, had been selected in the 'twenties' by Percy Lamport and his wife Mary, to meet the needs of a growing family, and in view of his mounting prosperity. As an executive in a big Insurance business, now in his early fifties, Percy was a minor magnate. Ultra-liberal Welwyn-origins accounted for his reading-matter: the *News Chronicle* and *The New Statesman and Nation* and other left-wing periodicals. And as a matter-of-fact, the richer he became, the more to the left these newspapers and weeklies moved. An enlightened interest in the Fine Arts was also, with him, of radical origins. He had become the possessor of an original Matisse, two or three Vlaminks, a half-dozen Marie Laurençins, the painter most exactly corresponding to his taste. Shaw, G. D. H. Cole, Priestley, Katherine Mansfield, Wystan Auden, *The Road to Wigan Pier*, *Father Brown*, was the sort of literature to be found in his study. So his cultural habits of thought were orthodoxly-liberal and unusually developed for a City man.

Such was René Harding's brother-in-law: it was Tuesday, May the 23rd, and René and his wife accordingly were to go to dinner in Hampstead; with 'Big Business' as René called him.

At 7.30 in the evening, as René stood beside the taxi, waiting for his change, his eye rested upon the superbly spacious house, so beautifully unlike the House that Jack Built. Nothing absurd about *this* house. How excellently abstract wealth was after all: it got rid of the idiosyncratic, the absurd! Lobb, the chauffeur, stood beside the Cadillac: so exactly uniformed, his face so excellently devoid of expression, *he* was not absurd.

(His *name* was, but not the chauffeur.) And as to the Cadillac,
no Cadillac can possibly be absurd. A few moments later René
and Hester passed the waiting car and began to ascend the
six steps to the pair of ponderous front doors. One of these
opened, and 'Rod' (Rodriques), most hysterical of spaniels,
rushed out, seething with the wildest joy. He was immediately
followed by Pauline—his owner, speaking legally, his goddess
in canine theology. Pauline was twenty, and though lacking
the fanatical abandon of her dog, possessed the impulsive
vitality of her years. On seeing René, with an ardour worthy
of Rod, she sprang at him, seized his beard, and flung her
arms convulsively around his neck.

'My bear-uncle! My old bear-uncle, where have you been?
What have you been doing with yourself? Oh, make your bear-
noise, René darling!' And René, lifting his bearded face in
the air, gave his ho-ho-ho laugh: and she echoed delightedly,
in a higher register, his famous ho-ho-ho.

Pauline turned to Hester, and another girl was now descending the steps. They were going to the Ballet at Covent Garden,
Hester was told: and then Pauline stood just below René, with
her face in profile, presenting him, for a few moments, a
heredity 'Welwyn eye'. Then she looked up, and enquired,
'When am I coming to hear you lecture? They say you are a
wonderful lecturer. May I come next week?'

René shook his head.

'Afraid not,' he told her. 'I shan't be there.'

'You always put me off. You despise my I.Q., I suppose,
that's it.'

As she got into the car she was wagging her finger at him.
From the doorway René blew her a bearded kiss. With a
deafening ovation in reverse from Rod, the Cadillac moved
away.

The quietness and gloom of the dark hall, after the noisy
scene without, almost startled René and he stopped. At the
far end a door was open, and through it Percy Lamport
appeared. Before the latter had passed into the hall, René had
put himself into rapid motion, at the same time crying 'Ah,
Percy!' His advance across the hall was at so smart a pace
that it caused small waves to dart and jump around the foot

of his torso—where the jacket had no support the cloth was prone to frisk. His bearded head was carried heroically aloft, as the superb figure-head cut through the gloom towards his smiling host.

Le roi René was not a man to be unconscious of style, in himself or others. He delighted to swim through space with the air of a Louis the Eleventh, bearing himself as a King of France hurrying to meet the Emperor Maximilian. He realized that his gait and gesture were too superb for his status or for the occasion. But this amused him. Sometimes he would deliberately act the king, or the statesman, about whom he was just then reading. De Richelieu he was very fond of impersonating.

These tricks and fancies, however, were incidental, and they never caused him to forget a mission or an opportunity. The present, he recognized, belonged to the latter class. He understood quite well with what object Mary had arranged this visit.

As ever, like an ill-conceived figure on the reverse side of a splendidly designed coin, was the unfortunate Hester. It would be a pity to exaggerate this, for it was nothing more than an irritable consciousness at times presenting itself, as of something amiss, but never strong enough to spoil the sensation experienced in his more flamboyant moments. But there was after all Hester to be counted in, as part of any picture in which le roi René was starring.

Just in a flash, as he swept across the shadowy hall, he saw the figure at his heels: the hips were placed too low and gave her gait a sexish drag, her neck was too long, which acted as a sort of pole to carry Big Eyes aloft.

Mary's face, Mary's gait did not advertise . . . oh, the horror of our lot. But *he* was goatish, he knew that: and all Hester was—was the Sandwich woman of his Achilles' heel: with some women a man must feel like a dog with a chicken tied around his neck. But he switched off the tell-tale image, as one switches off the radio when it gets too bad, and thrust his head a fraction higher and quickened his quick dancing step.

But now, driving the smiling Percy back, he entered the drawing-room like a conqueror. When he looked in Mary's face the forecast was favourable, there were no danger signals in her eyes, they just looked at him serenely. As to Percy, he was standing sideways, an eye in the side of his face, a darkly mischievous, mesmerized amusement carrying the gaze outwards to the horizon. Suddenly awakening out of his trance he proposed a drink, and all of them soon stood holding their sherry glasses, containing a wine as near to a tasteless abstraction as the best Rhine wine. Among other things, Percy was a member of the Food and Wine Society. Sherry is the last thing the Englishman learns how to buy.

René disapproved of his host's orthodoxy in the matter of painting, of his tame acceptance of fashionable pressure, and the values imposed. He regarded these values as an offence, when sponsored by a stupid man. Percy was a prize idiot, he had no right to these views—he should be collecting Academic monstrosities. So, refusing to take Percy's *avantgardisme* seriously, he nevertheless always enquired with great politeness about any new purchase, which was usually to be found on the walls.

'A new one I think.'

He had observed something which it seemed to him he had not seen before: the figure of a hanging man in some enclosed place, with a number of big-headed, round-faced marionettes, all expressing blood-lust and derision. One pulled at the rope, one lighted an immodestly-carved pipe of great size. A dog scratched itself, with a flea nearly as large as the dog squatting on its rump. He examined it an inch from the glass, *très amateur*.

'Ecole de Paris?' he enquired.

'No,' Percy told him. 'This is a Belgian etcher of the nineteenth century. His name is Ensor. I am not quite sure how much I like him.'

'No, I suppose it is not easy to make up one's mind straight away.'

'You have to live with a picture before you can say whether you really like it.'

'I can see how that might be.' René nodded his head sagely.

René stood gazing at the tongue protruding from the mouth of the victim. Meanwhile, the happy possessor of the picture

stood in profile, the one eye amusedly and with infinite knowingness simmering away all to itself. As René turned to speak
to him he had the mental comment, as his eye fixed itself upon
the profile, 'Un Ensor, sapristi!'

'I must say I rather take to this,' he declared aloud.

'You like it? I am glad of that. I find I like it more and
more.'

'It does grow on one,' the other agreed. René moved down
the room to where he thought he saw a new Marie Laurençin.
Laurençin heads all resemble one another to such a degree
that anyone not an expert may well find it difficult to say
which is which.

'I have not seen this one, have I, Percy?'

' "Clothilde"? . . . Yes, you have often seen the "Clothilde".
It used to hang in the dining-room not far from the door. I
mean on the same side as the door. I think it is wonderful.'

'Of course I remember it. How stupid of me.'

'It is not stupid,' Percy protested. 'With her pictures even
I sometimes forget which is which.'

'How extraordinary!' exclaimed René. 'I should have
thought . . .'

'I am not often at a loss,' Percy smiled.

René had noticed that they were now alone in the room.
Mary, he had assumed, had abstracted Hester purposively.
Percy looked up and said almost with violence, 'I want to
tell you how greatly I admire your action in resigning your
position at the University. It is one of the finest things I have
ever heard of. I congratulate you.'

This took René's breath away. For a moment he said
nothing and stared a little stupidly at his brother-in-law.
Suddenly he recovered, and almost shouted, 'My dear chap,
you don't know how those words have cheered me. I knew
you would understand. But the wholehearted nature of
your support, your uncompromising endorsement of what I
have done, well, it's like a breath of fresh air. Thank you,
Percy.'

'It is I who have to thank you for setting all of us an
example of fearless courage, of facing up to obscurantism and
hypocrisy, the conservative mind which crushes all the life

out of our institutions. To give up everything rather than be privy . . . to the intellectual fraud perpetrated in the name of education. My dear chap, it is inexpressibly fine, it is to have done a great public service. I wish I had half your guts!'

René listened in growing amazement. Did Percy mean that if he had the guts he would denounce the villanies of the great Insurance Companies?

Did he regard himself as a village Hampden manqué? Apparently his amazing brother-in-law derived pleasure from imagining a day when he would return as usual from his office, kiss his wife, and announce that they at once must pack: that he was saying good-bye to Insurance, that he was selling his houses, cars, and so on, dismissing the servants and that in future they would dwell in a three-room flat in Pimlico or Shepherd's Bush. René had often speculated as to what effect a life-long diet of revolutionary journalism might have upon a highly successful executive. It now was obvious that marxism was simply transmuted into romance, into British Dare-to-be-a-Danielism. As to whether Percy understood, or indeed took the faintest interest in what precisely were the principles behind his brother-in-law's unwordly action, René could only guess. He supposed that in a woolly way the good Percy labelled as 'idealism' any defiance of an established order, or institutions: 'idealism' being the word traditionally favoured by the revolutionary journalist for the impulse in the moral man to devote himself to the welfare of men-in-general. Clearly Percy's reaction would be just to affix the label 'idealism', without going further into the matter. He never went behind words or underneath clichés or slogans. Since they had never had any really serious talk, his brother-in-law could not be otherwise than quite ignorant of what René's beliefs were.

'Percy,' he said, with emotion in his voice, 'what you have been saying has had a tremendously tonic effect. I daresay you can imagine the view of the world is simply that I am a fool. I am not made of wood and such support as yours is a wonderful stimulus.'

Percy looked down at the floor steadily for about a minute, hearing himself praised; just as he would had he scored a century for his old school and was being congratulated by the

Captain of the Eleven or the Headmaster: 'Splendid, Lamport.
A faultless innings!' Then he looked up, smiling a little bash-
fully. 'Will you have another glass of sherry, René? It is some
stuff Simon recommended.'

And they moved back to the table where the sherry and
glasses had been placed.

Mary appeared followed by Hester, and she saw at once,
by the faces of the two men, that both were agreeably excited;
obviously their relations had been changed and cemented, by
some emotional impact occurring for the first time. Percy wore
an expression with which she was familiar. He had looked like
that when he had appeared for the first time in coast-guard
uniform, in the War to End War: or when, for instance, he had
broken with the firm of family solicitors on learning that they
had behaved with typical professional caddishness and dis-
regard for the laws of fair-play in a case which he had
entrusted to them. She guessed that her husband must have
gone quixotic in emulation of her brother, and that he had
just shown his mettle in setting about some windmill, to prove
that he was just as mad as René. Her eyes rested with a gentle
toleration on the pair of them. Perhaps, after all, they were
right and she was wrong. But she found it very difficult to take
either of them seriously.

At dinner a new consignment of champagne was tried out,
to the popping of corks and raising of glasses (*du champagne!*
just as if René had performed a remarkable feat forsooth).
After a glass or two René began ho-ho-hoing. The occasion
became almost festive, and Mary frowned a little as she smiled,
feeling among other things that it was bad policy for her to
appear in too *carefree* a rôle. Would Percy understand him?
He was very easy to misunderstand! And Percy would expect
him to behave with a proper gravity, his fellow-Quichote in
keeping with his recent heroism. So Mary remained a little
severe throughout.

When, however, Percy observed, 'What do you think,
René, about the Russian Pact? Are we going to have an
Alliance with Russia against Hitler, or not?', the face of the
ex-professor subtly altered: it did not become graver, but
rather a little soberer and immediately wary.

'No,' he said cautiously. 'No, there will of course be no pact between England and Russia against Germany.'

Percy looked almost startled at the aplomb of this assertion. 'You say *of course* there will be no pact. *The Times* seems to think there may be.' Percy looked up through the screen of his eyebrows, crumbling the bread at the side of his plate.

'That, I believe, is very unduly sanguine. All history points the other way. But it is quite usual for *The Times* to ignore history.'

Percy smiled. '*Sometimes*, certainly.'

'There is much affinity between the Russians and Germans. The Russians naturally will think that it would give us great pleasure to see the Russian and German dictatorships destroying one another.'

'But may they not,' Percy protested, 'desire to see Hitler destroyed?'

René shook his head. 'That is too simple,' he said. 'Russia would not *help* Hitler, with arms. But might agree to a limited pact with her. Why not? Moscow, after all, would relish the sight of Germany exhausting itself in defeating England or vice versa. One of the great mistakes the English make is to believe themselves lovable.'

Percy laughed. 'There is some truth in that.'

'Russia will never go to war if it can possibly avoid it, though it is said to be much stronger than is generally supposed. It will always prefer not to commit itself deeply. . . . For the rest, there are two things always to bear in mind. *First,* the Russian people are traditionally very averse to war. Unlike the Germans. Unlike us. *Secondly,* the Russian ruling class have always got on well with the Germans, and have made use of them whenever possible. The Armies have still been friendly when the politicians were bickering.'

There was a pause, Percy continued to eat in silence. Mary and Hester smiled at one another, as if to say, 'Men are very clever! It is a debate where our merely feminine views would be *de trop*.'

The host wiped his mouth and pushed his chair back. 'Your two cardinal points,' he began, 'may or may not be of the decisive character that you attribute to them. I am not competent to judge. What I do know is that I should be indeed sorry should the pact not materialize.'

'I too.' René vigorously nodded his head.

'What is more,' Percy continued, 'the situation would then be of the utmost gravity.'

'I agree, it could hardly be graver. For ten years now we have carefully progressed, as if that were our aim, into this terrible situation. It seems to me, in all seriousness, that there has been a great deal of deliberation in getting ourselves tied up in a worse and worse position from which nothing can disengage us.'

Percy stared at him. 'Do I understand you to say that it was on *purpose* that we find ourselves in this highly dangerous situation?'

'After years of the closest observation and exhaustive research,' René told his brother-in-law, 'I find it impossible to come to any other conclusion.'

At this unexpected dénouement, of what had succeeded his initial enquiry regarding the proposed Russian pact, Percy's first reaction was one of bewilderment. This was expressed in his face with a most graphic explicitness. Next, it could with a comic distinctness be observed transforming itself into something else. The bewilderment hardened into suspicion: Percy could be seen to cast a covert glance at the bearded oracle! Mary noted the arrival of second-thoughts with anxiety. For absurd as the phase of Percy and René's relationship appeared to her, in which the quixotic was in the ascendant, yet Mary would have far preferred that to one in which her husband came to look upon René as a lunatic. Nor was René unaware that he had gone too far. Formerly he had never moved on to an enlightened plane in conversing with Mary's husband, nor with Mary either, except for one lapse, which had not developed. He asked himself how he had come to be led into this, and why he had not contented himself with some conventional explanation. 'It was the prophet coming out,' he told himself, with an internal grimace.

René made no further move, as though to allow his oracular statement to take effect (though he sincerely hoped that it might not); meanwhile he gave himself up to the delights of a Coupe Marocaine, wondering what elixir it was which Percy's Greek cook had introduced into this exotic *entremet*. Mary and Hester, who both had memories of Pangbourne, were outside this political debate, discussing mutual friends. 'Old Mrs. Proctor,' Mary said, 'had been born in India, and told me she was a Buddhist, and was convinced that in her next incarnation she would be a Siamese cat.'—'I like old Mrs. Proctor,' Hester mused.—'I did too. Her choice of a Siamese cat accurately reflected her nature. She *was* a cat, but a Siamese cat!' And laughed.

But Percy was suffering another transformation. His face had cleared up. He was obviously once more in the clutches of some heroic emotion, it seemed to Mary. And at this moment he broke the silence between the two men, which must have lasted several minutes.

'What you said was a hard saying,' Percy told his brother-in-law. 'Just for a moment it was too much even for me.'

Greatly relieved at his tone, René replied ambiguously, 'The world is a hard place.' He was resolved not to permit himself any further departures from the beaten track.

'Indeed it is!' Percy answered heartily. 'But do you really believe that the Tories would be such ruthless monsters as to *arrange* a second world-war . . . yes, even connive at the successful emergence, or in effect *create* such a bloodthirsty little gangster as Herr Hitler, such a scourge of God, to advance their class interests by a shambles.'

René almost laughed outright. His brother-in-law was incapable of imagining any turpitude other than a Tory-capital one. It was a masterpiece of doctrinaire delusion.

'The macchiavellian Tory is capable of anything,' René asserted with suitable solemnity, having decided to convert it into a Party matter.

'You think he would go that far?' Percy leant forward. 'Do you think he would pull down the world about his head, if necessary, in order to have his stupid way?'

'Don't you? Consider the deeds of his secret service! He deals in political murder just as much as the Hitlerites or Italian fascists.'

'I still recoil,' Percy protested, 'at the picture of civilized

men, however corrupt, plotting the destruction of whole populations, and even sacrificing perhaps half of their own. I consider Mr. Churchill a very bad man, but scarcely a Borgia.'

René stroked his beard; he was thinking of the Borgias.

'All Tories are potential Borgias,' René laid it down (for
if he was so stupid as he had revealed himself, even so childish
a statement as this would go down all right!). 'I say it quite
seriously,' he added—for he believed he saw a shade of suspicion darkening his brother-in-law's face, and must plug it
in pretty stiff. 'The ruling class of a country, the traditional
ruling class, is completely ruthless. Human emotions are
luxuries which those desiring power must discard entirely.'

'You speak like Machiavelli,' Percy smiled.

'But the modern politician behaves like Machiavelli. This
is brought home to the historian, though he is very careful
never to betray the guilty secrets he has learned. It is more
than his place is worth. As the servant of the ruling class, he
cannot but become privy in the course of his researches to the
dark secrets of his masters.'

'But, René,' Mary interposed. 'Was Lord Macaulay, for
instance, in possession of these criminal secrets?'

'Of course he was,' her brother told her, smiling. 'But he
wanted to be a . . .'

'A LORD!' Percy almost roared delightedly

'Exactly!' René smiled.

'I think you are a pair of dreadful cynics!' Mary laughed,
all the jolliness of the dinner having returned.

'Well, I do not propose to reveal any of the dark secrets I
have myself come across. Let me take an incident which is
described in every history of the United States. I refer to the
sinking in Havana Harbour of the battleship *Maine*. At the
time the Americans were accused of doing this. The motive
would be obvious: namely, so to inflame American opinion
that war with Spain would be inevitable. Well now, when it
was said that the *Americans* were responsible for the sinking
of this ship, with enormous loss of life, the American Government was clearly *visé*. But the President was determined to
have no war if he could possibly help it. So would it be the
War-party of which Theodore Roosevelt was a prominent

member? Would they murder hundreds of their countrymen, gallant seamen, in order to precipitate a war? The answer is, to my mind, that they would. Indeed, they would blow up half the world to have their way. And this goes for all politicians in all places. Guests are no longer poisoned by their hosts, as was the case in the Italy of the Borgias. That is too crude. Hypocrisy has, in our society, put a thick patina over everything: there are a number of forms of violence which must not be indulged in. But whereas in the Italy of the Borgias massacre was confined to quite modest numbers, today a man (a politician) may destroy ten million people without it ever being remarked that he has behaved rather badly.'

They all had listened to this more or less attentively.

'It may have been accident,' Mary observed. 'It may just have blown up of its own accord.'

'No one ever thought it did that,' René replied. 'The more sinister explanation is practically uncontradicted.'

'The Americans are a nation of gangsters,' was Percy's comment, 'and you can hardly argue, because Americans were capable of such an action, that Englishmen would be liable to commit an equally foul crime.'

René laughed.

'Upon such a generalization as that "all Americans are gangsters" you cannot safely base an argument. Bryan, for instance, Vice-President in Woodrow Wilson's administration, was not a gangster. There are, let us admit, a few exceptions to the rule that all politicians are blackguards. Americans as a *whole* are no more gangsters than we are. Sorry.'

'No. I am sorry too. The good Americans—if there are any —are untypical.' Percy, like many of his countrymen, took up a very rigid position regarding the Yahoo on the other side of the Atlantic. The ex-professor pushed his chair back and laughed negligently.

'My illustration was unfortunate. I forgot how opaque the atmosphere of prejudice is. I should not have gone for my illustration to the United States. But there is no particular point in re-starting and taking my illustration from nearer home. By all means retain your illusions regarding playing-the-game and a race of "Very Perfect Gentlemen".' He looked at his host and smiled. 'Remember, though, that it is usually Tories who speak about playing the game. Do not be *too* credulous.'

Soon after this the two ladies withdrew. The men remained standing. After a pause, as though for *recueillement* on the part of Percy, that gentleman practically re-enacted the scene of just before dinner, with this difference that he had now drunk quite a lot, and his guest also resembled him in this respect. During his emotional expansiveness Percy became quite red in the face, and once or twice moved dramatically close to his brother-in-law.

'How is it, René, that we have never until tonight really got to know one another? Why have we never had any good talks before? It is really astonishing how little we have found to say to one another.'

René knew perfectly well the answer, why they had never had any serious conversation before. But he affected to be at least as astonished as Percy at that fact. He had looked upon Mary's husband as a man with whom he had so little in common that it was unnecessary to exchange anything more than commonplaces. But René crashed, almost with violence, with a heartiness even exceeding the other's, 'Yes, is it not amazing that all these years we should have been content to discuss the weather, or some child-murder or football-match . . . Marie Laurençin!'

They both laughed, looking around for one of the ubiquitous stylized inanities.

'It is extraordinary,' he went on, 'how something happens . . . and two people begin talking without any social inhibition and are revealed to one another. It is one of the most extraordinary things in life!'

'Absolutely!' Percy noisily responded. '*The* most extraordinary.'

'The most! It is like the discovery of Plastic.' René capped the whole matter. 'Just a jolly old milk-bottle, the sort the slovenly housewife leaves hardening away there on a shelf —too damned lazy to wash it out and return it to the milkman, and the stuff brought about by her slack habits is *plastic*. World-shaking discovery. A universal substance such as the alchemist dreamed of. Tea-trays, false-teeth, cups and saucers, eye-glasses, surgical instruments, flying-machines—all. out of a bottle of milk. We have been like the indolent housewife, you and I, Percy. We ought to be damned-well ashamed of ourselves!'

Percy did not entirely come up to his guest's comic picture of him, and there were times when he showed a certain uneasiness. So now, smiling a little dubiously, he remarked, 'We neither of us perhaps can claim to possess such staggering properties as are to be found in a neglected milk-bottle. But I think you are a very remarkable person: our talk tonight has given me furiously to think. And I like thinking furiously.'

'So do I.' René discharged a furious puff of smoke from his dilated nostrils. They sat down and talked a little more, Percy saying, among other things, what a marvellous insight his new friend had into American history. 'But of course it is your job,' to which the historian replied, 'It is in fact a pity that Englishmen do not know a little more how America came to be what it is.' Then suddenly Percy drew his chair, with some violence, near to that of René.

'Look here, my dear fellow, I have been thinking about this ever since Mary informed me of your splendid gesture, how you laid down your post . . . in a spirit of the purest idealism. Whenever I think of it I marvel—how many people would sacrifice everything for a principle, expose themselves . . . well, to penury? Now, my dear fellow, I am a relative and you must allow me to say this. In order to meet the difficulties which must immediately confront you, you must allow me to place at your disposal the sum of one thousand pounds.'

René began to say, 'I could not think of allowing . . .' But he was interrupted by Percy, waving such remonstrances away with an imperious hand.

'The sum I have mentioned means nothing to me, I can very easily spare it. Needless to say, it is not my habit to distribute cheques. But in *this* case I look upon it as a paltry sum, and let me say at once that if you should require more in the first year or two to keep you going, do not hesitate to turn to me. I should be ashamed of myself if I did not support you in any way in my power.'

3

'But really, old chap . . .'

Getting to his feet with a purposeful air, Percy said, 'Will you wait here for a moment, I shall be back immediately. I am going to my study to draw this cheque on the spot. Excuse me. I shall really only be two or three minutes.'

He left the room, and René, who had risen, went to the table and poured himself out another brandy. As soon as he was alone René's face contracted. Glaring down at his glass, he would appear to be concentrating for purposes of analysis.

The Absurd was once more puzzling him. This man he was with was so obviously not screwed down tight, and half-finished: kept attacking him—yes, actually *assaulting* him—with nonsensical approbation! Then he would shoot off, as he now had done, into the *néant*, soon to reappear with a cheque for a thousand pounds. Was this faery gold? Was he an emissary of Nonsense in person? Yes, would these thousand pounds only be convertible into a thousand absurdities? For such a figure could not possibly deal in a rational currency.

But René poured down more brandy and squared his shoulders. It was his brother-in-law . . . after all, who slept with Mary every night. Mary, stable as a rock, she would not be closely associated with so unstable an entity were she not assured that his money came from a normal mint. No.

Although he had drilled himself into tolerance of the Absurd by the time Percy hustled in, the first impact of the bird's-nest coloured thatch, the rimless glasses (put on to write the cheque), produced a mild spasm of alarm, of the type always experienced when Mrs. Harradson emitted, 'Oo, sir, Professor Harding, sir!'

But he forced an agreeably abstracted expression on to his face (no unseemly expectancy of what was about to happen, yet . . . in a musing of a happy kind, so that if anything *did* drop in his lap it would be received benignly, without too crudely abrupt a change of countenance).

'I say, Percy, I ought not to take this you know! I am quite serious,' he protested, as Percy placed an envelope upon the table beside him. 'You're a terrific brick!' (He supposed that 'brick' was the kind of idiot word that belonged to the vocabulary of this sort of homunculus.) 'But I know I should refuse!'

'Nonsense, my dear chap!'

René looked up quickly at the word 'nonsense'.

'I don't know what Hester would say if she could see me pocketing this,' as he picked up the envelope and put it in his breast pocket. He almost laughed at the thought of Hester's disgust at the sight of a thousand quid. 'Hester always says I have no proper pride.'

'She will soon get over it, I expect.' For this was rather in excess of what could be absorbed by the homunculus on the serious level.

'I expect so, poor dear girl. For she takes a more serious view than I do of our future.'

'Women are born pessimists,' Percy told him.

René nodded his head. 'They are the eternal Greek Chorus.' Then quickly placing his hand upon that of his host, which lay, hairy and sprawling, on the table, and administering a slight pressure, he exclaimed fruitily, 'I am your debtor for life, old man. I do not mean I shall not repay you this sum. I mean that when I *do*, I shall still be your debtor.'

'Nonsense!'

At this second 'nonsense' René shot up his head even more quickly, and examined closely the bird's-nest hair, the blankly shining eye-glasses. Had he read his suspicions? Has this old bourgeois second-sight?

But Percy resumed the dinner-table conversation, which had apparently given him an appetite for political and other discussion; or there had been something René had said which had stirred him into unaccustomed speculation.

'In my lifetime,' he began, 'the attitude to violent death has completely changed.'

'In mine too. We have become like the Orientals.'

Signs of animation were seen in the bird's-nest-topped head, with its glazed eye-sockets (for the glasses were still there). 'Orientalized, are we? You think that?'

'All I meant was, 'René clarified, 'that in the past it was always said that our attitude to death was different from that of the Oriental races. Today one does not hear that said, and I think that there is no longer any justification for saying it.'

'No, there is not. I do not mind being blasted out of my house by a "super-bomb" at any moment. This is a quite new attitude.—I mean my callousness about myself.'

A frown grew upon René's face, like a hieratic tree, during Percy's self-analysis. The last thing that he desired was a serious discussion with this auriferous Nobody. But such self-complacent revelation of callousness normally would have provoked him to didactic reproof.

'Ah ha, yes, very painful,' he muttered.

'Rather the reverse,' the callous one smilingly corrected. 'But I often have wondered,' he went on, 'whether the sort of orientalizing we have undergone was not due to the extraordinary growth of Jewish influence.'

(Ha! An anti-semite, thought to himself the surprised listener. One of the City Man's substitutes for thought—the fox-hunting still in the blood of the stockjobber. But he waited.)

'It is my opinion that the Jews have too much influence,' Percy continued truculently, glancing at his frowning companion; the frown still there which had grown under the stimulus of passing reference to high explosives and high finance.

'I should be interested to know your opinion, René, of the Jewish question.'

Stirring himself reluctantly, this frowning guest, whose profession it was to have opinions, drank his brandy slowly, ponderously put down the glass, and a shade grumpily gave his opinion.

'The Jews. The Jews are an alibi for all the double-dealers, plotters and intriguers, fomenters of wars, *und so weiter*. A useful tribe, they take the rap for everything.'

It was with a much colder voice that the bird's-nest-crowned mask drawled, 'So you regard the Jews as much maligned?'

'They certainly are maligned. They have their own advocates in plenty; I am only interested in justice, and I notice numbers of malefactors escaping on the backs of the Jews.'

Percy's disappointment was patent, he was even ruffled. 'In the Insurance business . . .'

'Ah yes, in the Insurance business you do meet a lot of bad hats with semitic cognomens.'

'You do indeed,' Percy asserted with asperity and then followed several accounts of fabulous Insurance frauds, and the part his company had played in same. The last of these stories was laughter-provoking, the delinquent possessing an eye for the farcical, and both narrator and listener became uproarious and mingled their laughs as they poured themselves fresh glasses of brandy. The bad patch in the conversation was over. Subjects in which the City man's passions were not aroused succeeded, one or two of which revealing an identity of view and so confirming Percy's new-found belief in his brother-in-law's wisdom. It seemed a long time to René since their wives had left them when his host got up and led the way to the drawing-room.

As all were moving about near the open front door preparatory to the departure of the two guests, René went up to his sister and kissed her, murmuring almost in her ear, 'Marie, tu est si belle, tu est si bonne!' The serene roman-face of the slightly-smiling Mary accepted the mariolatry blandly, squeezing her brother's arm. And over her shoulder could be seen in the light of the hall lamp the figure of Percy, his head once more in profile, his shining eye rapt in a dream of unutterable knowingness. René saw him as a large bird, a hen-bird, a bird's-nest upon its head, transfixed in a dream of exultant intensity; a bird who had just laid a splendid golden egg.

.

CHAPTER VI

How Victor Saw the Matter

'ARE you a subscriber to a Press-Clipping Agency?' Janet Painter looked across the marble table at her brother. He shook his head. 'You did not read my story about you then, I expect.'

'What was that?' René was watching a girl at a neighbouring table who had been sketching him he thought. He had seen no sketching in the Café Royal for a long time. Habits were changing among the native artists. Spectacled girls were always the hottest: her specs were the big rimless ones that went with myopic, fat, red-lipped, provincial Sunday School sexiness. As greedy for it, as red-cheeked lads for jam. She turned towards him and smiled. He pointed his bearded lips and puffed a pencil of blue smoke.

'The little beast carts that sketch-book around with her as a means of getting off,' he ruminated. 'She sketches men into her fat little net. Probably been trodden by several hundred Yorkshire Tykes or Shropshire Lads. Now up in the capital, is swimming around with that protruding fish-mouth of hers below the short fat nose.' He removed his eyes from the coarse bit of sex-bait and caught Victor's eye, which had been covertly feasting upon the same abject morsel. Not for the first time did he find himself cruising in the same dirty waters as Victor. They had so few tastes in common that *this* one he found particularly startling.

'Idealism,' his sister was saying, 'was the caption for my story.'

'Idealism?' René repeated. 'The World as idea and as imagination. I see.'

'Yes, I say the most brilliant of our "young" professors, whose book, *The Secret History of World War II*, created such a sensation last year. After enumerating a few of his more glittering academic honours, I went on to describe how at last

64

unable to bear the feeling of guilt, he had resigned his professorship. The sense of guilt had grown with his increasing sense of the evilness of the system his teaching was designed to support. Now, he, accompanied by his beautiful young wife, who with great bravery is following him into the wilderness, are booking a passage for Canada, where they are to start a new life. "Such idealism," my story concluded, "is not often met with outside the pages of a novel." '

'Oh, why didn't you tell me about this, Janet?' drawled Victor fruitily in his throat. 'How clever of you, darling!'

Mr. Victor Painter was Janet's husband, but his classily-barking patronage she took no more notice of than if he had been a familiar dog.

'Where has this story found a home,' René enquired, also ignoring the drawling noise.

'In the *Ladies' Realm*,' she told him. 'But I am slithering another one into the gossip of the *Daily Telegram*.'

Meanwhile Hester glowed appreciatively, actually blushing a little.

The four had just been dining within, in the smallish room where the orchestra performs.

The party consisted exclusively of René and his brother-in-law, Victor Painter, and their wives. This party had been proposed by René, with the purpose of passing an evening with Janet, his second sister: thirty-seven, eight years junior to Mary, and ten years younger than himself. She was dark and in some ways a slenderer version of Mary, and in character much less substantial too: Victor and Janet were a pointedly youthful thirty-seven. The ten years which separated René inflated by them to twenty. Across these twenty-odd, Victor addressed his brother-in-law as from a long way off. His learning and renown served to confer upon these inflated distances a proverbial likelihood. In Victor's manner, too, there was always something which implied that, as decade after decade passed, he automatically was destined to become the possessor of a similar learning and renown. If, at present, he was ignorant and quite unknown, this was merely owing to his youth (for the ten years he added to René's age, he took off his own); consequently it was in fact across no less than three decades, rather than two, that he addressed his wife's brother. |

To such a harmless rearrangement of nature and adoption of a false position René would not have objected (his beard alone was a testimony to his indifference to the Zeitgeist), had it not been for his brother-in-law's general vulgarity and distinct proclivity to 'bound'. ·

Victor was a product of Liverpool, and the accent with which·he had originally spoken was that peculiar to Lancashire: in no way inferior to B.B.C. English certainly, but that had not been Victor's view. He had come to London young, after a brief period as a wool clerk. It had been borne in upon him immediately that to speak as if an Old School Tie hung around his somewhat scraggy neck instead of a work-a-day necktie was essential for success. Giving proof of a certain histrionic endowment, he completely suppressed the locutions and tang of the Merseyside. He substituted the languid drawl of a Vaudeville toff.

As he strolled from one room to another of their little house, it was with so manifest an indifference to the lapse of time, that anyone could see he had been born in the top drawer, and that *Time is Made for Slaves* was his family motto.

His brother-in-law always listened to his throaty baying tones with boredom, and found it difficult to hide his contempt for this Ersatz gentleman. There had even been a moment in Victor Painter's life when his surname appeared to him a little compromising: and he had once considered changing it by deed poll. Did it not draw attention, quite unnecessarily, to how his ancestors had made their living? For *painter* signified, of course, a fellow on a ladder painting a front of a house. But it was not long before he learned that those privileged beings, the painters of easel-pictures, invariably referred to themselves as *painters*. So he was on good terms again with his name, and even a little proud of it. He thought of Lord Leighton and of Sir Alfred Munnings, and when asked what his name was by, say, a hotel clerk, he barked proudly, *'Painter.'* ·

Victor by profession was the third on the notepaper of a not-very-prosperous Publicity business. In this Janet assisted, in a spasmodic way. Lastly, since the nature of his job brought him into contact with a number of actors and literary people, Victor regarded himself as an inhabitant of 'The Art World', a typical attendant at the annual Three Arts Club Ball, and the kind of person the casual visitor would expect to see at the Café Royal, which he persisted in regarding as a 'rendezvous of artists and models', though it had long ceased to be that. How on earth Janet had come to marry this squalid coxcomb René could not understand: except he was obliged ruefully to agree that ten years earlier this melancholy, baying countenance may have provided the female eye with material for mild romance.

This being Victor, it may be imagined that it was in no way to be in *his* society, René had arranged this party. On the other hand it would never have occurred to Victor that René's suggestion that they all four should meet at the Café Royal, could be for any other reason than to pass an evening with him: to secure *his*, Victor's, opinion upon the course he had taken, in resigning his professorship, and to give him the inner low-down regarding that resignation. It was, in consequence, a little puzzling to Victor that so far his opinion had not been sought, nor had any account been forthcoming of why (the *real* why) René had thrown up his job. 'René is a deep dog,' he reflected. 'He has got something up his sleeve!'

René's objection to discussing anything about his resignation with the shoddy, flashy Victor was absolute: and when he saw that personage leaning over confidentially towards him, he met the intruder with a dark scowl. However, Victor proceeded, quite undeterred, to address him in a hoarse, throaty, confidential, brother-in-lawish manner (as though to say 'in the family things can be told which it is perhaps undesirable to broadcast outside').

'What, René, was the real story,' Victor asked, 'behind your resignation—I mean the real motive? Did you have some bust-up or something?'

René stared at him for perhaps a minute, and then turned his back. Janet laughed. 'All Victor wants to know is was there any dirty business?'

At this René turned around with not very good grace. 'Oh,
3*

I beg your pardon,' he said to Victor. 'I thought, for some reason, that you were talking to yourself.'

'No, nooo,' Victor drawled, and as he drawled astonishment could be seen changing into anger. 'I am not accustomed to speak to myself.'

'No? You wish to know . . . ah yes. Nothing at all is concealed. The occurrence to which you referred has no esoteric inner story. My original statement is all there is to say.'

'I see,' Victor observed drily. He was extremely offended. He looked down his nose, hooding his eyes and hollowing his cheeks, as he was accustomed to do with anybody whom he regarded as nearer to the bottom-dog level than himself. He had been becoming acutely conscious, as they sat in this sacred hall of fame, that this man, of whom he had always been rather afraid and cringed to, at times, was no longer the person that he had been. His status had suffered, to his mind, a catastrophic decline. It had required a sizeable interval, and almost two hours had elapsed since they met in the restaurant, for him to realize the new situation. (Upon the level, of course, which was valid for him.) With questions of *status* Victor was very familiar. As a Publicity Agent, *status* was a cardinal factor in the very existence of such a trade as his. And when one of his two partners passed down to him some 'name' of a client on the down-grade, no longer worthy of their attention, he enjoyed saying, 'Now, Mr. X., let us face it squarely, you are no longer front-page stuff!'

So with these backgrounds, when it came to the great Professor Harding turning his back on him and even giving him a bit of lip—oh. then, it was time that the true state of affairs should be emphasized. After all, René was now a man out of a job, and like any other man out of a job, he had to find a new one; and in all probability it would be considerably less good than the last. Hang it all, he, poor little Victor, had a job. It might not be a very good one, but there it was; any job is better than no job. So this fine brother-in-law of his had better get off his perch. He must be made to understand that (for whatever reason—and he, Victor, was not likely to swallow the *Idealism* stuff) he is no longer a professor of history, but just some vague free-lance person. He is not, even, a professor any longer. *Mister* Harding, if you please!

In his grandest manner, magnanimity in every line of his face, Victor addressed his brother-in-law, drawling drearily, 'I can quite understand how you feel, old man, I should be a little testy myself if I had just got the sack! . . . *You* haven't been fired, I know. You committed suicide, so to speak, fired yourself!' (and he ha-ha-ha'ed like the crowing of a rooster on a cracked gramophone record). 'You may even be in Queer Street for all I know. One does these things . . . in a passion. Then one regrets it ever afterwards. When it's a relative it comes home to one. . . . I am really awfully sorry; I sympathize with you most genuinely.' He sighed. 'What Canada is like I do not know. They say it is a tough place.' Then he said facetiously, with a broad smile, 'You may end up as a lumberjack! That would be rather fun.'

René had been looking at him with an expression of such concentrated contempt that it was a proof of how far he had sunk in Victor's estimation that that professional valuer of reputations did not quail. Janet had been listening only half believing her ears, when suddenly, at this point, she shouted, 'Victor! I wonder what you think you're talking about?'

'Me?' Victor enquired innocently.

'Victor, you are angry! I always know . . . your ears are sticking against your head. Apologize immediately for what you have just said.'

'Apologize! What on earth for?' drawled her husband in affected astonishment.

'Such a rat does not even know when he is being offensive!' René spoke to his sister. 'He is right. He has nothing to apologize for. If you marry a gutter-rat you should study a little the mentality of your . . . bed-fellow.'

'René!' Hester's consternation flung her forward upon the table and she clutched his arm in a foolish automatism. But now Victor's drawl came with a sharper note, as if it were difficult for him not to go a little quicker. He still used the back of his chair to hook his arm over, and addressed himself to his wife.

'Cads who insult their sisters . . .'

'Are you drunk? . . .' Janet screamed at him.

'No, no more than anybody else here. What I was saying was that cads who insult their sisters are certainly unfit to wear the academic regalia' (he drawled out 'regalia' with extraordinary unction). 'That they should *resign* is the best thing they could do.'

The two wives were white and motionless, both staring at René's face. As to signs that it registered the insulting epithet, the face in question showed nothing. All that the two women could see was a deeper red spreading where the beard did not cover it; and the eyes appeared to be growing more bloodshot every moment. Yet René was looking into the distance, and his head had an angle suggestive of the act of listening.

What René had actually been hearing was (a) the word 'Cad' and, at the same time, (b) the voices of two women behind him. They were carrying on the following conversation, not in a stage whisper, but in a loud undertone. *First woman:* 'I never had an orgasm with Fred not once, and we were married ten years. Ten years! Imagine!' *Second woman:* 'I don't believe I have had more than a half-dozen with Philip and we were married in '25 . . . or was it '26?' *First woman:* 'Heavens, what is the matter with these men. Philip looks as if he ought to do better than that. He is so athletic.' (She stopped.) 'Oh listen!' she hissed. 'A fight! A fight! I haven't seen a fight for ages!' *Second woman:* 'My money's on the Beard!'

The dialogue of the two women had already begun before the word 'Cad' reached René's ears, and that word had not sufficient authority to abolish the women's chatter. Cad held its place in the foreground of René's consciousness on equal terms with the inability of Fred to produce an orgasm.

As the two wives watched the inscrutable, angry and inquisitive listening face—that of the brother of one and the husband of the other—they each in their different ways considered what course to take should there be a sudden explosion: Janet had decided, when the storm broke, to fling herself in front of Victor. Hester decided to call upon the waiters to rescue Victor. If René were to injure his brother-in-law on top of the story of his resignation . . .! She dug her nails into her hand and tears came to her eyes. She heard the woman behind René cry, 'A fight! A fight!' and only just managed to hold down a scream. A waiter who, in passing, had heard the word 'Cad', and saw the furious bearded mask of the 'Cad', lingered to watch the explosion. As to Victor, his was the composure of a gentleman who has been called a 'rat' by a 'Cad'. He looked down his nose and delicately flicked the ash of his cigarette upon the café floor.

To this circle of watchers René's congested immobility looked as though it were turning to a state of chronic suspense. Meanwhile, inside the bearded head a battle raged. Many years of disciplining his choleric nature squashed the choler until it nearly split his head. The memory of his recent domestic explosion battled against his rising madness. And then Fred's ten-years-long orgasmless efforts grew and grew at the expense of the 'Cad', which shrank and shrank. After two or three seconds of this ever more violent expansion of the power of Fred, the 'Cad' collapsed. To the alarm and terror of everybody, Victor giving an involuntary jump, Hester clapping her hand over her mouth to repress her panic, René was convulsed with a deafening roar of laughter. He stamped and roared, amid the bewildered relaxation of the spectators.

'Can it be that he is yellow?' hissed one of the disappointed women in his rear.

Hester's face wore an almost maniacal distorted smile. Victor was far more angry than when he had been called a 'rat'. In his fit, René actually kicked Victor sharply on the shins, as he threw a foot out in a spasm of mad mirth. Victor withdrew his leg with dignity.

When his seizure was over, René looked at his watch, smiled at Janet and stood up. Hester, more gracefully, not to say languishingly, followed suit.

'We must go, Janet,' he said and moved away. 'Good-night, Victor,' Hester sang, as she passed the 'rat' of the party, contriving to look limp, and livid with rage, at the same time. 'Good-night, Essie my dear,' he sang back. 'You must be having an awful time. You have my sympathy.'

Janet accompanied her brother to the entrance hall.

'You don't seem as well as usual,' she said.

'Yes, Janet,' he replied at once. 'I am not worse than before. It is that preposterous little animal you wedded who requires a dose of castor-oil.'

Victor beckoned imperiously to the waiter and ordered a double brandy. The waiter did not say, 'Yes, my lord Duke,' but Sicilian eyes veiled themselves with respect and Victor felt much the same as the Duke of Marlborough, or the Duke of Somerset, must feel when they order a double brandy. The curious thing was that England still swarmed with Dukes of this sort in 1939.

'It's no use, darling, but your brother is not a gentleman,' Victor told his wife, when she had returned.

'No, darling? He lacks breeding, I suppose it is that. But may I ask what caused you to be offensive to him? What has he done to you?'

'Oh, nothing,' he drawled, sticking his shoulders up and waving his hand. 'Turned his back on me, but what of that? I am only a *rat*, after all!'

'You are a very vain rat,' she retorted. 'So because he accidentally turned his back on you, you start being *very* offensive.'

'I like ac-ci-dent-ally!' He caressed the word, undulating witheringly over it.

They remained among their respective thoughts for awhile, then Victor sat up observing, 'There are one, or I should say three or four, things about Professor Harding; I give him his title, you notice, though that is just kindness.'

'What are these *things* you notice . . .?'

'Well'—he drew a noseful of smoke into his diminutive lungs and expelled some of it again, watching its reappearance along the sides of his nose, looking as if he were squinting —'to start with he is not a man, who, except for his beard, would impress one as out-of-the-ordinary at all, is he? I mean, I should never take him for a *learned* man. His conversation is upon a very pedestrian level. I have never heard him mention any historical event: except once he said Queen Elizabeth had a beard, like his, but that *she* shaved hers.'

Janet laughed. 'How amusing. Did he say that?'

'There you are!' exclaimed Victor, '*amusing*. That is just it. Did you ever hear him talk about anything *serious*? Or do you ever remember him being in dead earnest?'

Janet laughed again. 'No, except when he called you a rat!'

'You are his sister, have known him all your life, and *you* say you have never known him to be serious about anything.'

'He worked like blazes at Oxford and got every sort of honour. I was only ten. But I was very impressed by the tall, solemn young man who was my brother, who was always reading in Latin . . . oh and German. No, I don't think you can say he is not *serious*. You don't understand him, that is all. If *you* were a learned man, we should all know about it, shouldn't we. René does not wear his learning on his sleeve.'

Victor's ears *did* tend to stick against his head when displeased, and now he lay back slumped very loftily in his chair, his arm hanging limply down behind it.

'I did not know him when I was ten,' Victor blandly protested. 'I can only speak of the present time, and I find him a common-place sort of fellow. . . . He even has rather low tastes.'

'That frightful tobacco, do you mean?'

'No,' drawled Victor with a particular anticipatory stress. ' No. Have you never noticed his eyes straying around, in rather . . . unexpected directions?'

'How do you mean?'

'Well'—Victor blew some smoke up at the once resplendent ceiling—'I caught him tonight smiling and blowing smoke-rings at an extremely vulgar-looking girl . . . with a rather pronounced *bust.* She had a pig face and yellow curls.'

'Dear me!' Janet laughed. 'What a little monster! Did she stick out behind too?'

'She *did*!' Victor assured her. 'And old René was ogling this little horror.'

'Shameful! And he a married man too!'

'You don't understand what I mean, apparently. One would hardly expect this great *Idealist* to take any interest in the protruding bosoms of such cheap little minxes. You would expect his mind to be full of other, and very different, matters.'

'The breasts of the nymphs in the brakes!' she mocked. 'But stay! I have caught you, my little Victor, before now— covertly eyeing the protruding bottoms of nymphs in the brakes of the Strand. Once I caught you *talking* to one. Take back those words about my brother!'

Victor laughed hollowly and a little sheepishly.

'You are more observant, darling, than I thought you were. But I am only young Victor Painter, junior partner in a second-rate Publicity racket! Nobody calls *me* an *Idealist*! I am just a little *nobody*. It's natural that I should take an interest in typists' bosoms. I have nothing better to think about. No one expects a little Publicity man to have any intellect. But the great Professor René Harding, who is so high-minded an idealist . . .'

'All right, all right, you poor little rat!' she broke in with a laugh.

Victor subsided, sulkily. Then he began again in his indolent drawl,

'I do not believe a single word about his scruples, and his horror of war! He nearly landed me one in the eye just now. It was all he could manage to pass it off with a vulgar laugh . . . like some drunken pork-butcher. His fanaticism! How can a man like that be a fanatic? He takes nothing seriously, he makes a joke about everything! He does not believe in any- thing! He just likes guzzling down all the good food and good wine he can get, and running after girls half his age! A fanatic!'

Exhausted by his diatribe, Victor closed his eyes.

One of the women at the next table leant across towards Victor, who opened his eyes when he heard her voice. It was none other than Fred's luckless wife. 'I hope you will excuse me for this intrusion, but I could not help hearing what you were saying, and I thought you would like to know that when the bearded gentleman passed me on his way out he winked at me. I thought this fact had some bearing upon what you were saying.'

Victor was as gallant as it is possible to be in a world so unresponsive to 'the Graces'. Then 'The Ladies, God bless them, God bless them, the Ladies,' was a toast which would have been echoed with fervour by the susceptible Victor. He was stirred to gracious volubility, by the perfume which reached him from the neighbouring table. But Janet was less fervent, though a little ornate. She said, 'Thanks. When next I see my brother I shall tell him that his optical salute was duly appreciated.'

CHAPTER VII

Rotter

ROBERT PARKINSON had a square head. It was like a fortress, and his body was a larger edition of that. He had a pipe, too, of a bulky type. He stuffed it, as he lay back in a strong soft chair, with plaits of bright yellow and black tobacco: a mixture whose stimulating pungency belongs to the family of smells including peat, tar, joss stick and burnt bacon. The sweet stench of his tobacco fumigated the heavily loaded bookshelves and such apparatus of learning as the half-foot-thick American dictionary upon a lectern, with an aggressive out-door to-hell-with-culture tang.

But his was a misleading personality. The thick-set body of a certificated master-sea-dog, and the almost startling aromatic violence of the smoke which blew from his mouth, twelve hours out of the twenty-four, were the camouflage of, as well as the fumigation, for a born book-worm. The fact was he played up to the accident of his physique, applauding nature's paradoxicality. Parkinson's accents were those of an educated don, and his dark eyes were as ruminative as those of a twelfth-century monk, a mellow schoolman, latinizing in his cell.

This was 1939, the last year, or as good as, in which such a life as this one was to be lived. Parkinson was the last of a species. Here he was in a large room, which was a private, a functional library. Such a literary workshop belonged to the ages of individualism. Its three or four thousand volumes were all book-plated Parkinson. It was really a fragment of paradise where one of our species lived embedded in his books, decently fed, moderately taxed, snug and unmolested. The London weather permitting, the sun warmed it for half of his working day. When the sun became too hot during high summer or thereabouts, which is a month or so at most, he departed, settling on the French Atlantic coast or repairing to Switzerland with a block of books in his luggage. Again, this was 1939. A good club was possible, the restaurants were good and not beyond his means, the London library supplied him for the absurdly modest sum of three pounds a year, with ten books at a time: in the butcher's shops was plenty of meat, the greengrocer's supplies of fruit and vegetables were cheap, fresh and plentiful, and all shops were well stocked with errand boys, and deliveries followed closely upon a telephone order. Elegant alcohol was available for the poorest professional man, an excellent bottle of Burgundy or of Bordeaux costing perhaps two shillings and ninepence. Such as Parkinson could ask a friend to dinner for an additional expense of around five or six shillings. And that powerfully sweet tobacco which he enjoyed smelling so much cost him little more than a fraction of what it would today.

According to any computation except that of the underprivileged, Parkinson was a poor man. There were many good things he had not the money to buy, his income was much smaller than that of René Harding. But what was it produced this blissful modest abundance that has been described above? Nothing more than writing a few reviews a month, one probably for an American publication, by whose editors his well-seasoned mind, whose judgements were delivered in an Oxford accent, was greatly appreciated. Why it is quite accurate to say that such a man nowhere today exists though he might receive the same remuneration for the same work, is because the pound sterling has lost two-thirds of its stature. It only masquerades as a pound. It is but six and sixpence. The work he did would be paid as though the pound were still the pound, for the periodicals and newspapers sell not very far above the nineteen thirty-nine figure. And accordingly their contributor must live in some other way than the way Parkinson lived. The Individualist Age, composed of a multiplicity of small paradises, is no more.

Whenever René came into his friend's study he regarded it with admiration. He ran his eye over the well-arranged shelves of philosophy, of history, of biography, of general literature, of politics: the French, the German, the Italian and other foreign books, confined to their allotted sections. For Parkinson was a man of method, and René was not. As to the spacious room, the heavy screens, the loaded lectern, and so on, René paid less attention to that. For he knew quite well why he preferred to stop where he was, in the House that Jack Built.

He occupied a separate flat, a flat for work only; it was inviolable. No one had ever ventured to disturb him. Had he been at the other end of London—or in Paris or in Rome —he could not have been more unmolested. Whereas, had they had a larger flat, in a finer house (not one of the Houses that Jack Built) he would have heard Mrs. Harradson's voice croaking 'nasty old man' in the passage outside his door, or it would have been the catarrhish voice of some other house-serf somewhere within earshot, or the gas inspector inspecting, or a new postman asking if a Mrs. Hungerford-Smith lived there, not to mention Hester's genteel flutings. So he did not envy Parkinson his work-room: dimly perhaps he realized that men like himself always were to be found in Houses that Jack Built, working in a book-lined area the size of a bath-room, which no charlady's finger ever touched: while for the Parkinsons there was always more amenity, more comfort, more space—which is not to scorn the Parkinsons but to define how these things are allotted, for one purgatory, for the other paradise.

When René entered the room it was quickly and quietly, without the empty fracas which is the rule with visitors; just as if he lived there and had been in the room five or ten minutes before. He went over to the fireplace and sat down. Parkinson did not rise. He made a little sign, which was a private salute, and with the other hand pushed over a box of cigarettes. Both of them knew that this was the last year of an epoch, and that such men as themselves would never exist on earth again, unless there were, after thousands of millennia, a return to the same point in a cosmic cycle. They knew that as far as that quiet, intelligent, unmolested elect life was concerned, they were both condemned to death: that the chronological future was, in fact, *a future life*, about which they both felt very dubious. They might survive as phantoms in a future England: or they might learn to live in some other way. It was with gravity that these friends sat talking, upon the brink

of a chasm, in comfortable armchairs, but not with pathos.
Once the fatality is recognized pathos is a disagreeable
vulgarity. Even the atmosphere appeared to be thinning out.
Parkinson and his visitor did not resort to words, merely for
words' sake.

Their interests were closest together, perhaps, in the field
of political thought, or the political-historical. René's political
insight was startling; predictions of his in the field of foreign
affairs, and the domestic scene as well, events almost invariably proved to be correct. His insight into the past was equally
remarkable. The first predictions of solar eclipses appeared
to the men of that time miraculous; and Parkinson almost to
the same degree felt a dumb amazement at some of his friend's
foreknowledgement of events, and hardly less at the light he
threw on past happenings. By now his 'belief in' this gifted
man was unshakeable. The species 'friend' has no exact
definitions and René Harding had no other complete friend
such as was this one: he only had men who were friends in
part. In a life, there is hardly ever more than one complete
friend, and rarely that. At Oxford this friendship had begun.
At Oxford or at Cambridge positions are taken up for life,
ascendancies forever confirmed, and the failure to secure first
place is a decision which is practically irreversible. There is
no democracy in youth.

From the first their interests were similar. At the university
Robert Parkinson had soon ceased to aspire to the first place
in the magnetic company of René Harding: and in the end
had come to look upon himself as a sort of disciple, and other
people tended to take some such relationship for granted.
During the last two decades René had written books which
were much discussed, whereas the other showed no signs of
ambition, and so time had endorsed the view that one was
the master, the other the follower.

Abstracting in this way the essentials of the relationship
of two people may be misleading, especially if one gets no
farther than the essentials. For instance, provided with such

an abstract as the foregoing, a person would undoubtedly be considerably confused in the actual presence of these two men. The first thing this person would notice would be that René's manner was anything but that of a master, of 'the boss' in this relationship. He was, on the contrary, the reverse of arbitrary, often deferring to his square-headed, squarely-camped and frowning follower. The first impression might even be that Parkinson was the taciturn but attentive leader, René a dashing follower. Actually, the last thing René Harding wanted to be was 'the boss'. There were three reasons for this. Firstly, he did not at all relish the rôle of 'boss'. Secondly, he had always had a great liking, and respect as well, for this unassuming but intelligent man. He prized his friendship and respected his judgement. Thirdly, had he had an appetite for bossing, he would have realized that in a friendship with an intelligent and unaggressive man, an indulgence of this appetite would be most undesirable, and would strain and probably ruin the friendship: for friendship of an exceptional order is allergic to the exercise of domination. Domination may in reality be present, but it must not be exercised openly.

René for a few moments sat passing his fingers through his hair, where the hat had pressed it down. Then he looked towards his friend.

'What did you want to see me about, Rotter?' he asked, using his pet name.

'I hoped you would give me a little help,' Parkinson answered. 'The *Bostonian* asked me to do an article about you and your work. I have now finished it, and there are some passages . . . Well, let's read them.'

He picked up some typed pages from a chair and began softly reading them. His dog-name, 'Rotter,' no doubt commemorated a period in his Johnsonian undergraduate days when he was addicted to monosyllabic disapproval. But all that a man so heroically built, with so commanding a headpiece would have to do, would be to bark 'Rotl' once or twice, and men would decide they had to do with a big dog-man and, with respectful affection, call him 'Rotter'. Misnamed, then, gently and evenly, with a minimum of opinionated forcefulness in the text, as unself-conscious as René, as if running over something for a typist or secretary, he announced the title. 'A Historian who is anti-History.' All this was routine. René lay back in his chair, his pointed fingers forming the apex of an arch, based in the elbows upon the arms of the chair. Neither he nor Parkinson looked at one another. All the latter did was to pause politely now and then, for a moment, and if René made no remark, to continue. However, René's comments were almost nil.

'This still young man has written a first-rate orthodox history, especially his noble study of the Tudors and Stuarts, of particular interest because of its tragic pattern of the frustrations of the Renaissance swimming against the full black tide of the Reformation. It was by this brilliant volume that, until very recently, he was known. He was regarded as a highly promising traditional young historian. Then, with great suddenness, the picture changed, the image of him in the public eye suffered a transformation overnight. His extraordinary work, *The Secret History of World War II*, that dramatic jump into the middle of the unfinished history of our time, appeared; and grouped with this in our present view of him must be several important essays and articles in learned reviews and in more popular publications. These also are of very recent date. Altogether, the book, conjoined with the smaller pieces, has made him one of the most discussed writers of the present time.

'Professor René Harding has not been on the stage long enough for the public to have made up its mind exactly what kind of figure this is who, more and more, is attracting attention by his unorthodox utterances. Is this one of those persons, who, by a skilful use of the technique of *surprise* and paradox, attracts more interest than he deserves? or is he, on the other hand, somebody enunciating a doctrine which is destined to do more than momentarily astonish us? Is he a really first-line figure, who has something to say of unique importance? It is my view that he is, indeed, just that. But before this comes to be universally recognized, there must be clarifications. It is necessary to dissipate the confused and misleading notions about what he represents, and to replace them by others, corresponding more to the facts. In this article I would like

to make a start in that direction. More especially I shall
attempt to discourage the misconception, so often met with
in connection with a thinker of this kind; namely, that his is
a purely destructive intelligence. He is, on the contrary, in
a remarkable degree, creative.

'I think I should begin by saying that René Harding is a
violent perfectionist. Accordingly he would be regarded with
disapproval by all those interested in humanity retaining its
vices, its most ill-favoured passions, intact. To illustrate this:
the exponent of a strict institutional Christianity would be
scornful. This is because the dogma of original sin, and indeed
the machinery of salvation in its entirety, requires men to
remain much as they are. It does not legislate for a terrestrial
community of saints. This is evidenced by the often-discussed
leniency of the catholic confessional, in the eager acceptance
of human fallibility. In that communion, a society of miserable
sinners is postulated, which of course accounts for the catholic
attitude to war. What greater sin is there than war, than
mass-murder? It is man at his wickedest, in his extremest
need of pardon and of salvation. So war is, for institutional
Christianity, a precious enormity.'

At this point René interposed. He murmured, 'Do not
involve me in your prejudices, Rotter. I am a friend of Farm
Street and of All Saints' too.'

'Sorry.'

The reading proceeded.

'But for the Marxist equally perfectionism is displeasing.
The class-war is as dear to the Marxist as is nationalist war
to the Christian. No improvement, no spectacular evolutionary
development, in the species for which it legislates, enters into
the programme of Marxism. Indeed, such an idea is entirely
alien to it. The type of improvement with which it is concerned
is in the bread-and-butter situation of men-in-general and
great amelioration in the conditions of work. Man is envisaged
as a *Workman*, not, more inclusively, as a human being.

'Not only is the perfectionist, or the idealist, disapproved
of by both these classes of men: it is quite extraordinary how
many different kinds of people there are interested in the
perpetuation of unintelligent and brutish human standards.

Then, of course, more inclusively and in a less specialist way, and without the dogmatist's intensity, men as a whole—the uncreative majority—oppose the designs of the perfectionist. Any kind of real perfectability, any tampering with their cosy averagism, their beer and football, their Scotch and golf, their "pools" and crime fiction, any tightening up of their slack mindlessness, any challenge to part with a fraction of their animality, is resisted by men.

'The reader should perhaps be warned that in the compass of this article I can hardly hope to give more than a caricatural idea of the views of Professor Harding. Reading through what I have just written I see how impossible the work is to telescope and to "pot". Our author does not suggest, for instance, that all history should be abolished, only that it should be approached in a different way with radically changed accents. The story of ideas, theory of the state, evolution of law, scientific discoveries, literature, art, philosophy, the theatre and so on, these are the proper subjects of history. Contemporary with these creative happenings are the proceedings of the uncreative mass, climaxed by the outrageous blackguardism of hereditary or elective government. The wars, civil massacres which should be treated as police court news, provide the basis for the story of mankind we encounter in history books. The explanation of this terrible paradox, that the state should always be in the hands of ruffians or of feeble-minded persons, is that the enormous majority of men are barbarians, philistines, and mentally inhabit an "heroic" age, if not a peculiarly violent Stone Age. And upon that popular plane the political world has its being. A number of creative "sports" are born into every successive generation of uncreative gang-rule. Though frowned on or even hated by the majority, these individuals nevertheless introduce into the dull and sodden stream of the average a series of startling innovations. They compel that strange couple, the "man in white" with his knife, and beneath him the prostrate patient whose lung he is about to remove, to behave differently. After much angry argument, they persuade the man in white to permit the etherization of his patient. This spares the surgeon the agonized convulsions and piercing screams of his victim, and spares the latter the agony and shock probably resulting in death. But the man who confers this benefit is violently abused by everybody. It would be superfluous to enumerate other instances. All such revolutionary innovations, as is universally recognized, have to overcome similar resistance upon the uncreative plane. Such inventive intrusion upon the still barbarous level is for ever complicating and violently transforming the uncreative life-stream below. Up to our age the official rôle of the *changers* has been that of ethereal visitors, having no part in the life they stimulate and refashion. The big boys, the great persons, have been, up to the present, the gilded thugs, and plumed and be-ribboned directors of homicide. But, with what may seem a baseless optimism, I believe that a novel situation is developing.

'The inventive and creative few are growing restless at the continued depravity of the traditional rulers on the popular plane, and the childish melodrama which they persist in perpetuating. The contrast between the debased level upon which governments function, and the glittering gifts which are forced on them by the creative intruders who are their contemporaries upon a higher but much less populous plane becomes, for the latter, more and more intolerable. More and more god-like powers in the hands of unintelligent and venal individuals (possessed thereby of a terrifying potential) is so obviously shocking that discussion of it has become a review and magazine item. The student masses have begun to regard the world into which they have been born with a cold eye, in a way that has never happened before. They are not all very intelligent, but they come to this situation with a new mind. They are beginning to look upon the proceedings of their masters as if they were looking down upon a plane of things beneath them. This is one very promising feature of the present scene. It is necessary to transcend the brutal plane of automatic life; and it must, of course, be the young, and first and foremost the instructed young, who effect the translation of average human life to a higher level. Among publicists, scholars, academic leaders, a similar disgust with the pitch of nonsense to which we have attained, and the persistent

criminality of the politicians, is another helpful sign. Clearly,
there is as yet an insufficient weight on the side of enlightenment to challenge the generations of Caliban. But more and
more people range themselves against the traditional world
of ruffianism and deceit which still lumbers on upon the
"official" plane, where all the values are those of a back-
alley brawl, or of an insurance fraud. The conspiracy to perpetuate the ten-millennia-long system popularly known to us
as "history" is well organized, however, it is necessary to
remember; and there is nothing to justify the hope of the
immediate end of the glorification of the unselective past as
"history". This is the point at which it should be observed
that the supermanism of Professor Harding is dogmatically
restrained. All he desires is to see the upper plane substituted
for the under plane: the only kind of superman he would like
to see installed is the superior man already there, the creative
minority. His ambitions do not lead to the setting up of a
Philosopher King. In a republic, a committee of Sages would
perhaps be the rulers. But into such detail he does not go. It
is resented as we should find the kangaroo resenting a suggestion that it would be an improvement if he were less of a
kangaroo, or should you propose to a hawk to reduce his
hawkishness. Having identified for the reader the idiosyncratic
slant of the mind of our author I will go on to his teaching
of History, or of no-History.'

René sat with his arm trailing over the side of the chair,
fingering Rotter's cat. He did not seem to be giving his closest
attention to what was being read (and indeed, such articles
had often been read to him before. Since Parkinson was a
most diligent puffer). When, however, his friend reached the
expounding of ideas it was evident that René was actively
listening.

'For René Harding, Jansenist, the past can only be visualized and written about as a crime-story. The criminals, of
course (and some are exceptionally unpleasant ones), are the
endless series of persons who figure as the heads of States.
Earlier, they were men and women disguised in some regal
fancy dress, the gilt bestowing a mystical sanction upon their
childishness, dishonesty or ferocity. Nowadays, seeing that

there has been so much unpleasantness about kings and queens, especially since the events terminating the eighteenth century in France—the heads of States disguise themselves as quiet little harmless people, just like you and me: but their outrageous behaviour, involving the deaths of millions of people, exceeds in horror anything in the historic past.

'If these persons are the star criminals of the story we call "history", the sympathetic characters, whether murderers or otherwise, are those inventive and creative persons who do their best to transcend the historical, and to jack-up the social level out of reach of the brutishness of these troupes of power-drunken individuals, who play the old game in new ways, but always to the same disastrous end.

'It is suggested by René Harding that the principal figures in the history-book should be those heroic creators who attempt to build something, usually to be knocked down by the gang of criminals above mentioned, with the assistance, of course, of the unenlightened herd. The actual rulers are not necessarily concerned in any way with these creative individuals; it is usually left to members of the ill-disposed majority forcibly to prevent the success of the designs of the creative few, or the contemporary wielders of power, may, for some reason, do no particular mischief; may omit to stage a bloodbath, debase the currency, pillage and tax to death the community, cheat them out of their rights, push them down into new slaveries. They may be absorbed in their pleasures, or once in a way they may even possess a streak of goodness. Anyway, in such periods, the creative minds are relatively free to carry out their civilizing work. Such work is usually destroyed within a few decades by a remarkable outbreak of bestial barbarity.

'Or, of course, these circumstances may invite the historian to look at them in another way. He may prefer to project a picture more reminiscent of Alice's adventures through the looking-glass. The mad kings, queens, duchesses, hatters and the rest are the more or less dangerous lunatics who surround the baffled hero. If this be the approach of the historian's choice, a great deal of gaiety will accompany the tale. This might be regarded by some as unethical, or even frivolous. There is nothing really very gay about Stalin, or Hitler, or

Napoleon. Menacing dummies as they might still be, in a world akin to that of Alice they would acquire a certain innocence, transformed by the alchemy of humour into a less sinister dimension. Professor René Harding admits as a possibility that history should be written as an Alicean chaos, or even as a violent burlesque. Many of the criminals in question, such as Henry VIII, might be treated as ghastly clowns, with the author of *Utopia* (in this case the murderee) attempting to advance the new humanism, but pounced on and beheaded in the end. Although he allows that this would be a quite legitimate manner of dealing with the historic material, Professor Harding prefers the tragic approach, reserving the full moral responsibility for the ogres involved.

'It is with the utmost concreteness that Professor Harding demonstrates how this new type of history would be written. Taking the twentieth century, the period best known to all of us, as his first illustration, he observes that, to begin with, the criminal in this crime-story is less and less the head or heads of the State. In the modern parliamentary democracy the ostensible leader is not the real one; and so the picture is more complicated than in the case of an Emperor or absolute Monarch. Let us take contemporary France. The little packets of drab personalities succeeding each other with bewildering rapidity possess too little power to be accepted as the real criminals. You have to look for your criminal among the sinister background figures, and in the pressure-groups pushing the little front-line puppets hither and thither, to left or right. A big rogue, like Clemenceau ("le tigre") does emerge, for a short while, in the world war (1914–18). But there has been, in general, a monotonous mediocrity in cabinet after cabinet. This has signified, of course, that all power was behind the scenes. It has been quite otherwise in Germany, Italy and Russia, where the front-line ostensible rulers were in fact the responsible parties. In Great Britain, during the present century, few of our first ministers have qualified as criminals in our crime-stories or histories. Certainly Mr. Baldwin, pipe in mouth, and quoting scripture, was a pernicious figure, but among his misdeeds there was no blood bath. Mr. Churchill, arch-militarist as he is, is merely taking advantage of a situation contrived by a great number of people of divergent interests.\Even we have had Lloyd George, with his Health Insurance Act, a splendid feat which places that minister in the creative category. On the other hand, there was a fat jewish-looking gentleman, with a lisp, a large cigar, and a homburg hat, facetiously named "The Peacemaker", who was on the sinister side. But in general the big criminal figure is absent from the lime-lit scene.

'Now this new history-making is productive of strange effects. According to the old method, we are shown a succession of potentates whose attainments are set forth in a favourable light even though it has sometimes to be admitted by the traditional historian that their intellectual stature was exceeded by some of their subjects. Beneath these loftiest characters in the historical plot, are shown lesser giants, for instance statesmen, cutting a great figure nevertheless, usually because of their aptitude for crime. Then, in the average history book, in what is little more than a foot-hole, we have a perfunctory account of learning, the arts, and mechanical inventions.

'Instead of this, what Professor Harding suggests is more like a description of the activities of two races of men, one destructive and the other creative. The destructive always wins in the end: just as we see, in this century, miraculous technical inventions, which could have set men free from senseless and wasteful toil, being seized on by the destructive race, so that, at last, things are a hundred times as bad as they were to start with, instead of a hundred times as good.

'The outline provided us by Professor Harding of how the twentieth-century would look in an intelligent history, differs absolutely from the kind of history we all know (that written by Trevelyan or Green, for instance). What we have called the "criminals" still play an important part, simply because the story is about something radiantly creative in humanity being invariably destroyed by something as malign as it is common and coarse; and this latter is, needless to say, the Criminal in question, only no longer given first place, and properly execrated by the reader. History à la René Harding is an essentially pessimistic narrative. Man is shown as an uncivilizable animal; the inferiority and destructive character of his appetite forbids attempts by the civilized minority to establish a civilized order. In a numerically feeble group there is great inventiveness: this, however is not forbidden, because *homo stultus* takes possession of all inventions, either using them as toys or applying them to destructive ends.

'History cannot be merely an account of all that is interesting, in age after age: the Divine Comedies, the great religious and philosophical systems, the feats of Galileo, Newton or · Pythagoras, or the arts, and the ideologies. As an account of what has happened that would be incorrect: for certainly all those things came into being, but that is only half the story, it is not "history". For all these things are products of man, and all have a more or less functional aspect. Once the aeroplane is invented, it is what happens to it afterwards, to what uses it is put, which is as much its history as its original construction.. It is the same with the radio, the internal-combustion engine, and the rest: and as to books, their publication is almost meaningless by itself; "history" is there to tell us who read the book and what the book did to him. Now, why Professor Harding's history is, as we have said, pessimistic, is because man in general ignores, misuses or misreads these various products of the creative mind, a mind not possessed by man in general. So this explains why so many uninteresting figures, and even, in the seats of power, such criminals must be still described, why it is impossible for the historian to escape from them. Just as the smell from the sewers must be described in a novel in which it causes the hero's death, so the new historian is obliged to describe what · is brutish and only fit for the garbage pail. To conclude, history can only be written as a tragedy, because all that is worth writing about that has come down to us has been denied its full development, has been nipped in the bud, or has been done to death. The world war (1914–18), is like a mountain range in the historic landscape. It is, at once, composed of mountains of criminal destructiveness, and a piling-up of tremendous creative inventiveness. Those four years marked in fact the mass-arrival of the cinema, the aeroplane, the motor-car, the telephone, the radio, etc. This is, as it were, a perpendicular wall of great height, a mountainous barrier, behind which the past world lies.

'The history of our century would not be one mainly of personalities (though, alas, they are there as ever). What we should see would be big, ideologic currents, gaudily coloured, converging, dissolving, combining or contending. It would look like a chart of the ocean rather than a Madame Tussaud's Waxworks; though there would be faces (one with a tooth-brush moustache), like labels of one or other of the big currents of ideas. Then there would be the mountainous blocks of all kinds, as though raised up by an earthquake: there would be the piling up of tremendous inventions, their instant conversion to highly unsuitable uses: the criminality of man rioting in the midst of these unnumbered gadgets. Then there would be the growth, in every society, of the huge canker of Debt. In more and more insane proportions, the Credit System would be apparent, developing its destructive bulk. One would sense nebulous spiders, at the heart of wider and wider webs of abstract simulacras of wealth, suspended over everything: hordes of men engaged for years in meaningless homicide: and vast social revolutions as the culmination of a century of plots, and propaganda of brotherly love at the point of a pistol, and *la haine créatrice*. So there would be arabesques of creation and of destruction, the personal factor unimportant, the incarnations of ideas, the gigantic coloured effigies of a Hitler or a Stalin, no more than the remains of monster advertisement.

'According to Professor Harding the Soviet leaders are mixed types. They *should* have been a new species in the history chart, but they are a species that has somehow failed, their creative impulse distorted. To parody the idea in Goethe's *Faust*, they are the spirits who willed the good and did the evil. But in them are seen a coarsely drawn sketch, of the new ruler who will no longer be the criminal of the crime-story, but the first of the creative earth-governors.

'Even Hitler, though a man of blood, has a streak of the new ethos mixed into him: a horrible paradox, but the militarist in his composition made short work of any contradictory impulse.

'Here we must note a rather curious streak of optimism in Professor Harding himself. Dreadful century as this one is showing itself to be, Professor Harding believes that it was *intended to be* really a new model: had it not been for an element which dragged it back into the past, that great mountain range, conveniently confined within the conventional limits of the year 1914, and the year 1918, has all the signs of being the giant backcloth for a new Year One. The Professor's belief may be regarded by some as of a naïveté worthy of Cobden and the Manchester School: but it is his view that the liberal idealism of the nineteenth century would, left to itself, have eventuated in a twentieth-century rebirth, wonderfully assisted by the burst of inventive genius coinciding with the liberal climax in the second decade of this century—that so supported, this idealism could have produced a new age of social justice, had it not been for the intervention of the Marxist ideology.

'His argument is that the incitement to hatred and civil war, the doctrine of the necessity of catastrophe, and indeed everything else about Marx's teaching stigmatizes him as belonging to the barbaric world of the wars of religion and the other things which it is our desperate wish to be finished with for ever. In 1920 the sudden expansion of Marxist influence, developing into a violent fashion, was a unique misfortune, because the world foreshadowed by Lloyd George's Health Insurance Act, and the increasing liberality on all sides, plus the revolution in Industrial technique, would anyway have led, under the leader-ship of such men as Beveridge, to a New Deal, unattainable by means of the blood-bath of a revolution.

'But this belief of Professor Harding's is, in reality, a revival of an earlier, generally held, belief. In the nineteenth century in England and America, and even elsewhere, it was universally thought that a new age of tolerance and intelligence, of "decency" and humaneness, had begun; and just as a great number of practices belonging to the bad old times of the unenlightened past, such as slavery, duelling, hanging and quartering, public executions, imprisonment for debt, child-labour, cruel sports, ill-treatment of animals and so forth, had been discountenanced and abolished (for ever, it was

4

supposed), so gradually all such odious survivals would disappear, and "The world's great age begin anew, the golden
years return". The time when nations would recognize the
wickedness and wastefulness of war was near at hand. This
belief was unchallenged in the english-speaking countries at
the beginning of the century, and such feeling lingered even as
late as Woodrow Wilson's Paris peace-making, or the Kellogg
Pact. But actually the world-war gave the death-blow to
this belief, and the happenings of the last two decades have
done nothing to reinstate it. The optimistic idealism of the
Nineteenth Century, although it is not identical with, inherited
something from the Enlightenment of the Eighteenth Century. The outlook of Professor René Harding may perhaps
more usefully be compared with the anti-past views of the
Eighteenth Century, than with the more sentimental aspira-
tions of the Nineteenth Century.

'Professor Collingwood considers this Eighteenth Century
contempt for the past—or at least for all the ages prior to the
Tudors, when the modern world began—as anti-historical, or
"not genuinely historical". He would look upon Professor
René Harding's anti-historical views in the same way.

'In order to facilitate an understanding of the work of this
new, anti-historical historian, a longish passage will now be
quoted from a recent lecture of Professor Collingwood's which
I have been privileged to use.

' "A truly historical view of human history," says Professor
Collingwood, "sees everything in that history as having its
own *raison d'être* and coming into existence in order to serve
the needs of the men whose minds have corporately created it.
To think of any phase of history as altogether irrational is to
look at it not as an historian but as a publicist, a polemical
writer of tracts for the times. Thus the historical outlook of the
Enlightenment was not genuinely historical; in its main motive
it was polemical and anti-historical."

'From this it will be seen, that Professor Collingwood
regards "genuine history" as accepting without demur the fact
that man's actions are in general irrational. He considers a
man who separates the story of the past into examples of
rational and of irrational behaviour, as no true historian. For

he has not the true historian's appetite for the good and the
evil, the rational and irrational, indeed whatever it may be
that can be proved to have *happened*. For him the true
historian must go to these happenings, of whatever kind,
without any prejudices, relating to ethics, taste, intellectual
fastidiousness, etc. He is, therefore, diametrically opposed
to Professor René Harding, whose view is that we should
reject entirely anything (notwithstanding the fact that it
undoubtedly happened) which is unworthy of any man's
attention, or some action which is so revolting that it *should
not* have happened, and must not be encouraged to happen
again. In other words, that it is time that men ceased proudly
unrolling the blood-stained and idiotic record of their past: it
is time that they should as a minimum become adult.

'The following is more from Professor Collingwood, analysing the eighteenth-century attitude of historians, which in some
ways is very reminiscent of this new objector to the past.

' ". . . writers like Voltaire and Hume . . . were not
sufficiently interested in history for its own sake to persevere
in the task of reconstructing the history of obscure and remote
periods. Voltaire openly proclaimed that no securely based
historical knowledge was attainable for events earlier than the
close of fifteenth century: Hume's *History of England* is a very
slight and sketchy piece of work until he comes to the same
period, the age of the Tudors. The real cause of this restriction
to the modern period was that with their narrow conception of
reason they had no sympathy for, and therefore no insight
into, what from their point of view were non-rational periods
of human history; they only began to be interested in history
at the point where it began to be the history of a modern spirit
akin to their own, a scientific spirit."

'Returning to what we were saying before we introduced
this very appropriate matter from an unpublished MS. of
Professor Collingwood, Professor Harding believes that the
Golden age of "peace and plenty", a typical Victorian dream,
was actually upon us on the eve of the World-War, and we
should be enjoying it at the present moment had it not been
for an evil principle of unexpected virulence.

'This seems to me to be turning the blind eye to that

non-Marxian barbarity, the great nationalist war of 1914–18, which made the russian revolution possible. But I suppose that Professor Harding would reply that that last great christian war would probably have been as Lloyd George asserted "a war to end war", had it not been for the social-revolutionary complications which it engendered. Finally, however, Professor Harding dismisses all this as a dead issue: for as he eyes the approaching war, and the vast mountain of Debt which will be of dreadful dimensions by the time this is over, not to mention all the other things involved and easily predictable, he sees no hope of anything but a plunge backward into the barbarism from which, not so long ago, we imagined we had emerged for good. The present century provides Professor Harding, as we have seen, with his first illustration. Some of his other illustrations are even more illuminating small working models of his plan for a new sort of history. The "century of genius", for instance, is particularly interesting, for we see political events of the first importance, according to the old idea, such as the execution of Charles I, and the Cromwellian epic: and then side by side with this, we are offered the spectacle of events of great magnitude of a different order altogether, such as, at the beginning of the century, the Tudor Stage brought to an abrupt close by the black-coated enemies of the Renaissance spirit—the Newtonian system, Milton's epic and Bunyan's allegory, the political philosophies of Hobbes and of Locke, the innovating scientific mind of Bacon, to mention no more, upon the plane Genius, rather than upon the plane of the gibbet and the headsman's block, the Old Testament battlefields of one of history's biggest ruffians, Cromwell, and all the other "great events" characteristic of *that* plane.

'In the historical blue-print offered us by René Harding, we see something like a tapestry of transparencies. We see what are the true great events, which gave the name "century of genius" to this period, as a white foreground frieze, and through this one can see, like a swarming of shadows, struggling Kings, helmeted and booted gang-leaders, Nellie Gwyn and Guy Fawkes and a thousand other things upon the mental level of the Dime novel, or of Fanny Hill, "infallible artillery", and of course pints of blood squirting everywhere. We have, in short, the two planes in starker contrast than perhaps in any other century; especially since the adherents of the old view of what deserves commemoration have a lot of Big shots, like Cromwell, to set up against the Newtons and the Shakespeares.

'I prefaced this study of Professor René Harding's work by stating that we have, in him, a perfectionist or, if you prefer it, an idealist. The term *perfectionist* is more expressive and perhaps, in this case, more useful. Now Professor Harding is not at all a naïve perfectionist.

'This is another fact to remember, of first importance. He is completely aware of all that ensues from such a position as his. To propose so profound a revolution on the writing of history can be little more than a gesture: obviously the historians could make no such change in their routine, unless, at the same time, men in general were in the act of revolutionizing their ways of thinking.

'So this is not merely a reform in the writing of history that is in question, but an implicit proposal for revaluation, moral and intellectual, throughout society. Which is absurd. Men do not turn their lives upside down in response to the summons of a professor of history. Professor Harding perfectly understands all this; he is not a deluded dreamer. But he simply asks, "What else could I do?" and proceeds quite undisturbed by the reflection that he is building a road which will be trodden by no one but himself, for perhaps a hundred years.

'Professor Harding's way of seeing the world is, then, analogous to the Vision of the Saints. But it is not necessarily in any way connected with saintliness. What this system amounts to, in reality, is a taking to its logical conclusion the humane, the tolerant, the fastidious. It is really no more than that with great rigidity and implacability, you pursue these things logically to a point where all that doesn't belong to them or that contradicts them is absolutely repudiated. But René Harding would say, "Why not take these things to their logical conclusion? what is the use of them indeed, if you do not take them to their logical conclusion? They do not exist, they are no more than mere words, until they are logically developed in this way: there is no half-measure in such matters."

'This is, of course, all very well: but in life nothing is taken to its ultimate conclusion, life is a half-way house, a place of obligatory compromise; and, in dealing in logical conclusions, a man steps out of life—or so it would be quite legitimate to argue.

'The questions above attributed to Professor Harding actually occur in his text. But he knows that they are purely rhetorical questions. He knows that they are sensible questions to ask—questions that *are* asked, from time to time, by men like himself: questions which would be quite otiose were it not for the fact they have a tonic effect, and that the conventional life of men (and of historians) would be even less satisfactory than it is without these uncompromising interveners. He feels that his is a function of authentic value, as a counsellor of perfection, in spite of the fact that it would be quite impossible to convert most historians to his standpoint, as it would mean the end of their careers. Conversions of such scope can only be attained under the threat of torture and death: and René Harding has somewhere admitted that he has put the cart before the horse, and that if he had not been tainted with scepticism he would long ago have given up history, and have attacked those more fundamental obstacles upon which history and everything else depends.

'In other words, this idealist carries a sceptic on his back. —Figuratively, the concentration camp (and it is not always figurative merely, at that) which awaits the anti-vivisectionist, the pacifist, he who proposes artificial insemination, the vegetarian, the egalitarian, and in fact all those anti-animal eccentrics, is a familiar landmark to this trained historian. I should perhaps say, however, that this implacable perfectionist is, in his personal life, gaily capable of unregenerate behaviour. He must not be visualized as a bloodless and solemn ascetic.'

René Harding's head swung slowly round, showing his comically-painful grimace of bouffonic reproach to his follower, who was actually slowing down before this occurred, in anticipation of such a reaction upon his master's part.

'Yes?' Rotter shot his question at the dumb show staged by

René, which he looked at sideways, his head still bent over the typescript. 'Anything wrong?'

'The *argumentum ad hominem* is justly disapproved of, and I see no reason why the American public should be invited to invade my private life. It does not affect the validity of an argument denouncing the evils of drink if the speaker is himself an alcoholic, though I suppose it would be tactful to do what he could to keep his red nose out of sight.'

The two friends gazed with their usual cold fondness at one another. In any article he wrote about René's work, Parkinson invariably, sooner or later, dragged in the historian's personality: in the first draft, that is, but removed it under indignant pressure when the typescript came to be read, as in the present case.

Rotter smiled sedately. 'I am most apologetic, but in indicating how, in your private life, you fail to discipline . . . to *prune* in the way one would expect you to, as a reader of your books, no disrespect was intended. My purpose was to dissipate the idea that you might be some pale little purist. You know how people speculate about the kind of man the author of a book may be, and how, from the standpoint of publicity, they should be prevented from imagining something disenchanting, which in fact is not there.'

René gave his head a violent shake. 'I think the recently introduced habit of thrusting under the public's nose a publicity photograph of a pretty girl to make them buy Miss So-and-So's book, if the book is by a male, a portrait as much like a screen-star as possible—this is especially done in America—I think this shows that the publishing business is attempting to rival Hollywood in cheapness.' Some such remark was usually made by René, during the discussion which followed the reading of an article; and Parkinson smiled appreciatively as it made its appearance. He sat quite silent. They were smiling at one another if they had been watching, with paternal satisfaction, the parts played by those two accomplished mimes, René Harding and Henry Parkinson.

'I think those personalities are quite unworthy of you, Rotter.'

Rotter laughed. 'They are deleted. We eschew the personal.'

'Thank you, Rotter.'

After this the reading continued. Although Parkinson always read such things to René, the text did not differ enough to escape monotony: Rotter had his formality for teaching René in transatlantic publics. The present article was, however, one of his best efforts. When Rotter's voice stopped and he put his manuscript down on the table, René stood up and stretched vigorously, and then complimented and thanked his friend with great sincerity, and his friend looked straight at him as if he did not hear what he was saying. Parkinson was one of those Englishmen who is calculated to baffle the men of other nations. His façade was at times forbidding, but his intimates paid no attention to it: they knew it was merely a screen stuck up by this 'sensitive', behind which he could give his feelings play, even if necessary drop a tear.

Why, in this instance, he looked so strong, was of course for English reasons. He was being praised; what he had written was the object of the most lavish compliments. Now, his writing he took very seriously, and consequently his sensitive nature was most exposed at that point. What is more, the man he almost worshipped was speaking of what he most prized— and, to add to this, René was better qualified than anyone else to judge the value of his writing. So naturally his stoniest and most unresponsive façade was kept stiffly in position.

But René's cynical eye, when it rested, upon Rotter, rested gently. All master-and-follower relationships, especially so matured a one as this, have in them something of religion and something of love. The pair are a love pair, and they are god and his dedicated. But when they are an english pair, the lovers are evasive, the devout is *sans façon*. There was even, at times, a mockery in the Rotter's eye. He knew he could only love from a position of complete independence: could only be devout with familiarity, and his incense was the reeking smoke of his pipe.

When the master-follower pair are a literary pair the sacred text is one thing for the master and another thing for the disciple. For the master the whole process of publicity is imbecile, and he is degraded in his own estimation when he thinks of himself squatting down to listen to a solemn exegesis

of his literary labour; to be seriously assisting at the building
up of a name, at the contriving of a superstition. To arrive, in
process of time, at a point when he will be described as 'great'
necessarily appears to him paltry and absurd, for he has no
illusions about the quality of those who are destined to employ
this silly epithet.

Under these circumstances, René would have far preferred
not to participate at this particular kind of séance. It was a
failure of understanding on good old Rotter's part to ask him
to do so. 'He even imagines that I like it,' he once reflected.
But he saw quite well that to enjoy the advantages of a kind
of minor god, he must not decline to provide the devout with
this satisfaction.—But what did he write books for? partly the
pleasure of writing them, but partly in order to attract the
absurdities which inevitably ensued. No, he was by no means
a perfectionist.

They moved over together to where the whisky and the
glasses were, and made ready a highball, fetching some ice
from Rotter's baby refrigerator. Standing, they talked for a
little about René's transatlantic plans. It was with exquisite
hard-boiledness that Rotter spoke of the departure of his
friend. The whole business depressed him so much that it even
affected his enthusiasm for his friend's magnificent rigidity.
Then they referred to the article again, and René asked him
why he made use of that horrid word 'perfectionist'. This
suggested a less than perfect taste on Rotter's part, and the
latter for a moment looked disturbed. Then he said, 'Why do
I employ the word "perfectionist"? Well, I realize that it is
not a nice word. But I am only a publicity man, and this
article of mine is for an american magazine. One must not hold
oneself at too great a distance from one's audience. And I
would say Okay or Sez-you if it would help your books.'

'I know you would, Rotter. I know you would make an
absolute hog of yourself. I must forcibly hold you back: you
write so much for the american public that in the end you
would ruin your style and bristle with the foulest expressions.'

Did René really mean it, Rotter mused, when he referred to
his style in so flattering a way? He could not stop himself—
quite idiotically—wondering this. Then, with a slight smile, he

4*

told René that he would be on his guard against the insidious
requirements of the Yankee public. They filled up their glasses
and strolled back to their chairs.

'Taking the beastly expression seriously for a moment,'
René said, 'I cannot see how you could have mistaken me for
a perfectionist.'

'No?'

'No. I do not desire *perfection* in the least. All I suggest is
that it is high time that people gave up over-valuing figures
neither more nor less noteworthy than a pugilist or a thug.
When writing *history*, hang it all, they should not accept the
world's estimation of what is valuable and important.'

'But most historians have the minds of a small-town bank
manager.'

'Of course, I know that. But there is no occasion to call me
a perfectionist because I think it is possible for the historian
to approach his material from a somewhat higher level; to
transcend the values of the market-place, and to attain to a
level which is all-over as intelligent as what is, at present, the
most intelligent. That would not be perfect, Rotter. It need be
no higher, for the present, than what would satisfy you and
me. Are *we* perfect?'

They both laughed. Rotter took up his article and threw it
into a waste-paper basket.

'If you do *that*, Rotter, I will refrain from comment in
future. You grow temperamental!'.

Rotter reached down and removed his article from the
waste-paper basket. 'I have just been asked by a Chicago
paper,' he then observed, 'to say something about Toynbee's
Study. Oh dear! I am afraid I have to do it.'

'Matthew, Mark, Luke and John, Bless the bed that I lie on.'

'Yes, I know.' Rotter laughed. 'But I should be obliged for
a little stimulation.'

'There is, of course, plenty to say,' the other answered. 'His
great merit is that he is one of the few people who abhor war.
But I think it is curious that a man with these unusual
scruples should be so little disturbed as he is by all the monstrosities of the past. For him, what is outrageous today is
anything but that five hundred or five thousand years ago.

'One would expect, for instance, this Victorian throwback
to bristle the moment he found himself, in his Universal
History, confronted by the slave-household of the Padishah.
But this does not occur. On the contrary, he dwells lovingly.
upon the Osmanli's nomadic masterpiece of despotism. He is
lyrical about "this marvellous system of human cultivation":
and marvels as much at the Mamluks as at the Janissaries.
Were he studying a colony of insects this objectivity would be
natural: but these were men. One would not offer this criticism
if he were a twentieth-century man.'

'No, he is not *that*.' Rotter took up a pen and made a note
upon a scribbling pad. 'Thank you,' he added.

'Then it occurs to me that the word civilization requires
careful definition.'

'You are speaking of the *Study*?' Rotter asked.

'I should have to refer to him again, but it is my impression
that he is careless about that. I suggest that you check up
on it.'

'I certainly will.' Rotter made another note.

'If, for instance, you say that culturally (or as "civilization") Rome is no more than a reflection of Hellas, and that
the Empire set up by the Church at Rome was merely a
prolongation of the Roman Empire, and that, of course, the
civilization of Western Europe remains essentially Graeco-
Roman (and that the *Roman* is Graeco-Roman is superfluous
since Rome was a reflection of the Greek civilization)—seen
in this way it is a continuous civilization from Pericles to
Mr. Attlee. In cataloguing your civilization—and making use
only of this very abstract term—alongside the Egyptiac, the
Sumeric, the Syriac, the Minoan, and so on you would lump
Hellas, Rome, and Western Europe as "hellenic". Now this,
culturally, leads to extraordinary complications. If what you
are studying is the growth, development, and breakdown of
civilizations, then there are so many breakdowns between
Pericles and Mr. Attlee (or, if you like, Stalin) that it is
difficult to think of what you label hellenic as one thing. To
pack Christendom and Hellas into one box would be much
easier if you could say that Christianity was just Stoicism: but
for bible-religion Christianity was mostly hebraic in temper.

'The labellers' difficulties are daunting. Since the monkish
civilization was latin, and since the italian humanists so
dramatically put on the market again the literature of Greece
and of Rome; since latin nations are the most intelligent in
Europe, and France has dictated culturally to the rest of
Europe for a long time now; since Italy was so incredibly
creative, you cannot shake off Rome, which was the child of
Greece—there is no other label for us except Graeco-Roman
or hellenic, is there?' Rotter scratched his head.

René nodded. 'Yes. It is rather a pity that the Italians
flooded northern Europe with their humanism, with Greece
and with Rome. Had northern Europe remained Gothic it
would have been more logical, wouldn't it?'

'I agree with you,' Rotter said. 'It would have been more
clear-cut. The old Testament is quite Gothic and would have
fitted in very well with the Norse mythology. We then would
have had a norse civilization up here, with Gothic sculp-
ture confronting, across the centuries, the figures of the
Parthenon.'

René laughed. 'Anyway, there we are. It is difficult to
prevent Mr. Attlee being labelled *hellenic,* from the practical
standpoint. But the *"breakdown"* question is another matter.
I have often thought how difficult it is. Toynbee, if I remember
rightly, made our civilization break down at the Wars of
Religion. He considers, therefore, that the Reformation did
the trick.'

'He is not the only one who takes the Reformation for the
start of the Great Decline.'

'But for different reasons,' René observed. 'But, outside of
dogma, the question of *breakdown* remains very difficult; and
for my part I believe it is today rather meaningless, seeing that
we have passed into what is potentially a world-culture just as
we are moving rapidly to what will be a world-society.'

Rotter gazed approvingly at his master. He reached over
and made another note upon his pad.

'Let us consider the breakdown business, and let us confine
ourselves to Great Britain. Let us survey the cultural situation
in this country from, say, the sixteenth century, when
humanism hit England, down to the present day.'

'I think I know,' said Rotter pleasurably, 'what you are going to do!'

'Well, it is just worthwhile to run through it,' René said politely. 'What we are going to consider is exactly at what point we detect the *breakdown* signs in our civilization. The Age of Faith and the Gothic art-form which accompanied it was not a *breakdown*, or rather not a *step-down* from what came before it. In the sixteenth century the Renaissance and humanism came to England and jostled about in battle with the Gothic: but, outside of dogma or of race, no one would assert that the Italian Renaissance was inferior to the Gothic. So there was no *breakdown* in the sixteenth century in England. Was there a *breakdown* in the seventeenth century? But that was the 'Century of Genius': it contained Shakespeare and Milton, and Newton, to go no further, and it hardly seems that there was any cultural breakdown there. The eighteenth century, if not so blazing with genius, is the most *civilized* of any yet. The nineteenth century in England was extraordinarily *different* from the eighteenth, its materialism leaving no room for the elegant scepticism it superseded. But it was no less civilized. It produced a terrific crop of cultural "high-lights": there was the Darwinian revolution, very great writers like Dickens, great political thinkers and a crop of first-rate scientists. There was no sign of *breakdown* there. We fought it on its borders, but we now realize how wonderful a century it was. How about the twentieth century? Are we civilized? The Man of Science would answer that we are even *more* civilized. Einsteinean physics and the discovery of atomic fission are not suggestive, exactly, of intellectual decay. The revolution in the Fine Arts, the academics describe as decadent, but the artistic pioneers appeal to me, personally, more than do the detractors. As to the social revolutionaries, they do not regard themselves as symptoms of *breakdown*. Quite the contrary. As the present-day "West European" intellectual sees it, there is just as much vitality in *his* civilization, however you classify it, as there was in Periclean civilization. And one should indicate here a further complication; our most admired artists regard artistic works of the Peak period in civilization as inferior to the primitive or so called "archaic" art.| The painters Gauguin and Picasso prefer the primitive art of Tahiti or of the Sandwich Islands to that of the High Renaissance, or of Fourth-century Athens. Is this still civilization? Or does it at this point break down? Is Civilization, when it becomes most civilized, no longer itself, or classifiable as Civilization? In other words, we have reached a civilized refinement where civilization is transcended. Now, the point of this review of the centuries, is that I feel that the great generalizers of birth and of breakdown run their abstract lines, arbitrarily, through all kinds of things. If it suited them, the *breakdown* line would go through the centre of the Century of Genius, or the century before, or indeed anywhere, regardless of the cultural vigour to be met with at that spot.'

'Yes.'

'Then I think that would be a profitable investigation.'

'I think so too.'

René sighed, and lit a cigarette. 'And I do not have to tell you, do I, that in my view civilization belongs to a period which is past. We no longer have to think about civilization.'

'There I shall be on familiar ground.'

Rotter made a note, and began to light his pipe. René pondered in silence for a moment then, leaning on the gunwale of his armchair, in an attitude suggestive of a surrender to happy sloth, he yawned and said, 'You are aware, no doubt, that there are many technical criticisms of *The Study*?'

'Yes.'

'Toynbee has been much criticized for doing violence to facts in order to crush them into the rigid frames of his theory. But I do not know how you intend to write about him. I should not be too tough if I were you.'

Rotter laughed. 'Toughness is not what I have to be on guard against.'

René stood up and stretched. 'I must go,' he said. 'Thank you, Rotter, for reading me that.'

Rotter got to his feet, smoking furiously. 'How is Hester?' he enquired.

At this René started, and then—there was no doubt about it—blushed. Very annoyed with himself, he countered, without answering, 'How is Kathleen?'

No blush came to Rotter's face. He answered placidly that Kathleen had returned to Ireland. 'I am now interested in a young lady called Josephine. She is a belgian discovery.'

René sighed. 'You seem very fond of foreigners,' he grumbled.

'Perhaps that is why I am so fond of you.' Rotter gave a soft growling laugh. The gallic half of René was not the part of him that Rotter liked least. The educated englishman's inferiority complex about the French René had often had occasion to be grateful for. He liked men with big pipes and square heads, who spoke with phlegm of this and that, their heads rising from clouds of smoke like a small mountain: he found that they looked favourably upon his french-gothic beard, and his dark celtic eyes. He began to drift towards the door, Rotter slowly moving with him. They did not speak until they were out in the hall and René had picked his hat off the rack, when Rotter asked him, 'Shall we be meeting soon?'

'Let me see.' René rubbed his eyes. 'I am spending a day or two with my beastly brother-in-law. The parson. When I get back, let us have dinner.'

They carefully abstained from all mention of the approaching end of the world. Both were tired of talking about it, and also tended to boycott it as a subject of conversation. They shook hands at the door. As René was hurrying up the street his critical frenzy had one of its regular spasms. He tore his best friend to pieces and himself as well; so much devotion was embarrassing; how could one really feel at ease with a parasite, and with what ridiculous assiduity he had encouraged this man to feed upon his brain. He went round there perhaps once a month to be milked, as it were. As the ideas imbibed in this way were observed to issue from Rotter's mouth, René would sometimes hang his head. If only Rotter were a shade less dependent!—but he shook off the critical fiend as he turned round into Marylebone Road.

CHAPTER VIII

An Agreeable Dinner-Party

WHEN René stepped out of the train on to the platform of Rugby station, he wished he had not come. This feeling was so strong that he nearly crossed to the opposite platform, to take the next train back to London. For the big rough word, Rugby, stank of Kerridge; that is the Reverend Robert Kerridge, husband of his youngest sister Helen. However, he checked this impulse to fly, and made his way to the telephone.

Kerridge! the very name was unseemly; the name of the Kerridges was probably 'carriage', but as the more archaic carriages doubtless spelled things as they pronounced them, Robert had inherited the surname Kerridge, or at least this was the philology sponsored by René, for the name of his brother-in-law. Apart from one's reactions to the particular clergyman involved, how much jollier it would have been had this been a visit to the Reverend Amos Barton of Shepperton, who one might have accompanied to the local workhouse, known as the 'College', sniffed the roasting goose, or exchanged a word with the one-eyed rebel, Poll Fodge.

How colourless was the existence of the Kerridges: how tiresome a 'pink' bank-clerk was Kerridge himself! Helen had indeed got herself embedded in a squalid *matière*.

Such reflections moving through his mind, he at last reached the telephone, and almost immediately was hearing the voice of his dear sister, who in many ways he valued more than anybody. He breathed the atmosphere of her voice, standing erect in the glass-box, and it was the voice of the Helen of yesterday, and this was the last time he would be in touch with her down here; for once he reached the Vicarage there would be Kerridge all round them, and it would be difficult to see her as distinctly as he now could hear her. Helen told him that Robert K. was down in Rugby shopping. They lived a half-

106

hour's ride outside it, but almost daily Kerridge bicycled in to shop, or to chat with some friends he had there. The news, however, that he was in Rugby, and not in Starbrook, had not even a practical interest, for René could not pillion-ride with him back to the Vicarage for there was of course no pillion, and had there been hè would have declined so close a contact with his relative.

Outside the station he found a taxi and came to terms with the driver. He was humming

> 'It won't be a stylish merridge,
> For we can't afford a Kerridge,'

as they started off. This almost springless vehicle punishing him badly, he speculated as to the likelihood of hackney vehicles no longer able to pass the Metropolitan police-test being shipped down to the provinces.

Rugby is a dull town, with none of the distinction that might be expected as a background for the ancient school. In the days of Tom Brown, yes: the approaches to the gaping gate, leading into the School House quadrangle, would still have possessed some style. But long ago the industrialism of the Midlands had converted everything into a drab uniformity.

As the taxi was turning at right angles in front of the great gate, he remembered how he had witnessed, on a January morning some years before, a snow-fight. There had been a heavy snow-fall during the night, and half the School House were in the dark interior of the gate-way preventing the rest of the School from entering. From all the outside Houses the boys had duly arrived to go to their form-rooms, and had been met by a hail of snow-balls. They laid siege to the gate, answering the fire of the School House from such cover as they could secure along the sides of the shopping street which led to the gate. Windows were broken and snow-balls also caused casualties among those attacking and those defending the gate. In the rear of the School buildings, a similar battle was in progress. It was a scene to René's mind, typical of this rough school.

They bumped along in this new street but very soon they

once more turned to right angles, and moved along the side of
the School precincts. Next came the Close, and as they began
to move forward beside the Close railings, René leant out of
the cab-window and looked at the line of School buildings
facing the Close, the Library Tower, and the windows of the
School House and Headmaster's quarters, from which Dr.
Arnold once would gaze down upon the Close, a biologist
scrutinizing work in progress. From this position, seated at his
study window, he was able to watch his burly young Christian
Gentlemen playing their own especial version of the game of
football. The spectacle would probably cause him to reflect
how lawless this school had always been, and how raw still
was the material with which he had to work. After all, Tom
Brown's School Days was going on under the same roof,
within a few yards of him.

It had been found impossible, in an earlier time, to persuade
its scholars to confine themselves to *foot* ball. Some passionate
young blackguard would snatch up the ball, and rush wildly
towards the goal with it, pursued by a howling pack of
agnostic Gentlemen. (And the Christianizing of such creatures
could be no easy matter.)—Since there was no means of
keeping this a ball-kicking game new rules had to be drawn-up
to regulate the rushing about with the ball under the arm: and
to limit, to some extent, the ferocity of attacks upon the man
who had run off with it.

Dr. Arnold was not a lover of tradition, and his head-
masterly blood did not boil, in retrospect, at the thought of
this defiance of the laws governing pastimes. The sight of a
mud-caked Christian Gentleman tearing down a field hugging
a dirty ball, and a dozen dirty Christians, as gentle as himself,
at his heels, seemed to him entirely as it should be. Did it not
harden muscle: and did it not add hardiness to a Christian
Gentleman's moral uprightness? In the School chapel the C.G.
in question would learn to smite people hip and thigh, and to
exact an eye for an eye, and a tooth for a tooth. The canes of
the prefects, as well as those of the masters, would harden this
Christian Gentleman-in-the-making in other ways: and fagging
toughen the little rat who was to become a Christian Gentleman, and teach him the beauties of Authority. His learning to

fear his redoubtable headmaster would be good practice for fearing God.

Then as to the spectacle of the ugly battles which would occur in front of the home-goal, it would not be forgotten by Dr. Arnold that many Christian Gentlemen had, a little later in life, to be trained as professional 'killers'. There were foot-slogging killers, and mounted (or cavalry) killers. As six furious figures fought for a slippery ball, rolling over and over near a goal-post, punching and strangling and kicking one another, the fresh-coloured rather jewish-looking face at the window (Jahveh Minor) had a gratified glint in his eye. Just then a boy passed immediately beneath where he was sitting, with a half-dozen books under his arm. He wore the School House Colours, and the doctor with some annoyance found he could not identify this pale and earnest face. He made a mental note of the features. The boy did not turn his head to watch the game. A little 'swot'. Arnold's pleased expression was replaced by one of heavy petulance. 'Tis a goodly sight, that knot of violent gentlemen in the great field beyond: but this bookish boy was in danger of never developing into a Christian or into a Gentleman.

At this point René, in imagination, left Jahveh Minor in his observatory, and moved on to a time when Dr. Arnold had abandoned his human laboratory at Rugby, and flung himself into the Civil War of Tractarians and Anti-Tractarians, raging around Oxford. He had no love for Tradition, it has been observed above; and this extended into the sphere of Supernatural Grace and the nasty stirrings of the Old Religion. He laid about him lustily. The arguments in favour of a priesthood stimulated his fighting glands to an extraordinary degree —for the delegation of Authority, when that Authority was God Himself, moved him to as violent an opposition as that he had incurred when at Rugby School he had delegated his authority to members of the Sixth Form, and even to Sixth Powers. This was very inconsistent of Dr. Arnold. For why should he object to God delegating His power to a priesthood, whereas, in his capacity of Jahveh Minor, he empowered the boys of the Sixth to act in place of him?

While such thoughts were unfolding in René's mind, the cab

had been proceeding on the road to Starbrook, and there, all of a sudden, pedalling along before him, he perceived a familiar figure upon a familiar bicycle. He would have known the neck anywhere. It was the Reverend Robert Kerridge: and it was with considerable satisfaction that he passed his brother-in-law, kicking up, he trusted, a fair amount of dust in the reverend gentleman's face. But the cab was not equal to the task of reaching Starbrook Vicarage so much ahead of the pedalling parson as to enable him to have more than a few words with his sister before the eruption of Kerridge. She was removing the tea things and he followed her into the kitchen, where she put down the tray and gave him a delighted hug. 'My darling René, how glad I am to see you. I have been worrying a great deal about you. We must have a talk . . . as soon as I can manage it.'

'Do let us.'

They moved back into the drawing-room, and they had just passed through the door when sounds announcing Kerridge's arrival came from without.

'I think that's Robert,' Helen said, and they both turned towards the door. There was a quick strong step in the hall and the Reverend Robert Kerridge entered the room with his customary *fracas*. 'Ah hallo. Was that you in the cab? I thought it might be!'

He moved forward a few steps, swinging his arms and legs, and displaying his glaringly white teeth, attempting to suggest the exhilaration of good-fellowship.

Described in this way, Robert Kerridge probably has a rather alarming sound. But to the average eye the hearty straggling of his legs and welcoming movements of his arms would indeed have spelled good fellowship, even if the white clerical collar did not in itself carry conviction. He was in his thirties, and according to average standards a tallish young man of regular features and agreeable expression. Looked at more analytically, he possessed rather too long a neck, while his eyes shone with too artificial a geniality through largish glasses. His fine, large, white teeth *were* too much in evidence. When he spoke, he chewed round and round with these teeth the words in his mouth, as if they were too big, and required

him to open his mouth wide and reduce them by mastication.
The words were all a dark blue. I mean that they had the
Oxford colours. The Oxford accent trailed after it the accents
of Croydon; but still, with the shining eyes and gleaming
teeth, waved about on the top of his long pink-and-white neck,
the accent did its work well enough.

There was a derisive something in the gleam as he straddled
about and rubbed his hands in front of René. Kerridge made
a hearty meal of the eleven words, 'It is a long time since
I last saw you, René,' his jaws rolling round in the act of
mastication.

'It is quite a time,' René drily agreed. 'Quite a time.' They
looked at one another with very little affectation of pleasure
on either side. The clergyman's aggressive politeness, with the
baring of his big battalions of teeth, was answered by a brief
amused smile, wiped off abruptly, succeeded by an air of
patient watchfulness, as one might keep one's eye upon a ram
of notoriously aggressive habits.

'I have missed you very much,' Helen said. 'But I hear all
about you from the family, of course. At least, all the family
knows.'

'Yes!' Kerridge crashed in. 'I was very sorry to hear about
your resignation. I always have trotted out at parties "My
brother-in-law Professor René Harding." It sounded very
well. I shall not be able to do that any longer now!'

'You can say instead, 'My brother-in-law, the author of
The Secret History of World War II' Helen reminded him.

'That,' Robert drawled, 'is not I am afraid quite so impressive. You know what I mean; a Chair of History is much rarer
than mere authorship.'

The young bank-clerk face of the marxist vicar retained a
pointed gravity for some time after the mention of René's
book. René's remained grave too.

'You both look a little glum,' Helen exclaimed. 'I will fetch
something to drink.'

'Won't you sit down,' Robert said, and threw himself into
a chair. René walked over to the window, and stood gazing
out of it. There was nothing to look at except a tree; but he
fixed a bored eye upon a baby twig. The voracious Oxford

accent of his brother-in-law, with drawling cadences, got busy behind him. 'What was the real cause of your resignation, René? Of course I have read what the *newspapers* say.'

René turned round. 'That is all,' he answered indifferently. 'Nothing is concealed. I simply did not any longer wish to teach what is called History.'

'So long as you can afford to indulge a very natural taste for leisure,' drawled his clerical relative, with a very casual laugh.

'Had I desired leisure I should have become a clergyman,' René retorted. He felt there was nothing else to do.

'I am afraid you do not understand what is expected of a clergyman, if you regard his life as one of leisure!' protested Robert languidly, stretched out like a holiday snap-shot in his chair.

'Has your morning been a very heavy one?' enquired René, advancing towards him, goaded into counterattack.

'Terrifically heavy,' Helen answered, as she entered with the drinks. 'Robert has been buying groceries, and having a heavy gossip with Jimmy Braybridge, the Vicar of St. Osaph's.''

'That is most unjust!' Robert drawled, more lazily than ever. 'I was discussing with Braybrook a question of great weight and moment.'

'Yes, the transport of a lawn-mower!' Helen laughed. 'Get up, Robert, and pull this cork!'

But René had the bottle between his knees, and there was the sound of a cork being drawn.

'A clean pull!' sang Robert and no one could say he was averse to others scrutinizing the inside of his mouth. 'Other things failing, René, you can always get a job as a waiter, can't you?'

Helen, frowning, breathed in her husband's ear, 'None of that, now!'

René shrugged his shoulders and moved towards the window again. He recalled the offensive words of another brother-in-law, namely Victor. These two very average sensual men could be said, couldn't they, to represent Everyman: so this might be taken as the world's reaction to what he had done. These mocking brothers-in-law could be set beside his mother. They all had much the same view of a man who threw up a professorship for nothing. He looked fixedly at the diminutive twig. He heard Helen's voice, speaking in an angry undertone, 'Robert, I hope that this time you will remember René is our guest! You do your best to stop him from coming down here by your rudeness. It is jealousy! You ought to be ashamed of yourself.'

'Jealousy! Are you in your right senses, Helen . . .' Robert began, but René left the room, as he stopped.

'Kerridge! Come out here, will you?' René called. The parson left the room with a disagreeable smile: but a few minutes later they both re-entered, and took up their drinks without further exchange just then.

After dinner, the clergyman excused himself, he had a letter to write. Brother and sister were alone for a short while.

'I am sorry, René, how difficult things are here. Robert has always been terribly jealous of you.'

'Of *me*?'

'Yes. And now, to make things worse, he is writing a novel.'

René laughed. 'A novel!'

'Yes. I do hope he does not become a celebrity! There will be no holding him!'

René made what is called in French a *moue*. 'Ça pourrait être bien curieux, quand même."

Helen smiled and nodded. She treated her husband as a precocious boy, from whom one must expect tactless outbursts.

The next morning a local woman came in to char. René at first regarded her with suspicion, but there were no signs of insanity. Outside of the London area such creatures as Mrs. Harradson are scarcely ever found.

Mr. Kerridge had a date somewhere. Shortly after breakfast signs of impending departure were visible. René was furtively attentive to these signs: and at length he was able to observe, through one of the front windows, the bicycle being wheeled to the gate, and through its iron work followed with joy the mounting of the bicycle. Finally, he watched with elation the

disembodied clerical hat gaining speed as it skimmed along
the top of the hedge. He waited a moment, then rushed back
into the kitchen, to announce to Helen that the coast was
clear. 'The wicked giant, in whose power you have been for so
long, has pedalled away on some mysterious errand. Hoorah!'
With his dancing step he led the way out-of-doors. Behind
him Helen, as eager as himself, danced at his heels in imitative
stance.

The Kerridges would have been very difficult to please if
they had not been grateful for the Vicarage which had fallen
to their lot. It had the dignity, the elegance of the eighteenth
century in every line, its well-cut red-brick, its windows and
doors picked out by the white stripes in their sockets, and
the white triangle balanced upon its white legs or convenient
columns, as clean and correct as white linen at the neck and
wrists in a gentleman's attire. A house which had escaped
by forty years the Romantic Revival. Also, the place was a
sizable one to allow for the considerable broods of sedentary
clergymen. And then the Kerridges had been presented with
a large garden too, and kept it in excellent shape—except that
it would have been better with fewer herbaceous borders. As
he danced past the Canterbury bells and delphiniums, René
said to himself that his sister at least could get away from the
obsessing india-rubber neck, white jaw-ornaments for ever on
show, and the two glittering panes of glass where eyes ought
to be: these herbaceous vulgarities would serve to sweeten her
imagination after a long tête-à-tête with the wicked giant
within, alecking away at his smartest, and perhaps attempting
to devour her with those hideous tusks.

As he thought of the two sets of piano-keys in Kerridge's
mouth, something possessive caused him to seize Helen around
the shoulders and draw her away more rapidly from the House
that Jack Built, as she decided that it was, inhabited by a
bankclerkish Giant, with big glass eyes and crunching tusks.
She clung to him, as if understanding that a Preux had come
to rescue her from a Giant oddly disguised as a Clergyman.

At the foot of the garden they reached a summer-house,
dating from Victorian days, a caricature of a miniature
pagoda. Once you got inside it, it was quite comfortable, with

a rug on the floor, a table and chairs, and at the back there was a window looking out on to a very minor ravine in part gorse-covered. They entered, went over to the window, which was open, and leaned upon its gritty sill, gazing vacantly out at the uncultivated strip of country, too far from the horizontal to be of much use to anybody.

'Now that we are alone at last, René, please tell me why you threw up your job? I did *not write* to you, because I knew that you would say nothing in a letter. Did you have the most fearful row?'

His sister's sudden question took René a little aback. After a short pause he laughed, and passed his hand violently over his face. His reply was a question.

'How long have you been married, Helen?' he enquired.

'Eleven years,' she said at once, as though she had had the answer ready.

'Well, I was appointed Professor of Modern History eleven years ago. Let us suppose that you suddenly left your husband. . . .'

'Me? . . . Why?'

'*Just suppose*. People would ask you in great surprise, what had caused you to take this step. You would answer, presumably, that you had done so because of his complete absence of moral understanding and because of the harm he was doing as a consequence of his lack of moral sense. At least this is what you would say if your case were a parallel one to mine, and your motives resembling my motives.'

'Ah, I see,' she exclaimed, in a tone of considerable relief. 'I was going to say . . .'

'But the answer I have imagined you giving to your inquisitive neighbours would appear to them of the most fantastic kind. What a reason to give! they would say. They would suppose that you had invented this to conceal the actual cause of the estrangement and separation. Later on, they would take you aside and ask you what was the *real* reason. You would find yourself in an embarrassing position, and in the end would almost wish that you had answered, "Oh, we just had a row, just a bad row!" Do you follow me?'

'I am afraid I do not,' Helen replied.

'No? Well, my case is rather similar to this suppositious one, in which you left Robert, explaining your action by charging him with moral obliquity.'

'Ah, I see what you were getting at!'

'Well,' René sighed, 'you will begin to understánd from this illustration, how difficult it is for me to know quite what to say. No one will believe that I am such an utter *prig*—that is how it must look to them—as I claim to be.'

Helen turned, and had a good look at the bearded face beside her, which in imagination, she always saw with a gay curling up of the ends of the moustache, nothing but high-spirited raillery and delighted exploitation of the absurd seeming to be happily mobilized behind those eyes. Even now his glance held nothing solemn in it. It swam and darted as it always did.

'I see how it must be, René. But it is so difficult to think of you convulsed with some ethical problem: yours is not exactly an ethical personality! I find it difficult myself to see you resigning your professorship, for *moral* reasons.'

René laughed, as he turned away from the windowsill. He lighted a cigarette, and dropped into a chair.

'Please give me a cigarette,' said Helen, as she sat down in front of him.

They both sat smoking for a moment, and Helen feared at first that she might have offended: but her brother then looked up with his accustomed smile. 'You put your finger at once upon one of the difficulties,' he told her. 'My personality is *not* that of a great moralist, is it? That is probably the reason for people's scepticism. You showed great insight, sister. But that is not *all*. If the issue were a simple one, or rather, if it were reducible to a simple explanation, I would have no objection whatever to making a public statement. But as it is, my personality is so out of keeping with the ethically heroical image that the bare facts elicit. You spotted that at once. *I* cannot be made to fit in with my story. To extricate myself from that misunderstanding, I should have to agree, *Yes, my personality is not that of a martyred moralist. But then I am not, first and foremost, a moralist.* From that point onwards everything is far too difficult to explain to the majority of people. To satisfy Tom, Dick, and Harry, some formula would have to be found—something as short as it was convincing.'

'But Robert is neither Tom, Dick, nor Harry, is he? Why do you not explain to him?'

'Because he is biased against me. And there is no particular reason why I should say more to him than to anybody else. But to *you*, I would like to explain a little, if you want to be bored.'

'I wish you would, René . . . I am not very learned!'

'It is not a question of "book-learning". There is nothing abstruse; my position could be made quite clear to anybody. If you were employed by some large concern, for instance, and in the course of some years you discovered that *everyone* in this considerable business was dishonest, and that the whole set-up was fundamentally a racket; when at last there was no longer any doubt that you were devoting your time and talent (such as it was) to something at once trivial and harmful, what would you do? It would be rather an awful predicament. Your salary is a good one; you are too old to re-direct yourself very easily. All your friends and relations attempt to dissuade you from resigning. Why be so fussy, so fastidious? they would argue. But now I come to the real point. Would you be a *great moralist* because you decided to resign? Not necessarily so at all. Any decent ordinary girl would find it distasteful and repugnant to spend her life engaged in activities which, without being criminal, were not honest and potentially very harmful. It would be, in part, no doubt, a *moral* issue: but equally, and perhaps in a more compelling way, it would turn upon questions of taste and of *self-respect*. We all have a considerable fund of inherited morality which we describe as "decency". And then there is a fastidiousness which is partly aesthetic, partly social conceit. We are presupposing a well-brought-up, rather particular, self-reliant girl. But why not? There are, happily, a number of girls like that. To sum this up: the term *great moralist*, if it were used of her in mockery, would quite falsify the true nature of the girl's action, in throwing up her job.'

Helen's face looked grave and a little embarrassed. She asked, with an apologetic air, 'You reason very clearly, René, but I fail to see, quite, what the imaginary girl employed by some people not quite on the straight, has to do with René Harding, Professor of History, who resigns his post.'

'Exactly!' René exclaimed, with much approval. 'My racket is *History*, you say. As harmless a thing as could well be imagined. What is *History* except dates—William the Conqueror 1066 and a list of the wives of Henry VIII? The past, the long-ago, is about as harmless as anything could be. That, more or less, is the general view of history, is it not?'

Helen laughed and nodded. 'I'm afraid so,' she said. 'I, of course, know a bit more than that. I have just been reading about the Court of Queen Anne. But I cannot see how there is much room for such a moral flare-up as we are discussing.'

'Well there *is*, even about Queen Anne's reign. All history is written with a bias. But if it is written with a state-organized bias, as in Soviet Russia, great harm ensues. For if you falsify past events methodically, you very soon authorize or indeed command that present events be systematically falsified also. And for there to be no standard of objective reality in a society is a very bad thing for the society in question.'

'I see that all right,' Helen told him.

'And do you also see, Helen, how I could not, in delivering myself of this explanation to Robert, have cited Soviet Russia, although it is the best illustration of state-falsification of History?'

Helen laughed heartily, as she always did at any reference to Robert's political views, in colour approaching that of the letter-box or of the setting-sun.

'We are getting along well,' René assured her. 'But History includes the present as well as the *past*. The World War was *history* as much as the Wars of the Roses. Mr. Winston Churchill is as much a historical figure as was the first Duke of Marlborough, about whom you have been reading in your Queen Anne book.'

Helen's face was still without the social smile: she recognized that her brother attached great importance to this interview, for some reason; that he set store by her understanding exactly what he was saying: and she was determined to concentrate, and to make her mind properly receptive. It was very rarely indeed that great exactitude was required of her understanding, and she sat very still, as though she were absorbed in some calligraphic feat.

'Now what it is essential to remember,' René continued, after a pause, 'is that any work includes the field of contemporary politics—twentieth-century politics. Whereas, up to a certain point, what you think, and what you say, about the Peasants' Revolt—about Wat Tyler and John Bull—has no immediate influence upon people's conduct, it is quite a different matter when you are writing about nineteenth-century Liberalism in England, or the deluded optimists known as the "Manchester School"; and when it comes to the twentieth century to Edward the Peacemaker, to the Duke of Windsor and to Mr. Baldwin—when it comes to writing about all this, it ceases to be history as popularly understood at all. It is more like analysing the character and behaviour of the members of one's family circle, neighbours or friends: or the notables of your borough or county, the local police or sanitary authorities, or local member of parliament. You see what I mean?'

He paused, and Helen said, 'I see.'

'The word history is synonymous in the popular mind with something *distant*. When *history* gets so near to us that it hurts, naturally we no longer regard it as *history*—and then, the so-called historian, when his history is *near*-history, is far less free than when his material is a century away. Any unorthodoxy is deeply resented, especially if he occupies an official position. Pressures are felt from all directions. All kinds of things are expected of him. He is supposed to conform to accepted views of every sort: more especially *economic* unorthodoxy is impossible. You are supposed to forget that the banks and great Insurance Companies exist: your view in all such things must be that of a child of ten years old. And as to *wars* (as to so senseless a crime as the World War), there you must speak of "anger of a great people demanding action". You must speak of governments giving way to popular clamour ("popular clamour" being the inflammatory banner headlines of the *Daily Mail* or the *Daily Mirror*): your history must sound not unlike an Armistice Day speech. You must turn no stones on the beach to see what is underneath them: you must adhere to the reality of the world of slogans, and you must never turn a slogan on its back.'

His sister looked up, smiling.

'Helen, I have only begun to say what it is necessary to run through to answer the curious as to the *real* reason for my resignation. I should have to proceed next to another point: namely, how events in the present century *reflect back*, and cause the historian to tell the story of the nineteenth century rather differently. I should say, *very* differently! And as to the nineteenth-century economics! But all this *n'en finit plus.* Apart from anything else, no one would patiently listen to the lecture which it would be necessary to deliver, for full enlightenment. To find a half-dozen words in which to explain why I resorted to so drastic a step as resignation, is quite impossible. From such explanatory words as I think up for public consumption people conclude that I am laying claim to an inordinate ethical sensitivity. My motives of course involve nothing of the sort. But it is impossible to compress into a sentence or two my reason for resigning without creating this impression.'

'I can see, I think,' Helen told him, 'how difficult all this is, René.'

'You have been very attentive, very kind. But you must, at the end of it, regard me as an abominable egoist keeping you screwed down in this summerhouse, while I harangue you.'

'Oh, René darling! . . .'

'The fact is, I very much wanted to have one member of my family who saw clearly what my resignation was about.'

'*One* does!' she interrupted. 'I have listened very carefully, René, and I believe I see already exactly what your problem is. It surprises me very much that this has not also been clear to other people, better informed than I am. My husband, for instance. . . .'

René gave a short laugh like a cough. 'It is because he understands so well that he appears so dense. *He* stands for the latest form of obscurantism.'

René sprang up and stretched, as he always did in such cases, as though to shake the concentration out of his body.

That he should want to shake it out was evidence of the fact
that he lived in two compartments. He shook off what was
mental as soon as he was done with it and passed over into the
animal playground of the mind—the sphere in which most
people of course pass all their time. He was half-brother to
Everyman.

He went over to the window, where he propped himself
as before, observing the blasted heath. 'What a glamorous
outlook!' he said. 'Is this hut supposed to represent life on
earth, and is that the great open spaces of the *néant?*'

'Something like that,' Helen laughed, who had come over
and was now standing beside him.

'I should have gone on with my disquisition,' René said,
'but I do not know how long we have. It is rather breathless
but let me shove in a further bit of elucidation if you can bear
it. I should have explained to you that in a full statement I
should be obliged to cite details likely to embarrass me.
Events in the twentieth century regarded by me as unworthy
of the historian's notice (since they belong to that barbary
which it is our duty to surmount), are thought of by many
people as of supreme importance. A *complete* statement would
merely start a row. Events of the last twenty years which
Robert Kerridge looks upon as world shaking, would not look
like that to me. And, of course, the pros and cons of my
resignation would depend upon values which some allow, and
some do not allow. It is really very complicated. In the
abstract, my resignation looks thus and thus; *concretely*, it
would look quite differently. So as not to get embroiled in all
those hot issues which tear our world to pieces today, it is
perhaps as well that my resignation should be accounted for
abstractedly. There is something in favour of people talking
nonsense about "a great moralist". Though, to add a last
touch of confusion, I am a sort of moralist notwithstanding.'

Helen frowned and cried, 'René! What a problem to set
your poor little sister. But I will work it out in solitude. I will
write to you when I have straightened things out. But I know,
instinctively . . .'

'You intuit.'

'I suppose that's it. I was saying that I am certain you are right. I know you better than anybody, and I know that what you have done is sensible and just.'

He gave her a quick hug, and said, 'I have you on my side, Helen. I knew I should. I am so thankful that we were allowed the time to have our talk. But what do I see! Merciful heavens (as Lady Brown would say). There he is! There he comes!'

Along the opposite crest of the little ravine, there indeed he was—teeth, glass eyes, rubber neck and all. For he was waving an arm at them as he pedalled. Helen waved back, in wifely salutation.

'You nearly hit me!' René gasped. 'Do not get too hysterical at the sight of old rubber-neck.'

'René! You must not call Robert old rubber-neck!' Helen exhorted him, wagging a finger.

'How you can degrade yourself by biting that rubbery substance!' her brother hissed as he made for the door. 'Hurry up! Be at the gate of the castle to greet your lord as he dismounts.'

'You go too far,' she complained, but did in fact hustle along, as though to reach the gate of the castle in time.

As René hastened forward to be present at the arrival of the Wicked Giant, he was startled by a soprano in the top register attaining to the shrillness of a steam-whistle in the next-door house. Deafened by the shriek, he passed the kitchen window and there was the charlady's face tilted back, observing him with the remote ethereal derision peculiar (he had supposed) to Mrs. Harradson, observing him in flight from the blast of the soprano. He realized that he had his fingers in his ears. He put his tongue out at her, and she vanished as if by magic. He stepped lightly and briskly into the house and Mrs. Huxtable, the Warwickshire charlady, emerged from the kitchen. . . . He promptly stuck his tongue out as if it were a reflex action. Mrs. Huxtable, as if knocked back into the kitchen with a sledgehammer blow, vanished: and a door, pivoting madly on its hinges, replaced her. It must be the country mind, he thought. She considered it quite in order to jeer at me in her gaze because I have my fingers in my ears, in order to bar ingress to the steam-whistle of a neighbouring soprano: but if I reciprocate by protruding my tongue, this affects her galvanically. Like Mrs. Harradson, she fails to conceal her disrespect. Disrespect shown *by me*, knocks her out entirely.'

'What are you doing, René?' came a pant from just behind. 'You are up to something I believe.'

'Incorrect!' he rapped back. 'I was merely turning over in my mind how Mrs. Harradson would have reacted. She would have gone into violent action—scrubbing, washing, or merely scuttling. She would respond as a town-bred charlady. She would play up with all that was comic in her; and throw a fit.'

'I am sure I don't know what you are talking about,' Helen told him crossly.

They were in the hall now, and they heard the tramp on the gravel outside of rubber-neck. While they had been talking he had pushed his machine in at the gate, and leaning it against a tree, entered the house with routine *fracas*.

'Ah, Helen, I have news for you!' he gave forth in a snarling gentlemanly drawl. 'Mrs. Pearson's bitch has been delivered of one fine black and tan puppy and a lot of less interestingly marked little animals.'

'Has she indeed?' Helen showed interest.

'I bespoke the fine one, as being what you wanted.'

Kerridge knew he was observed, and that it had been divined that he was in fact a Wicked Giant, but was determined to stand his ground, on his credentials as a young clergyman addicted to a working-class bicycle. He swung slowly over, from side to side, drifting his feet a little, elephant fashion. Though the dental display was almost non-stop, he never laughed. He was a machine whose Creator had forgotten to fix in a bark: or perhaps he had thought that the grin laid on most of the time made the ha-ha unnecessary. If the workmanship had this limitation, that there was a sluggishness and monotony in its reactions which made it smell of the *machine*; if the eyes behind the fixed spectacles were glassy, and if the feet seemed unnaturally heavy, his talk was as successful as a calculating machine. But of course this is how one would argue if one did not know that Kerridge was in truth a Wicked Giant, attempting to disguise his *wickedness* by invariably

5

smiling to suggest bonhomie, and that the creatures of Fairyland were big, always lumbered, and mouthed their words.

René at all times treated him correctly, as a young clergyman who had married his sister. But his uneasiness sometimes
amounted to horror. In René's composition, the Preux caused
him to feel that it was his sacred task to rescue Helen from the
clutches of a supernatural monster. If his sister were not
careful, she would find herself flying away some day, among
the stars, to unearthly mountains. She would find herself in
the blue mists of a world of rubber-necks. Top-booted and
white-bearded giants moved about with an intoxicated
gait, lifted their feet waveringly as though they did not
know where to put them down. She would be taken to
see them in their mildewed castles, bayed at by mournful
dogs.

The longer René stopped at the Kerridges, the more powerful the illusion grew that Robert Kerridge was a supernatural
impostor, that he was, not in fancy, but in cold reality, a
'Wicked Giant': happily he had never stopped more than a
few days. Had his stay extended into as many weeks, the
sensation would have become intolerable. It is quite likely as
the time to go grew near, he would have killed Kerridge. As
it was, on this second day, he was still in a playful region, the
atmosphere of Fairyland not yet so thick as to madden him.
There was still an even chance that this was merely a clergyman after all.

During lunch Kerridge announced that a housemaster at
Rugby, Grattan-Brock by name, was coming to dinner. 'I
suppose I should have asked you first, René!' he heavily and
archly minced. 'But he is a great fan of yours. He knows *The
Secret History of World War II* by heart!'

'I don't think that we should mislead our guest, Robert,'
Helen protested, looking very angry. 'Dr. Grattan-Brock, far
from being an admirer of René's, has violently attacked him,
and in my presence.'

There was a moment of silence, in which her husband
looked with such sullen displeasure at Helen, that instinctively
René gripped his knife, and looked, himself, perfectly
ferocious.

'I think, Helen, you should not make such statements. You do not understand these things. . . .'

'Oh, don't I!' she said, laughing. 'I know far more than you think! But what I am quite certain of, I am not *deaf*, is that Dr. Grattan-Brock, at this table, called René a fascist, an impostor, a poor scholar, and—yes—*a cad*!'

A most delighted 'ho-ho-ho' came from René, who was gazing with malicious enquiry at Kerridge.

'Dr. Grattan-Brock, however much he admires a book, does not dispense with criticism and analysis,' Robert Kerridge solemnly pointed out, frowning at an imaginary person hovering between his wife and her brother.

'Obviously he does not,' René said, frowning with an equal pomp. 'Spare the rod and spoil the child is his motto. He lays into those he loves, hot and strong: and considers there is no better way of expressing his appreciation of an author than by jotting down in his diary, "The author of this ill-written book is, *par dessus le marché*, an utter cad." In view of the great esteem in which he holds me, I must anticipate tonight, I suppose, some pretty plain speaking.'

While this persiflage was in progress, Kerridge crumbled up his section of bread, while he eyed his wife with glances far more eloquent than any words. Helen sat with bowed head, but she told herself with a crusading fervour that she was not going to stand by while her dear brother was made a fool of, however bitterly Robert might reproach her! René had opened his heart to her that very day, and she saw how the land lay. There were more loyalties than one; and loyalty to a husband did not wipe out all others.

Tea they had by the fireside as it had grown unexpectedly cold. After tea Robert Kerridge drew his guest aside, and, with affected embarrassment, informed him that Mrs. Huxtable had threatened to give notice: that he would be terribly obliged if René would not put his tongue out at the charlady. She was a very strict Presbyterian.

'I like that!' René protested. 'She was jeering at me because I had my fingers in my ears.'

'I have never known Mrs. Huxtable to jeer at anybody, René,' Kerridge said coldly.

'No? Put your fingers in your ears and see what happens!'
René's tongue suddenly shot forth from between his bearded
lips. 'One way of resisting rudeness! If you put your fingers in
your ears you will find this handy.' And again he stuck out
his tongue, afterwards sauntering away from his round-eyed,
pained-looking host, trying to decide whether the tongue was
meant for him or not.

The housemaster's arrival that evening was accompanied by
much stamping about in the hall, the drawling bay of the
Oxford Accent and the big-dog barking of the visitor. Dr.
Grattan-Brock was only a moderately big man physically,
however, though rather obesely stocky. He was one of that
numerous class of more or less learned English men (and in
this class may be included a few literate Americans too) who
believe that they are Dr. Johnson. Their voices roll towards
their interlocutor heavy carefully-picked words, reminiscent of
those which thundered in the small-talk of the formidable
Lexicographer. A bending of the brows will, at times, accompany these verbal discharges.

But something had happened to this shadow of the great
eighteenth-century doctor. Dr. Grattan-Brock had not come
under the spell of Marx, no housemaster could do that. He
might be a Morley-like liberal, but nothing stronger. But what
had happened was that Dr. Grattan-Brock had been very
active during the Spanish Civil War, and events leading up
to it. He had shown himself *outstandingly* liberal. He had
met numbers of fellow-travelling intellectuals (like Kerridge)
and even C.P. Party-men. From these frequentations he had
acquired a harshness wholly twentieth-century. This he had
incorporated, or worked into, the Johnsonian ponderosity.
But some subjects inflamed him and brought back those grand
days he had spent in Barcelona, and then the ponderosity
began to pound and snarl. As it was, he would go along nicely,
no-sirring and yes-sirring you for a long time, until suddenly
he would become the soap-boxer.

It was in Johnsonian vein that he began with Professor
René Harding. 'I am a reader of yours, sir. I am very grateful
to Robert Kerridge for affording me the opportunity of
meeting you.' René, on his side, was greatly amused. He was

his most urbane. He planned, by the extravagance of his language, to shame this local impersonator of Dr. Johnson out of his pose. He screwed up his mouth and its surroundings into a budding rosette of concentrated sweetness. His eyes directed upon the other a crackling glance (emitting something like a cloud of midges playing all over the person in front of it, in the last refinement of deferential gallantry).

'My brother-in-law and my sister, too, have told me so much about you. The privilege of meeting you is something, sir, I had never dared to hope for.'

The housemaster blinked a little at this but he accepted it as normal, and even managed an abbreviated eighteenth-century bow.

'The privilege, sir, is altogether on my side.' Then came the bow.

It was in this spirit that they all went in to dinner, with many courtesies on René's part suggestive of the great social and academic importance of Dr. Grattan-Brock. And had it not been for the incitements of Kerridge it is probable that the dinner would have passed off with Dr. Grattan-Brock basking his way through an excellent meal (for her early home life had provided Helen with a feeling for good cooking), and have gone home thinking what a charming fellow Professor René Harding was. It was Kerridge who first moved the conversation into dangerous channels. In a pause after a number of scholarly exchanges he was heard to say, 'By the way, Grattan-Brock, I was telling my brother-in-law that you had read his *Secret History of World War II*, and how much you had admired it.'

There was a disagreeable silence, all four suspending the meal and waiting. At last the housemaster shook himself and growled, 'Oh (arhumm) yes, of course. Indeed, I did, read your book, (arhumm). Are you writing another, sir?'

René laughed. 'No, sir. Not for the moment.'

'My brother-in-law is going to Canada. He is sailing in a few months.' Kerridge beamed at René.

'Canada! Extraordinary place to go to. Well, sir, I hope you will have a good trip.'

That the Professor was not returning, that he had resigned

his professorship, etc., etc. was, Kerridge saw to it, elicited. The housemaster began to be less ready to bask in the flatteries of this ex-Professor; and although René attempted a diversion with the architectural beauties of Strasbourg, which he had recently visited, Kerridge soon drove him out of Strasbourg, though Dr. Grattan-Brock seemed inclined to linger there a little. The St. Estephe, which was now circulating, was all the more conducive to pottering about in a French city, and perhaps becoming acquainted with *La Maison Rouge*.

A little later Helen, returned from a somewhat lengthy visit to the kitchen, found, to her astonishment, that the atmosphere had so worsened as to be alarming. Her husband and the housemaster were both turned, with accusing eyes and irritably knitted brows, towards René, who was looking first at one, and then at the other, without speaking. It was Kerridge, evidently, who was the leading spirit.

'Very well; but *The Times*, René, described you as fascist-minded, didn't it?'

'Did it?' René smiled. 'I do not remember that. But quite likely it did, since many people have been called that recently, simply because they had made a remark of an unenthusiastic kind about communism. So many youngish reviewers are romantic about Russia. It is quite absurd. I do not have to love Russia because Hitler, Russia's enemy, is so vile a man.'

'I do not think, René, that the critic of *The Times* would base a judgement on so stupid a reasoning as that.'

'No?' René looked around awaiting the next move.

'I must say, sir, that I myself have felt, at times, that you showed fascist tendencies,' Dr. Grattan-Brock began a little gruffly. 'It was just an impression, to be sure, but you have used arguments, sir, which have (arhmmp) surprised me.'

Kerridge showed signs of annoyance at the feebleness of the housemaster's co-operation. He leaned over and refilled his glass with wine, hoping that this might improve matters.

'I remember you pointing out to me, Grattan-Brock, a good illustration of what you mean. It was where Professor Harding made a comparison between Herr Hitler and St. Ignatius Loyola.'

'Yes, I *do* remember that. How, sir, you could compare that miserable gangster at present terrorizing Europe with the founder of the Society of Jesus I completely fail, sir, to understand.'

René shook his head. 'You have got that wrong, sir. I was not suggesting that those two men personally resemble one another; what I said was that they had functioned much in the same way. Both were "military-minded", both organized para-military organizations, both were reactionaries, both stood, or stand, for the old order in Europe, one had the Reformation (potentially), the other the Communist Revolution, to cope with.'

From the housemaster came a muffled snarl, from Kerridge a deep-toned bay of gentlemanly protest.

'But, sir, do you consider it seemly to speak in the same breath of this foul blackguard, this guttersnipe who has seized power in Germany with . . . with *anybody*?'

'Upon what plane, sir, are we discussing this? Upon the plane of contemporary political passion, or as History sees these things: not *subjectively*, sir, but subspecie aeternitatis.'

'Subspecie aeternitatis fiddlesticks! How can you bring eternity in to supply a monster like that with admission to a place where he can meet saints and heroes upon equal terms? I am ashamed, sir, to be sitting at a table . . .'

'No, Grattan-Brock, do not allow yourself . . .'

'It is quite clear now,' said René coldly, 'upon what plane this discussion is to proceed: upon the plane, that is, of passion, not of reason.'

Helen's voice rose full of an unexpected sharpness and firmness. 'But what is all this about? Will you allow a mere woman to ask a few questions? I cannot quite see what my brother's offence is. He is a historian, not a political writer. You, Robert, and you too, sir, I gather, are exclusively politically minded. You are talking at cross-purposes.'

'Classification is one of the historians' tasks,' René said. 'My only offence was, in the course of classification, to put the Iron Chancellor No. II (whose military obsessions I detest as much as you do), to put Herr Hitler in his right pigeon-hole. He has often been compared with Martin Luther. Quite apart from whether one admires or detests these two figures, as

a historian, the comparison appears to me erroneous. The
soldier-saint seemed to me a far better choice. Oh, gentlemen,
please.' René half rose in his chair, holding up a hand. 'This
is not to say that the German Chancellor is a *saint*.'

Helen laughed. 'You two seem to be taking up a most
unreasonable attitude. This Führer (little beast though he is)
has a certain place in history, which may be defined and
measured. He has to be pigeon-holed, however much we
would wish he could be abolished. Just as he has to be shaved,
and measured for suits.'

'I am afraid, my dear lady . . .'

'Most unfortunate illustrations. I do wish, Helen, you would
not talk nonsense.' Kerridge bayed disgustedly his complaint.

'You can't just slap down anything you don't like,' René
told him.

'I hope Robert will digest that,' Helen laughed.

'We are devoting too much attention to one point,'
Kerridge began. 'There are plenty of *other* things in *The
Secret History of World War II*.' Kerridge looked at Grattan-
Brock. 'Are there not, Doctor?'

'I was thinking just now, sir,' Dr. Grattan-Brock was
addressing himself to René, 'where classification is in question,
that your *Secret History*, sir, can only be classified as a
political work. You are as much a politician, sir, as we are
politicians.'

René's urbanity unimpaired, he turned towards the sour
and quarrelsome pseudo-eighteenth-century personality at his
side, and observed, 'In finding myself classified, sir, as one of
you, I suppose I should feel flattered. I am afraid I am unable
to return the compliment and invite you over into my class.
You belong irrevocably, sir, to the subjective order: I might
add to those who, with shouts and brandished fists, throw any
argument down on to a lower plane, out of reach of Reason's
arbitrament.

'Order, order!' called Kerridge roughly. 'Are you describing
my guest as a brawler and a bully? If so, I must really ask
you . . .'

René rose. 'I will immediately comply. I will withdraw to
my room, You have asked me to sit at this table in order to

attack me: because I do not tamely submit, you ask me to leave it.' He looked the 'Wicked Giant' in the eye. 'It is extraordinary behaviour for a clergyman.' He moved round the table towards the door.

Kerridge sprang up, crying, 'Now look here, René. *This* is extraordinary behaviour if you like! Do please be sensible and come back and sit down.'

René, standing with his hand upon the handle of the door, answered quietly, 'If you will allow me to make a few remarks, without interruption, I will return to my seat.'

A sound similar to the rumbling of the stomach came from the housemaster: at the same time Kerridge, who had resumed his seat, declared, 'As many remarks as you like, my dear fellow. Why should anyone interrupt you? It is not every day that we have a famous author among us.'

René walked back to his place to the right of his sister, who gave his arm a quick squeeze as he sat down. Everyone looked at him with various expressions. 'As I have been accorded permission to deliver a short lecture . . .'

'No lectures at dinner-table, not that,' sang rubber-neck.

'Yes, I was going to say . . . !' came a Johnsonian rumble.

'All right then. It shall be table-talk, it doesn't make any difference, provided I have my two hundred words in silence.'

'Shoot!' His mouth bitterly twisted, all teeth showing, the clergyman sat back derisively.

'Herr Hitler's air-fleet will doubtless smash up large areas of our capital. Our air-force is so inferior in strength (for some reason) that that seems inevitable. Why a few brigades of British and French troops did not march into Germany, at the time of the Rhineland coup, why Hitler was not made prisoner, and the whole Nazi movement forcibly liquidated no one knows, at least I do not. Let me say about this by now very powerful and menacing politician, the Führer, that *my* indictment of him is mainly on the ground of his insane militarism, and belief in force. This boils down to terrorism. Many people express a more or less insincere horror of the fact that he is a dictator. There is however one man who is at least ten times as complete a dictator as he: and there is much dictatorial power elsewhere. Myself, I object absolutely

5*

to political terrorism and philosophies of force. And War as well as other forms of organized violence belongs, for me, to the Dark Ages. I am not violent myself, because I am a civilized man. So far, so good. Now what I find is that those who are most juicily ferocious in their denunciation of the German Leaders are themselves adherents, or part adherents, of a terroristic philosophy. This appears to me hypocritical. Hypocrisy is a thing for which I feel a great distaste.'

René stood up. 'Now, I will retire to my room.' He stepped back and, without hurrying, left the room.

As he was leaving, Kerridge laughed bitterly, saying, 'I am afraid that my brother-in-law has always been a man of violent gestures. The French blood, I suppose. Oh, I apologize, darling.'

'The man is a thug,' exploded the housemaster, whose glass had never stood empty, Kerridge had seen to that.

Helen now rose, exclaiming rather hotly, 'Now I shall go to my room, too,' and moved off quickly in the wake of her brother, her husband shouting, 'But, Helen darling; you simply cannot leave us like that, we have a guest. It is impossible for you to do this!'

He, in turn, moved towards the door, and so, in a few moments, there was no one in the room but the housemaster who, with a wheeze, grasped his wine-glass fiercely, and emptied it at a gulp.

CHAPTER IX

How Much Can we Afford to Jettison?

THE next morning just after eleven o'clock The Reverend Robert Kerridge was exhibiting proudly his fine dental christianity to a fair-sized congregation in Starbrook Church —about twenty-five or thirty women christians, appreciative of his well-toothed and Oxford accent. About the same time René and his sister sat in a taxi-cab, chatting about Kerridge, on their way to Rugby station.

Almost as soon as the cab had started, Helen had asked her brother's forgiveness for the disgusting scene of the night before. 'It was perfectly awful, I have never seen or imagined anything so vile. And I just cannot understand it. I do hope, René, that you will try and think of us without thinking of *that*. It was utterly unlike Robert; I believe that he was temporarily out of his senses. He was abjectly apologetic this morning.'

René stopped her with a most hearty laugh. 'No apology whatever is required of you—for you to apologize is absurd. I owe you my deepest gratitude for rescuing me from a dragon.'

'A dragon? I believe you are capable of dealing with any dragon.' And she glanced sideways in a complimentary way at the Preux.

René shook his head. 'I am afraid not. There was a moment when I first caught sight of it, that I had that St. George-like feeling. But no—now I know better.'

'What is all this, brother, about mythological monsters?'

'Well, a dragon has made its appearance in this century. It is not a reptilian animal about fifty yards long which spits fire. It is a far bigger animal than that, and a far more subtle one. It is, if you like, a mental animal: one may identify it, almost see its fiery being in the minds of men. I have seen it, I have felt it. For a long time now I have known of its existence.

I know why it is here, I am afraid of it. I recommend you
very earnestly not to interfere with it, pretend you do not
see it, and if you do so, you have nothing to fear from it. Side-
step if you can its tumults, its earthquakes, its thunderbolts.'
'Oh dear me. This is terrifying. Do explain!'
'There would be no point whatever in my doing that. We
are little, powerless, shortlived creatures. What I am speaking
about is supernatural, of vast powers, and ageless. We cannot
possibly know why, at certain periods, these monstrous things
appear among us and then disappear again. Only, it is the
best and only advice. Mind your own business.' He looked
sharply round at her. 'But stop. For you there is an alternative: you can *ride* this monster. You have one of its scales quite
handy. Why not become *it?*'
'I become more and more afraid.'
'That,' he said, 'is an excellent thing to be. I used often to
marvel at the expression godfearing. What a barbarous thing,
I thought, to suppose that God should wish to be feared. I
have altered my mind. In order to live, we must do a great
deal of salutary fearing.'
Helen laughed and put her arm through René's. 'All the
same, you seemed to be standing up for yourself last night a
little bit.'
'I do not often find myself in bad company, because I am
careful to avoid it. But if attacked, I answer; quite mildly of
course.'
'I forgive you for that insult,' Helen laughed. 'We
deserve it.'
'I still get a little cross sometimes: to have everyone thinking in exactly the same way about everything, is, humanly
speaking, a nightmare. People attempting to make everybody do this I find nightmarish, too. Yet an orthodoxy is
certainly hardening all around us. There is a good illustration of this in the fine arts, the anti-academy rebels are automatically raising up a new academy. Upon your dining-room
walls there is that colour-reproduction of a painting by Nash.
It is a chilly and rigid affair, is it not? Those things do entertain me, the best of them: but I realize that they are a new
academicism in the making. Everyone is a zealot today, they

cannot paint a water-colour without doing so as if it were a religious rite. I read some of their writings. *You must* abstract. It is categorical, it is as if it were a branch of revolutionary politics. Oh, I do not like that *must* of theirs, I hate these twentieth-century *Absolutes!*'

'So do I, René. But it seems as if we have to live among Absolutes. Why do you not invent an Absolute yourself?'

'My Absolute is Moderation.'

'That,' she said, 'is an inherited Absolute. The French always pretend, at least, that moderation is their mellow goddess.'

'Yes, that Absolute of mine may be a legacy, as you say. With a dual national inheritance it is difficult sometimes to keep track.'

'Ah, these mixed marriages,' Helen sighed rhetorically. 'I sometimes think mother was a goose to go abroad for a husband.'

'I could not agree more,' he smiled. And they made merry for a moment over the possibilities of an all-gallic parentage. 'Perhaps,' René roared, 'we should have been on the Côte d'Azur at this moment. . . .'

'Eating *bouillabaisse*,' she laughed.

'Even so. *Endimanchés*, and in a restaurant, *une belle terrasse*, the masts of the port beneath our eyes.' He rolled about joyously upon the seat of the cab.

After this they talked a little about the family:

'What a united family we are,' he began. 'In France, and in Germany too, families cultivate that unity. It is not only a hangover from the Catholic World, it has to do with other things also. In a nation firmly organized, at least half-way down, into family-groups that really stick, there can be no *étatisme*. The family is the great enemy of the State conceived as one huge family. All that passionate affection developed within the limit of the family circle, is a thing which violently resists dissolution. And it cannot be expanded very greatly. Thin out that love until it fills the entire State and it has evaporated. Consequently, the whole character of the Society has to be changed (quite apart from the destruction of the Family) in order to establish *étatisme*. Since no one loves the

State, when there is *only* the State, there is very little of that warmth and sympathy which the human animal needs.'

Helen agreed, but observed that the Germans loved the State: a horrible kind of love, but still the State *was* loved by somebody.

'When members of a family are very united,' René went on, 'they are apt to have no sympathy to spare for anybody else. I, for instance, have been so devoted to Mother, and you know how I have loved you, Helen—not to mention dear Mary and Janet as well—that I have not had any real friendships, and have felt far too little sympathy for people to whom some fraction of love at least was due.'

'I can carry you out in that,' she told him. 'When I first knew Robert, for instance, I could not stir up any liking for him, try as I would, and even when we were first married, my sensations were so tepid . . .'

A perfect roar of amusement burst from René. 'Oh, Helen, how right your instincts were. I cannot understand how you can ever have mustered a farthing's worth of sympathy for him. How can one *love* a piece of india-rubber.'

So they had talked as they drove through the Sunday shut-down of a provincial English town. They had made the journey in a shorter time than expected, and when they reached the train, which was standing in the station, there was twenty minutes to wait.

The moment they entered the train and made their way along the corridor to a first-class compartment, René was overcome by an extraordinary depression, which his sister could not fail to detect. For a moment they sat in silence, and then Helen began to talk about his book. 'I must read your *Secret History* again. I shall understand it so much better now, after our talks. I shall plug you, to the disgust of my immediate circle.'

To speak in this way of his book would be the best way to cheer him up: such had been Helen's idea. But it had no such effect.

'It will sound absurd to you, it cannot do otherwise, all these warnings. But you really do not have to go on with your championship. Please put away my book, in an honoured position on your shelf, with a number of other books you have read and enjoyed. That is quite honour enough for me. But treat it as we do all those in such a class: leave it where it is. Do not laugh at me, take my advice.'

'I shall do nothing of the kind.'

He shrugged his shoulders, and remained silent. Like one of those masterpieces of impressionistic modelling, chiaroscuro suggested in sculptured heads, René's face appeared to her disintegrated, as if translated into a clay-coloured object of gouged and slapped-on bits. In the poorly lighted compartment, he sat, his head sagging sideways. His grief had made him into a 'Burgher of Calais' rather than a bearded apostle embedded in the gothic stone at Chartres.

However, in spite of so much discouragement, she persisted. 'I have always been so fond of you—I mean *personally* of course—that it has been an obstacle, isn't it odd, to my reading you. As if strangers alone were interesting! But I was very impressed by what you told me.'

He put his arm around her waist, and tears came into his eyes. 'We must part, Sister. I am afraid we shall not meet again. Everything is over with me, you know, I feel.' He put his head down to her shoulder, and she could feel him shake.

Helen was deeply astonished at what was occurring, for she would have said that it would be quite impossible for this masterful brother of hers so to shrivel up and cry like a child.

'René,'—she spoke to him softly—'why are you like this?'

René looked up, intelligence appearing to return. 'Sadness, you know, at parting,' he said drily. 'At leaving everything, at going away into a wilderness among so very solid a mass of strangers. And never to come back. Never to come back.'

'René!'

'The numbers, the mass of strangers, does not matter, they might as well be stones. Indeed, the thicker the mass of stony strangers the deeper the wilderness. Then the fact that Canada is four-fifths an authentic wilderness does not matter. It would be the same emptiness anywhere. The same ghastly void, next door to nothingness.' He lifted up his head, but did not look at her. 'You must understand what has happened to me! It is destiny. Through looking too hard at the material I was working on, I saw the maggots in it, I saw the rottenness, the fatal flaws; had to stop earning my living in that way. There is a very small chance that I can make a living there rather than here. I have no particular reason to go to Canada. I must go somewhere out of sight of what is going to happen because I know so well the reasons which make it impossible for it not to occur. How disgusting, how maddening, and how foully comic all the reality of death and destruction will be; I just cannot stick around here and watch that going on. Canada is as good, or as bad a place as any other. The problem is, to get out of the world I have always known, which is as good as to say out of the world. So Canada is to be my grave. I wish I had chosen for myself a warmer place —or that fate had. My former colleague, who has been in Winnipeg for some years, implores me not to go to the Dominion unless they offer me a professorship. He says the chances of anything of that kind are slight. He tells me that Canadians feel very strongly about vacancies in Colleges being filled by Englishmen, against whom there is a great deal of feeling. On the other hand, it would not amuse me, like some Russian emigré, to eke out an existence as a shoe-black. When my small capital is exhausted I shall make a painless exit from an existence only bearable under certain well-recognized conditions. There is no alternative existence *ici-bas* when you have got where I did; if you leave hold you shoot down like a lump of lead. You have just witnessed, I mean last night, how far down I have already got. Twelve months ago I could not have been treated like that. The kicking around has begun. It began with our rat-like relative, Victor: it continues with the Vicar of Starbrook, who gets in a local housemaster to have a bit of fun.'

Helen had been listening with lowered head, in wretched silence. At the concluding words, she recoiled a little, the reference to the doings of the Vicar of Starbrook stinging her unendurably for a moment. Then she leant towards René and said how all that he had told her had amazed her. 'I had not the remotest idea that you felt like that about your position.'

René looked up half-smiling. 'How did you think I felt

then? Of course you could not know. Now listen. I do not talk about this. I have spoken to *nobody* about it. No one has any idea what my reactions are, nor is there any reason why they should. I have just told you, I cannot tell why, except that I have always been so near to you. I do not want you to let anyone else know.'

'They shall not.' Her voice was low and trembling.

'Meanwhile, of course, I go about exactly the same as before. I believe I am right in saying that I show no signs of any emotional disturbance. What is more, to be quite accurate, I *feel* no emotion, except when I deliberately turn my mind that way.'

'I am so glad,' Helen told him, looking up. 'You certainly show nothing, and I am glad you have that ability to insulate.'

'No, I have not been sad. Saying good-bye to you is the saddest thing that has happened to me yet, or that ever will. You have always been what I love best in the world. I hate this parting . . . I hate this parting!' He clung to her with tears in his eyes.

Two or three minutes earlier the guard had called 'All passengers' friends out of the train.' And now, a moment before, the whistle had sounded and he felt the train beginning to move.

'You can't get out now,' he told her. 'You can catch the next train back to Rugby.' But the last words she did not hear, she had sprung up and was now rushing down the corridor. René was horrified, for the train seemed to be moving quicker. As he ran after her, people came out of a carriage and blocked the corridor. She was out of sight, and he entered a carriage and sprang to an open window, where he was just in time to see her jump from the moving train and fall on the platform.

The human body is not a square object like a trunk, and when it falls it tends to roll. In her case it rolled towards the train. But a porter seized her shoulders and stopped the roll. In doing this, he apparently lost his balance and went down backwards with his legs in the air. In the same instant Helen, now no longer a rolling body, but in command of her limbs once more, sprang to her feet, and René momentarily had the impression that it was she who was knocking over the railway porter. She moved out away from the train and placed her hands trumpet-wise in front of her mouth. He heard in his ear as if it had been the thin whisper in a shell, the two syllables of his name, 'René—René—René!' He frantically waved his hand.

Only when the station platform was out of sight, he drew his head in, and returned to his own compartment. Quietly he took his place in the window seat facing the engine. This parting had been so unexpectedly painful. He had had no anticipation of anything unusual, owing to his careful insulation from the centre of emotional awareness. As he had explained to his sister, he was able to fasten himself down to the unemotional daily routine: but suddenly, without any warning, floodgates of realization would fly open. The insulation would break down. In order not to be at the mercy of his emotions, he had been obliged to effect a division of his personality into two parts: he had created a kind of artificial 'unconscious' of his own, and thus locked away all acuity of realization. If a doctor had told him he had only three months to live, all the significance for him of this announcement would be hurried away and put under lock and key. He of course could not guarantee that something would not release it at any moment, but he had for so long mastered his reactions that it would be unlikely to burst out until permitted to do so. His callous self was so well insulated from the compartment of the imagination that he was able to pass as a somewhat unemotional man. On the other hand, he *did*, as in the present case, experience a certain number of violent surprises.

So he sat almost rigid in his corner; for the 'floodgates' in question had not yet shut-to. On the other hand, in the past forty-eight hours his nervous system had undergone quite sufficient strain, and he wished to return to the callous norm as quickly as possible. But this could not be instantaneous —his mental machinery was not so stream-lined as all that: so for a short while the glare of awareness was still present.

A number of things came under review, and not of the most agreeable. But he sometimes succeeded in exercising the right of selection. He now threw back the beam of his acutely awakened awareness upon the statement he had recently made to his sister. For he knew from experience that this heightened perceptivity was capable of distorting, and even of transforming, facts. Was he, in his parting with Helen, speaking in a moment of natural depression consequent upon the dinner-scene of the night before? Making every allowance for temporary depression, he could not see how any *real* account of his present circumstances could be more optimistic.

He might pull down over the reality a fire curtain, which was what his insulation system amounted to; he might gamble upon the *one chance in a million*, the chance that his fortunes would radically mend, and he find himself, in, from the worldly standpoint, as favourable a position as before. It was as open to the rag-picker to nurse a golden dream as it was for him to soothe himself with reflections upon the miracles of Chance. Certainly by eating his words he might teach in some comic little college in a neck of the woods. That appeared to be the summit of future possibilities. So the searchlight showed quite as empty a scene as, to his surprise, he had depicted in his farewell to Helen.

Now he had visited all the members of his family in turn; he had got a flea in his ear in every case except one, the exception being Percy. It is true that these visits had taken a different form in each case: he had done scarcely more than *show* himself to Janet and the egregious Victor—what more could he do, and, of course, why should he do that? To his mother and Mary he had made a very superficial statement: but again, what more could he do? With Helen, alone, had he attempted a real explanation (an explanation which would have been entirely wasted upon his mother and Mary). To Percy, there had been no need to say anything; it would, indeed, have been quite impossible to make him understand a single syllable. Percy *knew* René was a rebel and a martyr, that was what Percy knew and no one could have altered

that. And so these visits had been futile, as far as elucidations
went; no one was any wiser as a result of his visit than they
had been beforehand, excepting only Helen.

He had, in the course of his summing up, a moment of
gaiety in considering what reaction the Dragon of his recent
cab-talk would have had upon Percy. But, of course, Mary
and her husband would have decided that as a result of over-
work, his reason had been affected. What these duty-calls
had done was to destroy a school-boy picture of a circle of
loving-hearts. That junk, at least, had been got rid of, for
ever.

But he thought that Mothers must receive a brief analytical
scrutiny; something more had to be hacked away from the
old domestic monument. Now, one's old bitch of a mother
was a figure one approached with reverence, because she had
given birth to one. A fact of such importance that one *must*
reverence her for that; though indeed she had only loaned
her belly for the pre-natal drama. She is always supposed
to be awfully fond of Me because of her having permitted all
this to go on in the spare-room she's got down there, for Little
Strangers. Often one hears of 'her bowels yearning' for the
one-time occupant of the spare-room. The fact of course is
that, except for the extent to which she may be influenced
by the stream of waffle she had to consume on the subject of
her 'love', she must feel what most landladies do about their
lodgers. There is no evidence at all that a woman has any of
these beautiful sensations, invented for her by man. Once the
nursing-job imposed upon her by nature is over, and the 'little
toddler' has grown to be a noisy and bumptious schoolboy
as big as herself, and still worse, a little later, the obviously
extremely limited but absurdly self-important young man,
she must realize (if she has not realized it before) that she has
simply been made a convenience of by Nature; and, in any
case, that it has been a great deal of fuss and trouble about
nothing. (If instead of a schoolboy it is a big fat schoolgirl,
peering at herself in the mirror all the time, it is hardly
necessary, in that case, to stress what her *real* sensations must
be.) Women of the working class go on turning out 'Little
Strangers', because of the importance it gives them among

the neighbours, and as an insurance in old age. If by nature bossy, it gives the woman a little community to bully, scold, make favourites of: and eventually this little community will work for you—or that is the idea.

The dogmas of Western European religions and much romance have been built up around the figure of the Mother. Any number of tough old girls are quite ready to regard this as their 'big part'—just as formerly they would play the 'little angel' to some masculine moron, who had been taught to expect 'love' from that quarter—meaning a sort of combination of worship and 'bowel-yearning.' Many women, quite naturally, develop a superiority-complex listening to so much man-waffle.

Having arrived at this point, he was able to focus his eye upon the old french lady, very comfortably installed, in a St. John's Wood mansion-flat, with whom he played a tiresome little farce every time he visited her. No wonder *elle rigolait*, and was full of well-matured mirth. To see him arrive, walk quickly across the room, his face screwed into a certain expression, reserved for old ladies who at one time have changed one's diapers (and earlier of course have given one house room in their intestines) all that must fill so intelligent an old woman with amused contempt.—When she had called him a *fool*—which had so astonished him at the time—it was something she had often thought, no doubt, but had not, until that moment of exasperation, given utterance to.

To his Testament of Mothers he added a Codicil.—There were, of course, women in the Mother-part who are *Great Lovers*. But he could see nothing agreeable in such forms of incest, where one of the parties is anything up to fifty years older than the other.

René promised himself to analyse properly, when in his callous norm once more, the nature of family love; to analyse carefully the cement which caused the average christian family to adhere. He had done, in the past, a good deal of serious field-work on the Family. In England, he had concluded, there was little more than animal attraction left: and when we get down to the animal level we only have to think of the pigeons on our window-sill. There would be no maternal recognition

for a young pigeon who flew down upon our window-sill and
reminded the old hen-bird, sunning herself there, that he was
a one-time egg of hers. He would be roughly repulsed; and
in any case, recognition on the part of the ex-chick would be
just as impossible, and unless men would somehow communicate the idea to the younger pigeon, even if he recognized
the hen-bird as his parent, it could never occur to him that
she owed him any interest or assistance.

With the very slightest christian hangover, the mid-
twentieth-century English family still retained a traditional
cement, which guaranteed it a thin cohesion. For a middleclass family desirous of some show of blood-attachments, the
best solution would be to become a Mutual Admiration Society.
In his own case, his mother had provided the basic ingredients
of solidarity owing to her French Catholic origin. For the rest,
the Mutual Admiration Society was the best way of describing
what had existed there. When tested, as had recently been
done by him, it had proved sadly inadequate. So his family
was a junk he had no further use for. His sister Helen was
another matter. For her he had an attachment produced by
something far stronger than the usual old family cement.
But (he remembered something) he must salvage Percy from
this universal demolition of old ties.

His own personality came up for consideration, as it always
did on such occasions. This time he selected for special notice
the fact that his natural gaiety was an exasperating thing
to have been endowed with in view of the extreme severity
imposed on him by his destiny. He had been born into a time
supremely unfavourable for the enjoyment of *la gaya scienza*.
He then smiled his first smile for half an hour; for Rotter's
article came back to him with its dogmatic 'René Harding is
a Jansenist': and he reflected that one adherent at least of
Port Royal was not devoid of wit. But as soon as he had
riveted his eyes upon the obvious incompatibility of the age
and of his personality, he realized it was not quite so important
as he had supposed. Its main disadvantage was that people
found it difficult to associate in their minds tragedy and gaiety.
The motives for his resignation were, however, of the grimmest
semi-ethical order. Looked at from that angle, he was almost

a dour enough man to be typical of his time. Something in him was as severe and mirthless as those uncivilized forces with which he had contended. But something apprised him that his spell of unlicensed awareness was nearly ended. He was exceedingly tired and, after looking at his watch, he arranged himself in the corner and almost at once fell asleep.

CHAPTER X

The Passenger who Wore the Ribbon of the Legion of Honour

'THIS is the last boat out of Europe,' the young Swiss told him, 'the last boat.'

It was possible that no more unescorted passenger ships would leave this French port. Like people making a frenzied exit from a building which was on fire, the continental crowds pouring from train after train all had the automatism of a great emergency. Europe on fire again for the second time in a generation. On principle, René approved of any exodus, at such a moment. But he would have liked to see the entire coast of France humming with people in flight, thousands putting out to sea in rowing-boats, and this port packed with vessels flying panic flags, and all their sirens shrieking. This was too detached a young Swiss fugitive.

There were no women doing what the occasion demanded, no tearing of the hair, as the Muse of History ordains. In disgust he pushed his way through this inexpressive crowd, but one woman of the old historic kind scratched him and brought blood.

Hester was lying down in their stateroom. The plea was a headache, but he knew that she was frightened at going away from family and friends, upon a journey which René had never pretended could have a happy ending, nor that her absence could be anything but long. As he entered she was crying hysterically.

'Come, my darling. What is baby girl crying about?' He put his hand upon her heaving back. His voice had been so unusually kind that Hester clutched his hand gratefully. 'I am sorry,' she choked, 'just baby feelings as you say.'

'Baby feelings, I know them, I had an awful baby feeling myself just now.'

Hester gave a big hoarse sob. 'Mummie!' she gurgled. 'It

isn't all mummie, it's everything and everybody. I am going
away in this boat from everything I have ever known and
from all those I have ever cared for. No wonder that one
gets baby feelings,' she sobbed. 'I am sorry, darling, I know
what you're thinking, but I just can't help it. All this is too
much for me.'

René was much affected. The realization of what this would
be for poor Hester struck him now for the first time. He always
forgot that Hester was a human being, because she was so
terribly much the Woman. And then her world must appear
to him such a petty world, that losing it could hardly mean
very much. Indeed, it is rather what the grown-up traditionally
thinks about the child; it cries its eyes out and it is impossible
for the mature to understand that its heart is breaking, if for
no other reason because it breaks so many thousands of times.

But René looked grave and was really sorry, as much as
it was possible for him to be. It was the beginning of a new
way of thinking about Hester, although, at that time, it did
not continue for very long.

As he got down on the bed beside her, he muttered, 'Poor
old Ess!' tenderly for him, and Hester pushed aside her grief
and turned towards him her big—her too big—eyes, clouded
with tears. But then, alas, the usual thing occurred: alas,
because grief is a more serious thing than pleasure, and it had
been too unceremoniously pushed aside. The effect of that,
too, upon René was devastating, mocking, as it did, his
momentary glimpse of a human reality.

However, not long afterwards, thoroughly purged of her
mother, and all the endearing scenes of the life she was
leaving, Hester's mind turned to the function that awaited
them in an hour or so. She passed nimbly over René and
began opening up their cabin luggage, and picking out what
she would require. She was watched morosely by René, who
lay, a little somnolent upon the bed. She darted hither and
thither, as if pretending, as it seemed to him, to find something: and assuming a series of display poses, as though she
had been modelling for *Esquire's* most risqué draughtsman.
He wondered if she worked out these poses when he was not
there. What a way of spending one's life. She was the most

frightful reflection of himself, the image of his lubricity. Worse than pinning up *Esquire* in his room, he maintained a live *Esquire* colour-block—he had always been teasing himself after this fashion. Oh well, what more, what better, had he to do now, except that! Hester's obscene person must henceforth be his Muse, in succession to History. He was going to Canada in order to fornicate with Hester. What else!

When these reflections grew unendurable, and an outburst against Hester threatened, he got slowly up and dressed. He went out, saying that he must fix with the purser about their table for dinner. Going up in the lift to the main promenade, he found that they were out at sea. A powerful wind slapped him in the face, the ocean's reaction at the appearance of the flushed amorist. The ocean had nothing to offer him like the scented femininity in his stateroom down below. But what had the ocean got if it set itself up against Venusberg? He thought of all its wonders which had captivated men. Its trump card, perhaps, was that delicious solitude, of which the poet speaks. And, what in marine terms, he wondered, would be the equivalent of 'a green thought in a green shade'? That would resolve itself, it seemed, into a battle between blue and green. Ah, the ocean could produce something far more secret than a garden.

He walked quickly sternwards until he came to a spot where he was quite alone. He looked down at the romantic water. A beautiful mercurial substance seemed to be moving in one direction, they towards the other horizon. Moon and ocean were overwhelming and commonplace. Is it worth while to go on looking at this changing but monotonous element?

With business-like grimness the railway porter had said, 'They may be here at any moment.' This had been at Waterloo. But there had been no announcement that war had been declared; and this was the *Empress of Labrador*, and no one allowed the doings of landsmen to intrude upon the immemorial trinity of man, moon, and ocean.

Above the coast of France search-lights made the clouds look sinisterly bright, and a storm was advancing from perhaps Boulogne, announced by the appearance and disappearance of its flashes. The dully glowing clouds and moving beams made the scene look enigmatically dramatic, but there could be no battles in progress just yet. Hitler would dash into France, it was to be presumed. The frantic fool, the Brummagem Bismarck. But there was not time for the fastest vehicle to have rushed into France, had there been nothing to stop them. What René was witnessing, he imagined, was the preliminary lighting up of the clouds over France. Yet it already, from afar, looked like a battle.

They were five miles, perhaps, out of the French port. All these people, packed tightly into the *Empress*, were rapidly receding from the terror. In London, at the last moment, there had been a shuffling of berths, and René and Hester had been offered a stateroom on the *Athenia*, or on the *Duchess of York*. Since the *Duchess* was sailing on a Friday, René declined that suggestion of the shipping office, and declined the *Athenia* because it was not a Canadian ship. Had it not been for that, they would have crossed in the *Athenia*. Afterwards Hester regarded this as a typical action of her Providence. 'Kismet,' she was heard to remark. For otherwise, of course, a torpedo might have burst into the Dining Saloon as they were discussing the Menu with a Steward—or is it Waiter? At present, later events made evident, the *Athenia* was somewhere on its way not far from them. \

In the sequel the *Empress* may have passed over the same *Unterseeboot*, but the *Empress of Labrador* was not the name written upon the torpedo.

Meanwhile, all its lights showing, the grand hotel was on the swim again across the dark rolling abyss. Apprehension must be unknown. The multi-ribboned Master up in his little clangorous house aloft, ringing his bells and tilting his braided cap, never thought of the liquid element through which the *Empress* was passing. The Master had long ago stopped thinking of his ship as seen by the fishes. To ring a thousand bells, seaworthy and jauntily naval at the Captain's table, was all his life. Until the broadcast informing him of war had ordered him out of the spot-light, his imagination did not reach below the plimsoll line. René was as callous as the Captain; he believed as profoundly as did that officer in the magic character of the word *war*: though when he looked down at the dark and heaving mass, he agreed that the word ought not to be uttered until they were in the New World.

They entered the restaurant, *en grand tenu*. Hester's eyes were surely the cynosure of all other eyes. René saw a young woman nudging her mother. 'Listen, *ma poule*,' he hissed, 'if you don't damp down those "bedroom Eyes" they will turn us out.' As Hester supposed this was merely a comic and roundabout way of referring to her ravishing attractiveness, she squeezed his arm, and turned her exhibitionist eyes upon him, in a flood of such intimacy that he actually blushed.

They approached the table at which two Americans were sitting, a man and wife apparently, who smiled and bowed slightly as they sat down. René had in his buttonhole the ribbon of the Legion of Honour—about which it is always said that not to have it is more honourable than to have it. But the Americans did not feel that way about it. The man glanced at the name card at the place next to his, and at once muttered something to his wife. Hester believed that what he said referred to the beautiful young woman approaching (herself, in other words) in that exquisite black crepe and brooch of rubies.

The American spoke first. 'It is a great honour to be sitting at the same table with you, sir. Professor René Harding, I believe.'

René bowed a little stiffly. Hester slewed her head around and socially lit up her eyes for a moment. The American spoke again. 'I may as well say, sir, that my name is Dr. Lincoln Abbott. I am the President of the University of Rome, Arkansas. Ours is not a great College like Chicago or Cornell. But it has beaten both at football!' He laughed, but René knew what this meant.

'What does that cost you?' he asked him with a smile.

'Far more than I should like to say,' Dr. Abbott replied. 'We are committed to that.'

'A majority of young men are probably better employed at football than at having knowledge squeezed into their skulls.'

René politely observed, though he exhibited no signs of a desire for much talk. The President however was of a different mind, and after a decent interval of a few silent spoonfuls of a 'Bisque d'Homard' he started again. 'We, all over America, read your terrifying book *The Secret History of World War II* with the greatest interest. It is not often, if I may say so, that such a book comes out of England.'

René smiled with polite appreciation, looking at his plate. But he said nothing.

'I do not have to ask you, Professor, what you think of World War Two, which may be with us in a few days!'

'No,'—René shook his head—'you do not have to ask me that, Doctor.'

He knew that these academic titles were very dear to Americans, and that he would be addressed as 'Professor' for the rest of the voyage, though he had described himself as Mr. René Harding for the Passengers' Register. By this time Hester and the President's wife were discussing standard female topics. What the Professor thought of the Doctor may be summarized as follows. First, the Englishman's outlook was conditioned by an extraordinary Social artifice. All Englishmen of René's age, educated at a public school and at Oxford or Cambridge, became automatically that mysterious thing a 'gentleman'. This is an aristocratic invention (though not of course invented by aristocrats). In its way it is a patent of nobility conferred upon all men with a professional status. It is a quite illogical honorary rank, but life in England until the end of the thirties was profoundly affected by the spell cast by the two words Lady and Gentleman. It created a mystical and impenetrable frontier (to be on the wrong side of this was an irretrievable disaster).

The above may appear superfluous: but the social structure it seemed necessary to describe is already an archaism.

To turn, now, to Dr. Lincoln Abbott. The essential thing about him was (as registered by René's automatic self) that he not only belonged to another nation, but to another class. Since the Doctor's intellectual limitations were unmistakable, this table companion was not greatly to René's taste. The latter was anything but an intellectual snob, so one can pin

squarely on him a class-bar. Hester was guilty of such sensations, too: for 'ladies' had (and have) at least as strong a
class-bar as had 'gentlemen'—though neither may have had
(to keep it in the past tense) any more blue blood than a
fountain-pen—less, for the latter might at least protest that
its *ink* was blue. There were Americans and Americans; René
had met quite a few who had surprised him by not sending
into action the class-bar, though he did not of course put it
in this way.

Well there it was, they must consume their food in the
company of this man whose mediocrity was not mystically
gilded as would, at that date, have been the case in England.
On the other hand, a compensatory emotion gradually made
itself felt; one which, twelve months before, René could not
have experienced. He felt a kind of horrible attraction for this
man, a strange toleration: the shameful cause of this was
Dr. Abbott's immediate recognition of him as a famous author
—yes, and because the middle-west College President visibly
enjoyed sitting at table with a Legion of Honour. This was
terrifying evidence of the extent to which René's morale had
declined. With inevitable publicity he had turned his back
upon the world and so, *ipso facto*, forgone its esteem and its
honours—and of these he certainly would receive no more.
Yet here he was, at the outset of his retreat into the wilderness, wearing one of the most desirable Orders the world has
to give, in the restaurant of a transatlantic liner (why?), and
experiencing almost cordiality for somebody visibly susceptible
to that emblem of success. Thus it was that when Hester
remarked after they had left the restaurant, 'Ought we not
to get them to change our table?' René shrugged his shoulders
and answered that they might go farther and fare worse.

Dr. Abbott was not slow in communicating to another
academic notable (a luminary appreciably superior to himself)
the name and quality of the bearded gentleman with whom
he had been paired off in the restaurant. Dr. Milton Bleistift,
the academic notable in question, was a one generation
American: but his immigrant-parents had named their sons
Milton and Homer, and both were as American as Coca-Cola.
Dr. Milton said he hoped they would be able to persuade René

to lecture at his university—for he was a president too. This was said with a flattersome German deference, which gave a little added depth to the pleasurable sensations resulting from Dr. Abbott's reactions at finding himself sharing his table with a Star. Even Hester noticed what a good humour her husband was in—she failed completely to identify the cause of his cheerfulness. Nor did she do so when he remarked, in an offhand way, that it was, after all, a happy thought of Mary's to pay the difference between the First and the Tourist Class. The next afternoon he came into their stateroom exclaiming, 'This bloody ship is full of "Doctors". I have just met another. That makes five.'

Hester made a grimace significant of her feelings about any more Doctors. 'Yes I know,' he agreed. 'But I have no wish to talk to the English. You understand, of course, why.'

'Well, while you have been collecting American "Doctors", I have collected an Irish countess, Lady Malone. She is of course an alcoholic, and I am not at all sure that she is not a lesbian. I am going to tea with her this afternoon—she has a most spectacular suite.'

'Goodbye.' René scratched her head, which he only did when in an uncommonly good temper. 'Does Sappho know about me?'

'I am afraid so. She is an intellectual. She claims to have read *both* your books.'

'She must be a phoney countess. Watch out she does not pick your pocket, while making a lesbian assault.' René looked at his watch. 'I must go, Ess. My fifth doctor is awaiting me in the tourist class.'

This youngest of the Doctors was an instructor at Yale. His name was Oscar Gilman. They sat in the Tourist café (as it really was) and their preliminary talk lasted about one hour. The Englishman's class-bar had no application in the case of Oscar, who, in the first place, had no American accent. He simply *had not* an English accent, which was a de-parochialization, both ways. His subject was English literature; known to René only as an adjunct to History. He felt provisional respect for this colourless de-parochialized instrument for studying the tongue they both spoke. The fact that one was maturely bearded and in his late forties, the other scarcely more than thirty, was no obstacle to communion, or to such communion as they might have. As they talked, their thinking proceeded much as follows.—Oscar liked this bloke with the tawny beard (when thinking of an Englishman he substituted 'bloke' for 'guy'—showing his learning in foreign slangs). Elizabethan Englishmen (Chapman) must have looked like that.—René liked Oscar as one likes a pine bath salt. How many vaguely Scandinavian-looking young men there are in the United States, with the clean and puritanic appearance the Norse blood takes with it, and rather colourless, or coldly coloured clothes. This neutral breed is classless, though they give a sense of being of a well-brushed *milieu*.—Why, Oscar asked himself, was this bloke talking to him? Could it be love? Oh dear, that prickly *moose*-tache—Oscar of course knew everything, like all young Americans. No doubt he possessed a thousand devices for the concealment of ignorance. Those cold, level, well-guarded young eyes; he would bluff his way out of any difficulty. An empty clean look like a well-washed lavatory, socially very useful, probably recommended him to his superiors.—Oscar approved the jutting and ironic mouth. His eyes, he saw, were idly investigatory. Okay, if he likes to pick around in this trash-bin.—Whether this bright, clean mind was not too neutral.—I am being high-hatted, but that always happens with a limey.—What did this tight-lipped young man think about war? Probably he was one of those fatalistic, uninterested-but-dutiful, young Norse-looking Yankees, rather fond of doing nothing-in-particular until a bullet bangs them down, that sort of 'excellent military material', too brightly uninterested to stop a war coming its way. No use talking to him about that.—'He don't seem,' thought Oscar, 'to know why he's sitting here, I think he's making up his mind.'

What *René* showed an interest in discussing was Yale, what Oscar preferred to talk about was Renaissance in England, the influence of Machiavelli and Hobbes, and such things. When they got up, the clinically-clean young neutral moved back with him into the First Class, where he had business, and they parted with polite warmth.

René's temperature had fallen considerably. This first conversation in limbo, where the same language had been spoken,
where (at one point) the same interests had been invoked, but
no contact had been made, was ominous. America had reached
a very different level of consciousness, but it was completely
cut off from life, and a kind of cold smartness presided at the
new elevation. He felt that Oscar was a phantom: and that he
himself was becoming one too. He was approaching a land
of sterilized thinking, and reflections of another life. The
reality must all be on the cigar-store and pool-room level, or
the world the negroes live in. He thought he would read something relaxing. In his hand-luggage he had brought nothing
classifiable as work. Among the few books he had packed was
George Eliot's *Middlemarch*, which he had been told by Rotter
was a good book. He had read few of the English classics,
and thought he would turn to them now, for a little. With
the first volume under his arm, he selected a corner of the
ship where he felt he would probably be undisturbed. Disagreeable sensations ensued almost from the first page. He
began reading about the two young ladies, of about twenty
years old. Now one was an 'ordinary' girl; one so alarmingly
unordinary as to cause her sister to be frightened of her.
Both the young ladies are beautiful, but the high-minded
one slightly more so. A grey-headed, hollow-eyed clergyman makes his appearance (he comes to dinner with the
uncle of the two girls). A good-looking young squire arrives
at the same time. The painfully priggish young lady is quite
rude to the young squire, for being so normal, but finds the
unattractive cadaverous clergyman of fifty very much to her
taste, and he is engaged upon a work of great learning: how
appropriate; she will assist him in this lofty labour. In a few
months they are married. Lest the reader should be depressed
at the thought of what was in store for this poor young lady
in the arms of this elderly clergyman, something is provided
by the considerate author. When the reader is first taken to
the Rectory, a young man is discovered seated in the garden,
sketching it in water-colours. He is a very different kettle of
fish from his cadaverous uncle or cousin, the Rector. The
reader knows, something tells him, that *in the end* the leading

6

lady will enjoy the embraces of this personable young man.
He heaves a sigh of relief. Just to show that the young fellow
is a sport, when he sits down again to resume his sketching,
he throws his head back (his curls tumbling about as he does
so) and emits a short laugh. It is obvious that this young
man has the same feelings about the Rector's marriage as the
reader has. But after that the reader is taken down to a lower
social level. He is introduced to a stock figure, described as
a 'gentleman-farmer', who is inferior, but full of a disagreeable senile vitality. Prospective heirs are there, and one of
them he gleefully unmasks.

At this point René would go no further. This sodden satire,
this lifeless realism, provoked him into saying, 'Why am I
reading this dull nonsense? It is just like Rotter to have recommended a book of this sort.' He continued to ruminate. 'The
historic illusion, the scenes depicted, and the hand depicting
them, could be preserved in some suitable archive; but should
not be handed down as a living document. It is a part of
history'—with this he dismissed it.

He went out on to the deck and swinging his arm back
hurled the heavy book out to sea. After that he returned to
their stateroom, lay down and instantly fell asleep.

At dinner Dr. Lincoln Abbott remarked slyly, ' What
book was it, Professor, that I saw you throwing into the
sea?'

'That,' René told him, 'was a novel called *Middlemarch*.'

'You express your disapproval very forcibly, Professor,'
Dr. Abbott laughed. 'You should try one of our American
novelists, Professor. Have you ever read any books by Stein-
beck? No? Well I wonder if the *Grapes of Wrath* is in the ship's
library. Would you say it was, Mildie?'

He pronounced 'wrath' in so strange a manner that René
was at a loss to guess what he meant. Misinterpreting the
abstracted look upon the other's face, Dr. Abbott ground out
savagely, *Grapes of Wrarth*!'

René, however, yawned. 'No more novels this voyage,
Doctor!'

All of which convulsed Dr. Lincoln Abbott with amusement.

René gave him a sidelong look, half amusement, half alarm.

This side-long look of René's was interpreted by Dr. Abbott as a facetious rejoinder, the silent equivalent of a side-splitting wisecrack. It convulsed Dr. Abbott, who was always appreciative of mirthful sallies, with much physical exertion. But at this point, unfortunately, René was seized with a fit of coughing. This Dr. Abbott interpreted as bottled-up mirth leading to a coughing fit; and if he had been boisterous before, his contortions now, his gasps and splutters, were positively indecent. The noise they were making as a table was spectacular. This was a matter of great satisfaction to Dr. Lincoln Abbott. But René rose, and, with a muffled remark to his wife, moved out of the room, still coughing slightly. Hester accompanied him; as soon as they were outside René gasped indignantly. 'It is preposterous. The fellow is becoming matey. Something must be done about it. I must see the purser immediately and get him to find us room somewhere else.'

'I should not do that,' Hester said. 'We must be careful to avoid jokes, I think. I had better say that I have received a cable to say that poor Rosa is dying.'

The next day the radio announced the Declaration of War. At tea-time they were having tea in the lounge and the King's speech was broadcast. René took all this as a matter of course; and, indeed, the passengers in general appeared to be very little affected. This was natural enough, since most of them were on the ship so as not to be in Europe when this event occurred. With a frown Hester stared a little more than usual: whether this was authentic distress, or a desire to attract attention, it is difficult to say.

If this event had been taken as a matter of course there was another happening, not very much later, which was received very differently. The next morning people were seen standing in groups, speaking in whispers. A large liner had been sunk only a hundred miles away. The radio had been shut off upon the Declaration of War. And there had been no official communication. It remained, therefore, a rumour:

but it passed from mouth to mouth, and it seemed for some reason to possess authority.

It was not long after this that the Captain and two subordinate officers passed through the first class. He was severely uncommunicative: but hardly had this occurred, when the ship's loud-speaker enjoined all passengers to repair to their boat stations immediately, bringing their lifebelts with them.

Within a quarter of an hour passengers were lined up before their respective lifeboat stations. They were dismal little companies. Even the tennis-courts were crowded with hammocks to provide sleeping accommodation, and the ship was so full to overflowing that it was quite certain *all* passengers could not get into the boats. Passengers eyed one another nervously, speculating as to whether they could fight their way successfully to safety, or at all events to a place in a boat. René noticed a small, bilious-looking individual glancing at him angrily, if a little furtively. Obviously he was regarding this tall, bearded neighbour as an obstacle, if it came to scrambling into a boat. But most of the waiting passengers just looked depressed and impatient as they shuffled about in the drizzle. Their instructor, René thought, looked scared as he ordered them how to conduct themselves in case of an emergency, and explained the proper way to wear their life-belts. Some passengers, at this stage, affected a disagreeable jauntiness. There was one, the hysterical note in whose laughter caused the rest to turn a displeased eye on him. As to Hester, she was in the dumps again. She had her lifebelt over her coat and looked grotesquely dismal. René wore his lifebelt like a gentleman, that is to say as if he had been born in it. Looking down at his despondent wife, he reflected that he would have to administer some tonic again.

They were ordered to wear their lifebelts, or to carry them, everywhere. They must sleep in them, and come to meals in them. René grimaced expressively with his mouth at the announcement about meals. It was not difficult to foresee how excruciatingly funny it would appear to Dr. Lincoln Abbott to see the Professor eating a grapefruit in a lifebelt. He felt that that table *must* be changed, since fancy dress was the order of the day.

The ship's behaviour had attracted attention immediately after the Declaration of War. It had begun to tack, or to zig-zag. This was the time, also, when large pieces of canvas were lashed along all the promenade decks, screening the interior from the sea, to make it more sure that enemy submarines could see no lights within. Now, as night drew on, there was something else that the passengers noticed. It had grown distinctly colder. By the next morning, it was very cold indeed. And blowing a gale. They still zig-zagged, but were heading due north. Were they bound for Greenland, René wondered; and, unless they encountered an iceberg, would they remain in some gap in the icepack until a naval escort arrived? They had been entirely blacked out.

As they got farther north the ship started to plunge badly in the stormy seas. Waves were frequently dashed against the canvas screen and some of the water burst through upon the decks.

Hester was not only the prey to 'baby-thoughts', but became atrociously sea-sick. René, who was a good sailor, replaced the steward, and nursed her through this violent but harmless reaction to the wallowing of ships in briny abysses: to the motions of the rut of a rolling whale, as it were. All the movements of monsters sicken the parasite. The big ship is the only monster of which we have any experience.

For three or four days, their radio cut off very rigidly, both for reception and dispatch of messages, the *Empress* could scarcely have rolled more and it seemed as though they were practically stationary, except for the furious rolling, off Greenland was the general guess. Thus unreachable, and as silent as the grave, tossed up and down, continually in some high latitude, but not told where, at least they might suppose that they were in safety. But it was obvious, also, that sooner or later they must go back into waters frequented by the submarine; and there were some of them who wished that the Captain would decide to do so at once.

During his vigil with Hester, René did not fail to criticize the policy of the Captain. This polar adventure of his was ridiculous. Why had he not taken them a hundred miles or so to north or to south of the ship-lane, and trusted to their speed to have left behind any submarine. There would be some, most likely in ambush near the mouth of the St. Lawrence; those risks had to be taken.

However, a few days later the Captain appeared to have come to the same opinion as most of his passengers. He took them back toward Quebec; quite unexpectedly they found themselves in the Belle Isle Straits, and unmolested ascended the estuary of the St. Lawrence.

During their stay in northern waters it had been difficult to eat and almost impossible to drink. René had, of course, gone into the restaurant, where Dr. Lincoln Abbott was generally to be found, happily somewhat subdued. René was undergoing a severe mental strain during that period, and it would have been a bad thing for Dr. Abbott had his customary boisterous self indulged in playfulness. Naturally there were lapses. When the Doctor was flung out of his chair, he thought this terrifically funny; he picked himself up and came gulping back to the table with schoolboyish mirth. 'I wish I had my football equipment with me,' he chuckled. ('Equipment' was not the word he used but some term descriptive of the armour worn in American football.) Any other physical contretemps of this sort affected him in the same way; but on the whole the Doctor was a much more tolerable companion under these conditions. One afternoon René had made his way into the Tourist Class, and had a little talk with Oscar. He seemed somewhat self-conscious, and he suspected him of concealing the presence of sea-sickness, under a more than ever colourless abstraction of the self.

Hester did not recover speedily, nor for some time did she seem to forget her nightmare of riding a plunging leviathan. She was very weak, when she first came out on deck in the estuary of the St. Lawrence; and although the movement of the ship was by this time normally steady, she tended to cling on to things, and soon returned to her stateroom, where the stewardess brought her such food as she could eat. The long journey up this huge waterway was, for some, an avenue, made agreeable by the proximity, somewhere, of places and people, so new as to offer a temporary toe-hold to Hope. For others it was, of course, home. For quite a few it was 'the land of possibilities'. But to René the closer this land closed in as they advanced, the tighter the knot seemed to be drawn about his neck.

All the incidents of this crossing remained, in his memory, of no more significance than what is left in the mind after a cross-channel journey, only multiplied ninefold. The Declaration of War was a fainter impression than the first volume of *Middlemarch* flying through the air: but neither stood out in any way. For René, the period since the *Empress of Labrador* had left Cherbourg reduced itself to one terrifying self-revelation. His delight at being recognized by the preposterous little President of Rome was so awful a self-degradation, and only less his gratification at the respectful eyes behind the gold-rimmed glasses of Dr. Bleistift. That this should have had the effect of an earthquake in his emotional centres was—the moment the emotion had evaporated—an occurrence which staggered him. He stared at it twenty-four hours later as if he had seen a ghost. Who was this man, with the Legion of Honour in his dinner-jacket, sitting at a table with a common little American, reverently gazing at the ribbon? Who was this man warming himself at such a fire as this? Could it be the René Harding he had known all his life? Was this foolish creature indeed *himself*, converted, by some witchcraft, into the gentleman he was gazing at across an interval of only twenty-four hours? The state of nervous dereliction into which he had passed with such rapidity, after they had taken their place among the herds making the crossing on this great liner, was to him incomprehensible. Especially during the days while he was attending to Hester, he had this picture incessantly before him—of a degraded self, not known to him before, by some subconscious convulsion thrown up into time, and sitting there for all eternity at that restaurant table, with its ridiculous red boutonnière. He brooded for hours together over this obscene image of his past self. It had a terrifying fascination for him: at one time he lay back in his chair and howled with derisive laughter at it. Hester, startled at this, called out, 'What on earth are you laughing at, René?' He answered, 'Oh, just at a funny picture which suddenly came into my mind. You know how funny pictures have a way of popping up. This was a beastly funny one.'

These days of dark brooding in the rocking stateroom affected him so deeply that he felt at times almost half-witted. He found himself offering Hester smelling-salts when she had asked for a hot-water bottle: and was surprised to hear himself addressing the Stewardess as Helen.

This indelible impression was of so fiercely salutary a kind, here at the outset, that it even modified his attitude, and for good, regarding his way of thinking about himself (or 'what was left of himself', as he put it).

At Quebec he stepped ashore a quite different man from that beribboned Professor who had encountered Doctors Abbott and Bleistift a week before—that figure which he regarded. as a terrifying apparition, which might at any moment once more usurp his place.

He had learned his lesson, the lesson of final and absolute exile, quickly. He began immediately to forge for himself a more disciplined personality. If he had to die, and that was no doubt what it meant, at least he must do so in a manner that was not base and childish. He must not die with the Legion of Honour in his button-hole.

Mary's insistence upon elevating them from the Tourist Class to the First, which had evoked gratitude at the time of his degradation, now was very differently viewed. That was altogether the wrong way of meeting his fate.—It should not be in evening-dress with one of the world's honours reserved for the second-rate flaunted in his button-hole. Quite another costume was the only appropriate one. No, he should not have been a First-Class passenger—the distinguished Professor Harding incognito—that was a quite false idea. There was no honest way in which you could make sufficient money to travel First Class. His First-Class passenger act had been Mary's big mistake, whose mind was a First-Class mind. Either the life he was now to enter was an empty interlude, an apprenticeship to death: or it was a breathing-space, a period of readjustment, preceding the acceptance of a much simpler type of existence for Hester and himself. These alternatives would have to be broken to Hester. All details it would be time enough to settle when they had reached their destination, some very moderately priced hotel, which it would now be his task to find. She would have to be given the clearest explanation. Quite likely she would leave him, which might be the best solution. But all of that was detail. The general shape of the future was starkly outlined, for him, as if by some supernatural hand. It was the way things must fall out, when anyone refuses to live in the land of compromise. What immediately ensues must depend upon the circumstances of the man in question at the time of his decision. If he were a soldier on active service and if he laid down his rifle and declared his intention to use it no more, the consequences would be death, banishment or disgrace. If he were a salaried servant of a great insurance company and became a conscientious objector (to the financial system involved), and resigned his post, then the blow would be an economic one. But there were many other cases, which it is not necessary to specify, where ostracism accompanies the act of repudiation.

But such actions, no matter how greatly the circumstances might differ, lead to an estrangement from the norm of life. An individual who has repudiated publicly the compromise of normal living must thereafter be careful never to use compromise, or half-compromise, under whatever circumstances.

Sometimes rolling upon the floor of the stateroom, as he lost his balance, at the severest of the sub-polar storm, he analysed all of this down to the bedrock. His humiliation had been so great, he had at one point with difficulty restrained himself from confessing to the stricken Hester.

He emerged from those spasms of self-reproach outwardly unchanged. His behaviour to the Doctors was in no way modified when he met them on the decks or elsewhere.

The decks were crowded as they approached Quebec. Quebec, the gateway not so much to Canada as to the St. Lawrence and the Great Lakes. Among the chain of cities upon this riverine highway, the American outnumber the Canadian, and of course outclass them, commercially. This magnificent rock, more impressive than Gibraltar, is a catholic citadel, the importance of which was appreciated by René. As he stared at it, he did not see a colonial battle

6*

in the eighteenth century between a handful of French and
English troops, he saw instead a magnificent cardinal, assisted
by a herd of clerics, celebrating mass, in the Cathedral. He
saw the French population multiplying, the English dwindling,
and this rock symbolizing catholic power, rather than anything
pettily national.

The President of Rome University (and how clownish a
Rome that was) came up and remarked, 'Well, Professor, you
are looking at Quebec, and I imagine you are thinking of an
Englishman called Wolfe . . .!'

'You are wrong, Doctor,' René answered, 'the military
exploits of my countrymen, past or present, do not preoccupy
me to that extent.'

This was too much for Dr. Abbott, his sides began to quiver,
René perceived he was about to relish this hugely in his
characteristic fashion, as the latest drollery, of that 'caution',
his old buddy, the Chevalier René Harding. He fixed the
Doctor with an eye so forbidding that his comradely orgy was
nipped in the bud.—It would be a mistake to say that René's
manners had suffered no change whatever, towards his
academic fellow-passengers. There had to be a certain severity
which was not there before. Dr. Lincoln Abbott he regarded
as, in part, a phantom. Dr. Lincoln Abbott was for him, above
all, an historic figure: for was it not the Doctor who had been
the opposite member (or whatever the actors call it) to that
pitiable fool the bearded Professor with the Legion of Honour
stuck in his dinner jacket? The comic playlet staged in the
dining-saloon of the *Empress of Labrador* was something of
such importance to him that the 'Doctor' in that farce had
for him a special immortality. Once or twice, on the last day
of the voyage, Dr. Lincoln Abbott had found himself being
stared at with such intensity that it made him feel hot under
the collar. Had he put his tie on inside out, had he forgotten
to shave his upper lip, or was it B.O.? The first time he
encountered this scrutiny, Dr. Abbott hastened to his cabin,
and examined himself carefully, from head to foot, removed
his jacket and sniffed at his armpits, but was unable to
discover anything amiss.

The passport business, and then the problems with the vast

amount of luggage they had with them—passing the Customs on the ship and arranging for the safe disembarkation of the hand luggage—all this fully preoccupied everybody as they approached Quebec. All that René did by way of farewell to the Doctors was a curt nod in the Customs Shed. But Dr. Lincoln Abbott was not going to let him off so easily as that. He rushed at him, seized his hand, which he subjected to an hysterical pressure, reminded him that he had promised to come to Arkansas and lecture, and a half-dozen other things, while Mrs. President Abbott came round and overwhelmed the half-dead Hester with her solicitations and effusiveness. At last they shook off these good people and succeeded in getting on the track of their porters.

On landing two or three porters seized their hand luggage. René tried a little French on them, but as they were mostly Indians they were not interested. All they could speak was very limited French-Canadian, which is anything but identical with French. The Hardings kept losing these people, and finding them again with intense relief; but at last they were in a cab and being driven through the old city at the foot of the rock, which was not in any way noticeable. There is the French hand in a good deal of the buildings but on the whole Quebec is a cold city, which is natural enough seeing that it is under ice and snow for half the year. They spent the night there, but René was disappointed at finding so little that was truly French. The next morning, René rather stern, Hester still rather sea-sick, they left in the train for Montreal—but not to stop in that unusually fine city, but to press on to Momaco.

Part Two

THE ROOM

CHAPTER XI

Twenty-five Feet by Twelve

THE Room, in the Hotel Blundell, was twenty-five feet by twelve about. It was no cell. It was lit by six windows: three composed a bay, in which well-lit area they spent most of their time—René sat at one side of the bay, writing upon his knee on a large scribbling pad. Hester sat at the other side, reading or knitting or sleeping.

For the first year she had sat upon a piece of monumental hotel-junk, a bluish sofa. But it secreted bed-bugs, the summer heat disclosed, as it caused one occasionally to walk upon one of its dirty velvet arms.

Once the identity of the bug had been established, and before it moved from the velvet structure on to the human body, René acted. Overcoming loud protests from the management, who insisted that the bugs were innocent tree-insects, the sofa was expelled. Next Hester sat in a large blue velvet armchair. It was closely related to the sofa, but no bugs had shown up. Lastly, they were furnished with a fairly new and bugless settee.

It was René's habit to place an upended suitcase upon a high chair and drape it with a blanket. He stood this between his wife and himself, so blotting her out while he wrote or read. He could still see, over the crest of this stockade, a movement of soft ash-gold English hair, among which moved sometimes a scratching crimson fingernail. This minimum of privacy, this substitute for a booklined study, was all he had for three years and three months—to date it from the sailing of the *Empress of Labrador* from Southampton.

In summer René lowered the centre blind to shut out the glare. At present it was December, and another glare, that of the Canadian snow, filled the room with its chilly radiation. There was a small stack of books upon a chair to the left of him; he wrote in silence, hour after hour, dropping each page,

169

as it was completed, into a deep, wooden tray on the floor at his side.

They never left this Room, these two people, except to shop at the corner of the block. They were as isolated as are the men of the police-posts on Coronation Gulf or Baffin Bay. They were surrounded by a coldness as great as that of the ice-pack; but this was a human pack upon the edge of which they lived. They had practically no social contacts whatever. They were hermits in this horrid place. They were pioneers in this kind of cold, in this new sort of human refrigeration; and no equivalent of a central heat system had, of course, as yet been developed for the human nature in question. They just took it, year after year, and like backwoodsmen (however unwilling) they had become hardened to the icy atmosphere. They had grown used to communicating only with themselves; to being friendless, in an inhuman void.

The room, as mentioned above, was twenty-five feet by twelve about, but six of these, out of the length, you have to deduct for bathroom and kitchenette. Those figures still in no way express the size, because it was immense. Two human beings had been almost forcibly bottled up in it for a thousand years.

In the Rip van Winkle existence of René and Hester—of suspended existence so that they might as well have been asleep—a thousand years is the same as one tick of the clock. It was a dense, interminable, painful vibration, this great whirring, agelong, thunderous Tick. Bloat therefore the minutes into years, express its months as geological periods, in order to arrive at the correct chronology of this too-long-lived-in unit of space, this one dully aching throb of time.

A prison has a smell, as distinct as that of a hospital with its reek of ether. Incarceration has its gases, those of a place where people are battened down and locked up, year after year. There is a wrong sort of hotel; one dedicated to the care of guests who have been deprived of their freedom, and have been kidnapped into solitude and forced inertia.—The Hotel Blundell was the wrong sort of hotel. It was just a hotel, it was not a prison, but for the Hardings, husband and wife, it stank of exile and penury and confinement.

Their never-ending disappointments, in the battle to get work—wild efforts to liberate themselves, ghastly repulses—had made of this hotel room no more personal than a railway carriage, something as personal as a suit of clothes. As time passed, it had become a museum of misery. There were drawers packed with letters, each of which once had represented a towering hope of escape. Each effort had resulted in their being thrown back with a bang into this futility.

Number 27A, the number of the apartment (for apartment was the correct term for it), was consequently a miniature shadow, anchored upon another plane, of the great reality, which they had willy nilly built up about them in their loneliness. They must vegetate, violent and morose—sometimes blissfully drunken, sometimes with no money for drink—within these four walls, in this identical daily scene—from breakfast until the time came to tear down the Murphy bed, to pant and sweat in the night temperatures kicked up by the radiators—until the war's-end or the world's-end was it? Until they had died or had become different people and the world that they had left had changed its identity too, or died as they had died. This was the great curse of exile—reinforced by the rigours of the times—as experienced upon such harsh terms as had fallen to their lot.

Then they hid things from each other; as when one morning she saw a report of the suicide of: Stefan Zweig, refugee novelist. He and his wife had killed themselves in their apartment at Rio.—To begin life again, was Zweig's reported explanation, once the war was ended, would demand a greater effort than he felt he would be capable of making: he preferred to die and the wife who had shared with him the bitter pangs of exile accompanied him, with that austere and robust fidelity of the jewish woman to her mate.

But as she stared and brooded over this ugly news-item, during a laconic breakfast—the sun with a great display of geniality glittering over the frosty backyards—Hester recalled how earlier in the week she had praised electricity as against gas, for fixing food and as a heating agent. René had given his gothic headpiece a rebutting shake. The substitution of electricity for gas, he had objected, removed from those who were tired of life one of the only not-too-brutal modes of making one's exit from it: one available to anybody, costing nothing, requiring no specialist technique. A foolproof key to the *néant*. Just turn on the tap and lie down.—So she stopped herself from exclaiming about this tragedy, remarking instead that the egg ration in England was at present one a month.

But this roused him to controversy. 'I'd rather have that one egg and be in England . . .'

'Oh yes—you'd probably find it was a bad one when you got it!' she told him. There was no chance of their getting back to England; she discouraged regrets.

'All right, all right! I'd rather have that one rotten egg . . .!'

She gave in with a big sigh, no longer denying her nostalgia. 'I too, René!—I'd give all the eggs in Momaco for half an hour in London!'

However, ten minutes later her husband came across the Zweig report. He exclaimed 'ha!' as he glanced through it and then he passed it over to her.

For the class of things they hid from each other was not identical. René did not picture Hester with her head in a gas oven. His Hester was strongly prejudiced against death. What *he* concealed from her was rather newspaper announcements of appointments to academic posts, even of a quite minor order. He hurriedly shuffled out of sight anything with a hint in it of horridness towards himself: such as when a local columnist referred to the presence among us 'of a certain historian for whom history ended at the Repeal of the Corn Laws'.

'Zweig,' said René, tapping the paper with his finger, 'put down his act to his own incompetence, and to the future not the present.'

'So I noticed.' Her anger broke up into her face, giving her suddenly the mask of a tricoteuse, 'I would like to rub their damned noses in that sort of thing,' she exclaimed.

'Where's the use? It's human nature.'

'It's like *animals*! . . . Human nature!'

They took up their respective rôles at once. He became austerely watchful that no missile should get past which he regarded as irrational, and therefore unlikely to find its mark and kill its man. Thus it was no use calling people 'animals'. Just as well say they had hair in their crutches and armpits, and discharged the waste products of their nutritive system. ' We are animals,' René shrugged. 'Besides, he was just bored probably. I expect it was that.'

Hester shook her head. 'Don't you believe it! How about Toller. How about . . .'

'That's right enough. . . . It's pretty bloody for a german-speaking and german-writing man.'

'Pretty awful,' Hester retorted, 'for any temporarily displaced person. Among people who pay lip-service to "culture" as they call it—to the objects of this war, but . . .'

'Oh well,' he interrupted her, 'the devil takes the hindmost everywhere. Hitler had kicked him down to the bottom of the class. So the devil got him. You can't expect a lot of Portuguese mulattos . . .'

'Nor Canadians for that matter!'

René laughed: 'Ah, he had never had the misfortune to encounter them . . .!'

But René was wrong. The real backgrounds of this act of despair were made apparent—with, as René put it, 'a lousy naïveté'—by the literary editor of the *Momaco Gazette-Herald*. Zweig *had*, it seemed, encountered these dwellers of the far-north, for he had spent some time in Momaco, obviously in search of a refuge, of not too inhospitable a spot to weather the storm in.

But individuals of world renown, the starry few, are only welcome in such parts as unreal and glittering apparitions, upon a lecture platform. To 'stick around' is not well received. —In his obituary notice the literary authority of the *Momaco Gazette-Herald* recalled, upon a lachrymose note, how this most distinguished novelist, during his sojourn in Momaco, *offered me his friendship*. He was sorry now he had not responded.

René burst out laughing as he reached this climax of the obituary. '

'Means poor old Zweig tried to get some reviewing to do in their beastly paper. But that would be too big a name . . . overshadow the other contributors. So . . .'

'So!'

'But a pretty fellow. He might have left out that bit about how he'd snubbed him and how kind of regretful and contrite he was . . . kind of half feeling he'd done the poor chap in. What a rat!'

In such moments as this they changed rôles. Hester became sweetly reasonable.

'My dear René,' she mildly protested, 'you take this little bush-tick too much to task. He was only *advertising* himself, to his little circle of bush-bookworms. If a newspaperman can't advertise himself . . .!'

So they conversed, these two inmates of this lethal chamber. Its depths were dark. Looked into from without—by a contemplative bird established upon the maple bough about a foot from the middle window—the Hardings would have seemed (as they moved about their circumscribed tasks, or rested sluggishly, upon the bottom as it were) provided with an aquatic medium, lit where it grew dark by milky bulbs. So they must have appeared to the visiting squirrel, applying his large expressive eye to the pane, to discover if his presence had been noted by the two odd fish in the dark interior, who fed him peanuts, when they had the jack. Of the six windows, three, half the year, resembled very closely the plateglass sides of a tank in an aquarium. The green twilight that pervaded the lair of the Hardings was composed of the coloration from the wall of leaves of the summer maple, abetted by the acrid green veil of the mosquito netting. Green blinds latticed with use further contributed to this effect of water, thickening the bloomy cavity.

In the winter a dark pallor, or the blue glare of the snow, replaced the green. For weeks the windows would be a calloused sheet of ice, in places a half-inch thick. That was the only way the window ever got a cleaning. The Hardings had to go over them with a sponge, plunged in hot water, in order to see at all, and some of the callouses, of the density of icicles, required more than one kettle of boiling water. Immediately a new coat of ice would form, but the dirt of a twelvemonth poured down with the dissolving ice. The smoke of thirty thousand cigarettes, and a hundred fish, roasts, or 'offal', rolled down upon the window-sills. Of course the film of factory smoke from the chimneys of Momaco upon the outside surface of the window never departed.

'This is not real,' René insisted one day, as he sat looking towards the daylight from an inner seat, sniffing the rancid smoke from the grill. 'It isn't poverty. That is the worst of it.'

'No?'

'I am rich—in a city where people die every day from under-nourishment. Idle—and rich.'

Hester, her face flushed from the sub-tropical kitchenette, shook her head. She felt sick from the smoke.

'The pukka-poor would laugh at us,' he told her.

'The rich would laugh at us too . . . .they do.'

'Those top-booted blackcoated Jews out of the Ghetto in Cracow, who have a look in their eyes, you or I shall never have.'

'Not?'

'Their lips are pale with blood that has never been thickened with anything that would keep in decent gloss the coat of a well-cared-for dog.—And their lips are etched with the extra-ordinary bitterness of their sense of that fact. They have tasted every injustice. They live ten in a room. We cannot fill this room properly. There are only two of us.'

'I consider it full,' she answered.

He stared round, as if looking for somebody.

'No. This is a joke,' he said. He got up. 'The fat from our food collects in the bottom of the oven. If we scraped it out and ate it on our bread, that would be hard times—though in hard times there would be no fat in the bottom of the oven.'

'These are hard times,' she told him. 'Different from the poverty of a rag-picker, but in some ways worse.'

The Hardings were exiles, not from Poland, or France or Germany, but from Great Britain. They were not romantic political exiles but economic exiles—exiles by accident, frozen in their tracks, as it were, by the magic of total war, and the unavoidable restrictions upon travel that entailed, and the iron laws dividing dollar currency from sterling currency, and so cutting English nationals in Canada off economically from their own country.

As an 'involuntary squatter' in the Dominion of Canada René described himself, if he wrote to a friend in England. Locked up in this dollar country as solidly as if he were in Sing Sing—no farthing reaching him from England—he and his wife had been marooned. In Tahiti, a Swedish best-seller, the papers had reported, was an even worse case. He had no money at all and lived by what he could beg or catch in the sea. In Massachusetts, an American friend had written them, 'an English millionaire' was marooned. He scarcely had enough money for a pack of cigarettes. So this ex-professor was one of quite a lot.

But as an 'involuntary squatter' René had chosen to squat far too near to the University of Momaco. There are hard and fast rules about squatting in new countries, of which he had not been aware. It is not a good thing if you are a potential professor to squat too near to the institution where actual professors function. That is regarded as a little threatening. That is not well received.

So for the Hardings exile was complicated by other matters, which was what made it so peculiarly bad. Their isolation was now complete. People in Momaco were even tired of gossiping about them. They had at last really forgotten Professor Harding was there. But René had not forgotten *them*. As he sat crouched in his corner of the bay window, behind his palisade, he would sometimes take up a notebook, marked Momaco, and make a little note for future use.

'I remembered something just now, Hester,' he might remark to his invisible wife.

'What was it, darling?' For she knew by the tone of his voice that it was something she would be glad to hear

'I thought, "Oh, God. Oh, Montreal." '

'Yes?'

'What exclamation could Butler have found to apostrophize Momaco!'

Hester gave vent to a cat-like rumble of feline anger. She had long ago given up trying to find words for what she felt about Momaco.

This prison had been theirs for more than three full years. When René read reports in the newspapers about Daladier, Blum and the other French politicians in their place of confinement in France (Daladier described as tirelessly reading all the papers he could get and never speaking, Blum writing, Guy La Chambre complaining all day about the food, or so their Vichy captors had it) he decided that the all-important difference that he, René, *could*, if he possessed the necessary money, take a ticket to Chicago or for that matter to Mexico City, did certainly count for a lot. It was a big advantage. But he had not even got the money to buy a ticket for a spot thirty miles up the line and spend the day at a lake. He could get the money to just buy enough good food and a car-fare to go downtown once a week. The city limits were his limits and Hester's.

For a period of four months Hester had not gone out at all because she had no shoes to wear. All the shopping had to be done by him; and when the meat famine had come in Momaco, he had to go as far as the downtown market. This took up half the day; while she sat at home, at the mercy of her miserable fancies, counting the hours of this senseless captivity.

At last Hester could buy a pair of shoes. A New York friend had unexpectedly sent a present of thirty dollars. She cried a little. It was like a cripple recovering the use of her legs!

Through always conversing only with each other, their voices sounded strange to them when they were visited once in a way. Their 'company' voices were like the voices of two strangers. So if they had a couple of visitors—as once had

occurred—it was like having four people *as well as* themselves
in the Room. It was quite a party.

And the Room: that became something else. For anyone
from the outside to come into that, was like someone walking
into one's mind—if one's mind had been a room and could
be entered through a door and sat down in. René found he
disliked their Room being entered by other people. The less
people had come into it, until practically nobody came—the
more they suffered in it boxed up there in interminable lonely
idleness—the more he felt that if he must see people he
preferred to see them upon neutral ground. That they should
see where he and his wife had been so unspeakably miserable
he looked upon as an affront. If he had lost his reason he
would probably have burnt down the hotel, so that no one
should ever come in and boast, 'This is where we shut up that
dumbbell René Harding.'

If this was a prison, and it was, the three bay windows
twelve feet above the soil-level had a better outlook than most
jails. It could not be an authentic prison, anyway, because
of a coil of heavy rope hung at the side of one window—a
precaution decreed by the city fire headquarters. No prison
has a coil of rope invitingly attached by one of its ends to the
wall at the side of a window. That would be an odd kind of
prison—as this one was.

Momaco, the city in which the Hotel Blundell was situated,
was one of the greatest Canadian cities. It was a big, pre-
dominantly anglo-saxon city, though the french-canadian
population, if anything, exceeded the english-canadian, the
two together around half a million souls. It swelled and shrank
like a river: it swelled in boom years, when the mines of nickel
and gold were booming. It shrank if the mine interests
weakened. But it was always a big place: it had got so big it
couldn't shrink as much as the economic fluctuations decreed.
Now the war was swelling it to bursting: it was swollen like a
great tick with the young blood of farming areas, as the war
factories mushroomed up. The experts predicted a catastrophic
deflation, when Canada passed back out of total war into total
peace. But Momaco could never become a ghost city, like
Cobalt or Kirkland Lake, unless the Province became a ghost.

This bush metropolis had the appearance of an English midland city, which had gone in for a few skyscrapers. Its business quarter, in spite of a dozen of these monsters, was mean. It even succeeded very successfully in concealing them; as if having committed itself to a skyscraper, it resented its size.

Momaco was so ugly, and so devoid of all character as of any trace of charm, that it was disagreeable to walk about in. It was as if the elegance and charm of Montreal had been attributed to the seductions of the Fiend by the puritan founders of Momaco: as if they had said to themselves that at least in Momaco the god-fearing citizen, going about his lawful occasions, should do so without the danger of being seduced by way of his senses.

Had this city not been, with so rare a consistency, ugly and dull, the Hardings might have been less cooped up. Being friendless, there was no temptation to leave their neighbourhood, and be depressed by the squalid monotony. Accordingly the rows of backyards, twelve feet beneath their windows, constituted their unchanging horizon. The walls of the penitentiary were the houses enclosing the backyards. Their room was cell 27A. But they were blessed with an amusing and loquacious warder, in the person of the maid.

How much land does a man require? The landowner Count Tolstoi asked that. It is one of the massive fundamental questions. His answer was six feet by two, the space demanded by a man's body when he is dead.—Alive twenty-five feet by twelve is all right, with the dusty trough of half a dozen backyards thrown in, and a dusty company of maples—in which pursuing their beautiful lives robins and jays, starlings and doves abound: not to mention the eternal passerine chorus, or the small black Canadian squirrel who vaults on to the windowsill.

The Hardings even had two favourite pigeons, who always came together. They named them Brown and Philips, after the two well-known picture dealers of Leicester Square.—But Brown and Philips vanished, in spite of the great reliance these two birds had come to place on the Hardings' bounty. And their promenade—or sports-ground where they played

bread-polo—on the flat roof of the kitchen quarters, tacked
on to the next house, lost much of its glamour.

There was one occasion when an escaped budgerigar turned
up to the amazement of all the birds present at the time upon
Brown and Philips' sports-ground. 'Poor beast,' muttered
René. 'Look at it. . . . It has no pride—it's a lovebird, it
wants love.' A group of sparrows was repulsing its frantic
advances. So gaudy a novelty in the way of a bird was not,
it was plain, to their taste. 'That's not love,' Hester advised
him. 'It's his big heart, only. . . . How matey he is!' she
exclaimed, as he knocked one of the sparrows off a ledge, and
engaged the next in what René decided was in fact only
energetic conversation. 'He is a darling!' Hester insisted. 'He
does look so funny among all those sparrows, the wonderful
little lost ball of fire!' But a captor came up a ladder, tip-
toed across the roof and caught him in his hand. 'Back to
the cage, buddy!' said René. 'To die in captivity.' At that
moment Philips alighted heavily upon the neighbouring roof,
decorously arranging his lavender wings, and Brown dropped
beside him, with an eye cocked towards the intruder carrying
off the escaped prisoner.

The Hardings' Room was not by itself. It was one of a
family of over one hundred apartments, as they were one
of a family of people called 'guests', comprising one of the
six apartment-hotels of Momaco. The bathroom, lavatory,
and kitchenette made of it a complete living-quarters. You
need never move out of it, if you did not want to, or did not
have to go to work. By telephone—the instrument was on
your writing table—you could order all your food from the
groceteria, the dirty backyard of which you could see from
the bay window. During the meat famine it was even possible
to observe the carcasses of beef or lamb being carried in at
the side of the door, rush to the telephone and secure a small
hunk before they sold out.

In the flank of the Hotel, on its south side, was a drinking
saloon. To placate the Methodists a saloon or a beer-parlour

was called a 'Beverage-room' all over Canada. It did not pacify the Methodists, who would never be satisfied until Momaco was a hundred per cent bootleg city: and in the war they saw their opportunity.—A dirty and generally drunken waiter would bring you beer, or, if he knew you weren't a dick, bootleg Rye or Scotch. If you were a 'wine-hound' you could have what in Canada is laughingly called wine.

Should you find it undesirable to move far from the front door and expose yourself to the saddening and depressing sensations produced by the streets and alleys of Momaco, you were obviously well-placed to stand a siege. For the Hardings it was a siege. Their resistance was an epic of human endurance, and some day, René felt sure, would make Momaco famous.

The sense of the passage of time depended largely upon the recurrence of Sunday. You got lost in the week itself, —Monday was very distinct. You knew when the week *began*. Mondaymorningishness was an unmistakable something that entered the room as Bess came in at 10.30 with her sheaf of towels and sheets. She was swollen with a sense of accumulated wrongs—during the week-end all the insults of the week had had time to mobilize and organize inside her, in her lonely room, and on Monday morning she discharged these humours as she passed from room to room.

Tuesday and Wednesday were sometimes a little difficult to identify. Thursday and Friday had a way of getting mixed up: and Thursday and Wednesday were a no man's land in the centre of the week: it didn't really matter which it was, and they were usually indistinguishable.

Friday has this advantage over Thursday, that it is unlucky. You can't cut your nails. You can't start on a journey: if you are one of those people who are lucky enough to be leaving Momaco, you have to restrain your impatience until Saturday. Something unpleasant is pretty sure to happen on Friday anyway (especially in Momaco) that reminds you what day it is you are passing through.

Saturday has a very definite function of its own among the days of the week. It is easy to identify—it is the last day as Monday is the first. Shopping is a more urgent matter, because

of Sunday. It is your last chance until Monday to buy what
you want. And as to Sunday, no one can mistake *that*. From
the Gulf of Mexico to Hudson's Bay everyone is in bed until
noon, so it is only half a day. But it is the day of days, because
you know you have lived a week more, and with luck, or
ill-luck, will soon be treading another week—towards another
Sunday.

The radio roars all day on Sunday. It vibrates with the
tremulous thunder of the organ. From a million pulpits sing-
song voices assure us that war is a holy thing. It is a day of
verbal bloodletting, of exhortations to homicide and quivering
organpipes. It is at once—cooped up in an hotel Room with
a radio—an uncommonly noisy day, and a very blank one.
It is a vacuum, full of a fierce and sanctimonious voice, hollow
with bogus emotion, calling for blood, and another one, sweet
and tender, promising love to the brave. *Why* you should be
stridently homicidal on Sunday is so obviously because Christ
would desire it, for when He talked about the 'other cheek'
He was only fooling, and He likes a good old christian war
just as much as any other Christian.

There is *no* voice telling people that this is a very great
revolution rather than the stupid war every booby thinks it
is—because it will afford all the nations an authentic *chance*
(whether they take it or not, which is up to them) of escape
from the unmentionable chaos which brought it about, that
a more intelligent society *may* be in the making. One in which
the men of creative capacity, instead of wasting ninety per
cent of their lives wrestling with the obstructive inertia of the
majority, will be freed for their creative tasks.—Instead of
such voices as that, which would be far too real a thing to
be tolerated on the highly respectable ether, there is just the
old fustian. A loud voice saying nothing: the nihilistic screech
of the pep-doctor—the platitudinous drone of the reverend
gentleman in the god-business, assuring us that Jesus was a
kind of Elite Guard, and God a sort of Super-Thor, and that
we are headed for a Valhalla of mediocrity.

So Sunday is a good day to anchor your timetable to. It is
a day that is a vacuum in more senses than one, because it
is quite impossible to get any news on Sunday, or to find out

what is going on. *Nothing* apparently is going on, in a world
where nothing is more important than something, and nobody
than somebody. A war is going on somewhere no doubt—our
lovely boys are dying somewhere up in the ether waves,
piloting their ships, hounded by Zeros in unequal fight,
because some fool or knave prevented them having anything
but 'too little and too late'. But the children are not supposed
to be disturbed on Sunday. We are the children—so all the
news becomes emptily rosy.

But about seven o'clock Eastern war-time Jack Benny brings
far more than comic-relief. He brings a great gust of reality
and heaven-sent respite from Godliness—and from verbal
thunder of bulletins telling of battles that probably were never
fought (or not that way). A salvo of wisecracks dispels the fog.
We are back upon the earth again with Jack and Rochester,
among things that matter to men, and things that are good
for human consumption. Once more we are among things just
as real as this war is—if we were ever allowed to know about
it, or treat it as a real thing, rather than a dummy.

So the week wings by: really it is from Sunday to Sunday.
From, and towards, that great blank empty End of every
week. As the poet so justly sang in his melancholy youth:

> *From the Intense Inane to the Inane Intense*
> *My soul took flight upon the wings of sense.*
> *But very soon my soul flew back again*
> *From the Inane Intense to the Intense Inane.*

Sunday in Momaco, from x a.m. war-time to x p.m. war-
time, was the Intense Inane, to which the soul flew back as
to rest, after its flight across the other six days of the week,
so replete with a meaningless intensity.

But the Hardings, placed as they were, were painfully
reminded of another unit beside the week, namely the year.
It was borne in upon them that there are fifty-two weeks in
the year. Just as the week has a shape of sorts, so had for
them the year. Christmas is to the year what Sunday is to
the week.

But a year is a higher organism than a week. Its shape is
more distinct. By looking out of the window you can see more

or less where you have got in your weary road across the year, from Christmas to Christmas. Whereas it is no use looking out of the window to see what day of the week it is (always excepting Sunday).

As year succeeds year, marooned in Momaco, you become very conscious of the seasons, as if you were engaged in husbandry instead of being engaged in wasting your life— day by day, week by week, and year by year. Actually you can *see* the seasons, as these two people did, and watch them revolve with a painful slowness, if you have a window, and if that window is not of milled glass, as they are in the rooms where Japanese confine their political prisoners.

Not to be able to see out, thought René, must be truly fearful, when he read the interview with the American correspondent who had been exchanged for one of their nationals, after four months of solitary confinement: this man had told his interviewer that the first thing he noticed after his release—noticed with a thrill of delight—was that *doors had handles.*

René sighed. He looked over at the handle of his door. There was the handle—that delicious handle, signifying *freedom.* He sighed again. For *à quoi bon?* What was the use of having a handle to a door, if in fact there was nowhere to go outside the room? If anywhere you could go outside was worse than stopping where you were? What was the use of living in a free country, as a free man, where doors had handles and windows had no bars, if that freedom was of no use to you —was freedom with a bar sinister, freedom with a great big catch in it somewhere? From the big bay window where the Hardings sat all day long and in the summer all the evening, the seasons made themselves visible in the backyards of Momaco. They waited for the so-called Squaws' Winter which in Canada precedes the Indian Summer—for the feeble snow- fall which has to take place before the false lovely gentle summertime of the Indian can come in and make believe for a week perhaps. After that in Momaco there was no fooling. The first blizzard hit them soon afterwards.

The backyards became a strange submerged version of themselves; with a deep soft icing of the Angel-cake variety all

seemed phantasy of a sudden, its relation to what was underneath beautifully pathologic. Every branch or twig had on a
furry coat of snow that swelled it out as a kitten's hair puffs
out its miniature limbs. Festoons and lianas of this souffléish
substance of weightless young snow made a super Christmas
card of what had a short while before been a piece of drab and
brutal impressionism.

Icicles six feet long, and as thick as a man's arm, hung from
the eaves and gutters. The heat of the hot-water pipes could
some days scarcely be felt. Yet they knew that in fact they
were giving forth a heat comparable to that of a Central
American jungle. Below zero temperatures started when the
cold came down from Hudson's Bay and higher, and the Polar
Sea walked right through the walls of the hotel as if it had been
a radio wave and went clean through your bones. At 50 below
zero, in a place by no means perfectly dry, like Momaco, with
a sizable river running through the middle of it, it was as
impossible to keep it out as radium, in the imperfectly-heated
apartment of the Blundell. It walked through your heart, it
dissolved your kidney, it flashed down your marrow and
made an icicle of your coccyx.

If in Momaco there was never any temptation to make use
of your privilege of a free man, and stroll out upon the streets
beyond the door of the Hotel, there was the need for exercise,
and with eyes shut the Hardings would occasionally walk
round the block. But when it got really cold there was something that competed even with Momaco itself to keep you
indoors; if summer or autumn you were never tempted to
remember 'that you had a doorhandle', even less in the winter
did you desire to insist upon your quota of prisoners' exercise.

From the Hotel up to the main road was a matter of three
blocks. To walk it when the wind was from the north or east,
and when there was a wind, in this sub-zero weather, was a
feat for anyone who was a stranger to such things. Your face
would be wet with tears which would freeze upon the face,
or the wind would catch the tears as they came over the rim
of the eyelid and dash them on to your shoulder. Your ears
would become cauliflower ears, and the drums would set up
an ache, which would not leave you for some time. Your lips

would crack. It was very severe indeed. But this was only when there was a wind. If the wind falls the glass does not fall, but you do not feel it much any longer, even at 30 below. In sunny weather, with no wind, 5 or 10 below is just pleasantly fresh. It is the wind that does it.

. Bad as is the wind, in the periods of great cold, there is something even more disagreeable. That is the ice. It is very difficult not to slip: and people in Momaco often, walking too confidently along the street, break a leg or an arm. In general the Momaconians of the more prosperous—and as they believe more civilized—kind like to think that Momaco's winter is a marked but not excessive falling away from civilized standards of warmth. So they often dress improperly in the winter.

All shop messengers or errand boys have ear flaps of fur after October, and could not go their rounds without them. They are as sure-footed as goats, but they are beaten by the ice. Then splinters of ice have a function, and one pierced a boy's eye and blinded him outside the Blundell Hotel. So the ice is abnormally bad, whereas the snow forms an engagingly soft material to tread on. The snow is beautiful to look at and to walk on: but at Momaco, and of course farther north, it gets worse, there is a little too much of it. It goes on for too long, and it is the eyes that are probably the worst sufferers.

Blindness is very prevalent. You meet blind people everywhere, tapping along the edges of the sidewalks with their sticks. The number of people in Momaco who wear smoked glasses is surprisingly great. They get so used to wearing them in the winter, against the dazzle of the snow, that they are also very apt to wear them in the summer, against the dazzle of the sun. They become conscious of violent light in general. And the light is for some reason very violent. In the morning it seems to bang you in the face, as it glares in at the window. Canada is no land for those with delicate eyes.

There is perhaps something more than the ice, the glaring snow, and the pulverizing zero wind. That is the mud. René and his wife found, during the foul period of mud, such small sorties as in the summer they permitted themselves, impracticable. The telephone had to be resorted to. There is no spring in Momaco. There is a period of winds—milder than

the winter ones, but very fierce and quite cold, which is said
to come in March but which really comes in April. Everything
arrives a month later than it is supposed to do. May is very
violent, too. Off and on there is a great deal of wind in
Momaco; not so much as in Chicago or Buffalo, where ropes
along the sidewalks have to be provided for pedestrians at
times, but still it is far windier than anywhere in Europe,
except as you approach the Sahara. Unlike an ocean-wind,
it is charged with no pep. It is a violent annoyance: you are
being pushed around by an element you do not respect. When
it finds its highest expression is in the tornadoes of the central
United States. But Canada east of the Rockies is part of that
unstable system.

Suddenly in Momaco you get summer. The leaves all come
out overnight. Agriculturally, between frost and frost, it is
a summer of a hundred days. After that the cattle go back
to the barns, and often the cereal farmer locks up his farm
and goes south to California.

The summer is in two parts. There is the summer and then
a super-summer. The latter is a heatwave, which is hotter than
the Red Sea—only in Momaco you cannot console yourself
with the thought that, being 'east of Suez' there 'ain't no Ten
Commandments'. There are Ten Commandments in Momaco,
as in no other city in the world. It is the city of the Ten Commandments, all of which are so violently broken that they
can never be forgotten, as they can be in a place where no
one pays any particular attention to them.

The Indian must have been a gentleman, to have a beautiful
moderate summer of his own in November—in protest perhaps
at the indecent explosion of silly heat seven months earlier.
This sort of Yahoo Summer—in contrast to the Indian Summer
—has no rationale. For why should it occur in a country so
typically northern as is 'My Lady of the Snows'?

So in the hotel Room the seasons revolve and have a sad
repercussion. They deepen the solitude, like the ticking of
a great ominous clock. They are of the nature of a clock, as
much as is a sundial.

The face of each new section brought a new despair to the
two people in the Room. If the leaves appeared on the trees

7

again it was not a matter for rejoicing—it spelt another section of one's life wasted in corrosive idleness. If the leaves turned russet and yellow and fell off the trees, that was another disagreeable pang. It meant more months had been consumed, with nothing to show for it; months of so-called life in which nothing had been done except wait for the mail, which always brought discouraging news, or listen to the radio, which droned on in its senseless ritual, or write something which might never see the light.

So the seasons were a curse. They were less anonymous than the days of the week—for Monday did not snow, or Thursday make itself known by its great heats, or Friday announce itself by shedding its leaves. Really, if it were not for Sunday, one could more or less feel one was always living on the same day. The seasons kept reminding you of the stupid plodding feet of Time.

CHAPTER XII

The Hotel and what Contains the Hotel

RENÉ, as they settled down, willy-nilly, in this shell, began soon to develop a consciousness of solidarity with the environment. The *Hotel* in which they lived was surrounded by the *District*, which was surrounded by the rest of the *City*, which was surrounded by the *Province*, which was surrounded by the *Nation*, which was a part of the *Continent*. The North American continent, like the Chinese toy of box within box within box. And these boxes were all of a piece, all cut out of the same stuff. They were part of the same organism, this new North American organism. Their cells would have the same response to a given stimulus. And of these diminishing compartments the ROOM was the ultimate one, which they inhabited. It was an American ROOM.

Now since the reactions of all these parts of a great whole were similar, the history and fate of one could be taken to be typical, in one degree or another, of all the rest. The Beverage Room in the flank of the building, full of sudden violence and maudlin song (the head bar-boy taking his rake-off out of the cash-box): the Indian—drunk as all Indians had been ever since the Whites had landed—dwelling amid the sentimental screams of his blonde Teutonic squaw: the dazed and crippled mistress of all this, doped in her room, staring at a disorderly mass of business papers. Mr. Ellis across the passage from Mr. Martin, an old especially privileged guest, dozing upon his sofa, the radio murmuring at him, was apt to be incontinent when sober, and even sometimes when drunk, which was his customary condition; the janitor exhibiting his stolen medals to his french-canadian harem, his eyes popping out of his head in a bird-like ecstasy of nonsense, like a creature out of a Lear's Nonsense Rhyme, or a companion of Alice; all this was a microcosm of what was without—one of the Ward, the City, the Province, the Nation, the Continent.

It was of course crazy—or more accurately it was crazed. It was a highly unstable box, within an equally unstable larger box, which in its turn nestled within a still larger box, of great social instability, profoundly illogical. The degeneration of the Maison Plant, the Hotel Blundell, was but a microcosmic degeneration repeated upon a larger and larger scale, until you reached the enormous instability of the dissolving System, controlling the various States. All this one day, at a touch you would think, no more, would come rushing down in universal collapse.—Indeed, that was what the War meant. It was a collapse, a huge cellular degeneration of society. It was crazy as this house was crazy.

The coarse Nirvana of the ugly bottle, or of the powder or pellet of narcotic, blinded the participants. As the State, the City, the Household waded in a morass of Debt and Mortgage, the Room was charged with despair and decay.

As the ocean liner is a microcosm, so is the hotel. The hotel contains everything belonging to human society. The hotel in a sense is the city. The hotel is the State. The hotel is the world.

Now this particular hotel, appropriately seeing the continent upon which it was situated, was a matriarchy. At the helm of state was a woman, Mrs. Plant, a queen-bee throned crazily over this hive—a great, broken, lolloping, half-blind queen, and so the hive was a bit cock-eyed, as you might expect. It was in no way more cock-eyed than the city, however. I doubt if it was any more ramshackle than any State. It was madly ill-run. But are not all States ill-run? Are not most cities glaringly mismanaged? Of course. Human society is so fearfully and wickedly mismanaged that there is no wonder that if we pause—as we are doing here—to examine any part of it, that part is seen to be idiotically mismanaged too. On a small scale, however, we can detect the errors more easily. The State is after all 'the State'. It makes the laws, it has power of life and death. It is not necessarily more intelligent for that reason. Because a thing is big it is not necessarily more intelligent. Indeed the contrary is usually the case: the giant is usually less smart than the dwarf. And most governments, or 'states' conform to that rule, of the bigger the stupider.

For honestly you must grant me this, that no individual could
be guilty of the follies that most bodies thousands strong,
which we call 'governments', are guilty of. You will object
that what the governments have to handle are far more
complex matters than what a man would have to cope with.
But 'complexity' is no excuse really for stupidity. Most of
the things statesmen have to deal with are fundamentally as
simple as the running of an hotel.—The fact remains, however
much one may argue, that only one man in a hundred thousand turns out to be a murderer—and he ends his life on a
gallows, or the 'hot squat'. Whereas there is no civilized nation
that finds itself a proper nation until it has taken human life,
to the tune of a million or so. If you murder *enough* people
it's all right. There is that.

So the hotel in question was naturally ill-run. How could it
be otherwise—seeing that it was typically of Momaco—which
was typically of the earth: and of the universe. Somebody
argued that it was not so badly run as all that: that the
proprietress—or the 'Leading Lady', as she was described by
one of her female assistants—was a genial old cripple.

Certainly, when Mrs. Plant disappeared for a few days to
have her face lifted, immediately it dissolved into a greater
chaos than before.—But badly stuck together as undeniably
it was, the erratic clockwork of this Hotel never actually came
to a full stop.

In the little world of *the Room* there was a guiding principle.
The Room was not a matriarchy. But passing out of the Room
—number 27A—into the Hotel, as we are now doing, we go
down a passage, all the rooms of which are Something-A. It
must be that farther down the passage when they came to
13 and began resorting to A's, they just went on A-ing and
at 17 or 18 were still engaged—hiding the unlucky number.
This is not a reasonable explanation, I know. But what
reasonable explanation could there be for putting A after
every number?

Inside the front door of the Hotel was a large reception desk,
but it was generally empty. You looked in vain for executive
personalities. You filled in the forms required by the law for
the newly arrived guest, and then went on a hunt for someone

qualified to receive them, and to allot you an apartment. This large reception desk had been introduced into what the architect had obviously intended to represent the lounge of a vast private mansion. There were comfortable but faded settees, tables with periodicals at least six months old and three nude statues, about half life size, which had once been white, and which still gleamed dully in the Edwardian gloom. From a stained-glass window at the other extremity of this spacious lounge, some dirty blue and green light was admitted, and in the middle of the ceiling there was a milky transparency which distributed discreetly the electricity around this shadowy entrance hall. It must once have seemed impressively solid.

Not only was the reception desk usually unoccupied, but this lounge, or whatever it was, was likewise almost always silent and empty. It was not patronized by the guests. The Hotel executive were customarily either dyeing their hair in the bathroom, or upstairs telling the fortunes of the guests in teacups.

This was in the daytime. At night the 'Beverage Room', situated beneath the stained-glass window, was open. This did not necessarily involve a more inhabited look in the lounge; but there was more electric light and considerable noise penetrated the interior of the Hotel. On a hot night drunken songs would reach the open windows of the apartments overlooking the Beverage Room; for the Hotel Blundell was a crowded beer-saloon as well as a family hotel in process of transformation into a clandestine brothel upstairs.

Receptionists—house-keepers—manageresses there were, working in two shifts. Miss Toole had been ousted from first place while away on holiday in Ottawa, her home town, by Vera. Vera was the number one assistant to the proprietress, Mrs. Plant, when the Hardings arrived. A spectacled young woman, she was a sluggish, corrupt little figure. She only would function if you introduced a dime into her clammy fist. A dollar had the effect of an earthquake.

This young woman got drunk on Aromatic spirits of Ammonia, otherwise called 'Sal volatile'. The management advised the local drug-store of her weakness: but in the end they were obliged to dismiss her. She found employment in another hotel where eventually she died, through her indulgence in this strange intoxicant. It should be added that Miss Toole had been very much addicted to drink also, but in her case it was whisky, and this had appeared to do her no harm.

The Hotel from the outside was a pale stucco affair, straight up and down, of four stories in addition to the mezzanine. The banqueting room and various offices which originally comprised the mezzanine had been converted into apartments, though this floor had not been promoted to first story. It was only up to the top front of the mezzanine that the Hotel face was pretentiously ornamented, rather like the front of a French hotel, quite unlike its grim Edwardian interior. The three-story annexe ran at right angles at its rear, stretching along a street at the back for some distance; and led into the Hotel down two wide corridors.

If the Hotel was a jumble of styles, that was appropriate, for the population was a jumble too; not so much as it is in the United States, but still a mixture. The French stucco front, of this Hotel, the Edwardian anglo-saxon hallway, and the apartments on American pattern, plus the velvet furnishings which are English, displayed, in a mild way, the incoherence customary on this new continent where nothing can ever be one thing. The multiple personality of Canada depends mainly, it is true, upon the two dominant racial groups, the English and the French. The major weakness of this small nation lies in the implacable hostility of those of English speech, for those of French speech, which is warmly reciprocated. This is in part a religious cleavage; the protestant English, backward and bigoted, rage against the papist hierarchy ruling the French. Then there is the fact that *class* here is *race*: the Anglo-Saxon suffers from a Hitlerian superiority feeling, and the 'Peasoups' (as the French are called) have had to put up with a lot of contempt from the master-race. But with quintuplets and families of twenty or thirty children the French will soon outnumber the English.

There exists a strong Scottish coloration in English Canada. But although many Scots are encountered, the North Irish and English are certainly more numerous. 'Though still the blood is strong—the heart is Highland: And we in dreams behold the Hebrides,' lines in a famous poem, may once have made the blood feel strong in Canada. But the pipers are dying out, and the marked Scottish coloration no longer means what it did. It should be added that, although the recognized Indians, still living as such, are numerically and otherwise a feeble group, the French-Canadians have a great deal of Indian blood, and in many cases are purely Indian, french-speaking and usually bearing Scottish names, like McTavish or McIntyre. The Russian, Scandinavian, Finnish, Negro, and other groups are greatly inferior in numbers. Some enterprising slave-driver went to the Ukraine about forty or fifty years ago, and imported great numbers of Russians for agricultural peonage. All the railway stations of Eastern Canada were full for months of hairy men in sheepskin coats. Then at last they had all settled: and they too—unlike the Anglo-Saxons—are great ones for breeding.

It would be impossible to understand a ROOM in a Canadian hotel without obtaining a clearer picture of Canada than that possessed by the average European. So here is a brief account of the country surrounding the Hotel in which was the Room inhabited by the Hardings. On the map Canada is vast; but the habitable part is of a tape-like shape, exceedingly long and narrow. This elongated country north of the St. Lawrence and the Great Lakes, from Quebec to Vancouver, has its cities, hundreds of miles apart, strung out between the bush and the United States border; everything is east to west, and hardly ever north to south.

What 'Canada' means is this strip north of the United States, signifying north of the river St. Lawrence and the Great Lakes, which continuous waterway divides the two nations in the way the Pyrenees are the inevitable frontier between Spain and France. Although this watery barrier is on a grand scale, it is at no point, except Quebec city itself, very impressive, in the way that the Hudson River is.

As to the historic consolidation of Canada; the founding of French Canada, and the big, bold landmark of Quebec is all that people know anything about. Where English Canada begins, above Montreal, it is technically known as 'Upper

Canada'. The first settlers from the States meant by this expression *up* the St. Lawrence, as they paddled as far away from the freezing coast as they could get. For the Tories, who came north in disgust after the War of Independence, were so dismayed by their first winter in Halifax (and well they might be, in those bad cold days before central heating) that they swore that even Lady Washington was better than *that*, and with loud cries of distress, fled inland in a body, till they reached Lake Ontario. That is where the River St. Lawrence ends and the Great Lakes begin.

So much for the southern border of this strip of a country, as far as the Rockies. The other side of the strip, in Upper Canada, is the Bush. This is a fairly solid wilderness up to the Muskeg and after that the Polar Sea. If you start driving north in an automobile from Toronto, Momaco, or Ottawa, you begin passing through farmlands which very soon thin out, and then you come to the impassable Bush. Small lakes are ubiquitous in the nearer Bush and there are summer camps in these fly-infested lakelands, thirty or forty miles north of Momaco and Toronto. They can be reached by car.

The Bush-cities, built in the Bush to provide a small urban environment for those working in the mines, can only be reached by rail, or by plane. So these communities in the northlands are extremely isolated and surrounded by Bush. This huge wilderness, pressing down upon the cultivated strip, in Canada, is so undesirable a residence that it is difficult to see the Bush being pushed back very far, unless the world becomes so overpopulated that men will live in the Polar cold rather than nowhere at all. It is quite uncomfortable enough for half the year at Momaco and Ottawa, though central heating helps to banish what otherwise would be hideous conditions. Nature in British Columbia is somewhat more benevolent; the western prairies, with their hundred days from frost to frost, are certainly no warmer, but it is a different topography to Upper Canada; and the Laurencian mountains provide the Montrealor with beautiful summer camps. But the people of Momaco feel themselves shut in between the St. Lawrence and the Bush.

Any criticism of Canadians, meaning English-Canadians,

7*

is in general irrelevant. An anglo-saxon community living
under such isolated conditions, in so uninviting a climate,
could hardly be otherwise than they are. They are just average
inhabitants of Belfast, of Leeds and Bradford, of Glasgow,
poured into a smaller community, American in speech, and,
apart from the fact that they acquire an American accent,
they continue to exist exactly as they did in the British cities
from which they came. One must not be deceived by the
American accent. Canada is not identical with the United
States: it is quite distinct, because most of the people in it,
except the French, come from these islands. If you criticize
them you criticize the average population of Belfast, of
Bradford and Leeds, and of Glasgow. If you deplore the
materialism and the humble cultural level, you are merely
criticizing anglo-saxon civilization.

Canadians have all the good qualities as well as the bad,
of the Ulsterman, the Scot, the Englishman: and among them,
of course, are about the same percentage of gifted people as
you would find in these islands.

Momaco is rather nearer to the Bush than is Ottawa. Like
Ottawa itself, it has a large french-canadian population—
about one third of the Momaconians are French. A river
traverses Momaco and its main square is built beside the river.
There is a very handsome Catholic Church dominating this
square: and it is a market square also, which at times gives
it a somewhat French aspect. The river is, of course, apt to
be full of logs, travelling down towards the St. Lawrence. The
City is built in a plain and is extraordinarily flat except for
a hill at its north-east corner. The Hotel Blundell was situated
where the English quarter adjoins the French. Balmoral
Street, on which the Hotel Blundell stood, was a long street
which began quite well but ended very badly: it was largely
French-canadian at the bad end. The Blundell was on its
earlier and better part.

CHAPTER XIII

Affie and the 'Roaches

THE Hotel was a ship whose engines stopped every night about ten. The ice-boxes in the annexe vibrated no more, as the cool air, smelling of ammonia, was forced up the zinc pipes into them. It was like a ship becalmed, this dusty old passenger ship, the engineers knocking off for the night. About eight o'clock a.m.—the time varied, according to how drunk the janitor had been the night before—the Hotel shook and throbbed: the beat and hum of its engines was heard from down below: the ice-boxes in the annexe shook. The ship was on her way again, the good ship 'Blundell'.

A half-hour later René and Hester quitted the bed, like two flies dragging themselves out of a treacly plate. One went to the bathroom, the other to the kitchenette. By nine o'clock they were seated at breakfast, watched from every bough of the nearest maple by the patient eyes of their bird-chorus.

'Canadian and British governments announce that they have given instructions that German prisoners are to be unshackled on Dec. 12th.' René read listlessly the headline in the *Momaco Gazette-Herald*. Hester's eyes stared as ever, but more painfully now. She stared at a point between the kitchenette and the bathroom, where she appeared to discern a ghost lurking in the wall, of which she was not apprehensive, because it had been there so long. The classic conundrum as to whether the cow is still there in the field when you have walked away from it, or whether it vanishes the moment you cease to observe it, is apposite. For the analysis of Hester's new look, she felt like the cow in the field which is no longer observed by any human eye (because, from this angle, René did not count). She had been a violently self-conscious woman —she was a cow in a field excessively conscious of being observed; and for whom to be observed was *to be*. But it was

197

so long now since she had been under human observation—for
she did not regard her present environment as human—that
self-consciousness had left her: and the ghost she stared at in
the wall half-way between the kitchenette and the bathroom
was the remote phantom of those people in England for
whom, long ago, she had been the self-conscious object. So
she was still a staring woman, but she now stared at something
so remote as to be abstract, and with far less vitality than
formerly.

Emptying his third cup of tea, René rose. 'Well!' He spoke
with fists raised to the dirty heaven of the Hotel apartment,
as if this bitter *well* were an imprecation. His stretch took him
forward several thudding paces, like a man with locomotor.
'I guess I'll make this Room fit for a hero to live in. . . . Why
don't they say that this time? They don't say anything nice
this time like "a war to end war"! Effrontery!'

'Hush!' remarked his wife.

'Yes, I know.' He heaved a sigh that was loaded with stale
revolt, that was like a freshwater tear, that had lost even its
salt.

A pair of large tarnished scissors were at his feet: he picked
them up and dropped them into a work-basket that was a
miniature oyster-basket from Boulogne-sur-mer: picked up a
breakfast cup with an empty packet of cigarettes stuck in it,
a square-toothed bread-knife and a last night's beer-pocked
tumbler, and carried them to the kitchen. Watched by his
wife, as animals watch each other with sullen reserve in cages,
when one comes to life, René returned and collected his over-
shoes, the ice from which had wetted the floor, and his damp
Bond Street overcoat, and went with them towards the closet.
His wife got up and drifted with the listlessness of captivity
towards the bathroom, against the window-pane of which the
birds were knocking with their beaks.

'Some birds . . .'

'Yes!' he answered emphatically.

'Some birds get to think . . .'

'Undoubtedly,' he said. 'Tell Philips we can't afford to feed
so huge a bird.'

'Poor Philips.'

'Never mind! Shoo the pigeons away. Why allow
Philips . . .'

'It isn't Philips,' she said, watching the birds from the
bathroom door. 'It's two sparrows.' The knocking had
stopped. 'They have been looking at me from that bough for
the last ten minutes.'

'Tell them we don't like Canadian sparrows.'

'It's no use. They don't know they're Canadian. Besides,
they can't help it.'

René, who was sitting at the table filling his pipe, showed
exasperation. He felt she never properly understood. 'Bread!'
he exclaimed. 'Ask them how the hell they think we can get
all that bread! Where from? Ask them. Say we're on relief.'

She looked at him. She had fetched some stale bread from
the kitchen. 'We soon shall be, if . . .'

'All right. But don't be blackmailed by a gang of sparrows.
They're too lazy to dig for worms. They prefer to sponge
on us.'

'Oh well . . .'

'They think they're romantic because they've got feathers.
Say you've got feathers too!' She put her bread down and
began to cry a little, softly and stupidly.

The knocking on the window began again. With this she had
a burst of crying, and sat down heavily. René rushed to the
window shouting,

'It's Philips! I can see him.'

He struggled with the window which would not move. He
ran back into the room and fetched the screwdriver they used
for that purpose and prised it open. The birds had flown away
and were watching him from the neighbouring trees and roof
gutters. There were not many, it was too cold. He gave vent
to an unfriendly roar in the icy air: then forced the window
down, with as much noise as possible.

His wife was weeping beside the pieces of stale bread. René
felt sorry, but he could not forgive his wife for not seeing
through these parasites, just because they had violet wings.

'I don't know where I can get the bread for Philips, upon
my word I don't,' he grumbled. 'I was a nickel out yesterday.
Three cents of that went for Brown and Philips and a gang of

common little gutter finches.—Don't cry.—They know you're
an English sucker. These bloody peasants wouldn't give them
a crumb. Let them go to ɟ...'

He stopped.

'I hear the gas-gun. . . . Not at this time in the morning!'

His wife got up, wiping her eyes.

A big fact in the Hotel Blundell was the Cockroach.—What
Hester had at first taken to be garden insects at last became
more numerous. Then one day Bess came in as usual and
asked, in an indifferent voice, whether the Hardings had seen
any cockroaches. No, they answered (for they were always
both there when Bess arrived to do the room). They had *read*
of ' 'roaches' in American stories, but they had never *seen* a
'roach. .

After that, however, they began looking out for the cockroach. And soon they became convinced that the 'garden
insects' were in fact cockroaches.

These animals began moving in on the Hardings in droves.
For, in other apartments, war was being made on them, and
they began crawling in to the only apartment where they were
not interfered with. So the Hardings complained to Bess,
and an insect spray was lent them. This was no use at
all. Apparently all over the Hotel—all over every hotel and
everywhere else, from the Market down town to the Drug-
store at the corner—they were swarming.

The cockroach (with diabetes, one of the national handicaps
of the North American Continent) is about the size of a
bed-bug, but elongated, lighter in colour, and speckled, with
a detachable pouch full of embryos which it throws away when
pursued. It exists equally in the bush and in cities.—There is
another kind, which is black, called the German variety. But
the reddish one is what one mainly sees.

About the time the Cockroach began to obsess the Hardings,
and all the Hotel, it also became a burning question throughout Momaco, and even in Ottawa, the capital city of Canada,
it closed government offices. Fifty girl clerks struck, because
these animals were running all over their typewriters and over
their clothes. So the department had to be shut down and
fumigated. .

In the Beverage Room downstairs, they were crawling up people's legs and getting in the beer. Customers were leaving to go to other Beverage Rooms. Mrs. Plant was extremely sensitive about anything that happened to her Beverage Room trade. She took steps accordingly.

A man arrived to demonstrate the use of the gas-gun. The Hardings were the people with the greatest collection of Cockroaches, so it was to the Hardings' apartment that he was brought, but he merely came to talk, not to deliver an attack upon the 'roaches. He told them how he had been all over the city, rescuing people from this pest. The City Hall was full of them. Only yesterday he had been asked to go to a Jewish workers' establishment, where the floor was so thick with them that you could not walk without treading on them; and when a girl was going to put a needle into a piece of cloth, she would put it through a cockroach first. The girls were screaming and weeping.

Then he produced the gas-gun. Since that time this instrument had been in use in the Hotel day and night. But Mrs. McAffie had especially interested herself in the destruction of these pests: and it was she who almost exclusively handled the gas-gun.

It was about ten minutes before Affie made her appearance. Now, as a personality, or visually at least, Affie was in two parts. There was the normal Affie that went about the house discharging her duties as manageress; and there was the hooded, rather sinister and witch-like figure who appeared, gas-gun in hand, and, after knocking at the door, this was the figure which entered the room, enquiring if they wished her to go into action, or whether she should come later on.

They had always up till now postponed a showdown with the 'roaches. They looked at one another, and they did not have to speak to reach agreement: both thought that a showdown with the 'roaches was overdue. René beckoned Affie in. They both of them proceeded to remove, or to place under cover, things like cooking utensils, crockery, toilet articles and the rest. Some were brought into the room, and others locked in cupboards. Then Affie entered the kitchen, and turned the gas-gun on the ceiling. It filled the whole apartment

with its acrid fumes, and within a few minutes hundreds of
cockroaches were pouring from the ceiling upon Affie's head
and shoulders. This continued for twenty minutes or half an
hour, as long in fact as cockroaches continued to appear from
crevices and hideouts all over the kitchen and bathroom,
and succumb to the fumes. The floor was carpeted with the
bodies of these insects. Many of them fell on the face of the
gunner, and her cheeks were also streaming with the poisonous
liquid. She appeared to be devoured by an insane itch for
destruction; it was personal, not at all a matter of duty. She
did not spare herself, but seemed rather to enjoy the tumbling
bodies of the vermin sticking to her face and hands, or
garments—her hair being protected by the hood.

Some of the insects escaped from the kitchen or bathroom;
and from time to time she would put down the gas-gun, and
hurry out in pursuit, crushing them with the heel of her shoe.
Stooping down, she would sometimes pick one up, and address
it in the following way: 'Ah ha, you threw off your bag did
you. You hoped to save your brood, did you! Your auntie was
too smart for you!' with which she would throw it down and
stamp on it.

René soon left the Room, and Hester followed him in a
few minutes. 'That woman is possessed,' he remarked, when
Hester joined him in the Beverage Room. 'It cannot be good
for her to breathe in all that stuff. She is the only person in the
Hotel who takes on the job, and if anyone else touches the gun
she gets very angry. What do you suppose is the matter with
her?'

When they returned to the Room a half-hour later, the dead
'roaches were being swept away, and René hurried over to
a window which he propped open. The icy air entered the
rooms, but even so it took a long time to expel this stink. Affie
vanished, and already she could be heard in a neighbouring
apartment, blasting away at the 'roaches.

CHAPTER XIV

The Patroness of Rotten Janitors

MRS. McAFFIE was their favourite figure. They· developed an affection for this flying wraith, with the faintly rouged cheeks, who dashed, flew and darted everywhere, as though she desired to·get rid of every remaining piece of flesh on·her bones. She was·tall and still enjoyed,·in the manner of an afterglow, a vanished grace. She was known ·as Affie in the Room, where she was a welcome apparition. The hooded figure with·the ·gas-gun was· Affie·in. a sinister rôle which troubled them a little bit.

Mrs.·McAffie·arrived in succession to Vera. In addition to being an addict of Aromatic Spirits of ·Ammonia, Vera was insolent, lazy, thievish, sly and bad tempered. She shot off.her mouth at Mrs. Plant one day, and that was when she left. Then Mrs. McAffie was hired and a spirit came into·the place which was of·a different texture—more volatile and sprightly than had been there before. Her age was unknown and unguessable. She endeared herself to René in one of their early conversations by the sincerity of her horror at the new war. 'They are`taking our boys,' she said in an undertone, as if speaking to herself and the fact that·her eyes were dry was only because anger dried them up. 'They are taking our boys *again.*'

Affie took no tips. She was the only decent person who ever found her way, or his way, into the Hotel Blundell. And she paid for it.

When Affie read the ·tea-cups once, René,, who liked her, ·succeeded in thrusting a· dollar bill down ·between her shrivelled breasts, and · she ran hooting from ·the room. But when she saw that neither René nor· his·wife believed in her hypnotic assurances that they .should beware of a· dark man, or that· they would tread strange ground shortly, she refused to take ·another penny. She shot away, pawing the air, when he approached her with a dollar bill.

Affie had been married to an attorney in the long ago, dead some twenty years. She had acted as nurse-housekeeper. She had owned a shop up in the gold-mining country, where it is very cold. She came from a bush-city herself: but she had exceedingly bad man-trouble: heavy, incurable, starry-eyed man-trouble. Her old eyes sparkled, her old bones kindled at the touch of a male, and the male touched them as he was looking for money. Some personable deceiver had cheated her out of her nest-egg up in the gold-country. Her shop in Timmins was hers no longer. She often sat crouched at the telephone, in the zero weather, brooding. Her dream-man had spat on her old heart. When the glass went down to zero, the old wound hurt: she rocked herself in the lonely lounge. Naturally she did go on losing any weight she had, as she rushed like a witch all over the Hotel—carrying towels or sheets, or just running for the sake of running after her shadow.

When she slapped the face of the young punch-drunk janitor, she flew up the stairs, screeching and croaking with glee. The janitor was ten seconds behind her on the annexe landing. She had vanished with a hoarse cackle.—The Hardings heard the indignant roar of the alcoholic pugilist, a few feet from their door: 'Come down here, you bloody old cow, Missis McAffie, and I'll wring your f—— neck!'—Silence. She had adroitly evaporated. When Affie and her colleague Miss Toole retired to the bathroom, and she dyed Miss Toole's hair a most unreal brassy gold, and Miss Toole did the same for her in a dark brown, Affie, with her cheeks rouged and lips painted, looked for a while a not uncomely scarecrow, with the shawl held tight round her shoulders to keep warm, standing and smiling at the Hardings' door, on which she had tapped, presenting herself like a child who had dressed herself up in her grandmother's clothes—she having of course borrowed the bloom from the cheeks of a granddaughter, and stolen the brown tresses. She stood, tall, genteel, and at bottom severe, with the smile of a naughty girl who had been at the dye-bottle with her little pal Molly Toole.

Affie is the nearest approach in Canada to the decayed gentlewoman. Affie certainly had decayed. And subsequently it was proved that she had in fact dwelt among the genteel, as a respected attorney's lady, in Ottawa. She had enjoyed the amenities. As 'well-bred', she beyond doubt still regarded herself.

Affie was a bad influence in the Hotel. She was so cheerfully and openly on the side of copulation—in spite of her respectable and even outwardly solemn appearance—no matter who were to be the performers: she cried in her heart with King Lear 'let copulation thrive!'—that she would rent the rooms preferably to women who could be depended on to use them for that purpose, and turn away people whom she felt had leanings to virtue, though otherwise more desirable tenants. The Hotel as a consequence, in the 'transients' section, was in a state of chronic disorder.

This suited Mrs. Plant, however, since people would pay several dollars more to use the apartments for acts of discreet prostitution than for less Babylonish purposes. Thus it was that when two French-Canadian civilians came in with girls with over-bright eyes, asking for a room for the four for a week, they were given the room above the Hardings. This had never happened before; always they had had peaceable overhead neighbours.

For a week the Hardings slept little. Loud intoxicated talk of four unbridled mouths, bottles falling, feet scraping, followed by the heavy rhythmic crunch and thump of beds, a truly French-canadian crisis producing a furious pounding up and down, succeeded by an alligator quiet: the night-long periodic flushing of the toilet, and procession of bare-feet—sleep was impossible. They knew they had to thank Affie for this, and a coolness ensued.

But this unusual woman was not only the protector of harlots: she was the patroness likewise of rotten janitors. There was one, young, baldish, genteel-spoken—a bank clerk, a white-collar out-of-work. Affie called him 'Sonny-boy': said he looked like a boy she once knew.—*Was* she faithful to her memories? That antique casket of her heart exuded a strong nostalgic perfume. The more well-deserved hatred he aroused in the Hotel, the more passionately she protected him:

Sonny-boy omitted to stoke the furnace. The guests were stark with cold in their rooms, while he lay in a stupor induced by mixing brandy, port wine and beer. When sober he could not fix a fused light or put a washer on a faucet, let alone restart an element that had ceased to give off heat. But he stopped a long while in the Hotel. 'I have a privileged position;' he announced to one of the maids, who tried to move him off the bed in a guest's room where he had gone for a nap. Affie shielded Sonny-boy truly and faithfully, until Mrs. Plant sent for the police and had him ejected, screaming imprecations over the shoulders of the policeman.

These are two examples of the way in which Affie was bad. She did no good to the Hotel, but then Mrs. Plant didn't either. The latter lady liked young and inefficient janitors too, up to a point; showed remarkable distaste for industrious or sober ones. She only liked old janitors if they drank. Then she would just as soon have them as young ones.

The Hotel was a matriarchate, as is America, run by what Affie called the 'First Lady'—or sometimes the 'Leading Lady'—Mrs. Plant, its owner, and her attendant ladies, including a couple of Scottish maids, with impressive Glasgow accents.

There was a guest, as has already been mentioned, named Mr. Martin, who had been there some time, and had, apparently, a pipe-line to the proprietress. Whether this little Englishman had, in the past, stood (however unbelievable) in a tender relationship with the big jamaican proprietress, it is impossible to say, but there he was, in an apartment not far from hers, as one who could be appealed to in her absence. He did not much enjoy all of these privileges for, on one occasion, he observed, in confidence to René, 'I *can* fix a washer or a fuse *of course*, but if I did they'd never let me alone.'

This group of women, all except Katie, the old Scottish maid, were not repelled by the criminal classes. They accepted them on equal terms with other guests, and if the police descended on them at night, that was the business of the police

and the criminals, nobody else's. So there were criminals.
Apart from the fearful noise the police made at night, yelling
'Open up—the police!' as they hammered on the malefactors'
door, the Hardings found the large family of criminals, one
enceinte, the quietest people in the house. They never fought,
they never drank too much.

Affie thought that, as it takes all-sorts to make a world, and
as a hotel was a microcosm, one should have one's criminal
element. But since her main interests lay in the direction of
the sexual impulses, there were always far more followers
of Aphrodite, than there ever were picklocks and motor-car
thieves in the Blundell.

The Hotel Blundell was just an ordinary Canadian
Hotel. It was not a brothel like the Plaza or Marlborough
in the next street, and was less spectacularly unvirtuous
than the first-class hotel on the waterfront: the King
George.

All Canadian hotels had been for a long time drinking-dens.
This could not be otherwise, for the only place a Canadian
business man could drink the whisky all his ancestors drank
was in a hotel room. 'Hard liquor' was not sold for consumption in public: but it was sold at the government shops, called
Liquor Control Stores, in bottle. As the bottles cannot be
taken home and drunk there—to this most women object—it
is drunk in hotel-bedrooms. Harry Martin had an old friend
called Mulligan, who was the president of a big concern. He
was a very big man, clothed like a big shot, with the big
bullying voice and glassy eye of a tycoon. He came sailing in
every six weeks or so (the times varied) with a nurse in
attendance. He went to bed at once, and there he drank for a
week.

During these periods Mr. Martin and the nurse moved
cautiously in and out of the room, as if they were waiting upon
a sick man. He never left the bed—except to knock the nurse
down if she absented herself for too long. He urinated and
defecated in the bed, and the sheets were removed, rolled up
and burnt in the furnace. He also relieved himself in this way
in the bath.

One day the nurse would be seen no more, the bout was at

an end, and the president was back in his office, sober till the
next spasm arrived.

This was the only example in this small second-class hotel of
how the big shot lives, but it was typical of what went on in
thousands of rooms and suites all over Canada. It was (and
perhaps is) a product of Methodism, with its edicts against
pleasures that are taken for granted everywhere else, except
parts of the United States. The more expensive, or as it is
called 'exclusive', hotel is where the business man keeps
his mistress. At the King George Hotel a Mr. Cox, the vice-
president of a very large corporation—known in the first phase
of their stay at Momaco to the Hardings—lived with a floozy
of old standing. They had been there together for so long that
this had become his real home. He only was at his official
home, with the 'Mrs. Cox' of the telephone book, on
Thursday. At first you might be surprised that Mrs. Cox only
invited you to dinner on Thursdays, until you were put wise
to the true situation.—If you got to know Mr. Cox really well,
you were asked to partake of a very much more agreeable
dinner at the King George. And it was a far greater honour to
be asked to the King George on Tuesday or Friday, than to
the Cox home on Thursday.

When first in Momaco the Hardings stopped at the King
George. The first hint they had of what lay beneath the
methodist surface of Canadian life, in the dominion—the
formidable sabbaths, the wholesale restrictions on everything
that is agreeable or convenient, even taxicabs—was as they
left their room the first morning, and walked along to the
elevator. A door was open leading into a large room: upon a
bulky sideboard were ranged scores of large and small bottles
and decanters, comprising every form of spirit and liqueur
known to man. Both Mr. and Mrs. Harding stopped, licked
their lips, and passed on, laughing.

'Some cellar!' said René, using Winston Churchill's favourite
and typically out-of-date Americanism. At that time René did
not know, any more than his illustrious leader, that Americans
no longer said 'some' this and 'some' that.

'A cellar in a very exposed position,' Hester remarked.

'Exhibitionism, I presume.' René shrugged his shoulders. A

couple of moronic business sub-men passed them, and they saw that they entered the open door. They eyed René and his wife, in their English clothes, with dull, bold dislike.

What struck the Hardings most about these amazing *moeurs* was the way such things were reacted to by all these women, as much as by everybody else.

That, both René and his wife felt, was the proper manner —irresponsible detachment. Life was for Affie and Madame Plant a cinema performance. A violent performance. If it had no *kick* it would after all be dull. They disapproved of any kind of sobriety or restraint. That René did not beat up his wife, or was not seen drunk every night, was not in his favour. His irreproachable behaviour as a guest would be registered against him.

So these were the backgrounds of Affie, to which we shall shortly return. However, she was mischievous, but not inhuman. What René objected to in the American system—a modified form of which exists in Canada—was its inhumanity. They had got involved in a violent and unintelligent dance, in which all reference to the happiness and interests of the human individual had been abandoned.—In Canada, as in the States, Prohibition had been imposed upon a docile people. An absurd religion, the last of Puritanism, was accepted by them: it drove them out of their homes into hotels to find some natural relief. This could not happen in France. Even in Russia, with its revolutionary restrictions, the sale of spirits was not forbidden.

CHAPTER XV

The Marvels of Momaco

THE Monday after Affie's gas-gun fury they were numbed by a letter from home. England had been becoming farther and farther away until it was, at times, hardly real. Percy Lamport was in another dimension: and René's mother had grown to be little more than a picture of an old lady in a chair. When they received a letter from Mary, or even from Helen, it was as though they were on Mars and they knew that the denizens of earth were attempting to contact them. But they, on their side, were only able to respond very feebly to these messages across interstellar space. A difference existed naturally between Hester's reactions and René's: she did attempt to respond, sometimes, with the same eagerness as was shown by those who wrote to her. At other times she felt that it was impossible to find anything whatever to say.

The present letter was from Mary, and it went on describing things that were of importance to people over there, but about which they had scarcely the energy to think. Why did Mary assume that nothing had changed? Everything had changed so completely that the scene she wrote about appeared pallid and meaningless. She and Percy now lived about half-way between London and Oxford. Janet and Victor were still in London—had not the money to be anywhere else. But what had uprooted and changed the life of René had upset the life of the Lamports too. When the exile thought of London, it was of the old London.

Another, and very important, factor in making a receipt of a letter from 'home' so unpleasant, was that René simply could not imagine himself ever living in England again: for him England became dimmer and dimmer *for ever*. Letters, from people who had once been so dear to him, but who seemed to have no understanding of the fact that they inhabited the past (which was the same thing as a demise), letters of this kind were not pleasant breakfast-time reading. They darkened the day. A letter from René's mother was worst of all, for there all the past of his filial affection put up a fight against his relentless scepticism re the maternal.

So things began badly that morning, and René found it difficult to write an article, which it was urgent and necessary to finish. Having been plunged from university life in a great European capital, with an awful suddenness, into life in this barren abstraction of the Room (worse, of course, than had it been any tolerable occupation, or even such an occupation as a truck-driver or newspaper reporter) his personality had suffered profoundly. All freedom depended upon consciousness: but now, at times, he felt his brain clouding and blurring. His daily periods of semi-consciousness increased. It was as *dreaminess* that he thought of the semi-conscious spells, and indeed that was often what they were. More and more the 'waking hours' were rather patches of semi-consciousness than a continuous wakefulness. Or full awareness. Then one day he would not wake up at all, he told himself. He would just get out of bed at the usual time, and his life, on a far more primitive level, that of the functional coma of the animal world, would go on as the polar bear does, or the ant. So a great experiment would have come to an end.

The problems of consciousness had often preoccupied René: he thought of it as enlightenment, as a light unaccountably breaking in upon a darkness, and the mind born with this light modifying the creatures affected by it. In other words, men. He estimated that we were perhaps rather more than half-way across that, in geological terms, infinitely brief era of 'enlightenment'. Men, he felt, were *less* enlightened than they had been.—Slowly men awakened from the sleep of nature, or recovered from the madness of nature, as René preferred to say. Man had begun to look around him, once the dazzling light had been thrown upon his surroundings; and he saw where he was, though *why* he was there he could not imagine. Finally he discovered he was riding an immense ball—dashing around in a cold, black emptiness—which was warmed by a much larger, extremely hot ball. All this was a great deal more than the polar bear or the monkey knew.

The polar bear was mad, he was obsessed with being a polar bear: and many men were pretty mad also, incapable of looking at themselves from the outside. No one could imagine why man had abstracted himself and acquired the sanity of consciousness; why he had gone sane in the midst of a madhouse of functional character.—And History: with that, René's central tragedy was reached. History, such as is worth recording, is about the passion of men to stop sane. Most History so-called is the bloody catalogue of their backslidings. Such was René's unalterable position.

So, locked up in this Room, or as good as, for years on end, he felt the light not losing its intensity, but getting patchy. He knew he could not go on indefinitely living in this way without returning to the functional darkness, it was only a matter of time. As now he sat with his writing-pad on his knee, assiduously scribbling, and dropping the product into the wooden tray at his side, his awareness was at a low ebb; for what he was writing did not interest him (it was bread-and-butter work of a pretty awful kind). This ant-like work was interrupted by the entrance of the scottish maid Bessie, or Bess, as they called her. He laid aside his work, stretched back in his chair, and said, 'Well, Bess, what's cookin'?'

'Another nit-wit,' she announced, as was her custom: and they knew that another weak-minded person, in one of the neighbouring apartments, had outraged her scottish good sense. The small, malformed, spectacled, glaswegian hotel-slavey squinted up with humorous toleration at her bearded fellow-countryman—and the fellow-countryman side of it was important. For Bess never for a moment forgot that she was a stranger in this country, and her tongue was turned against all its inhabitants, and especially those in the Hotel Blundell. When her father and mother first came to Canada they rented a house in Momaco. For twenty years no one in the street addressed a word to them: they were all Canadians. Then the people in the house across the way left, and new people moved into it. To her mother's amazement the new tenants spoke to her one morning. They were Scotch. When Bess crossed the Atlantic to join her parents, experiences analogous to this were her lot likewise, and, outside the Hotel, she spent all her spare-time with scottish immigrants.

The nit-wits who came to lodge in this Hotel were innumerable: for every morning Bess had a new nit-wit to announce to the Hardings. But this was Monday morning; she entered the room with clean sheets and pillow-cases, and swollen with a sense of accumulated wrongs—as though on Sunday all the slights of the week had time to mobilize and solidly invest her in her lonely room, following her into church and acting as a pressure-group in the rear of her prayers. On Monday morning she worked off these humours, as she passed from apartment to apartment. She felt almost light-hearted as she reached the end of the third-floor apartments of the annexe. The Hardings inhabited the first apartment to be visited on the second floor.

The nit-wittery would consist of anything, from an enquiry as to whether Scotland was an island, to the nearest way to the Momaco hospital for diseases of the throat. A guest only had to open his or her mouth in Bessie's presence to betray half-wittedness. Then she also was a disseminator of scandal. Far more diligently than any bee transports its pollen, Bess collected and distributed information of a scandalous nature. René squeezed her dry of the morning's quota, and she always left the Hardings' apartment with a sense of being appreciated, and of having blackened someone's reputation. Both René and Hester understood quite well that they were not immune, and that 'those English nit-wits in no. 27A' formed part of her repertoire; but they always welcomed her appearance at about ten-thirty in the morning. Between Affie and Bess no love was lost: the latter took every opportunity of informing Mrs. Plant of any misdemeanour of Affie's that came to her notice, and always endeavoured to be the first to draw Mrs. Plant's attention to scandalous happenings, before Affie got a chance of doing so.

After the Bess interlude René laboured until lunch-time, Hester washing-up, attending to a rudimentary toilet, feeding the sparrows, and reading a library-book. After lunch René fixed the alarm on the clock, and they lay down on the settee for some more oblivion. They were awakened by the clock in time to prepare themselves for an unusual event. Someone was coming to tea.

The visitor they were expecting was Mr. Herbert Starr; and it was in the following way that a fraternity which they would never have expected Momaco to conceal became known to them. It was just after Easter of the year 1941, and Hester and René had taken off their overshoes for the first time that year, and went out to the market. They had for long known that Momaco was the never-never land, was the living-death, the genuine blank-of-blanks out of which no speck of pleasantness or civilized life could come. They moved disconsolately down the street side by side without speaking. René's lustreless eye, for the thousandth time, spelled out the words 'BINGO! Eight o'clock tonight' upon the notice-board in front of the Boer War Veterans' Club. A Boer War veteran hobbled down the path beside the budding shrubbery towards the gothic door of the club. This old man had been a springy young khaki warrior once, with a brand-new bayonet, gone to fight for gold and .diamonds. An 'absent-minded beggar'. Oh, God, oh, Momaco (and Magersfontein)! The Canadian sun shone with its deceptive brilliance, for it was not over-warm, as the veteran faded into the gingerbread gothic.

But everything was not dispirited and listless in Momaco. For suddenly overtaking him a figure swung past with swaying hips, and a violent arm sawing the air at his side, with little finger stiffly erect, having separated itself from the other fingers. A *man*: a fairy-man.

René felt a glow, as if a leprechaun had declared its presence when least expected. Civilization after all existed here: how eccentric to be so flaunting a fairy in such a region as this— he might have come swaying and mincing out of the pages of Proust. . . . Proust! Proust in Upper Canada: what a violent conjunction of images, he thought. Never the twain shall meet, one would say, of this chilliest, dullest West and that most civilized and urban East. How would Monsieur Charlus's lungs be able to breathe the air of Ontario?

René was quite cheered up by this. The sting had been taken out of 'Bingo'. As a prisoner whose cell is suddenly invaded by a mouse or rat will regard this animal with tenderness, as a link with the past, so he followed, amused and encouraged, the swinging hips, the single arm that sawed majestically up and down, employed for dainty but headlong propulsion.

He found that this fairy haunted the Beverage Room of the Hotel Lafitte. His hunting-ground was not among the cockroaches of Mrs. Plant's saloon. The other hotel, although french-canadian, had a much cleaner drinking place, with a better type of soldier.

A little later, perhaps three weeks later than this, he had gone down to a jewish newstand and shop that sold English and American papers, the only place in Momaco where such exotics were to be met with. There he was accosted by Starr.

Starr introduced himself as a mutual friend of a Glasgow intellectual, who had been given an official job in Ottawa. Starr said he had intended to write to René Harding, and suggest a meeting. Since then he had learned of his presence in Momaco, but *now* this most auspicious encounter meant, he trusted, that René would do him the honour to have lunch with him. He, Starr, would appoint himself the guide of Professor Harding in Momaco.—Was Momaco not *dull?* Why no. It was the most wildly exciting place probably in America or anywhere. But he would reveal to René the secrets of Momaco: and make known to him a number of people, of very extraordinary interest and charm.—Oh no, dull was *not* a word that could be applied to Momaco.

René's curiosity was mildly aroused, but not enough to prolong this conversation any longer than necessary. During a period of eighteen months Mr. Starr had been encountered mainly in bookshops, perhaps a half-dozen times. René had never admitted this anything but attractive little man behind his social defences. There was a certain event, coming at long last, which very slightly endeared Mr. Starr to him; but it was not until this December of the following year that he so far weakened that he had invited this queer little object to tea.

It was with no delightful anticipation that Hester and René dragged themselves from their siesta a half-hour before the established time, to act as hosts. As it was, it was a rather hurried marshalling of the cups and saucers, and arranging of the company-biscuits upon a plate was only just in place, and Hester's face powdered, when there was a gentle tap upon the door. Herbert Starr made his entrance, smiling and sidling, and all but kissed Hester's hand as he bent over it, saying to René as he stood up, 'Mrs. Harding and I have already met—unknown to her' (with an arch flutter of eyelashes in Hester's direction). 'It was a few weeks ago in a bookshop—I wonder if you remember, Mrs. Harding? We both wanted to look at *Salammbo* at the same time, but I relinquished it, observing, 'I will wait until you have finished with Carthage.' Do you remember?'

'Oh yes, I remember that very well,' Hester laughed. 'I thought it was extremely civil of you. I did not keep you out of Carthage for very long.'

'You did not—and I thought that very, very civil of *you*.'

Mr. Starr slipped smoothly into the chair indicated by René.

'Well, now you are going to lift the veil, aren't you, on Momaco?'

'Yes.' Starr was completely bald, except above the ears, and his ears seemed to cling back against his head, as the ears of dogs do when abashed or guilty. He smiled and smiled and nodded.

'It is a strangely interesting place, is it not, Mr. Starr?'

'Wildly—fantastically—interesting!'

'Has it always been interesting?' enquired Hester.

'Always? It is one of those places where you have to have a guide. I shall be your guide, and I shall make you acquainted with the most entrancing people. It will be a revelation to you both. I wish I had met you before, for it must have been very dull for you. I am so sorry.—But we will start tomorrow.'

'As soon as that?' René enquired, smiling. 'I am busy tomorrow.'

'Well, the next day.'

René and his wife laughed.

'Count me out,' said Hester. 'I am room-ridden. One says bed-ridden; why shouldn't one say room-ridden? I am room-ridden.'

'But how terrible!' protested Mr. Starr, with smiling politeness. 'Would not your physician allow you to go abroad, to have dinner with a woman who is probably the most intelligent person in Momaco?'

'I'm afraid not. His name is Dr. Fell. He has prescribed *this room* and I have got so used to it, I am afraid I should feel strange outside it now.'

'But how perfectly terrible.'

'I thought so at first. But it is amazing what one can get used to.'

'Oh dear!' Mr. Starr still smiled, but his smile was full of polite pain.

'I have my family of squirrels. They are the only people in Momaco who do not mind my being English.'

'English! But that is absurd. To go no farther, there are the Daughters of Empire . . .'

René laughed.

'Yes, there are the Daughters of Empire!' He turned to Hester. 'I will take a peek at one of these human marvels of Mr. Starr's.'

'You are laughing at me,' said Mr. Starr. 'But marvels they are.'

At length it was arranged that René should meet Mr. Starr at a restaurant for lunch, to make the acquaintance of one of Mr. Starr's marvels. She was a Mrs. Glanz. Her husband was a Buffalo German, and of course she was rich.

All Mr. Starr's friends were women, and all rich. He had once, twenty years before, been in New York. But a rich man left him there very suddenly with only a season ticket for a box at the Opera and no money. Since he had grown bald he had nestled in the lap of wealthy old women, whom he apparently drenched in a scented torrent of flattery, poured equally over their faces and their minds. But *he* was of humble origin: his brother was a workman, he revealed. It was wonderful, he said, how he went about in the most exclusive circles.

'If Mrs. Moir only knew,' he told them. 'But they think I am like themselves.'

At eleven-thirty, an hour before the luncheon engagement, Starr telephoned. He said Mrs. Glanz had started.

'How do you mean?' asked René.

'She has just left.'

'Left where?'

'Oh, she lives rather a long way off. Four miles.'

'It won't take her an hour to move four miles,' René objected.

But Mr. Starr was evasive or at least confused.

'But I believe, I certainly believe, she will be there.'

René remained silent.

Mr. Starr burst into a suppressed cough. 'You must really excuse me, Professor Harding, I get this occasionally. I have been lying down.'

'Not well?'

'I am quite well, thanks,' Mr. Starr said hurriedly, 'but I have these attacks. I hope you won't mind, but I have asked Charles Brooks to go to the restaurant and meet the woman, and introduce you.'

'So you will not be there yourself?'

Mr. Starr had a fit of shrill coughing.

Charles Brooks, according to Mr. Starr, was an Englishman, who worked in a publisher's office and wrote plays himself. René had not met him: so at one o'clock he telephoned the restaurant, asked for Mr. Brooks, and told him he was prevented from coming to lunch. To make his excuses to the lady.

'I don't know if I shall recognize her,' Brooks said.

'Why, don't you know her?'

'Never seen her in my life.'

René banged down the instrument and told Hester what had happened. Instead of Mr. Starr, there was a certain Charles Brooks (presumably gone there at Mr. Starr's request) waiting in the restaurant for a woman he had never seen, and therefore would be unable to recognize. In any case, from Mr. Starr's evasive and disjointed remarks, it did not seem likely that this unknown lady would be at the restaurant. 'I was right, you see, he said.

They discussed this further piece of Momacoishness with

some disgust. René knew it was his fault. Both he and Hester had scrutinized Mr. Starr, sceptically and derisively. From such a figure nothing could be expected but nonsense. He had not the money, anyway, to take people out to restaurants. Still, it was just more and more of Momaco.

'I have asked Brooks around this evening to have a drink,' René told her. 'He seems a fairly rational person. He *is* English.'

He found Brooks in the Beverage Room at the appointed time. He was a stocky, dark and fattish fellow about thirty-six. René's *Secret History of World War II* he had read, and appeared to know a good deal about him. He was a not unattractive man, frank and well behaved: with René's permission, he would put him in touch with a wealthy friend of his—it might serve to relieve the social monotony of Momaco. He then went on to describe the friend.

Mrs. Stevenson was a married woman (her husband stationed in England). She was his mistress. She had a daughter of eighteen, who was very beautiful. This bewitching young lady cried herself to sleep every night.

'Nothing between you and the daughter?' René said, frowning. He felt sure that there was something between him and the daughter, and possibly half a dozen other women. 'Certainly!' Brooks answered firmly and incisively. 'I have slept with her too.' But was it necessary to inform him about all this copulation, so soon after they had met, and in connection with an invitation to Hester and himself to be made acquainted with these persons?

'I see,' René observed drily. 'They appear to be most desirable acquaintances.' He gazed at this Cricklewood Casanova with a somewhat cold curiosity.

'Women like that, who have all the money in the world, are as easy as anything. I confine myself to them.'

'A capital plan.'

'None of those girls in Mansfield's [the large department store] would get on her back, you'd be fooling around for months.'

'I suppose so.'

Brooks had of course noticed that a certain displeasure

8

had replaced René's original affability. At this point he said,
'I hope you understand, Professor Harding, that I should
not suggest a *serious introduction* to such a woman as Mrs.
Stevenson. I even feel that I ought not to suggest that your
wife . . .'

'No, it is all right, my wife has become hardened to
anything in this place.'

'Oh, I am glad. I thought you might be rather bored. And
these people are quite indecently rich.'

'That is as it should be.' There was a short silence.

'Well, when shall I arrange for the party?' Brooks asked
briskly. 'Practically any evening you like. I am with her every
night, I can arrange it how you like. Would you prefer a big
party; four hundred people? She often throws big parties. It's
an enormous penthouse. She loves it. Or shall we make it a
smaller party? Some interesting people, that sort of thing.'

'It's as you like,' said René.

Some evenings later, Mr. Starr put in an appearance, his
ears pressed back on the side of his head. Brooks apparently
was not well. Nothing much: well, it was kidney trouble.
René burst into a 'belly-laugh'.

'I am not surprised,' he said.

But Mr. Starr had an aversion to direct references to
anything sexual.

'Brooks says, "You must rescue the Hardings socially."
Well, I have arranged that you should meet *Mrs. Moir.*'

Mrs. Moir was his Dulcinea. Mr. Starr had never spoken to
her, except once. A few words. But when he was at a party
Mrs. Moir was conscious of him all the time. He saw it. He
knew it. She wished to speak to him. They did, in effect,
telepathically converse.—*She* was one of the Marvels of
Momaco.

At Mrs. Taylor's—that was where they would meet Mrs.
Moir.—However, some weeks later he dropped in and said he
had not been able to get Mrs. Taylor going. Though she was
very rich she had complained that to entertain the Hardings
would cost fifteen dollars, Mr. Starr told them (they began
looking at him more and more disagreeably). She had totted
up the main items. There would be a little wine; then she

would have to hire a maid; there were many other things, such as tomato soup, which stood between the Hardings and a visit to Mrs. Taylor.

Hester got up, and saying that she must go down and try to find Affie, she left the room.

René scrutinized his visitor carefully, and he considered getting up, opening the door, and shooing him out. But instead he threw his head back disgustedly and yawned. What a ham! What an insulting old fairy, pack full of fairy malice. Ugh!

But Mr. Starr was very apologetic. Some severe things passed his lips with reference to Mrs. Taylor's parsimony. Mrs. Taylor was not a *Marvel* herself, though one of the charmed circle.

All these Marvels crumbled into dust, however, in spite of the intense genteelness of the conjurer. The fact that he had rather brutally recounted his squalid interview with old Mrs. Taylor—for he now mentioned that she was seventy years old, suggesting this as a sort of excuse—showed that he recognized that that comedy was finished. *This* sweet-scented manuscript was closed—though to life in general still clung the same cloying perfume, inseparable from the act of living with this Proust-drunken parlour-treader. Thenceforth the Marvels were not mentioned.

But Mr. Starr felt unmasked. A slightly nasty glint came into his eye. Hester returned, looked down at Mr. Starr, hesitated, and then sat down as before. Mr. Starr almost immediately took his leave. He did so with great dignity, as if he had been in some way offended, but was determined to take no notice of it. Hester was not looking in his direction during this ceremonious leave-taking. 'Must we continue to see that dreadful little man?' Hester asked rather angrily. 'He is making fools of us, in the way all these beastly people do if they get a chance. I do really think that we might dispense with his visits.'

'Yes, let's do that. The only reason I have gone on seeing him is that he is so comic.'

'Yes, I know he is *comic*. . . .'

In spite of this, when a discreet tap came at the door a few weeks later, they let him in, laughing at him as they said 'Sit down.' They were rewarded by further information about this remarkable little bald fairy. In the course of quite a long talk they learned that as 'Lord Herbert' he carried on a correspondence with a lady (a socialite in Montreal who was quite unknown to him. He addressed her in his letters as 'Lady Louise'.

René wondered how many of these transplanted domestics bestowed upon themselves titles of nobility, for certainly Herbert was not the only noble lord in Momaco: he was shown one of these missives which Lord Herbert had just composed. It ran as follows. 'Dear Lady Louise,' it began. 'How your last letter intrigued me—I could see your eyes moving as I read it, your very beautiful veiled eyes full of secrets. Your lips had a queer dear smile, as if you knew that I was watching you. I always watch you as I read what you write. There is a perfume in the words you choose. Did you know words secreted perfumes? They do. No one else arranges words that way. They are as personal to you as your arms or your hair.'

René tossed it back to Mr. Starr.

'Lord Herbert, you are a fair deceiver!'

'Not at all.—I make such money as my simple tastes demand by writing slogan pieces for Mansfield's. It's second nature with me to write like that. I think like that.'

'I often wondered, Mr. Starr, how you made your living,' Hester remarked, looking at his exposed scalp, though he was still a very dapper man—gnawing at forty perhaps, or else fighting stubbornly with the early forties themselves, the first and toughest, as only a fairy can fight.

He gave her a darting smile of recognition, and breathed softly at her

'Mee-owww!'

At his first visit it was soon apparent to René that Proust was the bible of Mr. Herbert Starr. He had peopled Momaco with Proustian figures. Mrs. Moir, or Mrs. Taylor, or Mrs. Baker, or Mrs. Glanz would be cast for the rôle of the Duchesse de Guermantes, or Madame de Marsantes. He had transformed Momaco so thoroughly that it was unquestionably, for him, a marvellous place, inhabited by diaphanous, secretly enamoured *grandes dames.* But it was, perhaps, merely a sideline of an advertisement-man which no one was intended to take seriously, any more than his literature on behalf of Mansfield's Department Store. But his proustian intoxication was a real thing at least. He lived himself in a proustian world, but he did not expect other people to follow him into it, however much he might mouth about it.

However much he may have got in René's hair, there was one person to whom Mr. Starr had introduced him who proved to be of some use. This was a figure which did not crumble into dust the moment you went in quest of it. This one feather in Mr. Starr's cap will be produced in the sequel.

CHAPTER XVI

The Word 'Brute' is not liked in the Beverage Room

RENÉ had a chat wtih Jim Greevy soon after he became a manager of the Beverage Room; he was standing in the reception desk for some reason, and displayed a beautiful black eye. But his expression was very disagreeable; it was obvious that he did not at all relish this manly discoloration.

'See this?' he growled. 'I got that doing my duty, Mr. Harding. For the *last time*. Would Mrs. Plant buy me a new pair of spectacles if these were stamped on? No. Mrs. Plant is not that sort of woman. I confine myself in future to taking the money. They can break up the whole blooming place as far as I'm concerned.' (He pointed to his eye.) 'A dirty little trouble-maker I had no option but to push out. As gentlemanlike as possible. As I turned to go back, what did the little bastard do but come up behind and land me this shiner. By great good luck, my glasses wasn't on my nose. Yes, Mr. Harding, if Mrs. Plant wants a bouncer she will have to hire one. *I* am not applying. I shall say to the boys tonight, "I am here to take your money. If you want to break · up the dratted place, it's okay with me. Pay no attention to me. *I'm neutral"*.'

Jim, of course, had his excellent reasons for wishing to remain where he was. All Mrs. Plant's Beverage Room managers robbed her, and Jim was no exception. But he was a serious, stocky, thick grey-haired, respectable fellow, liked by René: and Jim was the arch-neutral upon the nightly battlefield where he worked; a militant abstainer from intervention.

Momaco was a city without a theatre. It had the regulation number of cinemas; but these ran the repulsive average Hollywood Film, and were of no use to the Hardings. No French, Russian, German film was ever shown anywhere and so there were no spectacles to attract them out of their Room. From the café angle Momaco was even inferior to London, which has its Café Royal. Perhaps once a fortnight it had been their habit to pass an hour or so in the deplorable Beverage Room. They dropped down about six in the evening.

Later the Beverage Room was a place where one spoke with the voice of a giant, and, when contradicted by another giant, drove his tusks down his throat or stamped with hobnailed boots upon his talking-box. Either way, by heel or fist, contradiction, henceforth, was made impossible. With wassail came song. The songs, of nasal passion, cut by hiccups.

Many giants were khakied legionaries. But little young men were also fierce. René had stood and watched one night the bright-lit mouth of their drinking den. Six hot young men, five hatted ones—one was hatless and expostulatory. The bright light was on his flushed face, his young eyes flashing, his bitter red mouth making a bitter meal of hot words. He spat his protests at the five hatted ones—for René five black backs —and blood from between his teeth was spat out too.—One by one the hatted five smacked him in the mouth with a fist. The mouth bleeding, the eyes angry, the handsome face continued to expostulate. The hot words,' from the curled-up blood-filled mouth, kept on streaming out, a tragic fountain of rationality. These were clerks, not giants, but they liked argument no less than giants.

Beverage Room was a euphemism for Beer Parlour. Only beer was to be bought there, but the drinkers had bottles in their pockets, ranging from Niagara wine to methylated spirits. These were poured into the beer. The limbs of the giants were filled with fire, and the fire hardened in their fingers as they curled into a fist as homicidal as a revolver; or relaxed to use the finger-tips for an alcoholic caress.

From nine onwards, anyway, the Beverage Room was an ear-blasting resort of homo stultus at his most alcoholic. So, as usual, on the present occasion (the day following the visit of Mr. Starr), René and Hester went down to have a drink about six o'clock. René, like most consumers of 'Beverage', had a bottle in his pocket, which was Beverage, too, but not of the kind that might be publicly consumed in English Canada. It was Scotch. As soon as their beers were brought them by Jim, they were spiked by René; Hester permitting a little spiking of her first glass, just to be sociable. She loathed the mixture from the bottom of her heart. They clinked their glasses, and drank to Momaco suffering a similar fate to the Cities of the Plain. The place was unusually full for six o'clock. The hour for the gigantism of the North American was not yet in evidence. Giants there were already, big fleshly chaps, but not yet at the stage when they felt five times as big as they were.

René's personality suffered the routine inflation of those who spike their beer. Hester almost forgot Momaco, as René imagined for her the demise of Mr. Starr; and how, since he had been a good little fairy, going to a Starrish heaven, he would find himself in the salon of Madame de Villeparisis, the 'little old monkey'. At last the real thing! But there would be disenchantment. The performers would seem too violent, the women too carnal (like a lot of Jewesses, with the voices of men), and the wit, like the scent, would be too violent. Mr. Starr, deafened and stunned, would creep away, and without too much difficulty introduce himself into Madame de Villeparisis' boudoir; lie down upon a chaise-longue and, curled up like a little dog, *a tired* little pet doggie, he would dream of Mrs. Moir and of Mrs. Taylor, and the imaginary St. Germain upon the hill at Momaco. In that insipid make-believe, with the soft growl of Canadian voices, he was back in his earthly heaven—much to be preferred to the glare and rattle of the real thing, and the hard scintillation of the gallic wit.

Both René and Hester were shouting with laughter, the image of the shabby little pansy, with his hairless skull and dirty white silk scarf, curled up in the boudoir of Madame de Villeparisis, dreaming of an imaginary Madame de Ville-parisis with a Canadian accent; turned Mr. Starr into a little curled-up dog-man of Salvator Dali's. René became more and more exuberant, as he drank his fifth beer, and Hester's eyes, like starry lamps, hung over the table, as they both were sealed up in their private world of joy. She lifted her arm to drink, when her right breast and hip were inundated with beer—which however was not *her* beer. Her neighbour's glass bounced off her body, and fell to the floor.

: 'I've wetted you, lady. My hand slipped.'

Hester sprang up with a startled cry. All that either of them had noticed was that a dark man, thinking his own thoughts, which must be ill-favoured, was sitting against the wall. René shouted at him angrily, 'You clumsy brute! Are you unable to carry your glass to your mouth without upsetting it over other people?'

'*Brutes* are we, you big-mouthed old limey! An'mals, huh!'

This came from the table behind him. René turned abruptly to identify the voice, and, more in astonishment than anger, found himself, at a distance of five or six feet, looking into a face of a most unprepossessing kind. The mouth was twisted into an ugly sneer right across the face.

'Yes, sir!' the man drawled. 'That was me. Another brute. Why is you and that jane with you doin' us the honour, down in this saloon. . . .'

'René! Let us leave here.'

Hester pulled him by the sleeve. He sprang up, as a dark face, full of platonic hatred, picked itself out, and Hester's neighbour of the unsteady hand struck him below the eye. He swung at this hateful countenance with an unexpected precision, and the man went down, with a great deal of noise, between the two tables, Hester jumping away with a gasp. He was gazing at the man between the tables, and, with the other part of his eye, aware of Jim Greevy wiping the beer off Hester's dress, when he was struck very heavily on the left cheek, and bounded back to meet this new attack. It was with no surprise that he saw his assailant blotted out by a large person who seemed to move up from the floor, and heard a deep voice observe, in an as-it-were official voice, 'Do you want to say anything to *me*, Tom Thorne?' But there was so much noise by this time that he did not find out whether Tom Thorne wanted to say anything to the tall stranger. The next thing he really knew was a panic-stricken entreaty, 'Do come away at once, darling'; and while he was hearing this, he focused something of an entirely different character to anything

8*

else in this phantasmagoria. It was much more integrated and
purposeful. A crouched, medium-sized figure was dancing in
front of him. There was no angry face—there was hardly
any face at all. It was an engine rather than a man, or a man
who was so highly trained that his personality was submerged.
There was something very dangerous about this taut and
dancing body. The presence of this figure in front of him
admitted of only one interpretation, and he struck it with all
his force, as if it were an adder, or any other dangerous thing
in nature. The next thing he knew was that he could no longer
strike it because it was so near to him. The next thing he knew
after *that* was how the lightning snaps and is gone, and it hits
you, and he had been slammed in the stomach, and he was
shut up over the pain like a book that had tried to slap itself
shut. The pain filled the room, and he was crouched in the
middle of it, hugging his pain. He felt a warm cheek against
his, and there was a soft voice near his ear; it said, 'So you
like that, budd' (much too dulcet for a Canadian but still in
the accents of North America). A stallion kicked a tattoo—
four more like the first, until he became no more than a solar
plexus, and the room was a solar plexus too.

He stood gasping, with his neck stuck out, like a bearded
rooster. It was then that he saw the *face*—the face of the
engine, which had attacked him. It was a smooth, young, and
rather thoughtful face; just now it was looking at him with
a calm concentration, one eyebrow a little lifted. Before he
could be aware of anything more, he found himself hitting the
floor, his hands still pressed in the pit of his stomach.

The uproar was intense, and someone must have been playing about with the electric light, for the light kept going out
and coming back again. Then there was a deafening scream,
and simultaneously a boot hit him in the face, and then more
boots began hitting him, elsewhere. Three or four boots perhaps. Then that stopped, and there was a trampling all around
him, and sometimes on him.

The trampling went on, but it seemed to have moved a
little way away. He heard Jim Greevy's voice saying, 'Get
up now, quick!' He was pulled, and crawled towards a chair.
'Can you stand?' said Jim. He lifted himself with Jim's aid

upon the chair. There he stopped a moment, and then rose
to his feet. Hester, in a hollow voice, was imploring him to
try and come away, then Jim Greevy pushed him through
a door, and Hester and he found themselves in the staff
quarters. The uproar of a fight still reached them, but, he still
doubled up, they were able to reach the street at the back.
From there it was only a few steps to the annexe entrance.
'I will tell Mrs. Plant, you have been beated up,' Jim said as
he left them.

'For heaven's sake don't do that,' René answered. 'Jim,
say nothing to her.'

Back in the Room, René sank upon the sofa. He felt himself all over with his finger-tips. 'No fatal damage,' he told the
pale and shaking Hester.

'You must see a doctor,' she answered.

René shook his head; he felt so sick and dazed that he was
not able to cope any more just then. Hester flung herself in
a chair with a terrible fit of weeping. Her experience in the
Beverage Room had been such a monstrosity, there had been
so much hatred, suddenly released, and it had then filled her
with such a dreadful fear, not to mention the hateful humiliation of having beer poured over her head—all this she had
to meet without breakdown, and so now she broke into a
hundred pieces.

This was not an indulgence, but a necessity on Hester's part:
she was unable to control herself. But having acquired the
requisite relief, she rose and went over to the telephone. The
doctor arrived in a quarter of an hour. One of the most obvious
effects of the mêlée had been a stiffening of the arm, the loss
of use in the left hand, and a considerable swelling around the
elbow, with, of course, a great deal of pain. There were other
areas which demanded investigation as well. Of this invitation
to probe Dr. Mackinnon took the fullest advantage.

René made no pretence to like the doctor. He was per-
suaded that Dr. Mackinnon would, in the ordinary course of
business, make his scrutiny as painful as possible. The more
the examination hurt, the more justified would the physician's
visit seem. Were the patient to wince, or if possible groan, the
more serious would the case appear to the family: and so the

more likely they would be to ask the physician to return. That, at least, was René's account, when the doctor had left, and the patient recovered a little from his mal-treatment. Further, the fact that he did not recommend an X-ray signified there was absolutely nothing there but bruises and the dislocation of the left arm and a sprained wrist, and it had been unwarrant-ably alarmist to call him in. As the doctor refused to push the disjointed arm back into its proper position because of its swollen state, that was merely an excuse for returning several times. René said for two pins he would push the arm back into place himself. Nevertheless he allowed Hester to take the prescription to the druggist. Since his arm and head were both painful he would have been unable to sleep without Dr. Mackinnon's sleeping draught.

Hester, however, lay awake and listened to the screams of the woman in the apartment beneath theirs, it being the husband's nightly habit to half murder her. (Three or four weeks later the police were called in, and they removed the wife out of danger.) What a fearful place they had come to! She must try and prevail upon René to return to England.— As soon as he was better—it would be no use to begin talking of that now. She watched for some time to see that he did not toss about and do some further harm to his left arm. When at last she went to sleep, her dreams were so appalling that she kept waking up, and in the end preferred to be awake than to be asleep.

So the next morning, dressings on his head, a sling for his left arm with only a slight bend in it, and several band-aids plastered about on face and hands, René was propped up on the settee. The arm was a good deal swollen, and the pain had not abated: he kept this at bay, to some extent, with Veganin.

After breakfast at about the usual time, the screams of the young German woman continued for more than an hour. She was married to an Indian—a north American Indian, not a Hindu. Bess was of the opinion she nagged the Indian until he gave her a punch or two to make her stop: and that she often would scream before he had done anything: this made him so angry he would perhaps hold her upside down and shout 'Will you stop that —— noise!' This, apparently, was

the only way to stop her. But soon she would start again.
When the screaming began, René said, 'I feel sorry for that
poor Indian.'

Hester looked at him in surprise.

'Oh,' she said, 'Why?'

'If I were that Indian, I would take a pillow and put it on
her face and sit on it for half an hour.'

Hester stretched over and squeezed his hand.

'Darling, you have grown very ferocious in the last twenty-
four hours. Has that kick on the head turned you into a new
man?'

He gave his ho-ho-ho laugh, the first for perhaps two years.
'The fellow may have kicked some sense into me, there is
always that. I made an uncommonly sensible remark.'

'You think so?' Hester became aware of a contradiction in
her husband. He was not really gentle: she did not mean that
he was un-gentle, but he could not claim to be gentle. Yet
he had always exhibited an authentic distaste for physical
violence. At school he had been an athlete. But he tended to
avoid the more brutal sports. It was as a gymnast that he had
excelled. He had once told her how it had always thrilled him
to fly through the air in a large gymnasium. The sight of him
bandaged there on the settee, delivering himself of an exceptionally brutal remark (it was the sort of remark that most
men make, but he had been a refrainer) naturally provoked
her attention.

It was almost as though he had been privy to her thoughts:
for he remarked, 'We have had our baptism of fire, have we
not, in the violent life of this hotel. It is an astonishingly
violent place, but no more violent than the world of which
it is so perfect a microcosm.'

'Oh,' Hester murmured.

' How extraordinarily, when one shuts oneself up in a little
segment of the world like this hotel, it is brought home to
one what a violent place the world is.'

'This hotel is not typical,' she demurred.

'It is. The kind of bourgeois family we were brought up in
is highly deceptive. War is cheerfully maintained by everybody; our military aristocrats glory in "blood and sweat and

ţears". But if a bank clerk were given power he would kill
even more millions. So far no one has been *killed* in this hotel.
But thousands are killed on the roads, and millions over in
the battlefields. You are right, this hote'. is not typical. It is
a nicԋ quiet hotel—a rather mild microcosm.'

The Indian's wife gave a bloodcurdling shriek.

'That woman,' he observed, 'is asking *to be killed*, as loudly
as she knows how to.'

'I am afraid that you are right,' Hester agreed.

'And now we are in harmony with the hotel,' he told her.
'If I lived here much longer I should be a full-scale blood-
sacrifice.'

He was now himself again, Hester thought, and she looked
over at him fondly.

'Oughtn't you to get a little sleep?' she reminded him. But
there was a knock on the door: it was Jim Greevy, and instead
of sleep, René visibly braced himself, and stuck bravely out
his beard.

'How do you feel, Mr. Harding? You struck a very bad
patch. I did all I could. But it wasn't much.'

'We do not underestimate what you did, Jim. You were
splendid.'

'Oh rats,' said Jim, with violent modesty; turning to Hester,
'I wiped the beer off you as it was thrown over you! That's
all I did.'

'You did more than that. You sided with the limey—you,
an Irishman!'

'There is that,' Jim laughed. 'Tom Thorne is a dangerous
man. A year back he served a term of imprisonment for man-
slaughter. I would not have him in the place if it were mine.
He fights every time he comes here. And tonight he had that
Yank with him.'

'Ah yes, that Yank.' René patted the sling. 'I had this arm
over my face. That was when I was on the ground. That Yank
kicked it pretty hard.'

'Yes, I'll bet he did,' said Jim. 'He's a nasty piece of work.
Of course he's a draft-dodger; that seems to contradict what
they say. They say he's very well known in the States, at
his weight a champion. But if he is a champ, what the

heck is he doing draft-dodging? Uncle Sam looks after his
champions. He would not be wasted in Guadalcanal, I
mean.'

'Perhaps he's no champ,' René laughed. 'But he felt like a
champion to me when he was doing that tattoo on my belly.'

'No, he may be a champ all right, but there must be
something else. Anyway, he goes everywhere now with Tom
Thorne. That shows the sort of man he is. He ought to be
pushed back into the States. Last night I noticed he didn't
take on that big chap, you know, who went after Tom Thorne.'

'Oh, didn't he? The little coward.'

Jim shook his head. 'No. It would not be that. Everyone
knows that Fitz was a Mountie.'

'Ah, I see what you mean. As a draft-dodger he would
prefer not to draw attention to himself.'

'Yes,' Jim nodded; 'yes, that, and probably something
else.'

'So that big fellow used to be in the Mounties?' René
enquired.

'Yes. He's a good scout is Fitz. I knew he would not see
a stranger like yourself beaten up. All the same' (he rubbed
his hand over his eyes in a quick bashful gesture), 'I had just
stuck my spectacles in my pocket when I saw old Fitz get
up; and he knocked Tom down with a proper haymaker.
Tom Thorne is a man who doesn't usually find himself on
his back.'

'Mr. Greevy, I do think that was splendid of you . . .'

'Yes, Jim, it was jolly decent of you to get ready to do
battle in that way. The ex-Mountie's intervention was a
wonderful stroke of luck for all of us.'

'It was that. He is a very popular man, is old Fitz, with
all except thugs like Tom Thorne.'

There was a pause, and then Hester spoke.

'But what had my husband done to these people? It all
seems very extraordinary looking back on it.'

'Yes, that puzzles me too,' René said. 'What on earth had
poor Hester done? Why pour beer over her head? Apart from
its being blackguardedly, it doesn't seem to make sense, does
it, Jim?'

Jim smiled wryly, and gave his face another violent rub.
'Yes, Mr. Harding, unfortunately it *does* make sense to me
all right.'

'Sense of what kind!' almost shouted René. 'You mean we
are the kind of people over whom it is natural to empty beer
and to kick 'em in the teeth?'

Jim laughed nervously. 'Well, you put it that way, Mr.
Harding, but it is a fact that in such a place as I am the
manager of it is natural for almost anything to happen.—
Especially to strangers.—You don't make a noise like a
Canadian!'

'That's too bad.'

'It isn't even that. I might as well say it, it is the English
accent I'm afraid.'

'Mr. Greevy, you really mean that? . . .' Hester looked very
distressed.

'I don't like saying it, Mr. Harding, but you must have
noticed yourself that the English are not very much liked.
Let me be frank . . .'

'Please do,' René told him.

'There is always the high-hatting charge. You see, in such
a place as ours, Mr. Harding—who has a voice that can be
heard . . .'

'And why not?' clamoured René. 'Are we to speak in
whispers then?'

'No, Mr. Harding, of course not, I did not say that. But
you are a man who knows the world, and there *is* a time to
speak soft and low. People think you are swanking, the sort
we have down there, if you talk very loud about things they
don't understand.'

René gave an angry and dramatic sigh. Turning to Hester
he said, 'You see how it is, being English is an unpopular
thing to be. To be Scotch is all right, to be Irish is just fine'
(he winked at Jim), 'but being what we are, we had better
stop here in this Room, rather than go out and expose ourselves to the displeasure of the natives—everymanjack of
whom comes from the British Islands.'

René pushed over a packet of cigarettes to Jim, after taking
one himself. Jim looked uncomfortable. The direction the con-

versation had taken made him regret his frankness. But René continued, and Jim looked up a little apprehensively.

'What I would like to know is the degree in which these are war-conditions. In peace time is there this perpetual drunkenness and fighting?'

'Yes and no,' Jim answered. 'Everything is worse today. But the Canadian is at all times an ugly man when he is full of liquor.'

Jim Greevy now enquired whether the kick on the left arm had broken anything: and whether the bandage round the head signified anything serious.

René reassured him. He told him his arm was dislocated merely: it was painful, but would be all right soon. Shortly after that Greevy left.

'Well, that was from the horse's mouth. We were imprudent, even at six o'clock, not to quieten down our voices.'

There was a bloodcurdling shriek from the end of the passage. It continued solidly for three or four minutes.

'I wish someone would empty some beer over that woman,' Hester smiled mirthlessly. 'But she "makes a noise like a Canadian", so that is all right I suppose.'

CHAPTER XVII

Vows of Hardship

BLIZZARDS blew from the Pole downwards, though they were abominably vacillating, and this was a severe one. Hester had gone to the groceteria about noon: it was no farther than the other end of the block, but you faced north to go to it from the hotel. Hester had to move doubled up, and to stop a half-dozen times, and stand with her back to the ice-blast, which whirled around her as soon as she turned, so that she stood in a whirlpool of snow. Each time she stopped she was very quickly forced around again in order to escape the whirlpool: and at intervals this mannerism was repeated again and again. Her hair was full of frozen snow and her lips froze against her teeth when she reached the groceteria: she went up to the glass case, and stared through at the items for sale, odds and ends of butchery. These show-cases were such as are used in Museums for the display of antiquities, and to begin with this method of exhibiting meat is displeasing to English people. She selected four kidneys as a treat for René, for the evening meal, and two Idaho potatoes—or if not Idahoes they were almost as large..

This was christmas-type eating, a foretaste of what it would be incumbent on them to do in the way of extravagance in four days' time. But they would not have the money to have much of a christmas dinner: so why not spread the christmas dinner out? Christmas had made everything worse, and Hester had privately reached a state of mind where she would whisper to herself, 'To hell with economics!' as she pointed to a packet of frozen peaches in the ice-chest. Why did they not go to the British High Commissioner, say they had no money, and ask to be shipped home? They had known another Englishman who had done that: there was no difficulty about it. They could not travel together, but what of that if they got back to England. It was also in this spirit that, before she left the groceteria, she added half a pound of mushrooms to her other purchases. Fortified by the heat in the shop, she then went back into the storm, ploughing through the snow in her over-shoes. Her stockings were wet above the knee, and the whirling snow drove down inside her overshoes.

When Hester reached the hotel, she was breathless and uncomfortably hot. She collapsed upon a seat near the front door, tearing her ulster open to ventilate the burning interior. At last she was able to move through the hotel, and then, her heart still thumping, stumble up the annexe stairs. She burst into the Room with a protesting 'Oh', and sank on the settee, struggling to recover her breath. She did not indulge in speech for a while: then she said, to the amused René, 'Never, but never, have I encountered such a beast of a blizzard! It is like a million dervishes whirling around one.'—But when the contents of the shopping bag was revealed to René he was less amused.

'Mushrooms! Idahoes! What does all this signify? Is this Christmas?'

'I am sorry.' She exhibited contrition. 'I was demoralized. Very demoralized. Please put it all down to the blizzard: I lost all sense of time and space.'

These luxurious purchases, this succulent raw material spread out upon the table, obviously produced acute dejection in René, and filled him with the darkest forebodings. The fact that his left arm was out of action had made it much more difficult for him to work. To be behind-hand with his work raised up the spectre of insolvency, and Furber, that was worst of all—and then *par dessus le marché*, Christmas!

He gave up his afternoon rest, for he felt that the mush-rooms and the Idahoes pointed to the necessity of making up for the time lost resulting from the brawl of six days before. When tea-time came he showed great appreciation of the Salada and of some stale cookies, which had been rejected as compromisingly old when they were entertaining Mr. Starr. He appeared to be in an exceptionally good mood, so Hester thought she would speak to him of her growing unwillingness to prolong the occupation of the Room, and of her longing to shake the dust of this country off her thrice-patched shoes.

C

'Just look at that blizzard,' she exclaimed, waving her hand towards the window. 'While I was sweating and·freezing, gasping for breath, and trying to prevent my heart from beating a hole in my side, when I got back to the hotel this morning, I·said to myself, "Hester, you have been in this country long enough." '

René ho-ho-ho'ed. He did not suspect the existence of any purpose behind this *boutade*.

'We are great friends, aren't we, René, as well as lovers?' she said softly.

René was thinking of the work he had to do after tea: he did not take this in for a few moments: they were not accustomed to say things of that kind to one another. But then he turned squarely towards her, reached over and planted his hand on hers.

'The greatest pals in the world, Ess. I don't believe there ever have been such pals.'

'I don't believe there have been either, René.' He had taken his hand away and passed it through his hair, and frowned, as if confronted with some difficult problem. He stared at her intently. She became self-conscious at this scrutiny; she felt like some wild animal not accustomed to be looked at. We take our being for granted, our physical presence comes to enjoy the anonymity of furniture. What was he searching for, what information that he did not possess already?

'I see, I see,' he almost hissed, 'a stranger who has become a sister.' And it flashed through his mind how his belief in blood, in the Family, had taken him, in the crisis of his life, to a lot of strangers beginning with his mother.

There was only Helen,· and that was not because she was a sister. But here, all the time, was the person he should have gone to. 'Hardship! I am beginning to love hardship. It sharpens the sight. When I look, I see. I see what a grand woman you are. I used to think that you were scheming and frivolous—I am afraid that you must have seen that I thought that.'

'I sometimes feared you thought that,' she agreed. She saw her chances of an opening slipping away. She had trembled when he spoke so favourably of hardship.

'I, no more than you, *would seek hardship,*' he said, and she started, for it was as though he had been listening in to her thoughts. 'But honestly, being imprisoned, as we have been, here, has its compensations. This barren life has dried out of me a great deal that should not have been there. And you have become integrated in me. This tête-à-tête of ours over three years has made us as one person. And this has made me understand you—for most people I should hate to be integrated with. It is only when years of misery have caused you to grow into another person in this way that you can really know them.' He waited a moment and then went on, 'In the other world, Hester, I treated you as you did not at all deserve. I cut a poor figure as I look back at myself.'

'There is no need to say this. I don't know why you are saying it.'

'But it is no use talking in this uncomfortable way about ourselves, as if I were I, and you were you. I am talking to myself and we are one. Is it necessary to say that I would sacrifice for you any miserable thing I had—well, as I would for myself?'

So the appeal she had proposed to make must be indefinitely postponed; she left her chair, and putting her arms around his neck kissed him very tenderly. 'My darling, we have been hammered together as you say by a very ugly fate, but we would have been together without that. You attribute too much to fate. But there is this, my darling, that I would do anything you asked me to do, and go wherever you wished. I did not know that I would do that once. But I know now.'

'What a grand woman you are. And this tête-à-tête of over three years has made us one person, Ess. I treated you awfully badly.'

René was so moved that tears flooded his eyes, as he held her as well as he could. She had intended to say that she would, as she had said, literally go anywhere, although secretly she would pray that it might be a less hideous spot —she had intended at least to put in this mild reminder; but instead she found that she was crying too, and they remained for a long time clasped together in something like a religious embrace. René was thinking this being and he were vowed to one another, in a sacrament of which good fortune and good times had no knowledge, and she was thinking how she loved René, and how wonderful it was after all to be loved and she would not *pester* him about leaving this awful place if he did not want to, and the war must end some day, some day, and *then* they would return to England, and leave this hideous ice-box behind!

He had just said, 'Let's have another cup of tea, my sweet,' and she had picked up the heavy teapot, when a tap came at the door. They heard Affie's voice through the door. 'Come in, Affie!' he shouted, and like a mischievous black-suited spectre she remained fluid for some moments, half in and half out of the apartment.

'Come in. Don't hover,' René commanded.

'I'm not interrupting?' Affie asked.

Both of them thought, 'Ah, she's been listening,' and laughed. She came in, smiling down at them, pleased at being privy to all that went on in the house. She was not by nature a Key-hole-Queen. She was more like an aged messenger of Aphrodite, with a supernatural passe-partout, bringing for preference aphrodisiacs from Aphrodite, and possessing supernatural access to everything in the hotel. She had no need to squint through keyholes, as Bess always accused her of doing, though she may have done that, it is true, to annoy Bess.

'When I have swallowed this, come and vaticinate in my teacup, Affie darling,' René invited.

'I will see if there is anything I think you ought to know,' answered Affie professionally, deeply inhaling her cigarette smoke. Affie sat huddled up, as though in prophetic concentration with herself. Her childish affectation of solemn preparation for a scrutiny of their fate always pleased them.

This was a recognized method of minor-moneymaking in Momaco. Many tea-rooms advertised in their windows that fortune-telling teacup-readers were within.

When Hester and René had finished their tea, they whirled their cups round three times, which was the routine procedure. The tea-leaves duly plastered upon the insides of the cups, Affie drew near, crouched over the cups, and gazed first at one and then at the other for several minutes.

Then she said to René, 'Someone loves you very much, very
. . much.' She gave a side-long glance of fun at Hester, and
then straightened her face abruptly. She twisted René's cup
completely round several times. 'You are going on a long
journey. The man you are going to see is dark . . . with
horn-rimmed spectacles; tall, fattish with a flattened nose,
young.'

René and Hester exchanged a glance of high amusement.
Several photographs of the gentleman in question had arrived
in a registered envelope two weeks earlier. Affie continued to
brood over the cups. She approached her face to one of the
cups, rather quickly, and raising one eyebrow. 'You must be
very careful about this dark man,' she said. 'You will be
crossing water. . . . It might be as well if you did *not* cross
water.'

'I do not agree,' Hester remarked.

'How do you mean?' Affie frowned.

'It is my view that he *should* cross water,' Hester insisted.
'Cross a lot of water.'

Affie looked relieved. 'I only meant a small stretch of
water.'

'Yes, it is after all only to Victoria Island!' René laughed
—Affie showed no sign of recognition, when he said Victoria
Island. She transformed her scrutiny to Hester's cup. 'You
have many friends,' Affie told her. 'You will receive a letter
from one . . . very shortly. . . . It will contain good news.'
She tipped the cup sideways. 'You have a boot in your cup.'
She looked up with a smile. 'It is very lucky. A boot . . . is
exceptionally lucky.'

When, a few months earlier, Bess had been away for a week,
a woman who had formerly worked there took her place. She
had been an Englishwoman once, many years before. She was
quite uninhibited, and the reputations of one or two of the
members of the staff, past and present, suffered quite a lot
in the course of her incumbency. She was especially dangerous
for Affie. Among other things she informed them that Affie
steamed open letters, and glued them up afterwards: this
occurring in the kitchen, where the postmen left the mail for
the entire hotel. This piece of information threw considerable

light on Affie's uncanny skill of divination in tea-cup reading.
There was especially one instance they recalled when Affie
had foretold the arrival of 'a letter . . . with a funny sort of
stamp . . . Indian I think'. Four days later a stamped letter
arrived from Colombo. After that, it had become a sport, one
of the favourite sports of the Room, tracing Affie's revelations
to a letter steamed open in the kitchen. The 'crossing water'
business at the present séance, and the insistence on the
amount of water being inconsiderable, was easily traceable to
a dozen or more letters which had recently come from someone
in Vancouver, who urged René to come out there. He backed
up this request with glittering promises, assuring René that the
local University would immediately offer him a Chair. Where
Victoria Island came in was that the correspondent invited
them to stay with him at his 'properties', while arrangements
were being made with the University authorities. This man's
father was said to be on the Board of the University and a
very influential man. A photograph of his father was enclosed,
and he certainly looked a very influential man. This correspondent had poured registered letters in at the rate of two a
week: they had impressed Affie more than they had impressed
the Hardings.

They both of them felt quite certain that Affie would do
nothing really dishonest. She steamed open letters to improve
her sorcery and sharpen her prophetic insight. Also she was an
inquisitive woman, and she would be amused to learn that
No. 34 suffered from a venereal disease or No. 19A was, as
she had suspected, homosexual. Knowing *everyone*'s secret
gave her a sense of power. Once, when she had said, 'Professor
Harding, have you ever visited any of our universities?
McGill for instance?' he was angry as long as it would take
to pick up a pin. Then he said, 'Where did you learn that
I was Professor Harding?' 'That is how your letters are
addressed,' Affie answered. But René laughed and asked her,
'What were the christian names of my grandmother?' Affie
only answered, 'On the English side or on the French, Professor Harding?' At which they all three laughed a great deal.

On the present occasion, after exhaustively analysing the
tea-leaves, she rose to her full height, and bowed herself out,

like a figure in a ballet. But at the door she turned, and clinging to the slightly swinging door, as if she had been posing for Andromeda, but had suddenly felt rather faint, she addressed Hester.

'Wouldn't you like a fur coat as a Christmas present, Mrs. Harding?'

'Why?' Hester enquired, with the smile that she reserved, in this place, for this old woman clinging to the door.

'Oh, don't you like fur? Some people don't. I have just bought a fur coat.'

'How wonderful, Affie. You've made yourself a beautiful Christmas present, have you! Do show it to me!'

Affie clung harder and harder, more and more archly, to the swaying door. 'It's a cherry fox,' she confided. Then with a croak she vanished. René went ho-ho-ho, gently combing his beard. They looked at one another in mutual relishment of Affie's latest exhibition of prophetic skill, but they were debarred from speaking; for she certainly was listening at the door. All that René said was, 'Well, I am going on a long journey.' Hester responded, 'But the water you will be crossing will be of insignificant span.' And René concluded with, 'Yes, there is of course that.' And then they turned on the radio.

The News was beginning. Richly and persuasively the preliminary sales-talk rolled out. 'Be the smart Host,' it exhorted, 'When you're serving Tall Drinks!' After a final appeal, 'So be the Smart Host', came a cataract of bad news, though thousands of dead bodies of enemies made you feel the day had not been quite in vain. Before the news was over it was learned that President Roosevelt had accepted the rib of a Japanese Marine, mounted in gold, as a paper-knife.

'A nice Christmas present for the Great White Chief,' René observed. 'They ought really to scalp their enemies. Sawing a rib out of the cadaver is decadent, I feel.'

Hester seldom paid any attention to the roaring voices of 'commentators'. They all had a vested interest in a long, long war. They would never be heard of again when it *did* end: they hoped that the ten million pounds a day (or was it a minute?) military budgeting would go on forever. Hester came to hate these brash voices, but after a time it was nothing but a troublesome noise. They might have been talking Chinese for all she knew about it. René followed the nightly outpourings with close attention, if for no other reason, because the *Momaco Gazette-Herald* bought political articles from him, and that was one of the ways he had found to make a living.

The murder of all these millions of simple inoffensive people all over the world, whether civilians or uniformed herds, the enormous, irretrievable ruin being prepared for each and all of these countries, the certain slavery consequent upon un-payable mountains of debt, plunging all the combatants indiscriminately, whether 'victors or vanquished', into worse and worse inflations; all this burden of knowledge, and what was therefore for him a spectacle of ruin, for the first year or so had tormented him. Now, however, the torments had ceased, and his reactions at present amounted to an anarchic pessimism, destined to undermine his fierce puritanism, his 'perfectionism?', as it had been called.

He would hardly know, if they should meet, and have lunch together, how to converse with Rotter now. His letters to Rotter for a year past had been few and far between. Then at last, about a month ago, he informed his disciple that he had modified his theory. He had explained that his opinion of the past and of the traditional writing of History was quite unchanged. He even retained his belief in a sort of 'Enlighten-ment'. But he now felt that the powers of evil disposed of such stupendous forces that they must always, with the greatest ease, annihilate any opposition: and it is inherent in earthly life that this should be so for ever. Any 'Enlightenment' that might make its appearance would be like a taper in a tornado.

His disciple had written to him in a tone of such utter despair, that he had considered it best to provide some imme-diate balm. So he wrote that, after all, the taper would not be extinguished by the tornado if it were secreted in the mind, where, as a matter of fact, it was generally to be found. All that he had done was to deprecate the idea that it would come out of the mind, and *physically* do battle with the Dark-ness and the Whirlwind. Then it would be a case of a combat between a minnow and a cuttlefish. This latter seemed to have afforded consolation to the sensitive Rotter.

But René could find nothing with which to console himself, though he now grieved less over the universal catastrophe as he realized more thoroughly its dark necessity, its innateness.

That there was no intention of ending this war, until it had become a total catastrophe *for everybody* was now obvious to him. He did not communicate to Hester his views as to the probable length of the war. He just sat before the radio, and listened to the unfolding of new moves promising, as he interpreted it, the most stupendous evils—sat there, night after night, too shocked to speak at times: at others simply stifling the human instinct to communicate.

It had been over three *very long* years, and he was almost reconciled to the hardship of which he had spoken. Even, he had developed an appetite for this negation of life, and a sort of love for this frightful Room. It was this that Hester most feared in him: she watched with apprehension how he was making himself at home in their present surroundings—and even beginning to ho-ho-ho. He had no wish to be in a greater scene, where men falsified everything, and built up their small façades: where 'success' meant failure and betrayal. He felt he could well live at some distance from the scholars who used their learning to conceal, and the literary men who, after a few years' spectacular navigation, crept into some port where they could moulder placidly for the rest of their lives. He experienced no desire to be once more in those places where the intellect was rewarded for its surrenders, and where the mind became illustrious in proportion to its moral flaccidity.

When, however, the storm of nonsense, the menacing voices had ended, they walked with Fred Allen down his East-side 'Alley', and shook as they listened to Mrs. Nutzbaum, or to the Bard who always prefaced his remarks with the words, 'That is precisely why I am here!'

They followed the exchanges between Fred Allen and Jack Benny, which began with cracks about Jacks *toupée*. Or it was a lucky break, and Jimmy Durante ('such are the circumstances that prevail') served up Ombriago and filled them with vigorous joy. They did not turn up their noses, either, at Fibber Magee and his outfit: and they both felt the keenest displeasure if anything caused them to miss Gracie Allen, and even more so Henry Aldridge, that classical satire on the American Boy. In the evenings they were surrounded by these wonderful comedians, brought them by half a dozen U.S. Networks: and in the end the war-bulletins began to fade, and like all good Americans they came to realize that it was only the comic that mattered.

Before they went to bed Fred Waring wished them 'A Happy White Christmas'. They both spontaneously groaned, as Christmas was mentioned, and René rattled a couple of bits in his trouser-pocket.

CHAPTER XVIII

Mr. Furber

WHEN René laid aside his sling, his arm felt like a toy limb: it could not take on much more than the stroking of a beard, or picking of a tooth. He kept his hand in his jacket pocket. People respect a sling, but an arm with its hand thrust into a jacket pocket was liable to be bumped into or even playfully seized. But these risks must be ignored: René could delay no longer his going to Cedric Furber's.

Living as they did, from hand to mouth, to lay aside for more than a week or so his work at Mr. Furber's forced them to draw upon their emergency reserve. Formerly their only reserve had been the key books René had brought with him. The *Encyclopædia Britannica* was the bulkiest and most valuable of these.

But, one by one, they had all been disposed of. At present their reserve consisted of a slim bundle of dollar bills sufficient to enable them to pinch and scrape their way through one month. Thanks to Furber, they now had reached a point at which they did not have to fear hunger. Provided the arrangements they had been able to make did not fall through they could make both ends meet, and have sufficient slack to enable them, most weeks, to put by a dollar or two.

Before this period of relative stabilization they were only saved from complete insolvency by the sale of books. There had been one occasion when they had been unable to buy any cigarettes for nearly a month, and they had never eaten so little in their lives. There was a book shop run by an Englishman, a Mr. Salter, and it was one of the best in Canada— which is not a country of second-hand bookshops. Momaco was as unpromising as could well be found for such a shop. But Mr. Salter mailed his lists all over North America. In the book trade, from Santa Fé to St. Johns, Newfoundland, he was well known. Although things were appallingly difficult,

they had sold him so many books that René had decided to
break new ground, if that were possible, rather than to apply
to Mr. Salter again. But the moment came at length they
literally had no money left, or just a quarter and a nickel. So a
History of National Biography and another book were packed
and René started off for the bookshop. He found it closed;
Mr. Salter was probably at a sale. The heat was formidable,
perhaps a hundred degrees. René had not the money to go
to a Beverage Room, to kill time, so he decided to walk to
the city's main department store, Mansfield's. It was at the
centre of the shopping quarter, about a mile away. The great
square shadows of the down-town buildings were delightful to
walk in, but between one block and the next the sun eyed
him without intervening masonries, and it scorched his back
through his shirt. On the return journey he had a piece of
luck. He found himself walking behind a diminutive Jew, with
a large cigar. Normally he would have corrected such a situation, have got out of range. He did not do so now, but inhaled
the horrid smoke with delirious pleasure. Afterwards it was
without exaggeration that he would insist that never, but
never, had he had a smoke to compare with it. There was no
wind, and the stream of smoke was carried into his face, up
his nostrils, without interruption; suddenly the Cigar turned
into a side-street, in the most unexpected way: for it had never
occurred to René that the Cigar might do that. He stopped.
Should he follow the Cigar? No, he thought, he must not do
that: the man attached to the Cigar might notice that he was
being followed. Besides, the heavenly Cigar was already a
short way away, and he would have to run to catch it up.

When he got back to the bookshop Mr. Salter was there.
The bookseller not only bought the two books René had with
him, but put down twenty dollars on account for a third
book. This René duly handed over (with infinite regret) the
next morning. That evening the two castaways on Momaco
faisaient la bombe with a bottle of Niagara wine, a packet of
twenty Player's and a fried Chicken Maryland.

René's present problem was to resume his employment at

Mr. Cedric Furber's house. He tended to take Mr. Furber too much for granted, and that was an error, psychologically. This error derived from the fact that there was something paradoxically solid about this gentleman, and it had impressed René out of proportion to its value.

This is how he had come to meet his strange patron. It was a little over a year earlier that René had gone one morning to the only serious bookstore in town, that is dealing in new books. He saw (and avoided) Mr. Starr, who was looking at a display of the very latest English books upon a table near the door. If he avoided Mr. Starr, that gentleman did not avoid him; and it was not long before he heard his soft 'Hallo', as he was trying to locate a book in one of the less accessible shelves. This was at a later meeting with Mr. Starr. Their original encounter has been described elsewhere. Mr. Starr had spotted the nature of the beard, had seen at once that it was not an ordinary outburst of hair, and the way its bearer bore himself meant something unusual. This had involved a fairly long chat, but René had no desire to repeat it.

But there was no resisting Mr. Starr, and a further chat took place. He left the shop in order to escape from Mr. Starr (but Mr. Starr came with him), and as they came out into the street, they passed a tall and bearded man going in. The two beards took note of one another discreetly. René remarked that the other was tall and elegant. His elegance was the only thing about him that did not remind the spectator of Lytton Strachey. But Mr. Starr mincingly intercepted the bearded one, who looked down the melancholy expanse of hair with marked disapproval. The dapper figure in the grubby white silk muffler and seedy tight little overcoat got no advertisement from his acquaintance.

'How are you, Mr. Furber! It is a long time since we met.'— An austere silence.—'I would like you to meet Professor René Harding, the historian. I am sure you have read *The Secret History of World War II.*'

At the name there were flattering signs of recognition: the large dull brown eyes above the long mournful beard softened. From the hirsute lips came polite words. René had stopped not far from the entrance of the shop. In response to Mr. Starr's light touch, he turned about and faced the bearded stranger. Both bowed and smiled.

'Mr. Furber,' said Mr. Starr, 'has one of the finest collections of books in Canada.' Mr. Furber had a rather effeminate gesture of deprecation. 'I think, Mr. Furber, that Professor René Harding would be very interested to see your collection.' Mr. Furber bowed agreeably—he was not a man of many words. Mr. Starr had turned to René. 'A first edition of *Decline and Fall* is among his books.'

There was a pause; then René said, 'Oh, are you fond of Evelyn Waugh?'

'No! Gibbon,' Mr. Furber corrected, a faint smile playing hide and seek in his beard; 'a not unnatural confusion,' with a sidelong glance at Mr. Starr.

'And your Proust manuscript,' Mr. Starr reminded, telling Mr. Furber in a bored voice, for he was angry. 'And haven't you a book of Cocteau drawings too, Mr. Furber? Someone seems to have told me.'

Cedric Furber regarded Mr. Starr with the eye with which money in America looks at no-money. He looked appealingly towards René, as if to say 'must we suffer the impertinences of this unedifying citizen?'

'I should be very happy to show Professor Harding my books, if it would interest him.' And Furber gazed in owlish, unsmiling invitation at René, who expressed his desire to see the books, and a day and hour was agreed upon.

With a very insulting look at Mr. Starr, this new figure in René's life passed on. Lord Herbert was ruffled. But he gave Cedric Furber a 'build-up'.

'His father was one of the richest men in Canada. A small nickel king. Cedric's brother became the head of the business, on the old man's death. Cedric went to Paris, and came back some years later with one of the finest collections of French books in Canada.'

Everything was the biggest or best 'in Canada', not in Momaco, in America, or in the world.

'Where did he pick up that beard?'

'Disgusting, isn't it?' Mr. Starr made a dainty *moue*. 'I think he was born that way.'

'What an accouchement!' .   .   .   ' , .   . .

'Oh no! You will make me ill in a minute.' Mr. Starr put his hand on his stomach, and protruded his tongue above the dirty white silk neckerchief. Then he looked thoughtful. 'But he might be useful to you.'.   .   .   .   . .   .

Such was the manner in which René became acquainted with Mr. Furber. ..

In due course René had presented himself at the residence of Mr. Furber. It was a not immoderate-sized building; but of some pretensions, with a rather lavish use of pillars and pilasters, also a marble terrace thrust out from the main window of the Library. It was situated upon the sacred hill which dominated Momaco to the North. Cedric Furber's collection of books turned out to be quite considerable, but very rich-undergraduate like; the aesthete and dilettante presiding at the purchases, evidently, the scholar conspicuous by his absence. Having learned of René's predicament, resulting from the rigid Exchange restrictions, Cedric Furber suggested that he should assist him with his books, giving up say two afternoons a week to this, for which he was to receive fifty dollars a month. The assistance required of him was mainly consultations. It was a gesture of goodwill. Cedric Furber's horizons were beyond the confines of Momaco, and although his friends at the university of Momaco battered him with their tongues, Furber did not listen. The Englishman was known to everybody for his historical treatises: Furber himself was almost a foreigner, and knew that all his Momaco friends were fiercely exclusive. The tariff wall which protected Canadian industries from foreign competition was not the only wall protecting things Canadian from outside competition. The learned professions, and the teaching profession especially, had a 100 per cent tariff wall against all learning that was not strictly Canuck; whereas the products of Canadian factories only had a 25 per cent wall. Consequently Furber did not listen to the chatter. This was a private affair between René and himself.—He liked Englishmen, because they were more

9

genteel than his own compatriots. His own family came from
Vancouver, with interests and relations in Seattle and San
Francisco, which was the next thing to being an American, and
he looked upon the ferocious exclusiveness of these longer-
settled parts of the dominion with the eye of an outside
observer.

If the genteel meant a great deal to Lord Herbert, it also
meant a lot to Lord Cedric. His aestheticism was a by-product
of social snobbery. Books, old jade, clavichords and Baroque
art were functions of the leisured existence of princes, counts,
and dukes. He too, like Mr. Starr, was of the circle of the
Duchesse de Guermantes and of Madame la Comtesse de Villeparisis. And, like Mr. Starr, he was what the latter designated
as a 'tribesman' (this refers, of course, to the Pansy-clan).

Mr. Furber lived with his sister. She sculpted, in a big studio
at the rear of their residence, though she spent more time in
New York and Washington than in Momaco. She was so
'grande dame' that she could scarcely be seen. When she was
'in residence' René was ejected, when his work was over, by
a side porch leading off the library, lest Mayenne should have
to say how-do-you-do too many times to this mere historian:
mere college professor, even if possessed of a respectable
celebrity.

The procedure, when René arrived—in the end he always
presented himself at the side-porch, for he was no more
desirous of encountering the preposterous Mayenne than was
that embodiment of gentility to see him—was as follows.
Furber and he would pass into an 'office', adjoining the
library. Furber would sit at his desk, in shadow (and in a
comfortable upholstered chair); René would sit upon one of
the two surprisingly puritanic chairs, facing the light—the
glaring North American daylight—until his eyes as well as
his bottom ached. When—after several hours sometimes—
he rose, his bottom was numb, his eyes watering. Of the two
chairs there were times when he thought one was the less hard.
He would stick to it for a period. Then suddenly he would
switch to the other one, and for a couple of weeks adhere to it.

Furber would push over a pack of cigarettes, or a box, or a
case: for smoking was conceded. There would be several books

on the office table, newly arrived from the New York dealers
or elsewhere. They would pore over these, discuss the author,
the period, the binding, the dedication if any (a phoney, did
René think?), hurry off and search in reference books for dates
and other data.

At last the conference would break-up. They would pass out
of the office, and enter the library, René winking at a bust
of Bolingbroke as he passed it. The library was where he
was supposed to earn his fee, reshuffling and organizing and
bringing the catalogue up to date. But it was in the office that
he passed the majority of the time, in conference with Furber.

Once or twice he *had* been in the house itself, as a very great
favour. Once he had even been in the drawing-room—for a
few minutes, to be shown an engraving. In the study, which
was a room adjacent to the library, he had actually been asked
to sit down, and the chairs there were more accommodating to
the posterior than were those of the little office. Upon the
study wall were photographs of nude young men: of *one* nude
young man he thought. As he was looking at them he found
Furber watching him with owlish impassivity, with the most
tenuous hint of enquiry: as if to say 'Well?' There was an
obscene ink-drawing by Jean Cocteau, a photograph of a Dali,
photos of Roman aqueducts, a scene in the mountains above
Split, a view of Paris from the window of an apartment in the
Ile Saint Louis where he often passed a few months.

In order to mark the occasion, Furber offered him a cigar,
which he refused. Dragging his long legs, languidly and with
elegance, like a sun-doped stalk, Furber then led him back
again into the library.

When friends came to see him—'friends' in contrast to
someone in his pay—they were led laughing into the study.
René would probably be sitting on a ladder doing what he was
paid to do; pushing the books about, attempting to get them
into homogeneous groups. Usually no notice was taken of him,
although no doubt when they reached the study, it would be
explained who he was. Once or twice one of these people
apparently wanted to say they had met him, and he was
introduced. This was what was disagreeable, not the times
when, gaily laughing, they passed into the study. These

persons were almost invariably young; Mr. Furber seemed to
know no one of his own age. René judged that they were
young intellectuals of the better sort, i.e. the less impoverished,
or possibly young men at the University. It was unlikely that
they were rich, for Momaco, though wealthy, was so primitive
a place that Furber probably was the only man of wealth
upon the Hill who knew the difference between Pericles and
Petronius. So the study was the place where he was called
Cedric, where he instinctively went with a 'friend', and where
René was not allowed to penetrate. To be treated like a man
who had come to mend the clock would not have mattered to
René, had it not been for the ordeal on the wooden chair, with
so much harsh American daylight. For he felt that it was not
intentional.

His patron's father had been 'one of the richest men in
Canada'. There are thousands of such, but he, undeniably,
was a biggish nickel man. For this sensitive bearded flower of
his loins, this was to be born in the purple. He had inherited,
along with his comfortable fortune, the feeling of the gulf
between really big dough, and such money as René could ever
hope to make: scarcely enough to keep one's underclothes
clean. Also there was the 'hired man' superstition of the
American. You never drank, smoked, exchanged stories,
unbent with your 'hired man'—whether you hired him at
twenty thousand bucks a year, or thirty cents an hour.

As to drinking, Furber never did that. He smoked: but even
when he inserted a medicated camphorized cork-tipped 'Kool'
between his bearded lips, and ejected the smoke through his
heavy goatish nostrils, it seemed paradoxically *masculine*:
René registered surprise. For Furber, a rich lonely bachelor
of forty, was very old-maidish and strict. He was dreadfully
fussy about untidiness. It was unlikely that his epicene
instincts found expression in any practical way, though it was
hardly possible that he was unaware of their presence. The big
lips under his beard were dreamy and large and a little child-
like, his big brown eyes were bovine but intelligent. He knew
to what 'tribe' he belonged, but probably did not practise the
rites of the tribe. He liked watching.

In some ways he was considerate. Once or twice he had

enquired how René was getting on, and when René answered
by a grimace, he took five twenty-dollar bills out of his pocket,
and pushed them across the office table.
'Here, put this in your pocket. Don't mind taking it. I know
the jam you are in here in Canada. When all this is over, pay
me back if you prefer to have it that way. The war won't last
forever, will it!'
'I don't know.—Thank you. That will do a lot and I will
take it.'
'Tell me if you ever need anything. I will do anything I
can.'
There are few rich men who, unasked, help a man poorer
than themselves. As he sat there upon the numbing wood, the
cold hard light from the large curtainless window glaring in
his eyes, and gazed at the bearded sphinx lying back in
the leather office chair, René appreciated that actually this
strange creature was *kind*. He was almost startled with all the
inhuman ritual of the American rich automatically adopted by
this barbarous snob, yet Cedric Furber had the generosity of
the poor. How was this possible? Probably a good heart.
René thought better of him (one's opinion cannot but develop
a favourable upward movement when a man gives you a
hundred bucks if you have nothing). He even began to believe
that he had found somebody in Canada who liked him. He
kind of liked this inhuman old maid, too.
'How hard it is to experience gratitude!' René sighed one
day, after Cedric Furber had paid them one of his rare and
patronizing little visits, at the Hotel Blundell. They had just
enough tea to last them until the day after the next: but just
enough by means of their painfully elaborated system of one
muslin bag between them. The bags, prepared by Hester, were
the size of a large thimble:
Furber had surprised them as the first cups were being
poured out. Naturally they were compelled to press him to
have some. Graciously—with his usual bashful graciousness,
in Hester's presence—and probably considering it the proper
thing to do, so as to *ménager* the touchiness of the poor—he
consented.
'Oh *good!*' she exclaimed, so loud and forcibly that

Furber started. And she sprang up to fetch the next day's tea-bags.

'I don't usually take it . . .' he said.

As a great condescension and particular treat for them he would partake of a cup.

'Well—*just to please us!*' she hissed.

He blinked, and stared owlishly at her. Hester had ways of expressing her gratitude and pleasure that were at times as startling as at times they were well meant.

So the next day, as they had no money until (probably!) the following morning, they had no tea. And tea was the one thing they found it was extremely difficult to do without.

'How *difficult* it is to be properly grateful sometimes!' René mused again, shortly after Furber had sidled and wriggled his great height out of the door, coquettishly responding to their duet of crashing *Good-byes*.

'Why be grateful?' Hester enquired.

'Just a debt,' René said. 'One owes gratitude, as one owes money.'

'What is gratitude?'

'A certain *quantity*,' he answered, 'chalked up in the mind, as belonging to somebody else.'

'Quantity of what?' she insisted.

'Of whatever one happens to have to give.—One's life, for certain things. A spoonful of goodwill for others.'

Hester frowned crossly.

'Well,' she said, 'understand this. However many dimes a spook of that kind hands me, he doesn't become real.—He only gives it to pass himself off as a real person. He kind of half-likes you because you play ball.'

René laughed.

'All right,' he said. 'I'll keep up my intercourse all the same with the spirit world. He is gentle and a little spookish isn't he? I don't mind him. He can't help believing he's the Duke of Kent.'

'I would prefer the real thing,' she answered, yawning.

'You are such a stickler for the real. I prefer these fantastic shadows on the walls of the cave.'

She laughed and got up, as their squirrel was looking at her with one large pop-eye through the window, his head, like a neolithic axe-head, pressed against the glass, standing on his hind legs.

'To hell with Furber. Stupid great hairy pansy snob!'

'Well, I cannot agree. You can experience gratitude for that stupid great hairy pansy snob. I can only feel gratitude to people very different from that.'

The squirrel hissed impatiently.

'My darling, no nuts! No tea! We are like you but we have not your sex-appeal.'

The squirrel retired into the tree, hanging upside down like a bat, one eye fixed upon her, as she placed a half a Dad's Cookie on the window-sill.

Like Lord Herbert, only with far less reason, Furber took his surroundings very seriously. He was as solemn a Momaconian as anyone: going to all the hundreds of committee meetings which gave to every microscopic local intellectual a sensation of importance every day of the week. To articles in Momaco, or Ottawa or Toronto papers, or in reviews such as *Midweek* (of Momaco) or *Saturday Night* (of Toronto) he attached as great importance as if they had appeared in the *New York Times*, in *The New Statesman* or *La Nouvelle Revue Française*. He had no sense of proportion at all, and spoke of the new poems of some lady friend of local note as though she were Paul Valèry or Mr. Eliot.

The economics of the two people exiled in a Room are of the importance that economics always possess where human life is suspended above the gutter by something as gossamer-like as the beard of Mr. Furber, or as fabulous as an exceptionally good second-hand bookseller in Momaco. René also wrote fairy stories in French for a Montreal Magazine, and political articles for the *Momaco Gazette-Herald*. But Mr. Furber—odd as this would sound to anyone acquainted with him—was the most solid thing upon the Hardings' economic horizon. And that was why René was obliged prematurely to remove his sling and bandages.

If he had *not* done this, and had presented himself to Furber with one of his arms out of action, Furber would have insisted upon his not resuming his duties (such as they were) at the Library (such as it was). His 'job' would have been endangered, or this was what he felt, he would have received no money. He now, after a considerable walk in the snow, reached the entrance to the Library: he rang, and with unexpected promptitude Furber came to the door in response to the bell. His large round brown eyes opened themselves in what was plainly a feigned surprise. 'Well! This is an unexpected pleasure!' he said.

'Indeed?' René replied with a foreboding of something unpleasant. They passed from the small hallway into the Library, and there, at the foot of a ladder, stood a young man surrounded by books, scattered in all directions upon the floor.

'Since you did not ring up again—how long ago was it, ten days?—I supposed that the arm was giving trouble. Things were getting a little chaotic here, and I thought I would try out a young man who is waiting to take up a post in Ottawa. It really *was* rather urgent.' He gazed around the Library.

René kept his eyes on the ground and did not speak. He had become very pale. Furber noticed the change.

'Come,' he said, 'let us go into the office, and see what can be done.'

The new 'librarian' had almost at once retired into the study, or private sitting-room, it would be better to call it, reserved for intimates or social equals. René followed Mr. Furber into the office, and sat down upon one of the two hard chairs. Then he spoke.

'I am sorry,' he said. 'I appear to have been responsible for a muddle—I was unable to tell you a week ago—it was a week ago I telephoned—the exact day on which I could remove the bandages, and so on. But I was pretty sure I should be all right within a week, and that was what I said. That was stupid of me. I should . . .'

'Not at all, I should have communicated with you. But I thought you would have shown some sign of life if there was any chance of your being able to turn up so soon.'

'Yes, I ought to have telephoned,' René persisted. 'As it is' —he looked up with a half-smile, and an ironic glitter in his mongol tilted eyes—'I have lost my job.'

'No. I hope not. Just for the present I must stick to my

arrangements with this youngster' (and 'don't you have to stick to your arrangements with me?' René inwardly countered) 'but a little later on, I hope, we shall go on with our work.'

René gazed up into the hard, flat, American sky, and his eyes began to water.

'On the other hand, Harding, if you are hipped . . . if you are in any money difficulty . . .'

'That of course I am. So long as the Exchanges are shut down, and I have no appointment, I must be that,' René said. Furber always appeared to have several hundred dollars in his note-case, and he now put down on the table three twenty-dollar bills. 'As I have said before, pay me back some day, in the piping times of peace. Meanwhile please tell me, at any time, if you are in a jam.'

René duly thanked him, but he left a few minutes later. As he went out into the snow, down the steps which led to the library, and down the magic Hill which so oddly stuck up above Momaco, he saw in front of him something like a large black hole in the landscape whichever way he turned his head. It was as though his vision were in some way affected. He marched back to the hotel, or, as the snow in places had not been cleared away, it was rather a martial trudge, and his head kept up a feverish hammering. When he reached the Room, and laconically announced the news, Hester burst into angry tears. But soon she wiped her eyes and expressed her feelings on the subject of 'the double-faced, elongated pansy man, the dollar seigneur who stinks of culture as some people do of camphor.' She borrowed her expletives from René, recombining them, and altering them with half-humorous feminine venom.

'He is a worm,' agreed René, 'but he is a worm with a great big pansy heart. Sixty berries are not to be sniffed at.'

'What is the use of that?' Hester protested. 'Such doles, uncertain doles, are not going to keep us alive. Are they?'

'No.'

'How are we going to live now?'

'That we must see,' he said, frowning.

9*

They neither of them felt that the tea they then had, a little early for them, was a strong enough drug to shift their immense depression. They both were brooding, when Affie made her appearance, and got to work on their tea-cups. Obviously she had been listening to Hester's outburst, for she made some rather disparaging remarks about Fairies. She also foretold a sudden change of fortune for the Hardings. There was a number of small black specks in Hester's cup; this was *money*.—After having revived them, as she thought, with promises of gold, she gossiped about their immediate neighbours. The woman in 21A, for instance, who had gone away to have a baby three months before, was her first subject. Some weeks before the time had come for her to be confined her husband had vanished. This, it appeared, was a by no means uncommon occurrence. The woman, however, could not do otherwise than enter the Nursing Home, when advised by her doctor to do so. She had the child: so far so good. But that was three months ago, and the Nursing Home had refused to allow her to leave until their fees were paid. She was a prisoner. Meanwhile the child was growing into a fine big boy. Attempts to trace the husband were in vain. But only that afternoon the mother-in-law had put in an appearance, settled the bill, and the young woman and her child were back in No 21A. In a month or so's time, all the expense over, the husband would no doubt return. Such was the general rule in Momaco. She was a good-looking young woman: Affie felt sure he would come back.

In the Nursing Home, incarcerated though she was, she had had a splendid time. Now she was idyllically happy, with her baby. Affie looked a little happy with the happy mother.

René sat for a moment thinking of this. Then he made a pronouncement. 'It sounds primitive at first. But I do not believe it is so, really. The expense of bringing a new citizen into the world is borne by the older, economically better-placed member of a family. Then the male bird (temporarily absent) returns to the nest, and the care of the new-born is assured. If the male bird does *not* return, it means the female is unattractive. But she had no right to reproduce her graceless self: so the male, in this case, acts in the best interests of nature to keep away, and to refuse to help her to perpetuate her unlovely self.'

'That,' smiled Affie, 'sounds to me a little primitive.'

'And to me, too,' Hester softly clamoured. 'How about ugly men? Many of the greatest men have been hideously ugly.'

There were sounds of polite exultation from the female side. But René put this down at once.

'You think you have reasoned well. But the fact is that the children of the great are their deeds. Their biological offspring is generally the dullest or vilest.'

After a little argument they left that subject, to discuss a neighbour, called by the Hardings 'The Duchess'. Affie had the latest information as to the new type of drug she was taking. This drug addict was a lesbian, and she had been crossed in love. Hence the new drug.

Finally, René attempted to discuss the Russians who occupied the apartment immediately opposite their own. A young man and a young woman, and the mother of the young man, lived there.

But Affie became remote at once: this was one of the only apartments about which she observed a strict discretion. The young Russian was unusually good looking.

'Do you not know who that is?' someone had asked René with surprise. 'It is the "Toronto Kid".' He was well-known as a boxer. But somehow he had got to Momaco, and he did no boxing there. Instead of that he held people up and robbed them, with violence. Or so the detectives said, with whom René had spoken in the Hotel kitchen. There were two detectives who haunted the Hotel for some weeks, but they appeared to be quite impotent: for why did they not arrest the young Russian, if they really had the evidence, which they claimed to have, that he was the next thing to a murderer?

Another puzzling question was why the Hotel disregarded the warnings of the Police. If the Police informed the owner of a Hotel that a certain guest was a dangerous criminal it might be supposed that he would be asked to leave immediately. Not so at the Hotel Blundell. René speculated as to the probable reason for this. The only explanation was money. Numbers of men used to visit the Russians' apartment, and

they were always of an ostentatiously criminal type. This
alone would be sufficient corroboration of what the two detectives said.

But now the underworld came there no more. The 'Toronto
Kid' was the owner of a superb car, the wonder of the Hotel.
It still stood near the Annexe door, but its tyres had been
so badly slashed (who was responsible no one knew) that it
was completely disabled. The discontinuance of the visits of
gorillas may have had something to do with the tyre-slashing.

A more likely explanation of this fact, however, was the
presence in the Hotel, by night as much as by day, of the
Police. It had recently been an almost nightly occurrence for
the Police to visit the Russians. At two or three in the morning
Hester and René were wakened by the tramp of heavy boots.
This was immediately followed by 'Open up, the Police!'
shouted over and over again, and an imperious banging upon
the Russians' door, which continued until the door was
opened. This lasted sometimes for ten minutes. The women
would have to get up every time, no doubt. This was an
extraordinary persecution; it was obvious that the Police were
convinced that something was hidden there, and it was equally
obvious that they did not find it. But there was now what
seemed to be a complication. The Police, it was said, were
also on this young man's track as a draft dodger. Some weeks
before, duly manacled, the young Russian was marched off;
but late the next morning he was back again. What this meant
no one seemed to know. Not even Bess. If this was to do with
draft dodging, then clearly his claim for exemption had not
been disproved. If it was to do with a criminal charge it had
not the effect of stopping their nocturnal visits. The police
may not have succeeded in wearing down the resistance of the
Russian family, but they were successful in almost reducing
the Hardings to nervous wrecks. But, dominating everything
else, the mystery remained as to why the proprietor of the
Hotel Blundell did not turn these people out, and *that* veil
Affie not only refused to lift, but would not admit that it
existed. She, who was the incarnation of indiscretion! This
must indeed be hush-hush to affect Affie in that way.

CHAPTER XIX

The Janitors

OF the janitors most remained unseen, in the regions where the furnace was situated, beneath the street level. One cannot refer to those regions as cellars, they were not deep enough for that, and also there were many other things there besides cellar-like areas. There were, for instance, a number of rather squalid apartments, there was a small office, a storeroom, and the remains of what was once a saloon. All janitors, theoretically, must ascend to the upper part of the hotel: for it was one of their duties to attend to the windows or fix the elements in the electric cooker, or keep the elevator in shape. But the majority of janitors omitted, for one reason or another, to do this. What was mainly responsible for their failing to carry out these rather ill-defined functions, was drunkenness. The furnace they just must attend to, or everyone in the hotel would freeze to death: but everything else they were supposed to do could, at a pinch, be done by somebody else. More than half the time, for instance, there was an occupant of a fourth-story apartment, a Mr. Jacobs, who fixed the elements, and attended generally to break-downs in the lighting, heating and elevator systems.

Why all the janitors were so defective in honesty, industry, in restraint with respect to the bottle, or what goes with that, *das Weib*, has already been explained. It was because Mrs. Plant, Affie, and everybody else, on the whole, preferred them that way. The hotel had no use for an honest, hardworking, and sober janitor. He would be out of tune with the hotel, and the janitor is a very important functionary in such a place. Charlie, the present janitor, was an exception to all rules. And *he* did not stay all the time out of sight. Quite the contrary. Charlie was flying all over the hotel all day long and for half the night. He awakened in René a rather similar alarm to that he had felt for Mrs. Harradson. Charlie was a very large Norwegian, like a gigantic squirrel, with a small head, in which a wild pale-blue eye at all times lit up and was madly expressive. He enjoyed the unusual advantage of being *persona grata* with both Mrs. Plant and Affie. Affie displayed the breadth of her sympathies by the variety of characters she sponsored and protected among the long succession of janitors: and without that protection no janitor would be there very long.

She had been passionately devoted to 'Sonny-boy'. It was *she* who named him 'Sonny-boy'—the bank-clerk-like young man, who was the most useless of all the janitors. In a way she was equally fond of Charlie, the old jailbird, with his wild eyes and torrents of broken English, indeed so broken that not a particle was intact, unless it was the Norse intermixture.

She actually preferred a man to be a thief and drunkard. Having been a nurse might account in part for her tastes. She once described to the Hardings an experience of hers at a hospital, where she had acted as an auxiliary unqualified nurse, or such was her story. One day a violently protesting hag was brought in. They immediately thrust her screaming and kicking into a hot bath. She was a confirmed vagrant: her hair was full of hundreds of hairpins and also the greasy hide-out of a horde of lice. She, for some time, defended her head with a fanatical ferocity; it required all the muscular endurance and hygienic militancy of Affie and two other nurses to force her to surrender her head. They cleared out all the hairpins and effected a thorough delousing of her entire person, and in the end she turned out to be a delightful old woman, according to Affie; a professional wandervogel, an indigent tourist, sleeping in the barns when the dogs would let her, a mettlesome philosophic wit. Affie struck up a great friendship with this old wreck who had once been a tobacconist. So all her life Affie had had to deal with sick or eccentric people (her most permanent type of employment being that of nurse-companion) until perhaps she had developed an appetite for helplessness.—However that may be, the only kind of janitor she heartily disliked was a competent one, like a man called Jan—whom everybody hated because he was so clean, sober, and good at his job.

Again, her sex reactions were original. A big strong man said nothing to her. Jan was that, and this side of him was greatly appreciated by the Belgian woman who ran the house next door. Even the hairdresser widow on the other side appreciated this too, and Jan was greatly in demand on either side of the hotel—until the Belgian lady beat up the lady hairdresser one day just outside the front door, after which Jan deserted the hairdresser and went to live with the Belgian rooming-house lady. But to Affie he was nothing, she said he smelled. This, René thought, was because he was definitely of the workman or seaman class. Affie disliked all workmen. Charlie was an ordinary seaman too; but he was mad, and more often in a jail—everybody supposed—than in a ship.

But then there was something more than either of those things. Affie had an eye for life. In Charlie she saw the ruined Peer Gynt, but still a wild piratic lunatic. She loved his screaming laugh, his staring hyper-eager eyes. She knew he had lived with the Troll-king and played every scurvy trick upon his fellows, out of giddiness—and that he would at last be melted down by the button-moulder. He lied so much he chased himself, whirling in and out of his wildly blurted stories. If you caught him in a lie, he burst into a peal of shrieks and dashed off, leaping along the passages and up and down the stairs like a demented kangaroo. Solveig had been sitting and singing, ah for so long. But what does Solveig's song turn into if you stop and listen to it? Into a brood of bawling children. So he vaulted away, and until he died would be skipping and screaming with laughter, thieving and lying.

When René had occasion to descend into the basement during the Charlie epoch he would find it full of the rolling pyjama'ed bottoms of French-Canadian prostitutes. Their black Indian eyes blazed with merriment when they saw Charlie come leaping down, with a duck in one hand and a coil of rope in the other, which he was swinging round his head, as if he would lasso the amused harlots.

Upstairs, he and Mrs. Plant would engage in shouting matches in some room where he was working. He liked her deafness, it gave him the opportunity to scream. As she always talked at the top of her voice too, they made a deafening uproar. Anybody would suppose they were having an appalling show-down: but if they listened they would find that the First Lady and her janitor were only violently agreeing with one another.

It was René's good fortune to observe Charlie, in the midst of one of these transports, slap Mrs. Plant on the shoulder, nearly knocking her down, so great was his approval of what she had said. Though visibly shaken, she did not mind a bit. Nothing that Charlie did was wrong. When he robbed a store she might have been expected to mind a little. But she understood, or Affie did, that he was irresponsible, and that it was, like everything else, a prank merely.

One evening after tea, René and Hester were in conference, and both were speaking in low tones, for they preferred that what they were talking about should not be heard by Affie. Hester was frowning as she listened, then suddenly without warning the door flew open. There may have been a knock, but neither of them heard it. Charlie stood there panting, his hat on the back of his head, and the right eye, which did all the expressive work, was darting about, full of the maddest light they had ever seen in it. His hands too were in ceaseless movement, and one flipped out of one of his pockets with a baby packet of tea. As he held it out he was convulsed with crazy mirth, and he continued to pour out a jerky stream of largely incomprehensible speech. But 'want buy' was said a great number of times with great eagerness.

Charlie dropped a small packet of tea upon the table by the side of which the Hardings were sitting. A lightning dive into the dark hole of his pocket, and out shot a second packet, then a third, and a fourth, and a fifth, and a sixth, and a seventh, and an eight, and a ninth, and a tenth, and an eleventh, and a twelfth. So there were a dozen miniature packets of tea. As each packet was produced, he riveted a moist eye upon Hester, and when Hester and René began to laugh, as the pile of tea-packets went on increasing, he laughed with extraordinary glee. They were entering into the joke of the thing—that was as it should be.

They asked him how much he wanted for these packets of

tea, and he screamed with laughter at the idea of knowing
how much he wanted for them. Tea was in short supply and
the Hardings wanted the tea. All he knew was they wanted
the tea, and that he had the tea. He tried to twist his body in
a hysterical knot, coughing with laughter. Then he darted his
head down towards René and poured out a lot of urgent con-
fidences, mostly in Norwegian. René's nervousness increased,
and taking a couple of dollars out of his pocket he held them
up, he made an offer. Charlie almost tore the notes out of
his hand, and pushed the tea-packets over towards Hester.
Then he reached down into the other pocket, and with the
abruptness of legerdemain a huge cheese, actually processed
cheese supplied in cubes, flew out of his pocket and then, with
a bang, there it sat, immense and greasy, upon the table. This
big square of cheese seemed to strike him as the funniest thing
he had ever seen. He kept pointing to it, gulping with laughter,
as he jumped about. 'Cheese!' he shrieked. Hester and René
shook their heads. Charlie had one more try at getting them
to see the joke. Then he snatched the cheese up and thrust
it back in his noticeably unclean pocket, and darted out
of the Room. The Hardings had not the least idea of
the nature of this joke. But very soon they were to be
enlightened.

The next morning at about nine o'clock there was an uproar
at the foot of the stairs near which their apartment was
situated. Both of them jumped up and ran to the stair-head.
Charlie, screaming with laughter, was being beaten up by a
large jewish woman. She had torn his shirt to shreds, and
Charlie whirled his arms about in an attempt to beat off this
frantic woman, who kept spitting in a hoarse staccato, 'Dirty
teef. You shop-lift—you break my shop in, you tak my sheese,
I phone de pleece.' Charlie took a six-stair leap towards the
Hardings, his face strained up towards them in the usual eager
delight, but she caught him by the heel crying hoarsely, 'You
beast! You crim-in-all' Clutching the banister, he kicked her
off, and in a blue cloud of strips and tatters, he leapt past the
Hardings. Mrs. Plant, it turned out, had come up behind
Hester. That lady gazed after her tatterdemalion janitor, and
when he had disappeared at the other end of the corridor, she

turned to Hester, smiled and nodded her head, as if to say,
'Well, what an odd fellow it is!'

Very soon the police arrived, and took him away, which he
seemed to regard as the best joke of all. They were as morose
as the great jitterbug was elated, and they marched off dourly
with this tattered giant dancing between them.

This irrepressible jitterbug turned the hotel into the kind
of place it would have been had the Mad Hatter been let loose
in it for a week or two. He would have been found attempting
to thrust Mrs. Plant into a teapot or purloin the medals of the
Three Musketeers—'each for all and all for each'. As a matter
of fact those were precisely the kind of things Charlie was
doing all day long. His infatuation for medals led to a stirring
scene.

Charlie was in the Beverage Room with his favourite con-
cubine. They were sitting with a man who had a magnificent
Boer War gold medal. The prostitute was so impressed with
this medal that she left Charlie's side and sat beside the
bemedalled veteran.

'You have no medals, Charlie. You have no beautiful gold
medal like this. I don't love you any more.'

'I have I have!' he cried as he sprang to his feet. With a
banging of doors he violently vanished. Ten minutes later he
returned, his breast jangling with medals of the most convincing kind. A number of suitcases were in store not far from
the furnace room, and this depository was in Charlie's care
and keeping. Needless to say he had conducted a thorough
examination of the contents of this luggage (for no locksmith
was more expert than he), and in one large portmanteau he
had come upon these beautiful medals. There, provisionally,
he had left them.

When they were back in their apartment, René said, 'If we
were people who were inclined to forget, this hotel would
always be reminding us what a chaos we live in.'

'I suppose it would,' Hester agreed without enthusiasm.

'We have got into rather a brisk little microcosm. But''—he

looked at her placidly—'it is not brisker than the nations of Europe.'

At the usual time Bess arrived with her vacuum cleaner. She seemed glad to have seen the last of Charlie, for she did not at all share the irresponsible temper of the First Lady, or of the Second Lady. A small shop, which in England would be called a 'general shop', was the place Charlie had broken into the night before. It was situated in a neighbouring street, and both Hester and René were its patrons, from time to time. Bess growled on about the enormities of Charlie, and the disgraceful scenes that occurred down below, in the lowest row of apartments. She said that on one occasion she had seen Charlie completely naked, darting in and out, in a sort of obscene hide and seek with a couple of naked french-canadian prostitutes. It seemed that he was at the top of his form before he put his clothes on.

At the time when usually the Indian was compelled to hold his teutonic wife upside down, there was a terrific shriek of an abnormal kind, though René felt sure that it was the same woman. The earlier disturbance had probably whetted his appetite for such things: for he rose immediately, opened the door, and moved quickly down the corridor in the direction of the shrieks. The sound grew louder, and then suddenly stopped. Mr. Martin's was the first apartment you reached as you moved out of the annexe into the main building. René found him, standing just outside his door, and looking in his direction. In light-coloured flannel trousers and a pale jumper, the faded pink of his cheeks pulled down a little by the set jowl, the eyes gently hooded, he was in some way a spectral figure. From the stairs leading down to the street level emerged the Indian; not at all a daunting figure, but a pleasant, dark-skinned young man. He was shouting, 'Cut that out. Come back here, you bitch, d'you hear me.' But a moment later he was confronted by Mr. Martin, and he stopped. In a low voice of great impressiveness, he heard himself admonished, as though a text from scripture had been selected for the occasion, 'A gentleman does not refer to a lady as a bitch!' The Indian stood rooted to the spot, as though he had seen a ghost, who had given utterance to some frightful curse.

Mr. Martin stood, awful in his respectability, his mouth having scarcely moved to utter the tremendous sentence. Obviously he was perfectly aware that this was big medicine. The Indian, having glanced rebelliously once or twice at the Eternal Englishman, went back downstairs again in eloquent silence.

With a smile, René went up to Mr. Martin. He had decided that it was best to affect to have some errand in the hotel. 'Good morning,' he said, 'so Charlie has left us?'—'As far as I am concerned,' Mr. Martin replied, '. . . well, there are people I should miss more than Charlie.'

Over Mr. Martin's shoulder René saw the inflamed face, the small girl-hiker figure of the German-Canadian, whom he knew principally as a Scream. The Scream looked at him as any Scream would, as if to say, 'Yes, I am the Scream.'

Mr. Martin was sparing of his words, and, in any case, somewhat mentally congealed. But as René was moving on, he observed politely, 'I suppose your arm is all right again now, Mr. Harding? It was very rough luck.'

CHAPTER XX

The Private Life of Bill Murdoch

RENÉ wandered through the hotel, and dropped in at the kitchen. Affie and Miss·Toole were sitting at the table. They had been having their mid-morning tea, and Affie smokily scrutinizing Miss Toole's cup. The normal everyday expression of Miss Toole's face was one of astonishment. Her eyebrows were forever raised, and if she were chatting with a guest you would have said that the latter had been telling her some pretty tall stories—which, incidentally, she was scarcely prepared to credit. But now she looked not only startled but dismayed. René saw at once that Affie had been scaring the wits out of her. He had seen her at it before, and felt rather sorry for her victim. Once or twice he had met Miss Toole in the corridor lately, and quite obviously she was terrified. She was moving about like an automaton, literally 'scared stiff'.

René sat down at the table. Affie lifted her head slowly and looked at the intruder: for obviously he was that. 'And how is Professor Harding this morning?' She knew that he did not like being called Professor Harding, and the fact that she addressed him in that manner signified that she would rather have his room than his company. Plainly she had arrived at a point in her sorcery act at which the spell was working, but for complete success more time was needed. Another ten minutes and Miss Toole would be speechless with terror.

René pointed to the ice-box. 'Did you discover who took the chicken?' The last time he had been down there, there was perturbation; no one had been in the kitchen for ten minutes or so and it must have been during that time that the chicken in the ice-box had vanished.

Miss Toole's look of astonishment increased, and she shook her head. 'Mr. Harding,' she said slowly, in a tone of chronic

271

astonishment deepening into dismay, 'to think that one can't leave a door open for ten minutes!'

But Affie, bored, observed, 'Things are often stolen from the ice-box,' as if to close the subject. 'Who steals them?' René enquired.—'Your guess is as good as mine.' And Affie turned back to the tea-cups. René smiled at Miss Toole and sauntered out.

Back in the Room, René told Hester that the embodied Scream had sought sanctuary with Mr. Martin, and that she appeared perfectly safe there.

'How does that insignificant little man manage to . . .?'

'I wonder. Mr. Martin has succeeded in exploiting English respectability. This is rather a feat, especially in a country where the English are so unpopular. In the first instance he must have impressed Mrs. Plant terrifically with his genteelness. His voice is discreet, he exudes *it isn't done,* he always seems a little tired.'

'He is the kind of man one sees everywhere in England,' Hester said.

'Of course,' René agreed. 'He belongs to the sports-jacketed lower-middleclass. He is a small provincial haberdasher, or (if he were younger) a Trust House manager, or a seaside tobacconist.'

'Yes,' she nodded.

'Well, that is where *respectability* is to be found. The "decent fellows" of the Public Schools become, on that level, "One of the best", "a white man". He would be as white a man as you could find if you tipped him well.'

'You are hard on Mr. Martin,' she demurred. 'He is a harmless little man, is he not?'

'I believe you are wrong. He is not a very trustworthy man. But in a small way he has "made good" in Canada. He knows the Northlands: he is one of the innumerable "prospectors" one encounters, who have never prospected. I am sure he knows no more geology than the patter anyone picks up in the North. A few men come in here and have a drink with him every evening. They sit there in his apartment drinking Scotch, and talking of gold and nickel. I suppose the whisky is bootleg. They are the substantial men of the immediate neighbourhood. They do not get noisy, though they drink a lot. They sit there drinking easily and quietly, as sea-captains do in a port, narrating their adventures in strange seas. I do not know what his adventures have been. When we first arrived Mr. Martin spoke to me of his life in the Northlands; how he played the doctor with the Indians, and so on. I think that is genuine enough.'

Hester regarded her husband with ironical expectancy. He returned her gaze, and smiled. 'I say a mouthful about a very little man: a mild, soft-spoken, weak-kneed Briton. But such mild-mannered little Englishmen have often been at the bottom of very funny things.'

Hester opened her eyes a fraction more than usual, and stared, again expectant. For such hints of melodrama were not his line of country.

'If he has exploited his genteel personality, others might do so too,' René added, as though as an afterthought.

'Really, René!' Hester laughed. 'If anything occurs in this hotel . . . of a startling nature, I shall suspect Mr. Martin— or *you*, darling.'

The janitor who succeeded Charlie was greatly disliked by Affie. He was the ex-boxer whose face she smacked. Everyone described him as 'punch-drunk'. But to René it seemed that the punches that made him permanently muzzy and half-stupefied were in reality kicks that came out of a bottle. The kick induced by mixing two or more bottles of dissimilar alcohol.

This janitor's name was Bill Murdoch. His behaviour was infinitely bad from the first day of his arrival, when he nearly killed a man in the Beverage Room. He was lazy, drunken, and surly. If, in the abstract, as a worthless ruffian, he qualified, he was dull and an unattractive man, and no one, man or woman, could take any interest in him.

Inured as they were to dramatic noises, both diurnal and nocturnal, some weeks after Charlie's departure there was one which made them and the whole of the rest of the hotel sit up. It was in the middle of the night, and it seemed as though the house were being demolished by a giant. Both René and Hester were wakened by tremendous thumping in the basement. It was a blow which shook the annexe to its foundations, followed, at intervals of about thirty seconds, by blows of equal force. Almost at once the most blood-curdling screams were heard, appearing to come from somewhere below. Someone—or something—was battering with sinister power upon a wall; or so it seemed at first.

'This is too awful! What is happening!' Hester's voice was a little breathless. For once this noise sounded as though the whole hotel was involved: as if at length this giant footstep would be heard outside their own door, as if the attack were upon all of them. For the imagination is apt to inhibit the rational faculties: and the imagination is basically anthropomorphic. And thus, although the faculties responsible for mathematics would assure the anxious heart that these sounds were a product of some sort of hammering, and it was *not* Thor's hammer that was being used, nevertheless the imagination would have its way, would insist that the god Thor was in the basement, or else it would appear that these enormous thuds were the footsteps of a supernatural being.

It was the splintering and the crash of wood, which could be distinctly heard, which removed these sounds at last from the supernatural, and confined them firmly to the natural order. There was a final ghastly thud, echoing from the nether regions, the tearing and cracking of heavy wood, and a crescendo of screams, differing in quality from the German woman's morning aubade in sharps, to which the annexe was treated every morning, as the genuine M'Coy does from its opposite. These screams had terror in them.

All this frightful, menacing disturbance, in the heart of the night, was merely the lid lifted off the private life of Bill Murdoch. René went out and stood at the top of the stairs. There was no sound now except the distant stoking of the furnace. Mr. Martin had passed him—without recognition. His face had the same look of awful respectability, the cheeks of faded pink hanging a little dourly, the eyes hooded, as on the occasion of his reprimand to the Indian. Obviously he was prepared to say, 'A gentleman does *not* employ a mallet to batter a lady's brains out,' if that were necessary.—There were certain hoarse mutterings, and soon afterwards Mr. Martin reascended, going in the direction of his apartment. Again as he passed there was no recognition. Guests were not supposed to snoop, to poke their noses in things of that kind.

'Very official!' René thought to himself, and he speculated as to whether Mr. Martin were the real owner of the hotel, and Mrs. Plant merely a rather subtle blind.

He watched the small grey figure, with its genteel flexing of the knees, as it went down the corridor. And he thought he saw something white in the dark angle where Mr. Martin's apartment was situated. Yes, René pondered, there is more in Mr. Martin than meets the eye. He reproached himself with having been so unobservant. So quiet a little man, so harmless, so genteel.

In the morning, Affie visited them after breakfast. This, according to her, was what had occurred during the night. A Peasoup, living in a basement-apartment, cohabited with a woman not a French-Canadian. This man worked at night. The woman was quite nice, Affie reported; she came from 'a good family' in Ottawa. This made it all the more surprising that, not content with living in sin with a repulsive Peasoup (who looked like a defrocked priest, and Affie felt quite sure he was—and it was a great pity they did not defrock more of them)—not content with this flagrant exhibition of bad taste, she had—at night, of course, when the Peasoup was out at work—palled up with the unspeakable janitor, who was always too drunk to be of much use to any woman, and sent his shirt to the wash once a year.

Well, for some reason, the Peasoup had unexpectedly returned last night and failed to find this woman in their apartment. After a little investigation, he discovered her in the janitor's room very drunk, in bed beside the even drunker Bill Murdoch. He had gone away, secured something at once heavy and handy, and returned to the room of the janitor who was now alone, since the offending woman had succeeded in staggering back to her apartment. With a rain of gallic curses he rushed at the prostrate janitor who had not moved from where he was, or indeed had any consciousness of what was happening, and gave him a terrific beating with the weapon he had found in the furnace-room.

This had occurred at about twelve-thirty, as Affie timed it. She had been woken up by the commotion. Then about four o'clock the stunned and drunken janitor came to his senses, or enough so to experience resentment, and to be in possession of sufficient strength to undertake retaliatory action.

He banged with his fist on the door of the Peasoup's apartment, uttering the most unspeakable threats; he flung himself against it, and kicked it with great violence. But these were all very solid doors of good Canadian wood, and he made no impression on it. He seemed, though, quite resolved to get in somehow, and his fury increased as he found himself thwarted.

The Peasoup's sensations were not of the pleasantest, for he was a small man, and the janitor would certainly eat him alive if he broke down the door. So he escaped through the window, and he had been watched by Affie, hopping through the backyards, which were knee-deep in snow.

Unable to bring down the door by hurling himself against it, Bill Murdoch had fetched from the store-room a heavy baulk of wood about six feet in length. Supplied with this battering-ram he opened the assault proper upon the Peasoup's apartment. His imprecations filled the whole of the lower part of the house, and the woman inside, who had not fled with her mate, was terrified, it was plain to hear. Why she too had not escaped across the snow Affie could not understand. When at length Bill Murdoch battered the door down, she was beaten within an inch of her life. (Perhaps Affie exaggerated, but it was no doubt probably unpleasant enough). It was most likely that Bill was still too drunk to see that this was not the Peasoup, or else not very particular who it was received his retributive blows.

Somewhere about noon the police arrived, and the battered, bloodshot, cursing janitor was marched off. The uncouth quarters reserved for janitors were cleaned out, clean linen replaced the soiled, and within a few hours a new janitor was installed.

CHAPTER XXI

The Microcosm becomes an Iceberg

NOT much more than two weeks had passed when René received a telephone call from Mr. Furber, asking him if he would care to resume his duties as 'librarian'. The following afternoon René was sitting once more upon one of the two unsoftened chairs at the side of Mr. Furber's office table, offering his opinion as to the value of several books, and as to whether they would be an acquisition to Mr. Furber's collection. Regarding the first of these two questions, he had not the remotest idea what the answer was. He knew as little about the market value of a book, as he did of the value of diamonds or fur coats. As regards the second question, since most of Furber's books did not interest him, it was a waste of time consulting him as to the desirability of adding a little-known Marquis de Sade to the collection. But he had to affect enthusiasm, in order to retain his position upon one of the unsoftened and malformed chairs, reserved for those of very low income-brackets. But he and Hester were overjoyed: black Christmas was forgotten, and they prayed with fervour that he maintain his precarious perch upon Mr. Furber's awful chairs for many months to come.

The actual date of this reinstatement was January the eighteenth. The evening of January the twenty-second was spent as usual. First of all they listened to the bulletins, reporting acts of war all over the world; the slow unfolding of World Ruin, Act II. After that they listened to a talk by an American Expert on Asia. He was a very aggressive anglophobe, who once a week told the American public that 'White Empire in Asia' was at an end—and he made it very clear what he meant by that. He meant that England must immediately quit India, Burma, Malaya, the East Indian and Pacific Islands, Hongkong, etc., etc., etc. He also made it perfectly plain that the English must do this because they

were unpleasant people; not because the wickedness of white
people occupying and bossing Oriental countries worried him
particularly. He was not a moralist, like an English Liberal
or Socialist—he was not possessed of an uneasy White conscience. He was just a violent imperialist who objected to
other imperialists occupying all the territories that would be
better run by Uncle Sam. And England was after all a small
island, not much bigger than Long Island.

'Europe will be crushed between American and Russian
Imperialism,' René remarked absentmindedly. 'And England's
Empire will vanish like smoke—literally overnight, this war
being the night in question. I wonder if there is a single
Englishman, bar Mr. Churchill and a few dozen more in
politics and in banks, who knows that?'

'Is it really as bad as all that?' Hester protested.

'It is what we call History. The only thing that is *bad* about
it is that the civilization which is now enjoyed by France (and
if it were not for Nazis, by Germany) will be destroyed, and
there will be nothing anywhere to take its place. That is bad.'

But, as has already been explained, the ruin of these two
people's world was by now so much an accepted thing that it
had lost its power to depress. No cloud went with them from
the war bulletins over into the other programmes consistently
light-hearted, which immediately followed.

The night was exceptionally cold, even for Momaco. And
although the heating system was good enough, on such nights,
when it went to forty or fifty below zero, they switched on
an electric fire which was also provided. Even so, they felt
uncomfortably cold, and when they went to bed they placed
their overcoats on top of the blankets, and slept in a laocoon-
like embrace.

About three-thirty in the morning there was a sound that
woke both of them; it was a new sound that they had never
heard before. They did not know what it meant, they lay and
listened. Actually it was the clanging of the large bell, which
was installed in a corner of the entrance lounge. It was a very
powerful bell, which could be heard plainly in the Annexe: its
sound was harsh and unpleasant. The Hardings had never
taken any notice of it, but it was an alarm bell, provided

to alert the guests in case of fire. René sat up in bed and exclaimed, 'What is that? It is in the house somewhere.'

'It sounds to me like an alarm,' Hester said. There was a stir and murmur throughout the Hotel, upstairs someone was pounding frantically about. Then there was a tenuous screaming, from a long way off, and almost immediately afterwards the Indian's wife went into action. René jumped out of bed, turned on the electric light, and went over to the window. As he held the curtain aside, he said, 'There are flames. The Hotel is on fire. We must be quick. We must try and get our belongings out.'

Hester jumped out of bed, and moved quickly over to the window. Flames were coming out of the top of the Hotel, against the moon-illumined sky. It was a bright orange kicking against an electric blue. Both had the same experience, both felt incredulous. The idea of the Hotel, the shell in which they had lived for so long, going up in smoke and flames, they had to become accustomed to; the destruction of a microcosm gives one a foretaste of the destruction of the world, and René thought afterwards how much they had taken their especial universe for granted, and how far they had been from a realization of the destruction they were always talking about.

'What do *we* do?' asked Hester, her teeth chattering.

'The first thing is to dress. And *dress warm.* We shall probably have to get out. It is at least forty below zero.'

He tore their overcoats off the Murphy bed, and afterwards pushed it up into the air, until it fitted neatly into its cupboard, the doors of which he banged shut. Next he went to the clothes closet, lifting from its hanger his warmest suit, and picked up his overshoes. In a few minutes he was dressed, all but his overcoat. Hester, on her side, had disappeared into the bathroom.

There was not much noise in the Annexe. Everyone was engaged in the same way, no doubt, as were the Hardings. There was a sound of people hurrying along the corridor, which was probably guests streaming out of the main part of the Hotel, from which direction came confused noises, among them the screaming of women. All these sounds filled both of them with horrified apprehension, and in René, more than in

Hester, there was the sense of pressure, from a time that was now constantly narrowing. René had lifted on to the table a large portmanteau: into this he rapidly packed clothes, underclothes as well as suits and dresses, snatching them out of drawers, and pulling them out of the clothes closet. 'Won't that be too heavy, René?' was Hester's anxious enquiry. He seemed not to hear.

For some little time, smoke had been seeping in beneath the door. When he had piled everything in the portmanteau, he strapped it up, and then went quickly into the corridor. It was full of smoke. The young Russian was standing at his door, and smiled.

'What is the Fire Chief doing?' he asked. 'Where are the hoses? It is a quarter of an hour now since that bell went. The Fire Chief is a Peasoup. He don't like being woken up.'

'Ah, that's it!' René responded. As he was going back into his apartment, he saw Mr. Martin coming along the corridor, with the expression that would be there if he were on his way to point out to somebody that 'a meat-saw is not the implement a gentleman uses to saw off a lady's head'! The bottom of his flat cheeks of faded pink flapped very slightly, and he called out, 'The Hotel is on fire. Open all windows.'

'Needless to say do not open the windows,' René warned Hester. 'Come with me,' he continued. 'I must carry this out. We will come back if the smoke is not too bad.'

René dragged the portmanteau outside the door. Firemen now were rushing down the corridors, banging upon the doors, shouting 'Get out.' The fireman on their floor sprang over the portmanteau on his way out.

'Let me give you a hand with that,' said the Russian. René was glad of this help, and the portmanteau was quickly carried out into the street. There were a number of people gathered there, guests and sightseers. René caught sight of a woman with whom he had often talked, who occupied a house almost facing the street-door of the Annexe. She offered to take in their luggage, if they wanted somewhere to put it. Hester had carried out a suitcase, and this and the big valise were placed just inside the front door. Mrs. Waechter was the woman's name; she explained to them how it was that the fire had got such a hold. The hydrants had been frozen and it had taken them some time to get rid of the ice. It was only a few minutes ago that the water had been directed on the flames.

·They left Mrs. Waechter, and returned to their apartment. The smoke was thickening all the time, and they had not been in the apartment above four or five minutes before the water began coming in at the door, and they were soon standing with water over their shoes. 'So they *have* got their hoses playing at last,' said René. 'They must be shooting some back into the Annexe, to discourage the fire from spreading, I suppose.' But Hester was too tired and miserable to reply. They were both hastily collecting what had not found a place in the portmanteau, into another suitcase. René pulled the curtains aside, and the fire had now spread to the entire front of the Hotel. Massive smoke was apt to obscure the flames. At one moment a leaping tongue of fire could be seen in front of a full-bellied black cloud, spreading out as it ascended into the sky: at another moment small and nimble flames would tumble and whirl as though escaping from something hotter than themselves. They both stood dreamily at the window: their eyes seemed to be saying to the flames, 'Yes, all right. Leave nothing.'

.. As they left the room René stopped and looked back. He was not looking at a room but at a life. 'Farewell, three awful years!' he said. 'You will soon be ashes.' But he did not wish that to happen. The Room was him, it was them, they might never be so happy again. And that was a dreadful thought: but it is what we always think when we say Good-bye to something forever.

The Russian was still there at his door; his eyes were apparently immune to smoke, but two huddled figures beyond him seemed to have their faces buried in handkerchiefs.

' 'Bye,' said René. 'You are waiting for flames, eh?'

'I guess so,' the Russian replied, looking up the corridor. Leaving the Annexe, they crossed the road to Mrs. Waechter's, and put the typewriter, rugs, attaché case, and another small suitcase down beside the other things in the Hall. They went back to the sidewalk and walked slowly over towards the Annexe door. On the way, René looked at her and said, 'I have a lot of manuscript in that suitcase we stored. I am going down into the cellar: No. risk.: I will go no farther. than is safe.'

, But Hester's face, which was quite stiff with cold, took on a peculiar expression. The muscles which were automatically directed to produce an expression of anguish, only succeeded in realizing a dismal snigger, tears rolling down her cheeks, caused by the intense cold. She poked her arm; through his, however, and dragged him away from the Annexe, which they had reached. 'There is nothing in that suitcase that matters, is there? Do not go back into the Hotel,'- she begged him. 'No, I won't allow you to go down into the cellar, René. Do come away.'

. He tolerated this forcible removal for a few yards only, then he stopped.

'I shall only be down there for a few minutes,' he told her, as he moved back towards the Annexe door. 'I am only going to have a look: if it is impossible to do anything about the suitcase, I will come back immediately.' He disengaged himself, crossed the sidewalk to the door, passed inside, and ran down the steps to the basement.

Hester followed him up to the door, and there she took up her position, although there was a good deal of pushing to and fro.

René found that there was not more than an inch of water in the corridor below street level, but it was extremely hot. Striking a match, he moved rapidly along the left wall as far as the furnace room. As he looked in he saw that the furnace was still functioning, and the light from one of its doors disclosed the fact that someone was standing near it. He went in and found that it was the Indian, who seemingly was warming himself and smoking a cigarette.

'A good place when it's forty below,' said the Indian.

'Indeed it is,' René answered, warming his hands at the furnace. The Indian came forward, and with an expert deftness, opened another of the furnace doors.

'All clinkers!' he said contemptuously, waving his hand towards the glare. René recalled that his job was said to be that of 'an engineer', which might mean anything from janitor to the designer of marine engines. But he certainly had a janitor's or fireman's indignation with the quality of the coal.

'I am down here to see if I could get into the storage-room. I have a large suitcase there.'

The Indian shook his head. 'I shouldn't go much beyond this.'

'You think it is unsafe?'

'I damn well know it is,' the Indian answered irritably. 'There is a very heavy door a few yards along there. It is fire-proofed. The store-room is beyond that. But the fire has almost reached it I guess. And the store-room would be locked anyway.'

'I will have a peek,' said René. As he left the furnace-room, René heard the Indian mutter something.

He wondered, of course, why the Indian had strong feelings about what lay beyond the door. And also, of course, it flitted through his mind that this was rather an odd place for him to be. But he thought it most likely that this man had come down there on the same errand as himself—which would account for his irritability: then had remained in the furnace-room as the warmest place he could find.

Out in the corridor he struck a match, and through the smoke (which was not so thick down here) he saw, he thought, the door. He walked in that direction. Suddenly, with the unexpectedness which always accompanies such experiences, he ran into the door, from which he recoiled with an exclamation of surprise. This surprise, too, was paradoxical, for naturally the door would be hot since the atmosphere was absolutely stifling. He fumbled for the door-handle and snatched his hand away with outraged astonishment—in spite of the fact that if the door was hot its metal handle would certainly be hotter. He thrust his hand beneath his overcoat, where it was flexible below the pocket. His hand muffled in this way, he seized the door-handle and violently turned it, pushing the door an inch or so open. Hot smoke poured out in his face, and there was the stench of burning which was intensely pungent. He was again taken entirely by surprise and was almost overcome as the inrush of smoke all but choked him. Almost in the same moment that he opened the door he pulled it towards him again, and it shut fast, it seeming to René that it was a new lock, it closed so easily. He staggered, coughing and spitting, away from the door, and as he could hardly see he felt his way along the wall until he reached the furnace-room.

As he stood just inside the door he heard the Indian's laughter, who remarked genially, 'Had a look-see for yourself. You don't think you'll go in and fetch your case?' René laughed grittily and shook his head.

After a moment he said, 'I had a look. The fire is nearer than you suppose.'

'Oh no it isn't.'

'Have you looked in there recently?'

'No,' the Indian said. 'No need to do that.' He coughed and spat. 'I'm sticking around down here. Waiting for those guys to put the fire out. And this is the warmest place I can find.' He continued to ponder darkly over the clinkers.

With a Good-night René left the furnace-room and made haste to return to Hester. As he was moving along the corridor he recalled that during the instant while the door was ajar, and before his eyes had become full of smarting tears, he had seen a glow through the smoke. He computed that the fire was twenty yards or more beyond the door.

When he reached the street door he found Hester standing just outside it, up to her ankles in water. The water was cataracting down the Annexe stairs, and across the sidewalk into the gutter, freezing as it went. And everywhere else, of course, there was quite thick ice, on which they certainly would have slipped, had they not been wearing their over-shoes, whose india-rubber soles at least enabled them to stand. Without that they could not even have stood up, for they had not the life-long habit of walking on ice of the Momacoans.

Hester's face, as he first caught sight of it, alarmed him, for she was beside herself, it was clear, with fear, cold and discouragement. He must get her, he thought, into some warm room as soon as possible. As soon as she saw him a congealed grin of rapture disfigured her face. 'Ah, darling, that is good.' She was shivering, as he took her arm, and he led her as rapidly as possible across to Mrs. Waechter's.

This good woman hastened out to meet them, and led them into her parlour. Unsolicited, she proceeded to make a pot of tea for them, and when René spoke of the necessity of finding a lodging for the remainder of the night, she offered them a large room which happened to be empty. All this satisfactorily settled, René took his leave. 'You sit here for a bit, the tea will help you to *dégeler.*' Hester was so profoundly chilled that she did not resist very much, telling him only not to be too long away.

Mrs. Waechter came to the front door with him.

'The hydrants being frozen gave the flames a big start. I hardly think they will stop them now.'—'Nor do I.' And René told her what he had seen when he opened the fire-door near the furnace-room. 'It would take a stream of water as thick as the River St. Lawrence to drown all that. It has got too deep a hold. It started deep-down.'—'I guess it did.' And Mrs. Waechter shook her head.

René made his way round to the front of the Hotel. It was of course impossible to cut through by the side of the Beverage Room, so he made a wide détour. He slipped several times in his haste, the last time rolling over in the snow. After that he went slower, a little lame from his heavy fall. He came into the main road, which was now a brilliant and sinister scene, wildly lighted by the fire, and in a haze of smoke. Rather more than half-way up the block he reached a small hotel. Two firemen came up to its entrance from the opposite direction, and he stood aside to allow them to pass in. The first was dabbing his nose which was bleeding. They practically all of them suffered from nose bleeding, as the result of the great efforts they were obliged to make, in the appalling cold. Small icicles were hanging from the nostrils of the second fireman; and his moustache, where his breathing moistened it, was full of minute icicles too. Some of them depended in front of his mouth, where, however, his breath tended to melt them. Wherever there was moisture there was ice. These two men had come to the hotel for a cup of hot coffee. René also noticed later on various householders, giving the firemen warm drinks; women also brought cups of hot coffee to the firemen working the hoses.

The proprietor was a French-Canadian. He was a man who had spent some years in France and spoke French correctly. René and he had often talked together, and, when le sieur Jean Lafitte saw René enter his hotel, he called out genially, 'Ah, vous voilà sans domicile. Où ce que vous allez gîter a présent?' Monsieur Lafitte was in the best of good temper. He was making money, and his principal rival was in process of elimination. Inside was a small Beverage Room where coffee and sandwiches were being served. It was full of refugees from the Hotel Blundell. There was a great clamour, as everyone wished to describe their sensations, to disclose their losses, to denounce the fire, to show their wounds. There were women with nothing but their fur coats covering their pyjamas, everything else left behind. There were men with singed hair and children with chattering teeth, chattering with fear and cold. As René entered a man near the door was complaining that firemen had seized him and refused to allow him the time even to cross the room, and fetch his money from the pocket of his suit, in the closet. But the topic that dominated all the others was the problem of Insurance. The loudest howls, the most distended eyes, had an economic origin.

René sat down and talked to an old American whom he knew slightly, and who was alone—but not alone from preference. It was quite clear that he could hardly bear to sit there, maintaining an involuntary silence. He was a little bag of fermenting words which, if René had not happened to sit down, would have burst: and there would have been a little figure conversing heatedly with itself, in the accents of Michigan and Illinois. For René, he was a little mine of information, waiting feverishly for its prospector, in the form of a parchment-pale, kid face, all its wrinkles tautly stretched, the neat silver-grey American suit enclosed in the neat dark padded overcoat, and the neat grey hat hung on the back of the head, its brim rising above the bright ironically-darting grey eyes.

All René had to say was 'Well!' and he began at once; he was well-nigh incontinent. The fire, he blurted out, came up from the basement. It was already a well-nourished flame when it sprang through the mezzanine. And at this point the

American assured him that with it seemed to come a very
strong smell of benzine.

'You first smelt benzine when you saw the Flame?' said
René.

'Yes, but I smelt it everywhere.'

Obviously the old drummer had a firebug story to tell. 'I
had an apartment on the mezzanine. From the beginning of
the ringing of the bell, I had at most six minutes to dress and
throw my things together. When I first put my head out of my
room, when the bell rang, I saw a smallish flame: when I left
the room less than ten minutes later there were big flames.
The staircase, I don't have to tell you, forks up from the
lounge, joining the mezzanine balcony on either side. These
flames were thirty or forty feet from the entrance to my
apartment, and I, of course, had to go down the opposite side
to them. In the apartment where the fire first hit the mezzanine
the man was badly burned, and is in hospital.'

'I see,' said René.

The old American looked at him with his bright inquisitive
eyes. 'It was Mr. Martin who was ringing the bell,' he said
impressively. 'He had got there mighty quick. Your fellow-
countryman was pulling away there as if he had been ringing
a church bell for morning prayers. Of course most people got
out of my part of the Hotel when I did. Many must have lost
all their belongings. I had a grip and nothing else, and most of
my stuff was still in the grip. I got back here last night. So
packing wasn't any problem for me. Oh boy was I glad!
There's plenty of people's lost everything, and the firemen
were rushing about shooing everybody out of their apartments, throwing them out in some cases.'

'People in the upper floors?' René suggested.

'No, just everywhere. It was all so sudden. I heard the
elevator working non-stop, but that could not have lasted
long because of the electricity. No time at all. Of course in the
upper part of the Hotel many of them had to come down on
the fire-escapes. As they put their hands on the old fire-escapes
they nearly froze to the metal.'

'Was not the metal covered on the fire-escapes?' René
objected.

'I guess not. But maybe it was the metal fire-ladders of the Hotel they were talking about. That lot—it was two women and two men—lost everything. And are they mad—why, one of them went round with a gun looking for Mrs. Plant, and your compatriot, Mr. Martin, they would like to find him too! But the Management has done "the vanishing trick", as I heard a man say.'

'Any casualties, any dead?'

'They say there are seven Peasoups up in a top apartment, who didn't hear the bell. They must be dead by now. A fireman tried to reach them, but he could not pass through the flames. I saw a woman jump out of a window.' He pointed out of the window. 'There are three corpses right out there, along the edges of the sidewalk, waiting to go to the mortuary.'

René left him, still talking. Outside in the hall there were numbers of people: there was one man in a blue dressing-gown, thanking a woman for having bathed his feet (which were bare) in warm water. 'Where are you going to get some shoes?' asked René. 'I'm damned if I know,' said the man with a laugh, 'nor where I am going to get anything else. Everything I possess is burned by this time. The firemen pulled me out of bed, practically carried me on to the fire-escape.'

René pushed his way out into the street again, and moved towards the fire.

In front of the last house in the block, which was that of the *Friseur*, were three bodies with their faces covered, their feet on the edge of the gutter. Two reporters were bending over them, removing one by one the cloths which had been laid over the face. As René drew level with them they uncovered the nearest face. It was Affie.

René stepped quickly forward. 'Hold on a minute!' he said.

The two reporters looked up. They were French-Canadians, he noticed. Affie's head had a deep scar, reaching down to the left eye. One of the reporters pointed to the scar. 'Looks as if someone had hit her on the head,' he said.

'It does,' René said. Almost automatically he said to himself, 'She must have got that while snooping. She must have had her eye at a keyhole . . . and someone came up behind her.'—Aloud, he said, 'This was the Manageress.'

The two reporters opened their notebooks: 'The Manageress?'

'Yes,' René answered. 'Mrs. McAffie.'

René crossed the road to observe the progress of the fire. He had to pick his way among the fire-engines, which entirely blocked the roadway: but he found a path, stepping on and over hoses, shouted at by firemen, who would have him choose some other route. The irritation of these men increased as they noticed him shaking with laughter.

He was thinking, 'To be lying in the snow. Dead.' Perhaps he was dreaming. Here was something that was not in conformity with a waking reality. It was what was absurd in himself, that suddenly he had been confronted with. Sudden death presents its card with a leer. He thought now that he had seen a smile on Affie's face. He could not be sure of this but he thought he had. She had understood the Absurd. So it was that he found himself doing what the firemen thought he was doing; it was a convulsion of meaningless mirth.

He had now reached the other side of the road, and stood gazing up at the flaming edifice.

There were groups of people standing all along the sidewalk, and gazing up, as he was. The two who were beside him were talking, and one of them was telling the other how he had telephoned to a friend the other side of the river. This friend had informed him that a huge cloud of smoke was spreading all over the city. René moved along until he was actually in front of the Hotel. The noise was formidable, there was the throbbing of the engines, the firemen shouting to one another, the excited talk of the spectators, in addition to the roaring and crackling of flames, and occasional crashes inside the burning building, and less frequently, though more disagreeably, outside. A section, for instance, of burning wood and masonry fell almost on top of the men manipulating a fire-escape: for several fire-escapes were still feeling their way on the sides of the Hotel, watching for guests who might still be there and seeking to escape. The fireman kept people at a distance, and René was already as near as he could get without protest. The fireman passed him, and asked a woman who was standing in her porch if she had some old socks she could give him. He held up his hands, both of which were becoming useless with frostbite. He followed her into the house, and came out a little later with his hands bandaged.

The noise, the glare, the clouds of smoke, the roaring and crackling of the flames, this great traditional spectacle only appealed to him for a moment. But he could not help being amazed at the spectral monster which had been there for so long, and what it was turning into. It was a flaming spectre, a fiery iceberg. Its sides, where there were no flames, were now a solid mass of ice. The water of the hoses had turned to ice as it ran down the walls, and had created an icy armour many feet in thickness. This enormous cocoon of ice did not descend vertically, but swept outwards for perhaps fifty yards, stopped by the wall of the house of the *Friseur*; half submerging the Beverage Room in its outward progress. The flames rising into the sky seemed somehow cold and conventional as if it had been their duty to go on aspiring, but they were doing it because they must, not because they had any lust for destruction. These were the flames that still reached up above the skyline of the façade. But a new generation of fiery monsters, a half-hour younger, appeared behind them, a darker red and full of muscular leaps, charged with the authentic will to devour and to consume. And there were dense volumes of black smoke too, where fresh areas were being brought into the holocaust.

But René believed he could see a still fresher group of flames, which must be sprouting out of the Annexe. He moved farther on, where he could see the Annexe. It was still quite intact, but there was a very active flame which he felt sure was feeding on the first timbers of the Annexe. Two streams of water began playing on it, and it grew shorter and paler, but it did not disappear. He heard someone saying that the Fire Marshal was in the backyards upon which their windows looked, and that he believed the Annexe could be saved. They were fighting the flames in the corner, attempting to stop them at that point. He could see a dark group near the centre of the white strip where the backyards were.

'Well there it is,' René summed up for himself, 'a bonfire,

a very large bonfire. Every Murphy bed, and every settee had a latent flame in it, as the stuff of a bonfire. As we lived in our apartment, in our wonderful crapulous Room, we were kept away from chaos and dissolution by its strong walls and orderly shapes. But it can all be set a match to, and daemonic nature appear from nowhere and eat it up. Then he thought of war. 'War is so respectable. The rulers, the firebugs, dare not do more than kill a few million people. Theirs is a hypocritical destruction, it takes them years to go round bumping off small packets at a time. How much better it would be if they summoned a few million people to the Sahara and destroyed them all within twenty-four hours by poison-gas or some quicker exterminator. But no; they must pretend. They must say that it is a very holy cause that they are serving, and fool around for four or five or six years. Fire is not frivolous and hypocritical, it is not human. The Hotel will not be there tomorrow morning. Instead of it there will be a beautiful iceberg. What a pity that dear Affie could not have got herself embalmed in the ice.'

René did not return to Mrs. Waechter's the same way. He circled round past the groceteria. As he walked warily along, he reflected what a handicap it was, from the standpoint of the Fire, that there was no wind. The whole place would have been burned down long before this if there had been a good wind. It was completely windless, and a really beautiful moonlit night, if one had any time for beauty.

When at last he reached the door of the Annexe, he saw that the fire had not been stopped, as anticipated, but had its teeth in the beginning of the Annexe. It was already filling the street with smoke, and smoke as well as water was now coming out of the Annexe door As he was looking at the door, the young Russian came out of the smoke, coughing and patting his eyes with a handkerchief. He had only taken a step or two when another man who had also come out of the smoke loomed up behind him, and seizing the hand which held the handkerchief, fixed on the wrist a manacle, with almost as little trouble as if this had been a prearranged scene. The two men were now fastened to one another, but as if coming to life the young Russian hit the other in the face with his free hand, and they

10*

both seemed to slip and fall to the ground, kicking, struggling and shouting. But another man appeared from nowhere, and bent down over René's ex-neighbour, whom he hit with something. It was difficult to see what. The next thing René saw was the two men dragging and carrying the young man to a waiting car, which was parked beyond the disabled car of the 'Kid'.

So the 'Toronto Kid' had at last had to leave his apartment, as the police had foreseen. Had he been obliged to leave his treasure trove, or whatever it was, up there in the smoke, or had he got it in his pocket, or tied round his waist, or in the lining of his hat? Or had the women . . . ? But René had been so busy watching the capture of the 'Kid' that he had turned from the Annexe door, from which, as he now saw, the two women had also emerged. They stood at present, wailing and weeping, in the custody of two detectives, who kept their eyes very closely upon them, especially, of course, upon their hands. But this was a rapidly moving scene; and it was hardly a minute before a car drove up and the two women were pushed into it. The men jumped in behind them, and as the car door was banged to, the car was already under way and disappearing in the wake of the other one. The people in the street all seemed to be shouting, and it was not certain if they were shouting for anything more than pleasure at seeing three people pinched, or anger at the thought that one day the same men might find some excuse for pinching them.

CHAPTER XXII

Had I the Wings of the Morning

FOR the remainder of the night René and Hester attempted to rest, but the noise of the fire itself, and the noisiness of those putting it out, and those looking on, made this very difficult. The fitful rest they did, however, manage to obtain, made them, by nine in the morning, fresh compared with most people in the immediate neighbourhood. To gloat over the destruction, Mrs. Waechter related the highspots; how a fireman on the ice-cap over the Beverage Room had been killed by the collapse of a wall, and how the bodies recovered were said to number twenty. 'How lovely!' René exclaimed, and Mrs. Waechter thought what a brute he was. Only Apartment 27A and its immediate neighbours remained to be burned into unrecognizability. The Fire Brigade felt in honour bound to prolong the agony of these four or five remaining apartments. As a slight wind had sprung up, this was demonstrably impossible.

After an excellent breakfast they went outside, and almost the first person they met was Bessie ('another nit-wit'): she appeared to be mouching round in the hope of meeting Mrs. Plant. The wind made it ferociously cold and they invited her inside.

What Bess obviously hoped was that with the Insurance money Mrs. Plant would acquire another hotel, and that *she* would be the Manageress, now that Affie was gone. They both felt Bess had grown in stature because of this opportune demise. She was at present in the running (she felt) for managerial status, and, meanwhile, she had become the sole transmitter of gossip, and bearer of news.

The latter function she exercised immediately. The following are a few specimens of this. Would the Insurance Company pay up? This was her first line. The hotel had been secured by Mrs. Plant by means of mortgages: she had been in the

293

habit of boasting that she had never paid a penny for
anything. She would refer to this as 'The modern way'.
But the Insurance Companies had become notorious for their
scepticism, wriggling out of payment wherever they could.
They were not such 'suckers' as their English opposite numbers.—When asked by René on what these sceptical companies
would base their refusal to pay, she stared with the crafty
innocence of a slum-child through her hideous steel spectacles,
'Oh, I don't know.' She appeared to be as sceptical as were,
according to her, insurance companies. Bess said the account
of Affie's death in currency (though from what mint this story
came she had been unable to discover) was that she had gone
back into a part of the hotel where the fire was quickly gaining
ground, to fetch her Cherry fur. But that story did not agree
with the position in which her body had been found. 'Where
was that?' René had enquired. She, with a mock-innocent
craft, answered, 'It was not far from you. It was just beyond
the door of Mr. Martin's apartment. And that was early on
—there was no fire there then.' René confirmed that he had
seen her body in Balmoral Street, at a relatively early stage
of the fire. 'Where did you see her?' Bess enquired. 'Not far
from Lafitte's hotel!' he told her. And Bess exclaimed, 'Ah.
Right over there!' She was full of information about the goods
and valuables lost by the majority of the guests, and the
people who now were penniless and with nothing left but the
clothes they stood up in. These destitute fire-victims were
resolved to get the money out of Mrs. Plant: 'But what hopes!'
chanted Bess.

'Will they get nothing, then?' said René. But Bess knew the
law regarding Innkeepers' liability in the case of fire. It seemed
as if the law had been drawn up by Innkeepers themselves or
their personal friends. For, Bess assured them, in Canada,
Innkeepers were exempt from any claim for loss of damage
to goods caused by fire.

When asked as to whether she had managed to save all her
belongings, Bess tended to be obscure: but René concluded
that all this meant was that she had lost nothing, but did not
care to be so utterly without a grievance. Katie and Bess had
been lodged in a small apartment adjacent to the kitchen, in

the extreme rear of the hotel proper. The two maids only had
to carry their belongings the length of the ground floor of
the Annexe, and there was the street.

Asked if Mr. Martin was as elusive as Mrs. Plant, Bess did
not seem to like that question. She appeared to become quite
unusually cagey.

'Well,' said Hester, 'I last saw Mr. Martin when *you* (nodding at René) were down below, looking for the case that was
in store. As I stood outside the Annexe door, Mr. Martin
appeared, moving effortlessly down the cataract on the stairs.
His expression was at once mild and stern. Turning at the
bottom, he descended into the cellar, the way you had gone!'

'When I was down there in the furnace-room!' René said,
astonished. 'Well, he never got as far as the furnace-room.'

'There are apartments down there,' Hester reminded him.
'I suppose he went into one of them.'

Bess offered no suggestion, but appeared to catch sight of
something out of the window. And the subject of Mr. Martin
dropped.

Bess said she must get on with her search for Mrs. Plant.
They told her to come in and see them again: when they left
they would leave their new address with Mrs. Waechter. Bess
looked so prosperous and so Canadian in her outdoor clothes,
but her personality, no clothes could transmute. She remained
indelibly the small Scottish skivvy, with her morning greeting
of 'Another Nitwit!'

That day they went on foot to a neighbouring boulevard,
where there were two or three apartment hotels. It was a
long street, nearly half of which was in the French-Canadian
quarter, and its hotels were spoken of as swarming with Peasoup prostitutes, or at the best very liable to be that. But
after the Hotel Blundell such personalities as they encountered
did not suggest a knocking shop. At the Laurenty the executive and service staff were French-Canadian, and seemed quite
decent people. It was settled that they should move in on the
following day.

On their return to their lodgings René telephoned Mr.
Furber, who, to his surprise, was impressed by the fire, and
treated him momentarily as a social equal, because he had

just been part of the cast in a first-class local thriller, a banner-
headline affair. This was very American. Mr. Furber thought
less of him when he heard that he had lost nothing, had not
come down on a fire-escape, and had not been robbed by a
fireman of his wallet. But he received new stimulation when
René told him about the little Detroiter, and how there had
been a stink of benzine, how this had caused him to smell a
rat, and how *arson* had been whispered.

When Mr. Furber was told that they were now going to
live at the Hotel Laurenty, he tittered. He referred to it as
the 'Lorelei'. René's visit was fixed for the following afternoon, so that was taken care of.

Before leaving for the Laurenty the next morning they
walked around the amazing iceberg into which the Hotel
Blundell had been transformed. It was a magnificent sight;
a block of ice towering over everything in the immediate
neighbourhood. It was of course a hollow iceberg. The interior
could be inspected through what had been the street-door of
the main hotel-building, on Balmoral Street. What René and
Hester gazed into was nothing to do with what had been the
Hotel Blundell. It was now an enormous cave, full of mighty
icicles as much as thirty feet long, and as thick as a tree, suspended from the skeleton of a roof. Below, one looked down
into an icy labyrinth: here and there vistas leading the eye
on to other caverns: and tunnels ending in mirrors, it seemed.
To the right a deep green recess, as if it had been stained with
verdigris.

This hollow berg was an unearthly creation, dangerous to
enter because so unstable. An icicle weighing twenty tons,
rooted in an insufficiently deep, an aerial upside downness,
might prove too weighty a vegetation in this inverted world.
Probably it would hold in present temperatures, but a relaxation consequent upon thermometrical decline from forty below
to twenty below zero, might cause the hugest icicles to crash.
It was a cave in which no polar bear could inhabit, in which
the Great Auk could not lay its egg, and into which no ex-
guest could enter with his ice-pick, to search for diamonds
which, in his breathless exit, he had had to leave behind. It
was a sinister, upside down forest of ice, rooted in the air; a

piece of sub-polar absurdity, which would stand there till the
first thaws: but René saw it as a funeral vault for Affie, which
would be mysterious and inviolable for long enough to suit
her volatile taste. Her hooting cry could sound there in the
night—the only human sound that could be heard, for only
as ghosts could men qualify for admittance, and only Affie
be at home in this unearthly scenery.

The 'Lorelei', to give it Mr. Furber's name, was a far better-
run hotel than the Blundell had been, although Bessie, when
she came to see the Hardings there two days later, was
highly critical, and spoke disrespectfully of the French-
Canadian servants. 'I have never yet met with a Peasoup
who was clean,' she said. To which René replied, 'I am half
a Peasoup. Perhaps that will help me to put up with it.'

To which Bess tartly retorted, in her Glasgow prim-talk,
'It may be all recht for yew, Mr. Harding, but Mrs. Harding
is no' a Pea-sup.'

But what Bessie had come for was to inform the Hardings
that Affie was now at a mortician's, and that a service was
to be held there that afternoon. A number of people were
coming over from Ottawa, who had known her when her
husband was alive and when socially her position had been
very different from what it was at her death. The service would
be at 3 p.m. René and Hester told her they would be there.

These establishments known as 'Mortician's' consist, of
course, in a 'lying in state' for everybody. Formerly only
famous men and royal personages lay in state, but the
American democracy could not but perceive that this was a
bad example of privilege. So these morticians multiplied, until
today no one economically superior to a rat-catcher but is
stuck up in a mortician's upon their demise. So that afternoon
the Hardings were introduced to this American mystery: they
were led through a large waiting-room, and leading out of
that was the curiously mis-named Funeral Parlour. They had
only taken a half a dozen steps when, turning their heads to
the right, they found themselves gazing down at Affie. They
were in a small chapel. There were perhaps ten rows of chairs,
half of which were already occupied. Facing the latter was
the coffin in which Affie lay, rather more than waist high.

It was somewhat inclined, and arranged so that the chapel audience could see in part the face. Affie was fully clothed, in a green dress she had recently bought. Her face was heavily made up, powdered, and heavily rouged: and whether any facial injection had been practised or not, Affie looked much healthier and younger than she had ever looked in life. The scar had been in some way filled in, and the discoloration removed.

On the other hand, it was a little Affie that they now saw, so small a face, like a sleeping child. This immovable expression of a false content, the slight smile of the last sleep, and of the mortician's art, succeeded in making it look as though Affie, from the unearthly calm of this final phase of her self-presentation, were smiling at the people who had come to look at her, just as she would have done had she been conscious —had she been asked to climb into the box and arrange herself there, heavily made up. So Affie still seemed active in this last display. The only thing which destroyed the impression that this indeed was life, was the *smallness* of the face. It had not been a *child* who used to stand there, just inside their apartment, with a slight ironical smile, always *faisant des façons* with an unspoken 'Shall I come in? Am I intruding?' —(She, who had been listening at the keyhole for anything up to ten minutes.) She had not been of childish stature, but tall and straight, with a sense for style—not like a doll, with its feet together, arranged in a cardboard box for the Toy Fair.

Hester and René only paused for a few seconds to gaze down at the dead. They then proceeded to the rear of the rows of seats. 'A gathering of well-heeled bourgeois,' whispered René. But substantial citizens were arriving all the time, and continued to do so, until the last of the seats were occupied. Nearly all those present dated back a good time, to those days when Affie and her lawyer husband were living in Ottawa, before his unexpected death. The heads of most of those in the audience, the males, that is, had the wintry thatch which would also have been that of Affie, were it not that she and Miss Toole dyed their hair in the bathroom every other Saturday. And finally it must be said that Mr. and Mrs. McAffie must have been both prosperous and popular, for all these people to make so considerable a journey to be present at the last rites of Mrs. McAffie. The gathering was almost complete when not the least prosperous-looking of this *élite* attendance made her appearance. It was Bessie, in a handsome fur coat (borrowed, as Hester recognized at once, from Miss Toole). She came up to them a little shyly; and all three sat on chairs placed in the corner for such as had not reserved seats.

As soon as it was evident that all were present, from a side-door emerged a handsome young clergyman, notably contrasting in age with his audience. He walked over to the coffin, and gazed intently into it for nearly five minutes. Talking had stopped, there was a profound hush. The long and mournful inspection of the dead, as though he had been impressing upon his mind this image, that there should be no anonymity when he came to intercede with God, was a well-conceived part of this ceremony, René appreciatively reflected. Then the young man, with his excellently serious face turned sideways to the coffin, began to intone a psalm in a strong and hypnotic voice. René heard the familiar words, 'For man walketh in a vain shadow, and disquieteth himself in vain,' and this he recognized. 'Take thy plague away from me: I am even consumed by means of thy heavy hand. When thou with rebukes dost chasten man for sin, thou makest his beauty to consume away, like as it were a moth fretting a garment; every man therefore is but vanity.' René pondered at this point, I am consumed by the heavy hand, but he added at once to himself that the hand, although heavy, was not so heavy as might be expected. And so he gave expression to what distressed Hester most. He was the kind of man, as she had come to learn, who having lost both his legs would say how merciful God had been to leave his arms intact: and if he lost one arm as well, would resign himself on account of one limb remaining to him.

The splendid rhetoric was lifted in the air, by the aspiring voice of the minister, winged with an emotion, which everyone felt would carry the words to God's ear, where somewhere His head is bent to listen to the noble words of such professional advocates as this, to intercede for those blackened with sin, which He is asked, in His infinite mercy, to forgive, and to allow to enter into the realms of salvation, and when

in finishing, the pastor sadly sang, 'Oh, spare me a little, that
I may recover my strength: before I go hence, and be no more
seen,' the last few words dying out, to fade away into the
shadow, the intoxication of the small audience had begun:
and at the end of a short and intense hush, came the most
penetrating Amen that that chapel had ever heard—or so
everybody felt.

All the red necks and white heads in the audience were
bowed. The young cleric was performing before a small
assemblage of elders, and chanting to them of death. They had
travelled hundreds of miles to be chanted to of death, smiled
at by the painted corpse of a member of their social circle.

'Let us pray!' said the young minister, and the little herd
of white polls bent still farther and the lines of shoulders rose
accordingly. And after that a collect, and then another prayer
for the slightly smiling funereal doll in the wooden box. Then
came the culmination. The head, with its beautiful waved
hair, thrown back, the minister began in an exalted voice—
and this was his final and most tragic, his most solemn piece
of declamation, and a most fitting culmination to the brief
ceremony: 'Had I the wings of the morning, and could I fly
to the uttermost parts of the earth' was his idealistic opening.

All these white-haired, these hoary sinners, mourned that
they had not the wings of the morning—those powerful and
golden, beautiful star-tipped wings, stretching across the
horizons like aspiring clouds. And oh, if they could have a
part of the advantages of the Morning (Who does not die or
become Afternoon, but flies on and on towards the remotest
west) then *they* would fly into the unearthly distances, not to
the uttermost ends of the earth, but of the world and of Time.
They had a momentary glimpse of a remoteness, of a solitude,
somewhere behind the stars, where they would be unimagin-
ably far from where they had been, and what they had always
been. This soaring rhetoric armed them with a contempt for
the life they would so soon be obliged to leave, and this verbal
intoxication melted all the old husks, and noses were blown
in all parts of the audience. At the rear, Hester and Bessie
were both wiping their tears away, and René bit his lip to
discourage an unmanly display. But he thought wistfully of

the odious days in the hotel, and his heart was soft and inexpressibly sad, as he thought of the wild woman who had
inhabited that puppet there, from which she had mysteriously
departed.

It was with shame at the debauch of sadness in which they
had indulged that most of them shuffled out of the mortician's,
some casting resentful glances at the small painted figure which
had been responsible for this. But the fixed smile or half-smile
of what in life was sexual *câlinerie* answered appropriately the
covert scowls.—Those who were going on to the grave-side
remained in prayer within.

The Hardings returned to the Laurenty profoundly affected,
but resentful. How dignified and how *real* (for it amounted
to that) Affie had been as she lay in the snow, with a piece of
coarse cloth over her face, placed there, perhaps by Monsieur
Lafitte, as a sign of respect. René could have wished that that
had been his last glimpse of Affie. The vulgar peep-show with
the dolled-up face, at the mortician's, was so violently unreal,
that it blotted out the real. They would have to wait until
time had washed out that garish spot-lit image, before they
could see her again in their minds.

This hotel, like the Blundell, had telephones in every apartment. Shortly after they had finished their tea the telephone
began ringing. René lifted the receiver, and he heard the
familiar voice of Mr. Furber. 'Ah,' said Mr. Furber, 'have you
heard the news about your late hotel?' René told him that he
had heard nothing about his late hotel.

'Well,' said Mr. Furber, 'a guest, a certain Mr. Martin, has
been arrested.'—'What for?' enquired René, with genuine
interest. 'Did he set the hotel on fire?'—'No,' Furber answered.
'He has been arrested for the murder of the manageress, Mrs.
McAffie.' There was such relish in Mr. Furber's voice that
René knew that he would be giving less than satisfaction if he
did not display emotion. 'Now *that* is curious!' he practically
shouted. 'When did that news break?'

Furber told him that it came through on the radio, the

Momaco station just gave that piece of information and no
more, except that Mr. Martin is 'a countryman of yours'.

René gave his employer all the information he possessed
about Mr. Martin. He also told him that he had felt, of late,
that there was something enigmatic about that familiar figure.
He had thought that Mrs. Plant, the ostensible proprietress,
might be a blind, and that the hotel might be owned by
Mr. Martin. Since then, a member of the staff had gossiped:
had told him that Mrs. Plant would assert that she had not
paid a penny piece for the hotel, that it had been a mortgage
transaction.

Then Mr. Furber evinced curiosity about Mrs. McAffie: was
the manageress perhaps the mistress of Mr. Martin? René
laughingly discouraged speculation along those lines, explaining that Mrs. McAffie was at least sixty and Mr. Martin too,
and that no love was lost between the two.—When, asked
Mr. Furber, had René last seen Mrs. McAffie. 'Why?' René
laughed. 'You do not suspect me of playing a part in her
murder? I last saw her a few hours ago in a wooden overcoat
in a mortician's.'

Mr. Furber, it was obvious, was greedily devouring a big
juicy slice of 'crime-mystery' in the making. He was reluctant
to hang up the telephone, but unfortunately René was a man
out of whom could be extracted the truth, the whole truth,
and nothing but the truth. So at last he sang his good-bye.

Hester was then told what had happened, and her reactions
were quite different from those of Mr. Furber. The killing of
Affie horrified, and did not amuse Hester. Apart from the
corollary of weeks of impaired sleep and in the end insomnia,
she had been less tolerant of a nest of criminals opposite 27A.
She felt that their toleration had been counted on, that no
Canadian man and wife would have put up with it. Her
general attitude to all the uncouth features of their life had
been very different from that of René. But this little lower-
class Englishman killing their darling Affie (and it was still in
that way that she thought of her, in spite of the ghastly
debunking of the Funeral Parlour), that was *too* beastly. She
felt sick: She asked René to stop discussing it. And then she
began to react violently to her memory of the scene at the

mortician's. The painted face in the coffin, the rather sly hint
of a smile (no doubt the mortician's handiwork) had been
repulsive at the time, but was doubly repulsive now. Affie now
began to seem to be part of the whole beastly business. She
and all the rest of them were a vile crew. She and René should
long ago have extracted themselves from this ugly milieu. The
evening was, not unnaturally, anything but pleasant. Mr.
Furber rang up two hours later, which did not improve
matters. More news from the Momaco station! A fireman had
seen Mr. Martin strike Mrs. McAffie with what looked like a
new-fangled, slender cosh. He had come up behind her as
she was looking through the keyhole of the apartment. Mrs.
McAffie had turned her head quickly, still crouching, and he
struck her down, swinging his arm with great force, so the
fireman reported. Also Mr. Martin was the actual proprietor
of the hotel, and it was believed it was he who had caused the
fire; and was thereby responsible for the deaths of over fifteen
people. How many could not be finally decided until the ice
had melted in the Spring thaw.

After leaving the telephone (with great difficulty) René came
back to where Hester was sitting. He was of course unable
to suppress entirely what Mr. Furber had said, and these
further details increased her nausea relating to everything to
do with the place they had lived in for so long.

René attempted to dispel the gloom by tuning in to the
U.S. Networks—carefully avoiding all Canadian stations. It
was late in the evening, when the following piece of silliness
issued from their instrument.

> 'For a cowboy has to sing,
> And a cowboy has to yell,
> Or his heart would break
> Inside of him,
> At the gates of the home corral.'

Hester had been knitting, and now looked up with a rather
sickly smile. 'My heart will break inside of me, if I don't get
out of this place. I know you don't agree with me, but I do
greatly prefer the Brompton Road to any street in this awful
country.'

René did not reply at once; he sat with his elbows on his knees staring at the radio. Then he said slowly and distinctly, 'What I am wondering is . . . if we left here where should we go. One would not find, I expect, in every city . . . a Mr. Furber.'

Hester stared, or it would be truer to say glared at him as though he had just displayed an unmistakable streak of insanity. And in some way she was right. Even more than herself René was shocked; and something did find its way into his manner of thinking which was insane.

Part Three

AFTER THE FIRE

CHAPTER XXIII

Momaco or London?

THE destruction of the hotel by fire divided their life at Momaco into two dissimilar halves. The second half had a quite different coloration from the first. The years in the Hotel Blundell were more romantic, because to begin with, Canada was a great novelty, and novelty is synonymous with romance; and the microcosm which had gone up in smoke and fire was more blatantly microcosmic than what succeeded it.

The management of the Blundell lived and let live, hence a great deal of raw life was present, then the fact that it possessed a Beverage Room (which the Laurenty did not) brought it nearer to the great heart of the universe, and entitled it to microcosmic status. The Laurenty was not, of course, quiet at night—no Canadian hotel could be that. From the number of dark and shining eyes and waving hips to be met in its corridors it was obvious that it was in one important respect in no way behind the Blundell. But excessive uproar was not encouraged. This was decently occulted. The janitors did not come and go with rapidity, did not leave, shouting, between policemen: or if they did, there was no Bess to keep the guests posted in such scandalous events. A French-Canadian maid, averse from speech, attended to the Hardings' apartment.

But it was not only on account of the very different character of the hotel that this second half of the war-years in Momaco was so different. There was a growing dissimilarity, owing to a psychological factor; a tension, becoming more acute month by month, between René and Hester, and, independently, within both René and Hester.

With increasing distress Hester observed the development of a new outlook on the part of her husband. At the Hotel Blundell the sense of transience of the first days always remained: it was an abominable hotel, in an abominable city, which they were going to quit at the first opportunity. So everything was anything but static. But now the horrors of Momaco were never mentioned. In the first place, the violent impression which the fire, the murder of poor Affie, and indeed all the brutal unmasking of what they had been living in the midst of for so long had made upon Hester, was apparent to René. He realized that he had a new situation on his hands. Consequently, he was careful to avoid expressing his feelings about the daily annoyances peculiar to life in Momaco for a couple of uprooted English people. He tended to discourage the chronic bitterness of the Blundell days; above all, he resisted any pressure to evacuate Momaco immediately. Against the 'really it was about time to think of returning to England, since it was plain enough that this war would *never* end' recurring almost daily, he set up a defence-in-depth.

'I agree,' he would say, 'that the war is of an exaggerated and quite unnecessary length. But it will end suddenly one day.'

'Oh no it won't,' she would retort grimly. 'And what is more, you know that it won't.'

René knew, of course, that it wouldn't: and then he had so often, in the past, shown her that it could not, that he had to be very careful not to press too hard the opposite view.

'All right,' he would answer. 'Unquestionably it will still be with us next week, and next month. But if it has not ended next year, in less than a year, its end will be so near we shall be able to stretch our arms out and touch its ending.'

Hester would lose her patience. 'Nonsense, René, you cannot make statements of that sort to me. Even supposing we take all that seriously for a moment, what then? Do you mean to say that you have so little consideration for me that you ask me to live in this filthy hotel for another year? I might perhaps have stood it had it not been for that ghastly fire. No, René, I just cannot face it.'

Sometimes René would resort to amorous treatment, vigorously administered. She humoured him—but after their transports, he could see that she was not convinced. The logic of sex would have proved dazzlingly irrefutable in any other connection, but not in this. To leave this place, and to return to England, was now nothing short of an obsession with her. And this had become the major feature of their daily life. It was, for him, a huge obstacle which had, in some way, to be reduced to manageable proportions or to be circled round and left behind, or perhaps to be incorporated in the landscape as a permanent eye-sore.

René attempted to divert her socially. It happened that soon after they had taken up their quarters in the Laurenty, through the agency of Mr. Furber René formed several relationships which tended to produce a more normal appearance in their life in Momaco. They went out to dinner several times, to a few parties, and René was made rather a fuss of at one of these. But as to these events producing a better atmosphere they had, if possible, the opposite effect. They literally terrified Hester. In one horrible prophetic glimpse she saw them settled down for good in this monstrous spot.

The middleclass Canadian woman, as Hester supposed it to be, repelled her just as much as everything else about England's ex-colony. The Kensingtonian lady, wonderfully tolerant of the artistically bohemian, for instance, stiffened in the presence of these Americanly self-assured, pink-faced English parlour maids (as she thought of them). Her eyes hardened, and contempt visited her voice, as she observed them doing a little crude detective work: had she or had she not been presented at court? was what they desired to know. She admitted never to have bent the knee at court; well, she must be of a pretty inferior class. It gave her some satisfaction to tell them that she had never seen the Royal Family at closer range than one hundred yards, and then by accident; and as to curtsying, she was sure she would end on the floor if she attempted to do so. *They* nearly all seemed to have had the opportunity of curtsying at one time or another, if only as spectators of a royal progress down the main avenue of Momaco.

She realized that her husband believed that this new social life must be a great treat for her; that he looked upon this as a trump card in his campaign to reconcile her to Momaco. It was therefore with great relish that she gave him her opinion of the ladies of Momaco—of the dream-world of Mr. Starr.

René attempted to counter this by putting in a good word
for the 'rather jolly' Madge Weldon, or Jack Christie's wife,
'who seems to have a talent for malice'. Hester made short
work of them: and warned him that he must not count on her
to go to many more of these boring entertainments.

So the passionate solidarity of the two lonely exiles practically confined to 'the Room' in the Hotel Blundell had begun
to crumble. The destruction of their prison had resulted in
their coming out of their seclusion into a more normal existence. Momaco began to relent. But Hester retained the spirit
of the disregarded intruder in a most jealously exclusive
society: and, as she saw it, René had in fact broken away,
and, in however qualified a manner, gone over to the side of
the enemy—had made his peace with Momaco.

It was of course true that René was prepared to benefit by
such amelioration in their treatment by the Momacoan as
might occur: but that did not mean that he had changed his
opinion. He still thought the Momacoans stank. The essence
of the whole matter was Hester's desire to return to England
at once. So it came to assume the shape of a fantastic question:
Momaco or London? Naturally such a question was abysmally
absurd: but René would have said that that was not the
real question. The nonsense-question, 'Is the miserable half-
civilized bush-city, Momaco, or is the great metropolis,
London, the better place to live in?' was not what was posed.
The real question was quite different. 'Was London or Momaco
the better place *for René Harding*, in the year 1944? would
be the real question. Since the burning of the Hotel Blundell,
and the manner in which Hester had reacted to that event had
obliged René to answer that question, the act of answering had
brought enlightenment. He knew that he could never return
to London, now or when the war ended. That point settled,
Momaco was his best bet, not only in Canada, but in the
world. This thought would have been terrifying to a less truly
stoical man: as it was he knew that it was Momaco or nothing,
and he began to know this hysterically, fanatically, almost
insanely. For he knew quite well that it was a fearful thing
to know.

The only factor which remained actively dissident was

Hester. If she would not agree to come into his scheme of life, makeshift and admittedly unsatisfactory as it was, what would the outcome be? It was unthinkable that they should part. But if she was obsessed, he too was obsessed. In his case the obsession was never again to find himself in the pit into which he had allowed himself to step; from which the fire had mysteriously rescued him.

CHAPTER XXIV

The Party of Superman

THE first of the new friends made by René were Professor McKenzie and his family. It was through Mr. Furber that the introduction was effected. He asked René to drop up one afternoon to meet a man who knew and admired his work. Since the fire Mr. Furber's attitude towards René had mellowed. The Hardings had been, as it were, baptized in fire as Momacoans of sorts. Also René was now in the secrets of Momaco, for was he not an acquaintance of one of Momaco's most eminent murderers? one whose 'homicide among the flames' took pride of place over all murders of recent years throughout the Dominion, and had secured banner-headlines in the metropolitan press of the United States.—It was Mr. Furber's habit now to introduce René in the following manner: 'Do you know Professor Harding, the historian? He nearly lost his life in the Hotel Blundell fire: and he had got to know his countryman, Martin, quite well during the three years of his stay there. You know, the *murderer in the flames!*'

In these introductions, needless to say, the rôle of the Historian was a very minor one. It was as the buddy of a murderer that he made the grade. The large, dark, mild eyes of Mr. Furber studied René's face with sardonic interest on these occasions. For Mr. Furber acted the part imposed by time and place, and acted it with relish, but he was under no illusions, and understood how vulgar the part was that fate had cast him for. He realized (with contempt, for Professor René Harding had to 'take it') what the other must be feeling.

With Professor Ian McKenzie, however, he acted differently. The Professor was an 'old countryman', and had come out only two years earlier, to teach philosophy at the University of Momaco. There were at that seat of learning two or three spectacular teachers, to enable it to hold up its head among the larger city-universities. It even had a logical positivist from Cambridge (England) by way of a spot of *chic*—also perhaps of scandal; although, had they understood what logical positivism stands for, it would have scandalized the methodists as much as it did the catholics. As for Professor McKenzie, he regarded the lectures of the nimble little anti-metaphysical with bored indifference. However, a collision was carefully avoided: the little Cambridge horse-fly was the possessor of a small destructive outfit, if he had nothing else, and McKenzie was a shameless metaphysician. He had no wish to be reduced to atomic dust by this patent pulverizer of everything. This was especially the case, since no retaliation was possible, the logical positivist having whittled himself away to a colourless abstraction which hardly constituted even a token target.

Professor McKenzie was a smiling Scottish sophist of about forty-five with a faint and pleasing accent, as far as possible from the aggressive scotchiness of Glasgow. Pleasantly surprised, René found himself again, at last, in the presence of a man of his own kind.

They passed from the Library, where the meeting had taken place, into Mr. Furber's non-business quarters (panelled with the nude photographic torsos of the juvenile male), reserved for those to be treated on terms of equality. (René felt quite uncomfortable at this honour, for he felt he ought to show, in some way, to Mr. Furber, how delighted he was to be there.) The two professors were watched by their host with a bland anticipation of something mildly amusing. It was as though they had been two mettlesome dogs, who might be expected to scrap, brought in there by the brooding aesthete. Both more or less realized what was expected of them, for McKenzie had been in Momaco long enough to understand the only terms upon which a man of mind may be treated otherwise than as an inanimate object, in such an environment. In his own case it would be the well-known pugnacity of the philosopher which would gain him momentary recognition as a living thing. He was now, he knew, expected to fight. René had a pugnacious record too; the confrontation of two such mental matadors should be productive of a kind of slanging-match.

It was naturally quite impossible for these two professors to clinch at once: they had first of all to exchange a few amiable commonplaces. Where had McKenzie taught? How long had he been in Momaco,.etc. . . . ? On his side, McKenzie enquired when René had arrived (assumed surprise succeeding to the information that the Hardings were old Momacoans), expressed the hope that he would have the pleasure of seeing René again, if that gentleman was remaining in the city, etc. Mr. Furber observed these *boniments* with the bored impatience that a person would show if two charladies, presenting themselves for employment, recognized one another, and indulged in social exchanges, so holding up the interviews.

. Professor McKenzie,.more conscious perhaps of his obligations, was the first to act as a Professor should. There must still be a short interval, however, during which McKenzie was referring politely to René's latest book, *The Secret History of World War II*. After a few more amiabilities, McKenzie went into action (much to Mr. Furber's relief, who had begun to feel that he had got a couple of very tame controversialists before him, and that he might have to stir them up or to turn them out).

With the most disarming smile the Scottish professor began, 'I do not know whether you would agree with me, Professor, but what I feel is that you cut yourself off from mankind.'

'Do I do that?' René smilingly rejoined.

'So it seems to me, Professor. If you assert that the aims and actions of human society up to date—everything except the dreams of the poets and mathematicians—are not only unworthy of record, but should be consigned to oblivion, that means that you set yourself against human beings *as they are*. Now,. as you are aware, Professor, the position you have taken up makes you a Member of the Party of Superman.'

. 'What do you call the Party of Superman, Professor?' (They addressed one another as 'Professor'. Anything in the shape of a title was made great use of, as the Germans are wont to do.)

'What we may call the Superman party', Professor McKenzie continued, 'is those classes of men in the twentieth century, who reach out violently towards a higher step up the evolutionary ladder. A remarkably clear-cut example of this

is to be found in the arts. There the so-called Abstractists are
probably the best specimens of what we are talking about.
These artists are those who would banish from the visual arts
the external world as it usually appears to men, and relegate
such masterpieces of the past as those of Van Eyck or Memling
to the status of the photograph. In architecture there is the
skyscraper, and the geometric creations of Lloyd Wright. Or
if we turn to Music, there is the twelve-tone system. In politics,
of course, the Superman party is the Bolshevist, which is a
super-puritanism, demanding that we should eradicate such
basic human instincts as the profit-motive for instance. And
in literature we have the invention of super-languages, such
as that of James Joyce. Everywhere we have seen, from
the teachings of Nietschze (*Menschlich Über Menschlich,* etc.)
onwards, a dissatisfaction with life as it has so far been lived,
and is still lived by everyone except a very few: a demand that
man should remake himself and cease to live upon the paltry,
mainly animal plane we know.—And now you, Professor
Harding, wish to supermanize the writing of history. So far
you have not had much success. If you will allow me to speak
rather frankly, it has landed you in Momaco!'

. Mr. Furber laughed with the expectant glee of the spectator
(in the stage-box). René smiled appreciatively. He liked this
bright Scot. 'I do not belong to the Party of Superman,' he
then said with quiet indifference. 'But it is a mistake which
may easily be made.'

'I was mistaken?' answered McKenzie, gently ironical.

It was obvious that Mr. Furber considered that the argument had made a promising début, and hoped that it would
not be abandoned. René decided to oblige.

Smiling accommodatingly, René lighted a cigarette, and
began to provide the Professor with an answer. 'Always,
Professor, I have made it my business to keep clear of what
you call the Superman party.'

'Nevertheless, it is fundamentally your party,' repeated
McKenzie.

'No. I have always discouraged spectacular aims. We do
not have to go outside, or *beyond*, what we have got. The
problem is a simple one. Government is often in the hands of

II

criminals or morons, never in the hands of first-rate men. This is a statement which most educated men would endorse. We do not have to create Supermen, but to manage, somehow, that men of a reasonably high order of intelligence and integrity govern us. No Philosopher King; just first-rate, honourable, intelligent men, such as are easy to find everywhere.'

'Are you not forgetting, Professor, that "all power corrupts"; and that the ten just men who were elected to rule— or the two hundred, or ten thousand—would soon become as bad as any of their predecessors? It appears to me a more idealistic or unrealizable proposal to make the good and the bad change places, than to evolve a Superman, who is wiser than Man-up-to-date.'

'We quote Lord Acton too often, I think, Professor.' René looked at Professor McKenzie with polite enquiry. 'Don't you agree? Power does not always corrupt, but corruptible people too often secure it. Then, again, Superman would not be immune from corruption, unless altogether inhuman.'

'Superman would be above corruption, would he not?' said McKenzie.

'It would be interesting to know how people visualize their Superman—except, of course, the titan of the Comics, who is merely larger and more muscular. For myself, I do not much care to contemplate a *wiser* man than Socrates or than Pascal. There seems to me something strained about the idea of Superman. What kind of man would this "Superman" be? Would he still be a man? Would he be physically exactly like ourselves? Or would he depart from the human norm visibly? What do you think, Professor?'

'I suppose he would,' said McKenzie.

'In that case his life on earth, Professor, would be a very uncomfortable one, if he were allowed to live. The first specimen of this Supermanhood would never be able to breed up a family of Supermen. He would almost certainly be destroyed, or closely confined for life, before he had time to look for a suitable mate. So even if such a development were desirable, it may be ruled out as impossible. This is one reason, though not the only one, why I do not fly any higher than Socrates or Pascal, or Voltaire.'

'So,' Professor McKenzie smilingly reminded him, 'we get back to the philosopher-king.'

'And so we should, if we specifically demanded one of those three great philosophers, or their modern equivalent,' René agreed. 'You would never get men to accept such sages as rulers, anyway. I agree with you, Professor, men prefer to be ruled by a vulgar blackguard. This I have, in fact, frequently pointed out. A criminal ruffian is often very popular, especially if he knows how to advertise his frailty humorously.'

There were convulsive movements and a chuckling sound from the bearded referee.

'Do you, by any chance, mean,' said Mr. Furber, 'the Mayor of a great neighbouring city?'

'Yes, Monsieur What's-his-name is a good illustration,' René agreed. 'Almost a standard specimen of what we have somehow to root out. It is precisely this popular appetite for the criminal and vulgar that we must not be defeatist about. Must not acquiesce in. Look at this war for instance. Are we to be defeatist about that? Must we say such things are natural and inevitable as history amply proves?'

'Yes, I am afraid so.' McKenzie nodded, in dismal assent. 'The majority of men still are barbarous. But we have drifted away, Professor, from the main point, which is the quality of your new ruler.'

'Very well, let us return to that. First of all, we have to remain within the modest bounds of possibility. For our non-moronic, non-criminal, enlightened man would fall far short of those very unusual men, those philosophers whose names I mentioned (but only to indicate a *type*).'

'However much you reduce your claims, Professor,' the Scot persisted, 'an enlightened man, well endowed with quali-ties of mind and heart, free of all criminal leanings, is very hard to find, and would impress other men as exceptional. The impression of strangeness would not fall far short of that which Uebermensch might be expected to produce.'

'Well, Professor,' René smiled, 'I am afraid we shall have to leave out the possibility of you or me causing such horrified alarm that we should be put under lock and key before we got a chance of starting our blameless rule. Let us turn, rather, to

the question of the waning, and eventual disappearance of
Homo Barbaricus. I am sanguine; but I am afraid I am not
very successful in explaining why. However, let me try a little
more. In the first years of this century the feudal, land-owning
aristocracies, naturally in favour of the barbary which produced them, were still intact, except in the New World. Well,
are they *still* intact? Will not this war yet further stamp out,
or blast away, what is left of the old order, based upon
barbary? So at length the ruling classes who were traditionally
interested in endorsing the barbarity of the barbarous
majority, at least these classes have been almost eliminated.
This is a great asset, for those who wish to liquidate the
barbarous habits of mind of the majority.'

For some minutes Mr. Furber had been attempting to look
like a feudal aristocrat, or at least a Medici. 'You approve of
the Bolshevists, then, Professor Harding?' he asked.

'No, I do not,' René told him. 'But there is no such thing,
in history, as an event, or as a policy, or as a party, that is
all-bad, or all-good. It was a good, or that is to say a useful,
action to sweep away the feudal conditions in Russia.'

But McKenzie did not seem prepared to let that stand. He
leant forward, as he spoke. 'The truth is, Professor, that a new
feudal class takes the place of the old. And with it comes a new
barbary, and even a new Dark Age.'

'There is always the chance of that: indeed it is almost the
rule, that if you remove anything from the social body, in its
place something of the same sort appears at once. But, to me,
the Soviet Empire has not a very stable look. Its survival
up-to-date has been due entirely to the benevolence of the
West.'

'Oh!' protested Mr. Furber.

'It sounds to you a paradox? If you think a little,' René
said, 'you will see what I mean. Their strength is artificial,
dependent upon the paradoxical neutrality or, as I have said,
benevolence of Capitalism.—However, this is really irrelevant.
All that is in question is whether a new barbary, of a permanent type, is taking the place of the boyars and Junkers, and
this, naturally, no one can be certain about. All one can
say is that the evidence points in the other direction—

towards some kind of Enlightenment, a mass rebellion against the brutal and archaic character of political leadership everywhere.'

'I am glad of that,' Mr. Furber observed in a tone of worldly irony.

René lighted a cigarette, as a sign that he had nothing more to say on those lines. As usual Mr. Furber was saturnine, taciturn and superior. Then Professor McKenzie stirred himself, and it was seen that he did not feel, on his side, that he had exhausted the subject.

'Well, Professor, I take back what I said. I see that I was mistaken in placing you in the Party of Superman. Your position is a far more novel—and far more complicated—one than I had supposed. It seems to me to be based upon a profound psychological error. For how you expect your mild, intelligent, and blamelessly honest man to dominate the ferocious, intelligent, and unscrupulous man I fail to understand.'

'You are thinking too much of the past,' René told him. 'It is an essential feature of my programme that the egotistic, the anti-social type should cease to fascinate the multitude, and rapidly diminish in numbers; and in the natural order of things the more or less enlightened will greatly increase in number and influence. Then ultra-barbarous wars should have the opposite effect from leading to a more barbarous state-of-mind, which is what happens at present. A crescendo of violence should, rather, lead away from it.'

'And so you argue, the sheep should become so numerous that at last they overwhelm the wolves!' McKenzie broke in.

'It is a mistake to regard men like myself and Mr. Furber as sheep.'

All three laughed; and Mr. Furber protested, 'You must leave me out of it, either as sheep or as wolf. Nothing would induce me to take power.'

'But I depend, for my theory, entirely,' René proceeded, 'upon a rapidly growing scepticism and enlightenment, and on a shrinkage in the lone-wolf type.'

'You cannot substantiate that,' Professor McKenzie told

him; 'there is no evidence of the existence of that historical process.'

René sawed his forefinger from side to side, a reinforced form of a shaking of the head. 'You must devote a little more time, Professor, to this subject. This question has been finally answered, you probably believe, once and for all, in one of the supreme dramas of the present century. I refer to the struggle in Russia between the Bolshevists and the Menshevists. Both were revolutionists, but when, with unexpected completeness and suddenness, success was theirs, the manner in which Russia was to be ruled had to be decided. The Bolshevists, a small party, were in favour of a government as autocratic as that of the Tsars—in favour of taking power and ruling ruthlessly, just like those they had overthrown (or even more so). And their view prevailed, the Menshevists rejecting with disgust the arguments in favour of the use of power. You would say that the idea in my latest book is to reverse this situation: that, with me, it would be the Menshevists, with their compunction, their idealisms, who would rule.'

'Yes, that does seem to follow, does it not, Professor?' McKenzie agreed.

'You would also say that my "mild, intelligent, trustworthy men", as I think you described them, would, in order to rule, be compelled to acquire the unscrupulous ferocity of the typical ruler. You would say that, when it comes to a showdown, it will always be the Bolshevist type of good man who secures power, and that the sort of ruler I envisage is impossible, because a good man who is scrupulous and gentle could never wield power.'

'Yes, I should say that,' smiled McKenzie.

'But, as we know, to associate ferocity, lack of any compunction and so on (as in the case of the Bolshevist) with what is called "idealism", with an extreme programme of social justice, cancels out. It results in zero. The high aims with which the revolution started cannot co-exist with the wholesale coercion necessary to check counter-revolution. A rule of iron eventuates in a society no better than the feudal society overthrown.'

'So social justice is impossible, and we shall never be

able to get away from barbarity?' Professor McKenzie
enquired.

'Not unless some change in the balance in our Western
Society occurs, as a result of the horrible extremes of destruction which we are now approaching—turns the tide against
violence in all its forms. It has seemed to me that in the West,
and especially on this Continent, there is an awakening which
amounts to an Enlightenment. It is easy to be sceptically
amused as to the existence of such an awakening. But I believe
that this war, or perhaps the next, will make the continuance
of the monstrosities in question impossible.'

Professor McKenzie lay back in his chair, indicating his
acquiescence that the argument should cease at this point.
René sprang up, and with agitated strides went over to the
window. He looked out for some minutes; then, with an equal
precipitation, he returned to his chair.

Mr. Furber turned his head, and with his large, blankly
enquiring eyes followed René's rush to the window, and then
followed him back again to his chair. 'You are disturbed,
Professor Harding? Something in your talk caused you to rush
across the room?' Mr. Furber purred.

Every once in a while René became acutely conscious of
Mr. Furber. Things would happen which reawakened his
curiosity; and on this occasion, as he re-seated himself, and
found the owl-like glance focussed upon him, he was impelled
to turn Mr. Furber over in his mind for the fifth, or was it the
sixth, time. Certainly Mr. Furber's mask most successfully
suggested a distinct, and possibly a new zoological species.
His large and lustreless dark eyes brooded blankly, allowing
one to divine a lazy but inquisitive brain, belonging to some
aloof, observant, mildly interested *creature* of owl-like habits.
A long shapeless black beard hung down lifelessly, concealing
his neck and collar. As it stretched downwards from the base
of his nose, this practically mouthless expanse threw the onus
of expression upon the eyes. These hung reticent, with very
little comment, secretive but harmless, above the weedy,
pendant growth. The emotionless dull red of the mouth existed
irrelevantly *in* this; the india-rubber lips secreted no saliva
and moved very little.

While he was with this queer creature René always felt that he was engaged in field work as an amateur naturalist. It was like being a bird-watcher, and Mr. Furber a great dreary owl. For all the latter's lethargy, his indolent remoteness, he concealed behind the blank discs of his eyes the gentle *gaminerie* of a spirited young lady of eighteen or nineteen; and there were violent streaks of *canaillerie* as well. Was he a soft, good-natured, 'impish', old shit? No: he was not susceptible of a worldly classification after that manner. One cannot speak of an owl as a shit, for instance.

So René was tremendously conscious of Mr. Furber suddenly, because this big weedy object was sluggishly interfering with him, at a moment when his mind was inflamed, and was attempting to pounce on something, as yet undetected; and the acuity of his attention was diminished by the intrusion into the field of vision of a bearded idiot-child, of huge proportions. The idle man-watching (and if birds are watched why should not men be watched?) of this irresponsible aesthete, to whose den they had come, resulted in his intellect being drawn away from an important object, and riveted upon an unimportant object. In other words, the mental energy mobilized to cope with the great dilemma was diverted into an angry analysis of the blandly-gaping Mr. Furber. Professor McKenzie was momentarily forgotten.

'There is a problem,' he told Mr. Furber, 'a major problem, and I once regarded myself as the man destined to solve it. Three years have passed during which my mind has been asleep. Professor McKenzie here woke it up with a start. I believed I saw something which I had not seen before. I was somewhat excited. I went to the window. . . .'

'Why do you go to the window?'

'Why do *you* go to the window?' René retorted, in what seemed a silly *tu quoque*.

'I do not go to the window,' Mr. Furber answered.

'Well, I *do*. I always go to the window if perplexed,' René remarked.

'You went to the window? Why did you go to the window, Professor?' Mr. Furber spoke gently, as if talking to a patient.

'Has the window a mystical attraction for you, Professor?'
McKenzie asked.

René turned to him, grimacing que-voulez-vous-ishly.
'Whenever I am pursuing some idea, if it escapes me it always
vanishes through the window.'

'Don't you ever feel inclined to pursue it?' Mr. Furber
enquired owlishly.

'I have so far resisted the impulse to plunge after them out
of the window.' René looked darkly at the window, at Mr.
Furber's large and lowering window; and Mr. Furber, who
now appeared to feel that these Professor fellows had finished
their performance, and had better be sent packing, rose
majestically, remarking, 'I must get to work, I suppose,' and,
specifically, to his pseudo-secretary, 'Another parcel of books
from New York has just arrived. It looks as though it might
be a very interesting parcel.' He gently moved toward the
library, and the Professors, who had risen, moved gently in
his wake.

'I wonder if you and your wife will come and have a meal
with us, Professor?' murmured McKenzie, and they proceeded
at once to fix a day. This was a turning-point in the epic of
Momaco; the social void was to be filled with friendly faces,
and the first face was that of this agreeable Scot. None of the
rancour felt by his wife embittered for René this transition,
only contempt for Mr. Furber was experienced by him, for
that bush-toff, because of his brutal omission; for of course Mr.
Furber should long ago have made their life more bearable by
putting them in touch with a few chosen people. And then of
course René's attitude towards the academics (unknown to
him) who so passionately held down their jobs, and closed
their ranks against the stranger of renown—for *them* his attitude hardened if anything. René's mind was absorbed by
these considerations, as they passed through the library, and
Furber's new consignment of books faded away into thin air.

Professor McKenzie lived on the Hill, so he and René parted
at the foot of the steps outside, where a little fresh snow was
beginning to fall; René very warmly shaking his hand.

Heading rather precipitately down the hill, the author of
The Secret History of World War II was in a mental turmoil;

11*

and the more chaotic the brainstorm grew, the more his speed increased, until he was in imminent danger of slipping upon the ice, and rolling down the hill instead of walking down it.

Since his last talks in England, over four years ago, he had had no contact of any kind with anyone more scholarly than the mushy Mr. Furber. Needless to say it was impossible to communicate with that stylistic owl-man. When at last, after these years of dumbness, the silence was broken, and communication began again (as he and Professor McKenzie disputed), the ideas hurt as they sprang up, arguments were painfully forced out of a rusty dialectical machine. A rough parallel to this would be the case of a man who had been wrecked upon a desert island and never spoken for many years, until at last a ship anchored off the coast of the island, and the castaway found himself speaking once more: lips, larynx, vocal chords, sinuses, tongue, all going into action again together after this portentous lapse, would do their work in astonished familiarity.

But it was the *subject* of this first act of communication which was so moving. All his life-work (so long neglected), and the very heart of what he had always been thinking about as well, had been burst open, as it were, and scrutinized, by a stranger of intelligence. A shaft of hard light had been cast upon an intellectual structure, and it had shocked him into seeing what he had never seen quite so objectively before. Now that he was alone, he attempted to arrange what he had seen, and to arrive at some immediate judgment.

It was rather similar to Dunne's problem of recording dreams. Upon waking, the most vivid dream fades with extraordinary rapidity. Usually ten or twelve seconds is all one has to turn an objective eye on and to describe the main features of the dream one has just had. Often its disappearance is far more speedy than that, and a few seconds are sufficient for it to vanish entirely.

At the end of his conversation with McKenzie, René was in the situation of the awakened dreamer. There had been a revelation of some kind. The mind was in a peculiarly sensitive condition, as if about to attain for him a new insight. But the 'interference' of the mischievous owl had stopped him before he could see what was as it were hovering indistinctly in the atmosphere. So now, rushing along over the snow and ice, the snowfall also increasing somewhat in density, he hoped that he might recapture what had escaped him under the ironical scrutiny of Mr. Furber's disintegrating futility. But anyone who has vainly attempted to call back from oblivion a dream, startlingly life-like for the few seconds it survived in waking life, will understand that *nothing*, neither standing on one's head, nor any other physical ordeal, will restore what has so abruptly clicked out. The memory is in league, it seems, with dreams, for nothing will persuade it to function regarding what has occurred during sleep. As he hurried forward, in place of what he hoped might be vouchsafed him again, was the face of Mr. Furber.

He reached the Laurenty fatigued and discouraged. As he entered the sitting-room of their apartment, snow on his hat and shoulders, Hester's quizzical stare, that new phenomenon, irritated him more than usual. She was celebrating a victory for which his dismal expression was responsible—an eloquent comment, she felt, upon how *well* his new social enterprises were going!

René sat silent until she brought in the tea. After he had swallowed three cups (chain-drinking) he was restored, and enabled to meet her stare on equal terms.

'You look rather tired, my pet,' he observed.

'You feel better now?' she answered. 'When you came in, *tired* is not the word I should have used to describe what you looked like. I should have said that you seemed on the brink of collapse.'

'Indeed?' said René, still smiling comfortably. 'Mr. Furber's house is a good way away, and I rushed along to tell you the good news. Our first invitation to dinner in Momaco!'

'After three years and a half.—How delightful! I do hope you *accepted*.'

'It was not by people like McKenzie that we have been ostracized. He is a surprisingly nice chap, who arrived long after us.'

'Is that why you looked so radiantly happy when you came in at that door a quarter of an hour ago?'

'Purely physical, my dear Hester, I had just been walking hard,' he answered, 'forgetful of the fifteen below.'

'So you said just now, darling,' she said in a wan tone which announced defeat, but not resignation.

A little later he went into the bedroom and lay down. It was very unusual for him to do this: he only lay down on the bed in the daytime when unwell. His purpose at present was to isolate himself, and to make another attempt to secure contact with a mind lit up by controversy and on the verge of discovery. But this withdrawal disturbed his wife, as he should have seen that it would: and before he had time to get his intellect in focus there was Hester standing beside him, scrutinizing his face with anxious eyes. 'What is wrong, René?' she asked him. 'Aren't you well?'

He rolled off the bed with an exasperated laugh. 'Absolutely nothing is wrong, excepting that when I am attempting to contact my Muse, someone intrudes, and asks me what is the matter with me! That is what is wrong.'

Hester was relieved, denying herself the regulation pique of the officious wife. His arm around her shoulder, René propelled her into the sitting-room. There he explained to her the cause of his withdrawal. It was a little difficult to be explicit, but he made her see what was happening, what an unsatisfactory rôle the memory was playing, and how a little seclusion was to be desired.

Hester cheered up with surprising suddenness. The word *work* was, for her, a magic vocable—work, that is, with its old significance; the sort of work which he had always done before he came to Momaco. Indeed, a big factor in the formation of her implacable hatred for Momaco was precisely that no work could be done there. Momaco—the place which was the grave of a great career: the barren spot where you ceased to think, to teach, or to write, and just rotted away. So the news that thinking was at last going on again filled her with indescribable joy. This re-birth of his normal intellectual life would surely, sooner or later, lead him back to England. For there

was no Public here; no publishers, no anything that is necessary for such enterprises—bold and dazzling enterprises—
which were as natural to her husband as they were necessary.
Hester felt happier than she had at any time since the fire. She
even began to make plans for finding a new home, when they
got back to England; one nearer to King's Road, Chelsea, a
better shopping neighbourhood for her, and where she would
be within easier reach of her friend Susan.

. The fact that Professor McKenzie's wife was an Englishwoman, and one who had come out to this deadly spot since
the outbreak of war, caused her almost to look forward to
their dinner engagement.

CHAPTER XXV

Dinner at the McKenzies

TWO days later, in the evening at six o'clock, Hester was examining herself in the glass, in a way she had not done since, in her stateroom on the *Empress of Labrador*, she was getting ready to accompany a Knight of the Legion of Honour into the first-class restaurant of the ship. It was now a different face from what it had been then. The stare remained, but it was no longer one of ladylike vacuity. It now was purposeful. The purpose was to escape from Momaco merely, but it might have been that of a woman confined in an iron chest, bracing herself to push up the portentously heavy lid.

René, on his side, was taking his evening suit out of the clothes-closet, wondering how much weight he had lost, and looking to see whether the moth had eaten a hole in the middle of the back. When at length he had tied his black tie and put on his jacket, and moved over to the long glass, he saw what the world would consider a very distinguished-looking figure —tall, well-shaped, with elegant, well-brushed beard. This life-size Royal Academy portrait of Professor René Harding impressed him disagreeably—it stepped, for him, straight out of the past of foolish ambitions, and of metropolitan self-importance. But Hester, who was watching him, from where she was sitting attempting to put a discreet gleam on to her nails, did not share his disgusts. With her hands immobilized, she sat following him with her eyes: then one tear, and after that another, began to roll down her cheek. She put down the shammy-leather pad, dabbed her eyes with her handkerchief and then jumped up. Going over to her husband she exclaimed, 'Darling, you look wonderful!'

'I'm afraid I do.'

'Don't be silly, René.' She kissed the splendid object, upon the beard not far from the mouth—a mouth worthy of an Air Marshal. 'René darling,' she said coaxingly, 'do wear your

328

decoration! I will go and get it for you.' He was speechless
with indignation—literally he desired ardently to protest with
enormous violence, but something stuck. The scene in the
restaurant of the liner rose up in his memory, in all its shameful absurdity. He must put that disgraceful emblem in the
waste-paper basket; or still better make a present of it to the
hotel proprietor. A woman is always on the side of the lousy
world. And then of course they want to demonstrate that
their man is a bigger shot than the other woman's husband.
So he stood, preparing to stamp on the decoration when it
arrived. But Hester, who was in the bedroom, could not at
once put her hand on the ribbon, and René had begun to
think of something else. All of this was giving Hester a great
deal of pleasure. More pleasure than she had experienced for
many a long day. This was all helping to reconcile her, to
make her accept life in this detestable dump. And so, after
all, if the Legion of Honour can be utilized to gild the road
upwards, from the winter of their discontent in Momaco No. I
to Momaco No. II, which might become, if not 'glorious
summer', at least not quite so oppressive a spot—well, if the
wretched decoration would help to that end, why not bedeck
himself with it—at the risk of appearing someone he was not
to McKenzie?

When Hester returned with the insignia—and a self-
conscious smile—instead of encountering the reception she had
anticipated, René was sitting with his breast at the ready,
inflated to receive the accolade, his face wearing a beatific
smile.

'Ah!' he exclaimed, as she approached with the ribbon.
'We shall make our début in Momaco society impressively
beribboned.'

They were obliged to telephone for a taxi, for René had
omitted to enquire by which route Carmichael Road was
approached. The French-Canadian driver took them through
the Peasoup quarter by the side of the river, from which
seething slum they shot up the road at the foot of the little
mountain where the McKenzies lived.

Carmichael Road was a rock-flanked, slightly curving road,
on almost the lowest slopes of the hill upon which Mr. Furber,

and all other illustrious persons, dwelt. It was extremely clean
and prosperous-looking. Subsequently Professor McKenzie
explained that this had once been a highly respectable district,
but the Peasoup tide flowed in underneath it, between the
base of the hill and the river, and the householders on the
other side of the road (the McKenzies were on the inner side)
found themselves gazing down into Peasoup backyards. As
a consequence, house-rents in Carmichael Road dropped,
sharply, until they had reached a level accessible to impecu-
nious professors. This had suited the McKenzies excellently.
There were some quite good French-Canadian shops down
below within easy reach, and for their part they did not object
to French-Canadians.

René, as an older Momacoan, instructed this relative new-
comer as to one feature of Canadian life which he might not
as yet be quite clear on. 'Class is Race, in this country,' com-
mented René. 'No Nazi could feel more racial superiority
than the English Canucks of Upper Canada.'

On the way to Carmichael Road René attempted to converse
in French with the taxi-driver. The latter repulsed him in
pidgin-English. But as his face was almost purely Indian, and
with traces of the 'nobility' of the Redskin, René tipped him
well. There were about fifteen steps to climb, winding up
between jagged rocks, in order to reach the house, which was
well built and substantial. Professor McKenzie opened the
door.

There was a fairly large living-room, in which they found
Mrs. McKenzie playing the piano—an early Beethoven Minuet.
She was a woman a few years younger than Hester. Laura
McKenzie was an attractive person, who was aware, but not
tiresomely so, of what could be done with eyes of light blue-
green in the shadow of a mass of dark hair. Regarding her
simply as a big sex-trap, to lure a male into a situation where
offspring may result, she also, thought René, realized the sex
value of the piano—of a mazurka of Chopin's or a Pavan for
a Dead Infanta according to taste. Hostesses who, on the
arrival of guests, are discovered playing the piano, received
from René a very bad mark. The figure rising from the key-
board to greet one was not popular with him. To break off in

the middle of a Nocturne to shake one's hand with a dazzling smile was not a device which recommended the woman
who made use of it to·René. That a room into which guests
are destined shortly to arrive should be impregnated with
mazurkas or pavans appeared to him in as bad taste as if some
perfume had been sprayed into the air a few minutes before
the guests' arrival.

So the minuet that was still in the air prejudiced René
against the McKenzie interior. He glanced sideways a little
- uneasily at Hester, to see whether the music had made the
same undesirable impression upon her. But apparently she
had no objection to a hostess clothing herself in the raiment
of Beethoven in order to welcome her more adequately; and
she showed no signs of feeling that Mrs. McKenzie had put
on stilts, and was culturally high-hatting her, or something
of that kind.

There was something that Laura McKenzie had, not visible
to René, which, from Hester's standpoint, put in the shadow
everything else. And, as an efficient observer, that invisible
something should have been the number one article for him
to check up on. She was a lady, that was the all-important
(to René invisible) something. What he had been looking for
was the kind of thing which could influence *him*; and this was
a rather usual shortcoming of his.

It was the tones of the hostess's voice, not the notes of
her piano, that mattered. And, staring blandly, Hester swam
towards those tones in an entirely satisfactory way, her
husband considered.

The four people sat down, René saying to his host, 'What
luck to have found so nice a house as this,' and it was then
that Professor McKenzie explained the reason for so charming
a residence being attainable by people in their income-bracket.

A sweet, swarthy, merry-eyed French-Canadian maid
brought in upon a large metal tray four cocktails and a shaker,
and everybody's tongue began to move with more agility.
Hester disclosed her obsession, and said how dearly she would
like to be in England once more, instead of this horrible place.

'I do not think you would talk like that if you had had our
experiences for the first two years of the war,' their hostess

told her, and it was obvious from her tone that *she* also suffered from an obsession, of an opposite kind from that of Hester.

'Oh, I am sure I should not be affected by that, a hundred bombs would be better than Momaco!' the latter forcibly asserted.

'It is not the *bombs*,' Laura McKenzie cried, 'I have never been within five miles of a bomb. You would find there were far more disagreeable things than the occasional bomb—unless of course you were in London.'

'All the same . . .!' intoned Hester. 'Never the less . . .!'

'The amenities of Momaco, I know, are few,' Laura McKenzie replied, 'but I still think that you are extraordinarily lucky to be in Momaco, quite extraordinarily lucky.'

A painful contraction of her raised eyebrows made Hester look suddenly like a hopelessly miserable child, who had lost something she could not replace.

'You have to remember, Laura,' McKenzie warned his wife, 'that our guests have had a terrible experience since their arrival here. Apart from anything else, their hotel was set on fire by a ghastly little man, a murderer as well as a fire-bug . . .'

'An Englishman, I think,' Laura sharply intervened.

René began to feel that they would never reach the dinner table if this went on. Only a very little more of this dogmatical woman plugging Momaco, and Hester would leave the house. Something must be done at once to save the situation. He shook the party with what he hoped would pass for a sudden, uncontrollable laugh.

'Here we have someone as obstinate as yourself, Hester! I never expected to meet anyone as fanatical as you on the subject of Momaco.'

McKenzie followed suit. He seized his Laura by the arm and recalled her to her duties as a hostess. 'Rein in your rage against the billeting-officer and the hostile constable, and the air-raid warden! We have guests . . . let us forget our personal grievances.'

'Sorry!' said Laura. 'I was on my hobby-horse, was I? And I met someone else riding a hobby-horse of a different colour.

I apologize.' She smiled at Hester. 'This war has made a savage of me.'

McKenzie then brought forward a less controversial topic. It appeared they had mutual friends named Saunders.

'You know the Saunders, don't you?' McKenzie began. Soon they were all talking about the Saunders, saying how nice Jessica was, and what an intelligent chap was Tom; and the Saunders drew them closer together, especially warming the homesick Hester; and still speaking of the Saunders they moved in to dinner in the room on the other side of the front door.

A Barsac which could almost have passed for a Château Yquem drew serious commendation from René, who appeared in the rôle of a sniffer and taster. Next he and McKenzie began speaking of the drink problem, for the control was very tight, with the result that bootleg alcohol was exorbitant. McKenzie had been given the name of a 'blind pig', who was reputed to be a little more reasonable than most. The place of this illicit merchant was not far from the Laurenty. 'Half the "blind pigs" in Momaco have their business addresses in our street,' declared René, 'but not at our end of it. There are several "blind pigs" in our hotel. One of them, with whom I deal, knows the French vineyards quite well.' He gave the address of this man to McKenzie, and McKenzie gave him the new address he had received. The name of this one was the Sieur Fondot. Were there no 'blind pigs' down below in their French-Canadian quarter? René enquired. But it appeared that that traffic mostly was carried on in the district beyond the railway track.

Upon the wall of the dining-room hung a photograph of a beautifully-built seventeenth-century English house, in what appeared to be what was left of a park. The trees seemed to belong to another time, when 'lazy tinklings lulled the distant folds', which they do no more. Laura's father was a parson, and this was his rectory in Somerset. René demanded rhetorically if there were anything more beautiful in the world than red Somerset, with its red earth, its red rivers, and its wealth of ancient red-brick manor-houses, rectories, farms and inns. And Hester's staring eyes grew misty as she thought

of those sacred counties, in the warm south-west of England
—from the indescribable beauties of Shaftesbury and the
neighbouring villages to the landscape of Lamorna Birch,
and the splendours of Tintagel. Laura was a little cynical and
aloof, when it came to a sentimental tripping around the land-
scapes of her birthplace, but she allowed that it was first-class
hunting country.

But Hester was in no mood to be put off by the cynic. She
was fond of wine, and especially of sweet wine. The Barsac
was finding its way round her veins. She had a sleepy, happy
look as her eyes rested upon the old rectory in the photograph
hanging directly in front of her, and, then, finding herself
once more in civilized surroundings.

It was at this idyllic moment for Hester that Laura
McKenzie felt impelled (perhaps because she divined her
guest's gooey state of mind) to speak of the English country-
side as she had last seen it.

'It may be that in another couple of years I shall be feeling
the way you do,' said Laura, with a jangling about of the
brilliant cold blue and green spangles of her eyes, in the
shadow of the impending dark avalanche of her hair. The last
thing that Hester realized was that the eyes and hair were
the human equivalent of the sumptuous and delicate scene
in the West Country which had acted on her with such
nostalgic force. It was a south-English combination, a feminine
romanticness of so special a kind that it could not come from
the northern counties, would seem very strange in France or
Italy, would be far too theatrical in Germany and probably
could not be found in Scandinavia. This is only to speak of
the *kind*, not of the quality.

'*We* were not living, for the first two years of the war, in
anything as pleasant as that.' (Laura waved her hand towards
the photograph.) 'Do you happen to know that bleakest of
counties, Essex? Well, we had to find some sort of a place to
live in quickly. We rented a small and ill-furnished house
about thirty miles outside London. To get there you pass a
dirty forest, an East End forest, and roll through the dirtiest,
sootiest, flattest slums ever seen. After an hour or so of
chugging through sooty, dank, dispirited fields you reach

Crackbrook. No one pretends that it is a show-place, or beauty-spot, but I cannot make you understand the degree to which to mention it in a guide-book would be disloyal. We lived for two years in Crackbrook.'

'If it was so unattractive, why did you go there to live?' enquired Hester, in a tone of bored protest. Why must she be told about this repulsive place?

'All the less brutally ugly spots had already been occupied. We were late-comers.'

'I see,' said Hester miserably. She looked towards Professor McKenzie. But the two professors were absorbed in harrying some little problem which had made its appearance, and been spotted by René.

Laura McKenzie smiled, and remarked, 'No use looking at *him*. You must hear what an awful time we had. As soon as war became certain it was decided that no speck of light must be visible to a night-raider, and wardens were appointed to see that this did not happen. No other nation "blacked-out" in this way. But as if the war were not enough, "war conditions" were so luxuriated in by that blood-sweat-and-tears merchant . . .' Her husband turned quickly towards her.

'Laura, I believe you are about to speak of a man to whom we all should be grateful . . .'

'Rubbish, darling,' said Laura, 'but I will say no more lest it might offend. Anyhow'—resuming her conversation with Hester—'I was telling you about the black-out. It is still in force. The most disagreeable type of men volunteered for the job of air-raid warden. We had a real beauty at Crackbrook. He prowled round our house every night. If a chink of light was visible he thundered upon our door. We were fined, most unjustly, several times, and then I took no more trouble to conceal my low opinion of him.'

'How unpleasant! Weren't you able to black-out your windows?'

'Of course I was!' Laura McKenzie told her. 'But there is always a chink somewhere.'

'I suppose there is,' sighed Hester.

'But if the Warden was an enthusiastic snooper, the Billeting Officer was an alcoholic old sadist, for whom the war was a

heaven-sent opportunity. She hated me, probably because I
was the only woman in her part of the hamlet who did not
fawn upon her. The house we had rented was small, and there
were three of us, with our seven-year-old son. But there was
a tiny room upstairs that was not occupied. One afternoon,
after a bad night of bombing in the East End, several bus-
loads of children and cripples arrived. This frightful woman
planted a crippled boy of twelve on us. To my protests she
answered that I had a spare room, and that no one else had
any accommodation for him. People who took in a cripple
received thirty shillings a week, and some of the local people
were glad enough to take one in. There must have been *someone* who would have been glad to have him. But there was
nothing for it. The Billeting Officer and the constable were
buddies, there was no one to. appeal to, so we had this
Jewish child of twelve (she had picked a Jew for me!) until
one day he disappeared. He complained one week that I
was under-nourishing him, and the Billeting Officer got my
week's sustenance money docked. The cripple was excessively
aggressive, and on one occasion he struck Ian with his crutch.'
    'How frightful!' Hester's face screwed up into a painful
grimace. 'Surely you could appeal to the police?'
    'Of course, but the police was the fat, red-nosed "boy-
friend" of the Billeting Officer. The cripple said that my
husband had hit him first!'
    'How disgusting!' Hester looked as if she were about to cry.
    'Well, I need not retail how horrible the shopkeepers be-
came. If you gave them large tips that was all right. If you
did not, you were treated atrociously. Some of them must be
getting quite rich; especially of course owners of food shops.'
    'How horrible!' Hester was now actually weeping.
    Professor McKenzie looked around at this moment, and
saw the tears emerging from the miserably staring eyes, he
then looked angrily at his wife.
    'You have made Mrs. Harding cry,' he said.
    'Sorry.' (This was apparently what Laura always said, when
she offended.) 'I did not notice . . .'
    'I am not crying,' protested Hester, very confused. 'It is
the Canadian light—it often makes my eyes water.'

They then began talking about the difference between soft English light, and the hard relentless Canadian variety. Professor McKenzie had had to go to an optician, and René, too, said he thought of having smoked glasses for the winter time, against the glare of the snow.

'Things are all right in the north and west of England, I believe,' Laura told her shrinking guest—a great concession showing that she was really a kind-hearted woman. And with that Hester's ordeal was over. There was no further mention of the unattractive sides of the English character, or those parts of England which were hard on the eye. The excellent cognac which accompanied her coffee re-mellowed her, and put a melancholy sparkle in her eye, for she was extremely susceptible to good brandy.

When they moved back into the living-room, René enquired if any Canadians were to be expected as after-dinner guests. Upon learning that no one had been asked to meet them, René removed his ribbon from his jacket, and put it in his pocket.

'Hester asked me to wear this, in case we should be called upon to meet some of the natives. I hope you didn't think I stuck that in my coat for you!'

'I think your ribbon is a well-deserved and colourful emblem. I wish I had one, and I should always wear it if I had!' McKenzie added.

'I am quite sure you would not,' retorted René, 'except in the company of the ignoble.'

It was not long before René asked Laura McKenzie if she would please play them something. Without fuss she went over to the piano and played several pieces very well. Asked to play some more, she played several more pieces, until René said to himself, 'She is going to play for the rest of the evening.' However, although entreated by René to continue, she *did* stop after the second batch. The Hardings learned that Laura had just begun her career as a pianist when she married. 'I had not the money,' she informed them, 'to hire halls, so I should certainly have failed.'

As a couple, René said to himself, the McKenzies were good-lookers. A dark, slightly-built man, McKenzie wore the no-longer popular 'side-boards'—without being 'dressy' he was careful about his clothes; and Laura, with a complete absence of self-consciousness, wore rather expensive ones. It had not escaped René that he was the object of a very friendly feeling on the part of his host.

The McKenzies appeared to be on especially good terms with the rector of the Anglican Church dominating the Hill; a very large church, almost acting as cathedral to English-Canadian Momaco. The Reverend William Trevelyan was an Englishman, and René supposed that Laura McKenzie's connection with the Church was at least a contributing factor to the more than usually cordial relations subsisting between the McKenzies and the rector. In any case, they seemed to wish René to meet this clergyman without delay.

The English colony in Momaco was especially, almost uniquely, strong; and the Reverend William Trevelyan was a person highly influential in Momaco. Quite half the board of governors of the University belonged to his flock. This fact alone demonstrates the unusual position of the English in that city, for, in most of the great cities of Canada, the English occupy a very minor position. McKenzie explained the meaning of the Reverend W. Trevelyan to René; it was arranged that Trevelyan should be informed of the presence in Momaco of this very original and well-known historian.

'Trevelyan's response will be immediate, I feel quite sure of that,' McKenzie affirmed. 'He is a man of considerable intelligence. This is rather rare, I imagine, in the Church of England.'

Hester was a quietly unconvinced witness of these proceedings, as though one man were proposing to the other a sovereign cure for indigence. She half turned, with a half-smile in the direction of her hostess. She left the house with rather mixed feelings about Laura McKenzie; admitting to herself, and later to René, that Laura was a curious, a bitter and arrogant woman, but quite amusing notwithstanding.

When the Hardings took their departure, the McKenzies looked at one another; McKenzie said, 'I like Harding;' his wife observed, 'She's a funny one, but she has her points.'

CHAPTER XXVI

René becomes a Columnist

THE next day, McKenzie telephoned. His Reverence would much like to meet the author of *The Secret History of World War II* which he described as 'very naughty'. Could René and his wife come to dinner the next night?

The Trevelyan dinner was a great success. The clergyman appeared to like René in spite of the 'naughtiness' of what he wrote. He had read a little history, and he liked discussing, from a churchman's angle, the years immediately succeeding the setting up of a separate English church in the sixteenth century. This, actually, was a period with which René was particularly familiar.

René, on his side, was not at all displeased with this contact: he felt there was a good deal of shrewdness underneath the cleric's rather flourishy talk. The following Sunday the Hardings were at the morning service in St. George's Church, and René's tall bearded figure was noted with satisfaction by the Reverend William Trevelyan. The church, to the astonishment of the Hardings, accustomed to the empty churches of England, was full, Victorianly full. The greater part of the congregation was English. Hester found herself surrounded by English people: though, unfortunately, just ahead of them was a Canadian couple; and the pleasing illusion which she might otherwise have enjoyed, that she was once more in England, was denied her. The Canadian voices, whose responses were louder than those of anyone else in their neighbourhood, and the lusty rolling of the R's, spoilt her enjoyment of her favourite hymn, 'For those in peril on the sea'. It was, however, consoling to feel that there were other Britons suffering the horrors of Momaco and that she was not a solitary martyr.

During the next few weeks they made the acquaintance of numbers of people, some of these, both Canadian and English,

339

were just people it was thought the Hardings might like to know; others were big shots, of potential use to René. One of these was the proprietor of the *Momaco Gazette-Herald*. This was a contact of great significance, for René was offered a weekly column in that paper, which was so well paid that it changed their economic position overnight; and so radically, that they moved from the Hotel Laurenty to an apartment-hotel in a more desirable quarter of the town.

One would have supposed that this last event would have stirred Hester into a certain elation. But that was not the case. She even warned René against the dangers of this new prosperity.

'Whether Momaco ignores you or fêtes you, it is always Momaco. Do you really want to spend the rest of your life in this awful city? The fact that you have been recognized all of a sudden, and have been given a newspaper job which will enable us to live comfortably, changes nothing. You do not want to be a journalist, do you? This column merely keeps us alive. Is that all you want to do, René? Just *keep alive?*'

Formerly René would have laughed, in the hope of wearing her down by mirth. Now he looked at her very seriously, for she was a problem which had to be faced with all the resources he possessed.

'A city is good or bad, attractive or horrible, according to the people it contains, and which of its citizens you happen to know. You call it "horrible" because of horrible conditions under which we lived for three years. If we had lived under similar conditions, London would be horrible.'

Hester laughed. 'These class-room arguments get one no-where,' she answered. 'It may be a good piece of logic, but it has no connection with the reality. London was where we were born. I might agree with you if I had been born in *Momaco*—though I should know it was a pretty poor place to be born in (if I had any intelligence).'

René drew in his breath. 'If we are speaking of *realities*, then let me say that I have no intention of stopping in Momaco longer than I can help. So your argument that because I have got a good job I shall therefore live here forever is fallacious.'

'Thank God for that!' said Hester with a bitter fervency;

getting up and going into the bedroom, there leaning out of
the window, inhaling the milder airs which were blowing from
the south.

René came into the bedroom behind her. She started and
stiffened as she heard him. Was he proposing to resort to the
venustic argument of the bedchamber? She hoped he was not.
She had never denied him her body, but she wished he could
understand that copulation was nothing to do with logic. But
this was not what he proposed. When she turned round, he
took her hands. 'Hester, I had something else to say. One of
the people in Momaco is myself. Another is yourself. The fact
that *you* are in Momaco changes Momaco a great deal for me.
Now today you have written to several people in London, to
Susan, to your Mother. You love London, and are homesick,
because perhaps a certain half-dozen people are there—you
love those people collectively more than you love me? You
would rather be in London with Susan, perhaps, than live
in Momaco with me?'

'You know I would not,' she replied. 'You know that the
question is absurd. But your question implies something that
is not true. It implies that my motives are purely selfish in
desiring to leave this place and to return to London. That is
absolutely untrue. Listen, I would throw myself out of that
window if I knew that my death would result in your returning
to England, and that nothing else would do so.'

This was typical of the way their half-disputes would end.
In a half-threat, or in something he felt it wiser to ignore or to
turn his back on. After all, the open window was there. But
on this occasion he turned on her reproachfully.

'If you threw yourself out of that window, it would achieve
nothing except to break my heart. It would shatter London
as much as Momaco into a million pieces.—Momaco—London!
—How I have come to hate those names!'

An almost sinister expression of loathing was on his face
as he said this. The effort to conduct these conversations upon
the normal social plane had really grown to be beyond his
powers of nervous endurance; to present a face undistorted
by passion, to employ the innocuous forms of civil speech,
instead of springing at her and shaking her till her teeth

rattled, howling in her face, 'Bosh, bosh, bosh, bosh! Quack, quack, quack, quack! Listen, intolerable sparrow! London is as useless to me as Momaco is to you. There are no conceivable circumstances which would ever make it possible for me to *work*, to teach, to exist intellectually in London, after my resignation. *Here* it is possible for me to work and here I stop —here I stop. I do not need you to tell me ten times a day that it is not worth while to work here, to work in Momaco. *Of course* it is not. I know that—I know that . . . better than you can ever know it. I am, let me assure you, *madly* aware of that. But I also know that I will never again become a nameless piece of human wreckage. I may not be much. I may not amount to much. *But* my shoes shall be shone: my pocket-book shall be packed with newly-printed notes: my quarters shall be in the smart clean part of town—*shall* be— and there is an end of the matter. If you say *London* once more I will paint you all over with the word London in big red letters, and tie you up, and mail you to Susan.—That is a *mild* ending for such a pest.'

So, at this period, suppressions were always involved, often resulting in muscular anomalies in his mobile face; he did not say anything more than politely he was supposed to say. But his face had the most extraordinary expressions sometimes, ranging from snarling smiles to a fakir-like ferocity.

CHAPTER XXVII

. The Black Fly

WEEKLY, until the summer, René wrote a war-commentary for the *Momaco Gazette-Herald*. He introduced into the column no controversial matter whatever. Objective judgements, with regard to the progress of the war; opinions as to the probable outcome of moves made by either side; explanations of what each move signified from the standpoint of military strategy—there was nothing more provocative than that. If the political issues were dealt with, only acceptable material was employed. At the end of the half-year his column had come to be greatly valued, and not only in Momaco. Those who had been responsible for his securing this job had nothing to reproach themselves with, their judgement had been sound, and their cordiality began to take deeper root.

In the first week in August, the Hardings went to a summer camp, about forty miles to the north of Momaco. There were a number of small lakes in the Bush, and at several places the Momacoans had built huts and arranged centres for the hire of canoes. What the seaside is for the English these lakelands are for the Momacoans. The English-Canadians and the Peasoups were rigidly separated, the English having the best sites.

René, in the interests of economy, selected a place where the English and French camping grounds almost met. The English, while paddling too far Eastward, might occasionally catch sight of a brown-skinned Peasoup disporting himself in the water; or a canoe-full of little inky-haired Peasoups might paddle past a Nordic Blond sunning himself in front of his hut (reading some Nordic literature, like *Forever Amber*, or a Western story). They would gaze at one another across the glassy water with racial disapproval.

This position, so near the Peasoups, was naturally inexpensive. But it had other disadvantages besides the inconvenience of catching sight of a few Peasoups. As luck would have it,

the camp-site René had chosen was occasionally visited by
what the border-people of the U.S. know as 'the Canadian
Fly'. However, they had a few days of blissful silence, of
fir-scented lakes, of plunges into icy waters by moonlight.
Hester was almost happy.

'How lovely this is!' she exclaimed. 'Before the Canadians
came I think I might have quite liked Canada.' To which René
answered, 'You mean *before the English came.*' For the first
time for months she could be seen throwing her head back and
laughing. She bathed continually, she did some bird-watching;
one night, at their starry evening meal, she got a little tipsy.
And then she was bitten—or is it stung? Whatever the black
fly does she was bitten or stung. Within twenty-four hours
Hester was a mass of bites, unable to sleep or eat. René, whose
bites were less severe, took her back with the utmost despatch
to Momaco, where she lay for a week or more in a high fever.
René was not well himself, and he listened morosely to
Hester's ravings. Canada was the subject throughout—'God-
forsaken ice-box, heavenly summers presided over by the
Black Fly. . . . *Please,* René, *never* let us leave this beautiful
country . . . you won't, will you? I could never forgive you
if you did so!'

The McKenzies had had their holiday in July, a trip into
Vermont in preference to the fly-blown joys of little Bush
lakes. Laura came over at once, when she heard what had
occurred. She enrolled a young Canadian friend of hers, Alice
Price, and the two of them fulfilled all the functions of nurse,
bell-hop, entertainer. They shopped, they rubbed in ointments,
they prattled, they cooked, they administered ice-packs, gave
cold spongings; and last but not least enabled René to concentrate upon his own bites. In Hester's case there was a poisoned
mind enormously complicating the problem of a poisoned
body. The amount of bitter vilification of Canada that Alice
Price was obliged to listen to would have caused a more
chauvinistic young woman to depart, her eyes flashing angrily,
quite early in the proceedings. But Alice was a second-
generation Canadian, with an English father, and had
listened to diatribes hardly less vitriolic from her own
parents.

As the fever abated, and Hester emerged from the torment, able once more to converse with restraint, the two young women undertook a sort of occupational therapy, trying to persuade her to knit or do crosswords. Then they entertained her with gossip of the Hill, of the University, of the city at large; and Laura would read her bits of letters from England. They did everything that was possible to ease her back, expeditiously, into normal life once more, and their ministrations were responsible, René believed, for preserving Hester's sanity intact, and sparing them all from an *open* breakdown. For a breakdown of health existed all the time, needless to say, and Hester, as much as her husband, was not more than fifty per cent normal. At the time of the execution of Mr. Martin she had gone about muttering to herself. They had hastened the process of hanging Mr. Martin by the neck and dropping him into the earth, as if it were hardly decent for him to continue to breathe. The proceedings shocked Hester profoundly. She dreamed frequently of the doll-like face of Affie, as they had seen it in the mortician's. Several times, in conversation with René, she insisted that Mr. Martin was not an Englishman. On the actual day of the execution, she was very nervous, and on one occasion when the maid (who supposed that they were out) entered unexpectedly, Hester stifled a scream, and, springing up, rushed into the bedroom—there, a few minutes later, René found her convulsively weeping, and it was a long time before she quieted down.

René's reactions to the trial, of course, were of a very different character from hers. Actually he went to the Courthouse on two occasions, and had a good view of Mr. Martin in the dock. He looked a very wizened bit of spotless respectability, in his striped flannel suit. He treated the whole proceedings exactly as he had the use of the word 'bitch' in addressing himself to a lady. His eyes remained hooded, and the skin of his face was of the same faded pink as before. He answered the counsel for the prosecution as if that gentleman had been a janitor, accusing him of some misdemeanour on the principle that *attack is the best defence.* Obviously the janitor, or janitor-like person, had realized that he was about to be denounced by Mr. Martin, and was forestalling Mr. Martin's attack by shooting at him a series of questions designed to cover him with obloquy. Mr. Martin, with the faintest of sneers, in a voice as thin as paper, answered him as though it were really beneath his dignity to have any truck with such a fellow. Once or twice he burst into derisive laughter—but laughter that was so noiseless and polite that it could hardly offend very deeply. If the judge asked him a question, Mr. Martin turned towards him as one gentleman to another, both of them above the mêlée of the Court, rather amused at the extravagances of those taking part.

Once René saw the prisoner catch sight of an old acquaintance in the public benches, and raise his hand with a gentlemanly restraint, his slight smile, with a faint amusement in it, suggesting as clearly as possible that here were two friends who found themselves both as spectators of a very curious, and somewhat degrading, spectacle.—Asked why he had struck down the Manageress, Mrs. McAffie, he became, for him, rather violently indignant. 'If I had been doing what he accuses me of, the fireman could not have seen me, because the passage was full of smoke. I had my handkerchief over my nose and mouth on the only occasion when, with great difficulty, I returned to my apartment. It was impossible that any fireman could have been farther along the passage than my apartment, as this fireman pretends that he was. The fellow must be suffering from some delusion, or else he is one of those people who enjoy seeing their names in the newspaper.' When confronted with the elongated cosh, which he agreed was his, and asked how it came about that there was human blood and human hair upon it, and that the hair was that of Mrs. McAffie, he simply replied that the police had stuck the hair there, in order to build up a case of homicide, so that their charge of arson would appear more probable—if anything could make that probable.

René got the impression that this little Englishman, whose god was Respectability, was playing the whole time for the benefit of his old friends and drinking companions, and was not seriously concerned with defending himself. He probably knew that there was no escape, but he wished to leave the scene the upright, cool and collected gentleman they all knew

so well, *visibly* incapable of the crimes of which he was so
absurdly accused.

From any standpoint, René's existence at this time had
become anything but identical with that of Hester. So many
of the plans of action which suggested themselves to him met
with bitter opposition, or were treated with disagreeable levity
when communicated to his wife, that he ceased to communicate them. Whatever he might plan assumed a continued
residence on that side of the Atlantic—this was quite sufficient
to cause her to feel no interest, and to react hostilely. Up to
the period of the fire he had informed her, from day to day,
of everything he was doing, or intending to do. As castaways
upon Momaco they had lived together, in an idyllic communion in which it was unthinkable that they should hide
anything from one another. Now he would consult her upon
nothing of serious moment. So they went back to a régime
which had obtained for some years before his resignation of
his professorship. At that time, aware that she would violently
disapprove of the 'quixotic' course that he was adopting (for
from the first he knew that his revolutionary principles regarding the writing of history must lead to a dangerous showdown
with those responsible for him), he had maintained a stern,
and it had at times appeared a brutal, silence. Hester was no
'intellectual', in any case, and he had never attempted to
initiate her into the mysteries of his new theory of History.
During the years of their semi-animal existence in the Hotel
Blundell all that had been changed.
    But, apart from anything else, now he was mobilizing him-
self for new efforts—he was projecting a new volume, dealing
this time not with contemporary history, 'secret' or otherwise, but with an even more radical analysis of what we call
'history'. This project he did not even mention to her. He
just spoke of his 'work', when necessary. There was a third
room in their present apartment, and this he used as a study.
He would say, 'Well, I must get to work,' as he made his
way towards it, and the assumption was that he was going

12

to work in connection with his weekly column in the *Gazette-Herald*. Before long it must have been apparent that he was engaged upon other work than just that. As he did not mention what is was, Hester knew that it was something she would regard with aversion; and she never asked him anything about it. Finally, he kept the door of the small room locked, 'to keep out the maid,' but this also kept out Hester.

If René had now returned to a compartmenting of their married life, to some extent, such as he had practised in the crisis-period in England, she too took a step backwards in one little matter. He noticed that the change he received when he gave her a few dollars for housekeeping was not very accurate. Since he needed as much as possible of any money not employed in mere living, to buy books (in some cases his own books, a few of which he had rebought from the second-hand bookseller) he was obliged to stop this leakage. Nor could he guess what Hester needed money for, beyond pin-money. The dress situation was not acute. She had brought a good number of garments with her to Canada. These had been rehabilitated, since he had come in possession of money again, and two new dresses had been purchased. Nevertheless, there was increasing evidence that Hester was bent on amassing a little money. He began watching her, as in the old days. But now she knew she was being watched.

CHAPTER XXVIII

A New Book on the Stocks

THE Black Fly episode was responsible for cementing the friendship of Laura McKenzie and of Hester. The extra-ordinary kindness shown by Laura was so much appreciated that Hester's weekly letter to Susan compared her to the Lady of the Lamp. When entirely recovered and able once more to pay visits, and accept invitations to tea, she approached Laura like an affectionate dog. It was Laura herself who made the comparison with a dog.

'She reminds me of a sickly dog with big sentimental eyes, dumbly thanking one for a good turn one has done him,' she told her husband; and, 'she is awfully like a big sad-eyed bitch, who has had a rotten time, and reacts hysterically to kindness. She *is* like an animal. There is something *shut off* about her, as if attempting to communicate in spite of some handicap. I think she is frightfully nice, but she embarrasses me rather. I feel I ought to know dog-talk! I also have to conquer an instinctive desire to stroke her.'

But Laura did manage to adjust herself to the big, mooney, thankful animal. They would go down-town to the department stores together, attended a lecture or two at a little Club and jointly accepted invitations to several cocktail parties, notably a large, more socially pretentious one at the house of the Rushforths, Nancy Rushforth being one of the half-dozen Canadian women with whom Laura preserved a continued relationship. Alice Price, also, at this time was someone whom Hester mildly cultivated. She had some nice talks with Alice's old father, but, as she found listening to these two Britons engaged in vitriolic analysis of everything Canadian undermined her morale, Alice did her best to keep them apart.

As it can be seen, Hester now allowed herself a limited participation in the social life made available to her by the new conditions. Her husband, as he observed this change of front, this compromise, experienced an intense satisfaction, akin to triumph. A little more of this 'normalcy' and the trick would be done, he told himself. The beaming smile with which he greeted her on her return from some mainly female social event, amused, but also annoyed her. Become conscious that she had surprised his too visible delight, especially after she had said, 'Don't grin like a Cheshire cat, for goodness' sake,' René disciplined himself into an attitude of unconcern.

If Hester was fairly often in the company of the Professor's wife, René with even more regularity, and with much more serious purpose, was in the company of McKenzie. As he built up his new book, hammering it into a solid logical shape, he discussed with the professional philosopher a number of points about which he was doubtful. McKenzie's was a very good mind of a routine kind, and it had not the insidious partisanship of Rotter's to make it a dangerous tool to use. If academically critical, McKenzie was generous; and even more than that he felt considerable sympathy with René's ideas. The philosopher was, of course, the proper specialist to consult; a historian would have been of no use whatever. This was a philosophic, and particularly an ethical work that René was projecting, and this new friend was just the man he needed for consultation.

His book was to be of a soaring and heroic dimension, and under the circumstances he was not able to provide the argument with the massed references, quotations and illustration the wholesale character of the book seemed to demand. The second-hand bookseller *rented* him, so to speak, an *Encyclopædia Britannica*, and one of the best American Encylopædias. Of the hundreds of other books he required for reference he found perhaps a dozen in the Momaco libraries. He could only hope that an opportunity might be afforded him, before the completion of the book, to pass some weeks near a great library.

Of the abstract questions which had to be tackled, there was one which has been mentioned already at an earlier stage (for it was a question dogging his former essays on those lines), uniquely threatening. McKenzie and he spent the best part of three weeks debating it. It was at the root of all this type of thinking. It was a dragon necessary to meet and to overcome, before going any farther. This problem of problems can be compressed as follows: if one condemns all history as trivial and unedifying, must not all human life be condemned on the same charge? Is not human life too short to have any real values, is it not too hopelessly compromised with the silliness involved in the reproduction of the species, of all the degradations accompanying the association of those of opposite sex to realize offspring? Then the interminable twenty years of growing up (of nurseries, and later years of flogging, of cribbing, of the onset of sex); twenty years of learning to be something which turns out to be nothing. In maturity, the destruction of anything which has value by the enormous mass of what has no value. In other words, the problem of problems is to find anything of value intact and undiluted in the vortex of slush and nonsense: to discover any foothold (however small) in the phenomenal chaos, for the ambitious mind: enough that is uncontaminated to make it worth-while to worry about life at all. And as to condemning the slush and nonsense, the pillage and carnage which we have glorified as 'history'; why, that throws us back upon the futility of our daily lives, which also have to be condemned.

Then we come to this: human existence, however well it was lived, would necessarily be upon a petty plane. For weeks René dragged McKenzie down into the morass where everything slips through your fingers as you try to grasp it, into the permanent instability of antinomy. They both felt like two all-in wrestlers, slipping about in an arena of warm mud, from which they would emerge covered from head to foot. In the end a precarious metaphysical foothold of sorts was found for René, though toe-hold would be a better description for it than foot-hold. René felt that a philosopher of greater range than McKenzie might have helped him to secure himself more satisfactorily. In the course of their relentless debates he had at once bumped up against the limitations of his new friend. McKenzie was a follower of Collingwood. The neurotic and competitive stamp of the author of *Speculum Mentis* would be something he could not approve of. He was an easy-going, modest individual. But his position as philosopher recalled

Collingwood. He possessed a strong ethical bias, which caused him to criticize Oxford Realism, the Moorites of Cambridge, and all sad, bleak materialists, as Collingwood was wont to do. Like Collingwood, he would describe the Realist of the Cook Wilson type as progressively throwing overboard all positive doctrines whatever; with a shout of joy jettisoning the last embarrassing doctrine, so that he now would be devoid of anything theoretic at all—except the theory that he must adhere to nothing positive. There is, in Collingwood's account of his own career, a passage where he describes the bad effect upon the youth of the second decade of the century of the radical nihilism of the Cambridge Realists—the proposal to extrude ethics from the body of philosophy of Bertrand Russell being especially cited. This reaction against the destructive character of these contemporary groups, in both the Universities, which made Collingwood so remarkable a figure, was a reaction taken over intact by McKenzie: and this was the kind of reactionary direction which marked his teaching at Momaco. He therefore was just the man to make it *too easy* for René to find a metaphysical foot-hold at any price, if the latter had not been very much on his guard. Nevertheless these debates with the learned and steady Scot were of very great use, and McKenzie was unsparing of his time, and placed his well-stored mind at René's disposal, and his skill as a trained debater.

'If everyone who was going to write a book,' he said slyly to René, 'took as much trouble as you do to establish their right to do so, there would be fewer bad books!'

Having arrived at the point where he knew, with certainty, exactly just what he stood on and why, and, again, for what reason he was giving himself this trouble (namely, 'because outraged by the events of the past thirty years beyond endurance'), he began hacking his way into the jungle of the past. His slogan was as follows: 'The past thirty years is typical, not exceptional.'

A number of specimen events (events in which no undeniably great personality, like Jefferson, were involved) were selected from British and American history. Nothing but the lowest type of criminal mentality or else the dullest average mentality was revealed under analysis; and yet the actors in these events are treated by historians as of the first calibre. This, as he pointed out, might be used to indicate the way in which history ought to be written—so much of it as need be written.

Then he engaged in an important and original piece of field-work. With the aid of a number of quotations from speeches and articles he demonstrated how ludicrously inflated was the language in which politicians referred to one another, and how *la grande presse* followed suit, or sometimes led the way. They are all 'great' for one another: how often does one not read in the newspapers one statesman using this word about another; or one will read in some account by a columnist of a member of the present Cabinet, 'Whether Mr. X is as great a brain as Mr. Y', or 'Even the masterly intellect of the Chancellor' or 'Such giants as Mr. Jones and Mr. Smith'. It could not be disputed that many occupations require a higher intellectual endowment than the parliamentary life; yet to hear proudly prominent parliamentarians talking about one another (and *you scratch my back and I will scratch yours* is a principle in constant use in parliaments) one would suppose that they were referring to some intellectual giant like Isaac Newton, or William Shakespeare, not a twentieth-century First Minister, or Chancellor of the Exchequer. Only the other day we could read one politician describing another as 'the greatest man of his age'. In this particular instance it might have been true to say 'the greatest politician of his age', but that is a very different matter.

At a dinner attended by billiards fans, or cricketing enthu-siasts, an unusually fine player of one of these two games of skill might be eulogized as 'The greatest man of the age', though certainly a billiards player might more deservedly be so called than a politician. Great proficiency in some craft in which a man is passionately interested would certainly seem to him the most desirable excellence, the *greatest* excellence, that a human being could have. What is unfortunate is that politics is a game that is played with *us*, not with billiard balls.

If we ask why such veneration of their political leaders is

accepted as reasonable by the public, the answer is obvious. Anyone who *leads* them must be a very important and remarkable person. Democratic politics possess a magic property, they are able to turn a nobody into a somebody. The secret of this magic is the substitution of quantity for quality. That is, of course, precisely what democracy, as a creed, sets out to achieve. But how, in democratic politics, the value 'great' = quantity may be seen in the following instance. If an atom bomb were invented which would wipe out a nation of fifty million people, the little politician who decreed that it should be dropped would achieve historical greatness, because, by his action, fifty million people had been killed. (It is typical of the values of History that the inventor of the bomb would have no historic significance.) But this is perhaps too artificial an illustration. It is, in fact, only necessary to cite cases with which we are all familiar. Any man, however insignificant his personality, who pushes round fifty million other people, as do the heads of the great departments of State, automatically attains thereby a quite unreal—a *quantitative*—importance; for instance, the Chancellor of the Exchequer, who, by his Budgets, so deeply affects the lives of fifty million people, or, as another instance, the Secretary for Foreign Affairs, who may, by his action, plunge fifty million people into a bloodbath. Even more, the First Minister, who is able to influence, for good or ill, fifty million people, by reason of the extraordinary number of individual destinies responding to his will, assumes, as a consequence, what one might describe as a quantitative distinction, which is what alone appeals to History.

History is the record of the quantitative; it is quite indifferent as to whether the happening is fortunate or unfortunate, provided it happens to the maximum number of people. As a consequence, space is devoted to a great number of events which are completely irrelevant, except for the fact that they affected great numbers of people. In the course of this impartial recording great advertisement is given to criminal, or to unintelligent, persons and their mass-responsibility. Unless the notion of significance can be detached from this misleading 'quantity' association, no proper History can be written. But, *pari passu*, this misleading valuation would have to be rooted out of daily life.

If, however, any very radical and wholesale action were to be taken regarding this quantitative blight applicable to all History; or if a new attitude were to be introduced, banishing the record of the silly, the criminal, or the commonplace (which, as it is, relegates History to the plane of a crime-yarn, a Western Story, or a body of statistics), then it would be necessary to attempt to expunge from our daily life, as far as possible, the things we condemn in History.

Needless to say, René was obliged to take into account how any interference or reform of History would be objected to by many interested parties, whose wishes could not be ignored. To take one illustration; the Catholics would not give up the reign of Henry VIII in any axing of the past, for that reign is rich in evidence of the kind they want. But what was being proposed by René was not a destruction of books, but a new approach to History, so that a new type of History should be written. Or, since he was not conspicuous for his optimism, he hoped that constant criticism of this kind would discredit, or discredit a little, the present approach. Beyond that, he hoped that the discredit of a certain kind of event in the past would reflect forward (to some extent) to how we all acted today.

He founded these slender hopes upon the frightful close-up of typical History which we have all had during the past twenty or thirty years. We have all seen great generals, great statesmen, great presidents, engaged in the conduct of great wars, accompanied by great victories. Everything has been *great*. At the end of it all we feel a little depressed by so much greatness. Is it too much to hope, René demanded, that these experiences, giving us a front row of the stalls view of all the great actors, will cure us a little bit of our taste for what we know as 'History'?

So far the projected volume covered ground almost identical with René's earlier work. But at this point he parted company with the somewhat frail optimism of his pre-war thinking. The idea of an increasing number of enlightened people was still there, to some extent, but he did not any longer feel confident

12*

of any but modest results. Having more fiercely than ever
derided the monotonous, unvarying mediocrity and criminality
which History regales us with; having with more violence than
before related this to our own mediocrity, he then proceeded
to go over, lock, stock and barrel, into what Professor
McKenzie had called the Party of Superman. We obviously
would perish ignominiously if we continued as we were at
present. We must train and compress ourselves in every way,
and breed an animal superior to our present disorderly and
untidy selves.—He added that there was very little chance of
our doing this, but that it was just worth stating that that is
the only possible solution.

Here it must be observed that the violence of thought which
was characteristic of René received everywhere an additional
edge because of the mental instability developing in him just
then. There were, at times, excesses of virulent expression,
which amounted to blemishes, and even sometimes diminished
the effectiveness of the argument. One might even go a step
farther, and find in his adoption of the Superman position a
weakening; the acceptance of a solution which formerly he
would have refused. His life altogether was being mechanized
upon a lower level—in everything expediency counted more
with him. And although in the sequel his work might *look* the
same, there was an insidious softening of the core which only
the expert could detect. He was writing a book ever so slightly
too much as part of his new plan of life, from which the old
integrity and belief were missing.

However, these labours had the effect of drawing the two
professors together in what became a genuine friendship.
Impressed by what René was attempting, McKenzie spoke
enthusiastically to Trevelyan of this distinguished work which
was in process of construction in their midst. At Trevelyan's
suggestion the University authorities were stimulated to offer
Professor René Harding six Extension Lectures, the subject of
which was to be the emergence, in England, in the sixteenth
century, of the new secular civilization. He analysed all the
ingredients of the late sixteenth-century melting pot. The story
of how the culture of the Italian city states had found its way
into England is, of course, a stock subject, but René's inter-

pretation of it was the reverse of a parochial one; he saw those events as if he had been looking at them from the heart of the Continent.

In the course of this work he paid frequent visits to Ottawa, where he found the excellent Library in the Parliament Building of the greatest use. On the first of these visits he and his wife lunched in the restaurant in Parliament House, as the guests of a member of the Government, whom he had come to know through his new Momaco friends. They had a table beside a window. From this position upon the towering rock on which Canada's Parliament is built, an imposing view might be obtained down over the fast-moving river which separates the provinces of Ontario and Quebec. Even Hester was impressed by the finest capital city of the new world. Unfortunately, as they were returning to their hotel, the Lord Elgin, the recent fall of snow achieving the same result as expensive laundry, they met a Highland regiment returning to their barracks. Alas, the wild music of the cold little island mountains of Scotland, and its bedizened clans, reminded Hester of Harrod's and De Bry's, where a piper often advanced along the gutters of the Brompton Road, and Hester would sometimes give him a threepenny bit. The alien snow, the parliament that was not Westminster, and the thought that again Momaco was their destination turned her mind back into the well-worn channel of hatred of the land in which they found themselves. On their way back in a parlour car, she expressed herself as follows, 'There is far too much snow in this country, and Ottawa is just as bad as Momaco. I always felt, in reading the Russian novels, uncomfortable at the thought of so much snow.' And René answered, 'I always manage to read Tolstoi without feeling cold.'

The appearance of Professor René Harding, in cap and gown, in a lecture room at Momaco University, attracted considerable attention, and even drew a fair-sized audience. Trevelyan, for instance, only missed one lecture; at the end of the series, he congratulated René warmly, and he said, 'It is a great piece of luck for this little place that you happen to be here. How wonderful it would be if you could occupy for a short while—for I realize that you will not wish to stay here once the war is over—if you could be induced to accept the History professorship while you are with us! Blackwell is leaving, to take up a post in the United States . . . if you were offered it, would you accept?' René signified that he would.

CHAPTER XXIX

A Chair at Momaco

WHEN René landed in Canada, he landed as a dead man, or as good as dead.

His first three years and three months at Momaco confirmed him in this assessment of the situation in the most absolute sense. He could never imagine himself emerging from this deadly shadow, this burial alive; what is more, like many men who find themselves in the position of the 'White Russians', or the Huguenot exiles, he prepared to begin to live again, in a very different way.

He was strangely resigned, accepting his change of fortune with matter of factness. But what had begun in Mr. Furber's library, a meeting on which at the time nothing seemed to hang, had assumed quite serious proportions. With his six Extension Lectures, and his weekly column in the *Gazette-Herald*, he actually had rather more than his professorial fees before his resignation from his job at home in England, and a substantial surplus remained when he had 'paid his way' every month. There was enough to buy quite a lot of books, so, in sum, he was just as strikingly well-off as, so short a time ago, he had been badly-off.

During the Spring of 'forty-four, as a weekly columnist, his task was not very onerous, for there was nothing much of a spectacular kind going on. This relative calm endured right up to D-Day in June (and this great event was accompanied by another one, the arrival of the first flying-bomb in England).

During these easy months he was able to get on with the writing of his book and the subject of his lectures was such familiar ground with him that the doing of three things at once was not at all a feat.

It was in May, when, one morning, a very portentous-looking envelope arrived by mail. He sat down at the breakfast

table and perused its contents; then, with apparent indifference, he flung it over for Hester to read.

It was an invitation addressed to him by the Registrar of the
University of Momaco to occupy the post of Professor of
Modern History in succession to Dr. Blackwell.

She read this document calmly, without speaking, and René
studied attentively another letter he had just opened, but both
knew that a showdown was imminent. René's hand shook a
little, the one that was holding the letter. He noticed this and,
tumbling forward upon the table, read it flattened out upon
the tablecloth.

At last, with great deliberation, Hester pushed back to her
husband the letter from the Registrar. 'What are you going to
do about this?' she enquired sharply, fixing upon him a weary
but remorseless eye.

'Accept it, of course.' He said this so categorically, that she
recoiled as though something heavy had fallen upon the table
between them.

'Oh.' She drew in her breath, it was a short, quiet gasp.
'You propose to accept?'

He nodded. 'Of course,' he said. 'Would you like me to turn
it down? Should I turn it down and in a year or so return to
England, and see if I can secure a post as History Master in
Mill Hill School, or take on the marking of examination-
papers? Such jobs are frightfully well-paid. I think we might
manage to rent a top floor in Pimlico. You would have to do
the washing. We could not afford a laundry. But we should get
by somehow.—Would it be better if I did that?'

Hester, whose face had been convulsing itself in a tragic
mask, released, with a sort of howl, a torrent of tears. René
sneezed violently, and noisily blowing his nose, went into
the bathroom. He was neither dressed nor washed: vigorous
sounds of another kind were immediately set-up, the dashing
about of water, puffing and grunting, in obvious competition
with the obstreperous cataract of grief.

Hester stuck to it for a minute or two, then fell angrily
silent.

As a rule René was a whirlwind dresser, but today he
took longer than usual. When at length he appeared he was

unusually spick and span. His present clinical respectability, his dazzling Bengal-striped shirt, his aggressive tie were in the starkest contrast with the old days in the Room. It almost seemed as though he had wished to demonstrate what well-laundered, well-heeled advertisements of well-washed prosperity they were, in contrast with the grubby pair who would gaze out of the Pimlico window, never visited by the window-cleaners, at the sluggish Thames, the colour of dirty bath-water.

The scent of the conifer-packed soap emitted by his well-scrubbed person seemed like a theme-scent in his corporeal and sartorial attack upon the tearful propaganda for the most smoke-sullied spot on earth—for the unheated houses, the rain of greasy soot-flakes of London; the smells of cabbage, of beefsteak, of washtub, and of sink, overflowing into the small living-room, where sat the man snarling over a welter of examination papers.

The demonstration was unheeded—by nostrils closed against pine, and eyes blind to a Bengal-stripe. He sat down opposite to her at the table, and picked up and arranged his letters.

'I think this is a most terrible thing,' she announced militantly.

'Do you? What?'

'The fact that this tin-pot little University offer you this . . . professorship'—she made a contemptuous noise, like a delicate bark. 'If you had known ten years ago that you were going to end your days as a Professor in a small colonial city, what would you have felt like? It is awful, René.' Her voice broke, she wiped her eyes. 'Worst of all is your attitude. You are as pleased as if you had received a . . . what is it called? . . . a Regius Professorship at Oxford. You were trying to hide your pleasure just now. You went into the bathroom and washed, to try and wash the childish satisfaction off your face.'

René laughed. 'Do not be so idiotic, Essie, you know quite well I was escaping from that flood of tears. As the weaker animal, women used to emit them as the devil fish emits ink.— But is not all this water archaic?'

'I am afraid that my position is as inferior a one as that of a Victorian wife. He who pays the money calls the tune.'

'Nonsense,' came his reprimand.

'I cry because I have no money of my own,' she told him.

It was only just over four and a half years, the scene reminded him, since they left England, and ceased to be that couple living in the House that Jack Built—he looked across the table objectively.

In their new and rather smart apartment, she in a new house-frock and brightly American, looking not a minute older than in those last days in England, he began to perceive the resemblance between the new and the old. How in those near-far days she would plot to receive payment for bayadère-like transports, in the form of a fur coat, and she still was plotting now. But today her plots led to other ends; and their nocturnal entanglements were no longer thought of as utilizable. Why? (he stopped to ask himself). Why had they ceased to be that? *Why would she of course not think of that expedient today?*

She no longer thought of fornication from the commercial angle, nor so lightly, because she had bid adieu to youth. The years in the Hotel Blundell had been a profound ordeal, and counted as ten years at least psychologically.—Did she love him still?; this wandered, as it were, across his mind. The answer seemed to be *no*; that had taken its final leave, no doubt, around the time youth had officially departed. No, he decided, love had nothing to do with all this. One would have to look behind the fire, and the hideous events accompanying it for anything like love. But she was a great planner, was his Ess, had always been. She was very deeply worried because she felt she had nothing to bargain with.

'You are a great plotter and planner, Hester,' he said gently. 'You are always deep in thought as to how you can get me back to England. You will have a break-down—why not take life easier?'

'I can't . . . I can't see you throwing away everything you have wanted . . . and lived for. This place seems to have cast a spell over you. Left to yourself, you would be quite content to sink into the petty existence of a little teacher in a colonial city . . . like Professor McKenzie. You were not a little routine teaching hack like him.'

At an impatient gesture of René's she pulled herself up.

'Professor McKenzie is quite a nice man, I am saying nothing about that. As you know, Laura and I are good friends. But you, René. You are something different, aren't you? You mustn't mind my saying this, but in the past you would not have taken any notice of such a man. Now you consult him. You take him into your confidence. You trust him as an equal. . . . You have changed a great deal. You have let Canada get you down, René.'

René threw himself back in his chair.

'All that is an out-dated way of thinking, Hester—I know it is difficult for you to understand. You cannot be expected to see how this war will change everything. As "Peter Pan" Nehru says, nothing after it will be the same as it was before it. You urge me, you implore me, to return to England. But England will be a very different place . . . poor, instead of rich —a second-class country, a drab shabby society, not at all what we have always known.'

She stiffened; with a touch of melodrama. 'I do not care what England is like. I am much too old to change my way of thinking and feeling. I would far rather have England penniless, England in rags, England with no more power than . . . oh Ireland or Iceland, than any other country in the world.' She stared bleakly into the future.—Susan, and Mummy, and Gladys, and Stella—she felt their warm British shoulders on either side of her. As she looked at René she made the mental comment, 'René darling is half-a-frog, of course.' That excused him for not seeing these things exactly the way she did.

'We have talked about this so much that we repeat ourselves. Still, I must as usual make the attempt to correct your way of looking at all this, Ess. I may have to stop here a couple of years more, but that will be all. After that there is an excellent chance that I should be asked to go down to some large American University; Yale, Chicago, something like that. The United States is surely a big and important enough place to satisfy your ambitions on my behalf. Apart from that, I am sure you would like it. You would go on being more Kensingtonish than ever, whereas I could hardly make myself into a Yankee. We could go to England, we should not be

locked up in the States. But I should not like to go to England
with my hat in my hand, as now would be the case.' He leant
across the table and took her hand in his. She gently withdrew
her hand, and looked up at him steadily.

'You see the picture the wrong way up, Ess, in a most
funny, pathetic light. Yes, you see everything through spectacles which both of us acquired in Hotel Blundell days. I wish
I could convince you of that.'

There was a silence during which she gazed at the tablecloth. She had moved very little while they had been talking.
She appeared riveted to her chair, in a despairing concentration. She did not seem to wish to move, or to rise from it, as
though she felt that, if she did, it would be her last chance
of deflecting him, that there was something final about this
interview

Then she lifted her head and looked at him coldly. 'All
right,' she said, 'you deceive yourself. You have an uncommon
capacity for self-deception, my dear René. I am sick of talking
to you about this business. Accept, full of joy and self-
congratulation, your dirty little job, and you will see, some
day, that I was not so wrong as you think.'

That was the last time that they had any extensive conversation of this kind. She seemed to have given up as a bad job
the effort to convince him of his mistake.

In the summer they went to the Gaspé Peninsula, in
the purely french-canadian Maritimes. With Hester the place
called to mind Normandy and Brittany, those adjuncts of
Kensington like the Oberland and the Rhine. She felt quite at
home there sometimes, except for the Canadian-English which
the *habitant* used on occasion.

The change of scene, however, and the sea air, benefited
her, as it benefited him. At one moment he became *almost* his
old self. It was not until the time came to return to Momaco
once more that the tension made itself felt again. In the train
on the way back they spoke very little; and it was a rather
gloomy pair of returned holiday makers who left the train at
the Momaco terminus.

CHAPTER XXX

Police Headquarters

IT had been necessary for them to curtail their holiday, so that René might have at least a month in which to prepare for his work at the University. It was unfortunate—for one of the big Churchill-Roosevelt Conferences (and one in which the former gave a great deal away) was occurring at Quebec —but the weekly column on the *Gazette-Herald* had to be abandoned, for René wished, during the Fall, to work intensively on his book in such time as could be spared from the preparation of his lectures.

At the apartment a certain number of letters awaited them. There was a letter with the London postmark for René. It was from Mary, informing him of the death of their mother; this had occurred in the third week of July. Her interest in the War had not been very great, but the national excitement at the invasion of France communicated itself to her; and then the sensational arrival of Flying Bombs (for her, as for everybody else, a recommencement, an all-over-again-ness,. probably of a worse kind) almost coincided with D-Day. These dynamic accelerations in the world about her, these new tensions, seemed to have been responsible for her death.

It was at their dinner-table that this, and other mail, was read; and the letter from Mary was pushed across the table for his wife to read. As she perused it, she began to cry. Dry-eyed, René found himself watching her, speculating on the exact nature of this grief. Of course it was quite natural and proper for her to receive this news in this manner. They should *both* have been in tears. And then he began to think of these two women together, the mother and the wife: how similar was the attitude of both in one respect. In the eyes of wife, as much as mother, he was a *fool*, though the obstructiveness of the younger woman, at the present juncture, was far more intense, corresponding with the egotism involved. As a matter of fact he was mentally focussing Hester for the first time, was frowning and staring hard at her, as though he had detected some unsuspected *physical* attribute, not remarked before, of a displeasing kind. She looked up at him suddenly. She had been crying less than he supposed, and was quite able to see the harsh scrutiny. She continued to look, and the vertical lines of a frown prolonged upwards by a swollen vein bisected her forehead. This, with her protruding eyes, produced an almost demented expression. 'René,' she said, 'what was it that caused you to hate your mother? You never told me.'

René had at once removed his eyes; and now, at her question, he answered without emotion, 'I did not hate my mother. You are quite mistaken if you think that. I do not cry like you, that is all.'

'That is not true,' she said, as she stood up, and, swaying a little as if she had been drinking, she went into the bedroom, and he could hear her throw herself upon her bed.

'A demonstration,' he thought, 'to leave me here on exhibition as a heartless brute. The idea being that the women are a sensitive, rather noble lot, invariably suffering from the lack of finer feelings of the male side of the creation.' René resented his mother being brought into a dispute between Hester and himself. What had occurred between his mother and himself was very much the affair of the mother and the son. It was a private matter.

From the time of their return from the Gaspé, René began a furious labour—there was little opportunity for domestic tensions. Hester made no enquiries about his lectures; subsequently she was not present at any of them; nor did he make any reference to them either. He withdrew to his room 'to work', without specifying the nature of the work; and later he went to the University to give his lectures, but all he said was that he was 'going to the University'. It was his hope that, quite suddenly perhaps, seeing that he was succeeding, she would relent, and everything would slip into place as if it had never been awry.

How closely packed the working-day was may be judged by the following circumstance—belonging to a period some months further on. On Christmas Day René worked in his study up to tea-time. They had arranged to go to Momaco's giant hotel for dinner, to celebrate with the McKenzies, who were bringing their son, Duncan, now ten years old. After a brief tea René returned to his study: and he hardly gave himself time to dress. Hester, on her side, had gone to see Alice Price, and to have a good talk with Alice's father about a certain country, which both of them loathed, and another, which both of them loved—romantically, uncritically. Mr. Price was quite a well-to-do man: but his well-known lack of Canadian orthodoxy, and his habit of continually criticizing the country which was responsible for his small fortune, had probably been the cause of his daughter's not marrying. She was good-looking, a typical Canadian, but already thirty-five.

When Hester got home to dress for the evening, René was drinking a cup of tea; and when at half-past seven the McKenzies called, in a hired car, to take them to the hotel, his toilet was still incomplete. It was with a flushed face of wry apology that he at last entered the car, saying, 'I worked too late; I have two jobs on my hands: you are a sensible fellow' (to McKenzie), 'and content yourself with one.'

The King George Hotel was an example of the colossal in hotel-building. . . . Certain of its massive and sinister vistas were suggestive of Gnossos rather than of Momaco, of hieratic rather than of capitalistic architecture. Their French-Canadian waiter had a countenance that went with the architecture. Lines of ponderous square pillars marked off the dancing floor from the lines of tables, and behind the pillar-line there was more depth than in the Château Laurier—which the architect clearly had had in mind, and had hoped to outdo. When they arrived, a rumba was in progress. Leaving McKenzie Junior at the table, the two Professors disappeared into the barbaric mêlée, Laura waving her posteriors expertly in the embrace of René. Hester, less disposed to borrow from the expressive buttocks of the Black, wobbled her own a little mournfully.

They decided that they would drink champagne. Before long they were pulling crackers, and transformed by paper

hats into pantomime figures, McKenzie with an eyebrow pencil
having given himself a very dark moustache. Chicken Maryland, with fried pineapple and sweet corn and potato mixed,
was the centre of the meal. (They had rejected unanimously
Turkey Momaco, Reine Pedauque.) Young Duncan McKenzie
looked rather green for a moment, after consuming a Bombe
Glacée Messaline. The Moët frothed as it should, and flames
from the large Christmas Pudding very nearly started a con-
flagration; Hester's Alsatian peasant-cap burst into flames,
but was extinguished with great skill and promptitude by
McKenzie, who clapped his hands upon the flames. A smell
of singeing bore witness to the part that Hester's hair had
played in the excitements of the evening. Theirs was a conventional Christmas celebration, and there was a great deal
of dancing: the taste of the French-Canadians, who were
prominent in staffing and stage-directing this monstrous Hotel,
was of a 'Rasta' type, the orchestra preferring rumbas and
tangos to anything else. René carried on an intermittent conversation with a French party at the next table—Parisian
French, not Momaco French. The noise soon became terrific.
There were one or two academical figures here and there, and
two of these joined them at one point. It was undeniably a
wonderful idea to have had their Christmas dinner in this
saturnalian fashion.

   With their last bottle came the final toasts. All of these
toasts, naturally, looked towards the future happiness or
success of each member of the party. When René's new
academic adventure was being toasted, it was noticed that
Hester watched, with an exclusive concentration, the scene
on the dance-floor. 'And now, René, your book!' exclaimed
McKenzie. But even to that she did not respond. This glass
that never rose to celebrate, but which got emptied all the
same, in toasts that were undivulged, at the last chilled this
Christmas Party, and left an uncomfortable sense of something
wrong: although, on the whole, the evening might be described
as a great success.

   When the Hardings got home, as Hester was drawing off
her gloves, she summed up: 'A pretty penny that has cost us.
What was it for?'

René looked at the cross and staring face with compassion. 'Mais quel entêtement, nom de dieu!' he said under his breath. As a consequence of his appointment at the University, if for no other reason, René was obliged to go to a certain number of parties and functions, as well as to dinner engagements or casual visits to the houses of the friends he had made. Hester almost always accompanied him. Such a demonstration as she made on the occasion of the Christmas dinner was not a typical occurrence, she usually conducted herself quite normally.

So when, one night, she failed to turn up at the house of the Chancellor of the University, at the time arranged, 7.30, René was very surprised and correspondingly uneasy. He had dressed at the University, from which he went directly to the Chancellor's house. It was an important dinner: the President of McGill and other academic notables were to be there. Of course, no great harm would be done should she not appear; if it turned out to be a *coup de tête* on Hester's part, some plausible excuse could be found. What he said, on the spur of the moment, was simply that he could not guess what had happened to delay her.

It was half-way through the meal that he was called to the telephone outside in the hall. When he picked up the receiver, someone said, 'This is the Police.' He was asked if his wife's name was 'Hester Lilian Harding'. His heart took a painful jump and stopped dead. He said quietly 'Yes', when the voice asked him to come immediately to Police Headquarters at Rochester Avenue. He asked no questions. Upon the back of a visiting card he scribbled a brief message, and told the man who had accompanied him to the telephone to hand it to the Chancellor.

In Momaco (unlike Toronto) taxis are allowed to ply for hire, and he found one almost at once. Rochester Avenue was not far, and as soon as he entered the door of the main commissariat of police, someone said, 'You Professor Harding?' —He was then conducted into a room in which a police officer sat at a table, who sprang up, saying 'You Professor Harding?' before any sound had been made by his escort. But after that, as they stood facing one another, the police officer appeared embarrassed. 'It's a warm evening for April, Professor,' he said. 'I'm glad you came right over here without delay. I was sorry to disturb you, Professor, I'm more sorry than I know how to say, Professor. . . . Hell, this isn't easy!'

'What is it?' René asked sharply.

To hunt other human beings seems to reduce the face to a coarse muzzle and baleful eye. When this simplified face attempts to portray pity, the effect is alarming.

'Will you kindly tell me at once what my wife has done,' demanded René.

'What did she do?' echoed the policeman. And René noticed the change of tense.

'She did nothing?' he asked; his lips trembled. 'If she has done nothing; why did you demand my presence here?' The aggressive tone provoked the reappearance of the unmodified jowl of the dogs of the Law.

'She did do *something*, Professor. She threw herself under a truck.'

René was trembling, and swaying a little. He glared silently at the police officer, as if the latter had said that his wife was a liar or a thief. Then he staggered forward, and supported himself upon the table with the flat of his hands. The policeman said, 'Lean on me,' and led him to a chair. He retched once and vomited a little, turning sideways to do so. The man rang a bell on his desk, and soon a glass of water was produced. René attempted to rise. 'Sit there for a while, Professor,' the policeman told him: he knew all about shock. He could see that this one had almost knocked this limey cold. He sat in his chair smoking, and noting something in a large book.

At length René got to his feet and said, 'Where is she? Shall we go?'

'Okay, Professor.'

The man walked beside him, his eye in the corner of his head, ready to catch him as he fell. They stopped, the policeman drew from his pocket a large key, opened a door.

René was not conscious of passing through the door, but almost immediately he found himself leaning bodily upon the policeman, his head almost on the shoulder of his escort, and looking down on a much-soiled collection of objects. They were arranged in the most paradoxical way. Like a *graffito* the essentials were picked out. He recognized the low-bottomed silhouette of a female figure, the clothes shapeless and black with blood. Slightly to one side there was a pair of legs in horrible detachment, like a pair of legs for a doll upon a factory table, before they have been stuck on to the body. At the top, was the long forward-straining, as it were yearning neck. Topmost was the bloodstained head of Hester, lying on its side. The poor hair was full of mud, which flattened it upon the skull. Her eye protruded: it was strange it should still have the strength to go peering on in the darkness.

René took a step forward towards the exhibit, but he fell headlong, striking his forehead upon the edge of the marble slab—the remains being arranged upon something like a fishmonger's display slab. As he fell it had been his object to seize the head and carry it away with him. To examine his legal right had been his last clear act of consciousness.

CHAPTER XXXI

The White Silence

TWO hours later, his head bandaged, René lay in a bed in the Momaco General Hospital. He was staring, with a dull and confused expression, at a young man who sat beside him.

'Nothing,' he said thickly.

'Had she no inherited pre-disposition? . . .'

'Please leave me,' René muttered.

'You have nothing you can tell me, Professor?'

'Leave me.'

The *Gazette-Herald* reporter coughed. An interne came up behind him, and bent down, mouth to ear. The reporter rose, coughed, looked at the patient, and moved away on tiptoe. This was The Silent Ward, as they called it, for a thrombosis secured admission for a patient to the White Silence, a place so quiet that, to be any-more silent, it would have to be death.

René's brain was silent too. All that entered it resembling a thought was a painful feeling that he was alone, that he had been removed from life and shut into a white solitude. The white interne was a mechanism. He could not understand the nurses. They had not learned how to speak. Wherever he looked he saw a round spot of light, but soft, as if it belonged wherever it happened to appear. The interne was watching him. He came over, and fixed white spectacles upon his nose. The eyeholes were circles of white muslin.—There can be no proper silence while the eyes are allowed to bang about. Now that the visual turbulence had been cut off, and sight reduced to a white circle, an all-over muting of the consciousness ensued. Even such stimulus as white-coated interne removed, the mind began to dream of white rivers which led nowhere, which developed laterally, until they ended in a limitless white expanse. The constant sense of loneliness ended, in the white

372

silence, as a necessary ingredient of the white silence, which was all that was desired—the negation of the visual; and an aural blank which had more quality than white, was not such a negation, and was as soothing as a caress. But at last consciousness ebbed quietly away, and René lay in a dreamless sleep, alone in this place dedicated to silence, totally removed from life.

It was only very gradually that this remoteness and peace began to be invaded by fragments of the glaring and clanging world outside this muted and spectral seclusion. It was the specialist's purpose to forbid ingress and access to anything belonging to the passionate universe without, from which René had accidentally been cut off. Everything was done to preserve the salutary aloofness.

But in the graveyard of the senses, one by one, the most brutal memories were resurrected. Before he left the hospital René was in possession of the full burden of consciousness once more. As a first step, about ten days after he had been brought in, the nerve-centres restored to proper functioning, he was removed from the Ward of Silence to a bright and pleasant room. And it was in that room that the struggle began, the struggle as gradually as possible to re-admit to the mind what had been excluded from it: and the re-admission was apt to be anything but gradual, and threatened to disrupt the vessel into which it rushed. For approximately a week he was left alone there, until he was regarded as strong enough to receive visitors: which protective measure left totally out of count the mental visitors who crowded in. The first to enter the room without knocking was, it was natural, Hester. And when the nurse found him sobbing upon the pillow, every effort was made to get rid of this terrible and disturbing visitant. For it was well understood by the doctors who she must be. But there was no expulsion of Hester. She was always there very soon, and obsessed the patient. Sometimes she would be as she was in the days of the Room, of the 'vows of hardship'. At others she was the *graffito* woman of the police mortuary. She would enter as he was half-asleep, with her eyes protruding, her head thrust forward, and the deep line of her frown prolonged by a swollen vein bisecting the forehead. The nurse would perhaps appear, to do one of the innumerable, irrelevant things nurses find to do, and he would lie glaring at the wall; and she would go up to the bed and give the pillow an idle poke; and say, 'Te voilà qui ne dors pas, René.'

But at last they decided to let in the world of flesh and blood, if only to counteract the more dangerous imaginary visitors. McKenzie was the first to arrive, and the only one for a long time. 'You have been very ill, René,' he said, 'you have had a terrible time. I have made a number of efforts to see you. Is there anything at all I can do? Laura would like to come and see you. Would that be all right?'

René continued to stare at him, even to glare at him, holding his hand tight.

'Do not trouble to talk, René. I know how hard it must be for you. Do not make any effort.'

René tried to smile, and it changed his face into somebody else's. 'I struck my head . . . they told you, of course. I suppose there was concussion . . . yes, concussion. I have got over it, at least I have got over the concussion. Of course I'm rather shaken you know.'

'I can well imagine.'

'It will be impossible for me to see any people.' His eyes filled with tears. 'I must leave here—Momaco, I mean.'

'Why? René, that would be a great pity. Wait a bit. Do not decide anything yet. You are in no state . . .'

'I have decided,' René said.

'You must go and rest somewhere. It is clear enough that you will not be able to work for some time. They are quite decent people at the University; they will give you sick leave, with pay you know. I will see about that. Allow me to see about that for you.'

René empowered him to do anything, and said he would be most grateful if he would act for him. He gave him a bunch of keys, lifting up one, and saying 'the front door'; lifting up another, he said, 'the desk'. There was a small address book; that was all he wanted. And then he became very tired. Muttering some apology, he turned his back upon his friend and was almost at once asleep. McKenzie left quietly, and informed the nurse that her patient was asleep. He asked if he might see the doctor who had been dealing with this case.

The next day McKenzie called again, bringing the small address book, mail, and some fruit. He was at once admitted. René had told them that he wished to see no one else. The mail was left with the doctor, to be delivered as and when he saw fit: with the warning that one of the letters was probably from the patient's dead wife. That day René said even less than the day before. He confided that he thought he would go to a certain place, if there was a vacancy. He would stop there for some time. Perhaps he would stay there a *long* time. It appeared to fatigue him profoundly to talk, even with anyone he knew. Having imparted the above piece of information, as before he presented McKenzie with his back, and rapidly fell asleep.

In a few days he got up, for the making of the bed, and a week later than that he gave signs of a rather more normal condition of mind. What was occurring beneath this frozen surface was a series of painful readjustments, followed, as was the case with McKenzie's visit, by sleep. He slept a great deal of the time, the doctors saw to that. Meanwhile he had written one letter: upon the envelope was the following name and address:

> Father Moody, S.M.,
> Registrar,
> College of the Sacred Heart,
> Niagara, Ont.

and to this letter a reply had been received at the hospital, but was in the keeping of the doctor, as was the mail from the apartment.

Neither to doctor nor to nurse, any more than to McKenzie, did René utter a word upon the subject of his wife's death. He continued to refuse to see anyone. Mr. Furber, for instance, greatly excited by the banner-headlines 'SUICIDE OF COLLEGE PROFESSOR'S WIFE', and the tittle-tattle scraped together by the reporters, made frenzied attempts to be admitted 'for a few brief moments' to see René. But René became hysterical at the idea of seeing Mr. Furber, so that would-be visitor was permanently banned.

The Hester he saw at present was a living and moving one, one that he had loved, a witty, at times malicious one; but one who had become as much part of his physical being as if they had been born twins, physically fused—or better, one might say, for physical amalgamation would be unpleasant, identical twins. It had been a fearful estrangement between them when she made a return to England a supreme issue, a life or death issue. She still, in death, spoke of England. But all he spoke to her about was forgiveness. Could he ever be forgiven? No, forgiveness was of course impossible. Once or twice he thought he must get back to England, and if he should ask her forgiveness *there*, then the sweet face would smile as if to say, 'You have returned! We could not *both* return! But you found your way back. That proves that there really was love in you for me.' And he several times started to plan a return to England—to England and to penury. The phantom was tenderer when England was in his mind: when he was thinking of all the profound advantages England had over any other English-speaking country.

At the time this communion of the dead and the living started, it was only the decapitated Hester who was present to him. His impulse in the police mortuary to seize and to carry off her head was realized in the imagination. In trembling horror he grasped the decapitated head, and pressed her dear face against his. And then the lifeless lips moved and grew warm. With amazement, and soon with delight, he felt the warming lips glueing themselves against his. His entire body responded, for she was no longer merely a head. Love had brought her to life again. He imagined, in a sort of delirium, this miracle. Never again did she return as Hester decapitated and legless. But that fearful reality was always present, somewhere, out of sight, never out of mind. He always knew that fundamentally and irreparably she was the *graffito* woman of the police mortuary, and only in memory something else. Attempting always to conjure this horror, he implored Hester to keep together—to be her old self. And so he went on from day to day, in the mental reality of his daydream, secured by his hospital seclusion. He did his best to preserve this delusion; he felt that if it stopped he would then be compelled to face the overpowering reality. So it was an escape device.

The reason played no part at any time in his subterranean adjustments in the hospital. To *think* was impossible. The implacable severed head, and the blood-stained severed legs on the one hand, and then the neurotic collapse in which his head injury had left him, made the continued exclusion of the reason imperative.

Then one day, when he was physically much stronger, the doctor came in and handed him his mail. The psychiatrist sat by the side of the bed while he opened the letters. First was a personal letter from the Chancellor, expressing his sorrow at the terrible misfortune which had overtaken René; next one from the Registrar, informing him that it was the hope of the University Board that René would absent himself from duty for as long as was necessary for the complete restoration of his health, his fees to be paid during that period uncurtailed. There was a most charming letter from Trevelyan, expressive of a genuine appreciation of the stricken Professor. Next several letters from Canadian well-wishers, Alice Price and the père Price for example. Then came the last two letters.

There was the not very beautifully engraved envelope announcing the *College of the Sacred Heart*. The letter within, in the crabbed peasant fist of Father Moody, was cordial in the extreme. The personality of the rubicund priest, who had visited him a year or so earlier, and offered him a course of lectures, if he had the time to give them at Sacred Heart College, was visible in every awkward scratch of the pen and crudely friendly word. The Father Superior, to whom Father Moody had spoken, had expressed himself as delighted if Professor Harding could come right away.

Last was the letter from Hester. He looked at the envelope, looked up at the doctor, who smiled encouragingly, and opened it quickly. He read—whitening as he did so.

Almost at once he put the letter down, still holding it with his hands. 'This,' he told the doctor, 'is a communication from my dead wife.'

'Indeed,' said the doctor.

'Yes,' he answered. 'She has written me. I think I will read it when I am alone.'

The doctor stood up. 'Well, I will leave you.' He passed through the door, and took up a position behind it, from which he was able to observe the patient. He did not have to wait. René lifted the letter again, and as he began to read, he was softly laughing.

CHAPTER XXXII

The College of the Sacred Heart

THE College of the Sacred heart, shortened for familiar use to 'Sacred Heart College', was a Catholic Seminary. The College buildings were, in part, originally a Fort. A cloistered square had been contrived in the heart of the Fort building; and all round this square were the long corridors, off which, upstairs and downstairs, were the cells of the priests, the College offices, the Chapel, and the refectory. The lecture rooms were in a large building in the rear, and also the dormitories of the Seminarians; behind that was the playing field; and behind that was the home-farm. On this the priests and Seminarians worked. Since most of them were the sons of Irish dirt-farmers, the farm work was carried out expertly. It was not irksome to anybody, and the priests took it in turns to work there, regarding it as a useful and pleasurable form of outdoor exercise.

About three months after he had left the Hospital, René sat, one afternoon, at the window of his cell. He was dressed in a cassock: he still wore his beard. It was a warm afternoon, and his cassock was open. The College was situated in the wine country of Canada, bordering the United States. The roar of Niagara sounded sleepily, like the sound of the ocean not far away. The window of his cell faced towards the river, which was the water of Lake Erie concentrating itself to plunge down at Niagara, as one of the most famous waterfalls in the world, though the slowly moving water of the River Niagara had nothing ominous about it, and, except for the roar as you approached the precipice, a man might slide over the top without at all realizing what was about to occur.

This training-centre for the priesthood was a well-disciplined community, whose life moved hither and thither in response to quiet orders, or to a settled routine. It was an idyllically peaceful place for the victim of dynamic excess to go to, or

13   379

for those wishing to shun the tumult of unplanned life. Every
sound in it had been dutifully muted. There, beneath the great
wing of the Roman Church, sat the hospital inmate, but now
gathering strength and wilfulness every day. He was in another
kind of Ward of Silence, but passion had taken possession of
him once more, and he was no longer a suitable inmate of
this place of ancient rules, where to consult the unconditioned
will qualified you for expulsion. For you cannot have *peace*
upon any terms but obedience to law.

The peace of the scene, the restful monotony of the lives
of these people, whose minds reflected the massively built
Summa of all philosophies (providing a static finality in which
the restless intellect might find repose), had proved in the
end nothing but an irritant to René. His intelligence was too
dynamic, his reason was too bitterly bruised, for a static bliss.

When he had arrived in a taxicab, three months before, he
was still only fit for silence, and he believed that for the rest
of time he would want nothing but peace. He had regarded
Sacred Heart College as a magical hospital, an ancient place
of healing; what was taught there, a mystical psychiatry. Without any reservation, as he entered the Registrar's office, René
was profoundly thankful that so extraordinary an institution
as the Catholic Church was still there intact, exultantly
human. What other institution—which *was* an institution—
lived as the guardian of the great human values of antiquity?

Father Moody was a very kind and pleasant priest, who
stood behind a long thick counter which was higher than his
navel. He stood there with both his hands flat upon the counter
before him. René could scarcely credit his good fortune as the
figure of the rosy-faced young priest, his eyes, blazing with
childish benevolence, was electrified at the sight of him, his
temples flushing a rich joyous pink, his hand outstretched
across the solid counter, behind which he functioned.

'Professor Harding, well! Why did you not let me know that
you were to arrive today, and I would have met you at the
station at Niagara! Did you come over in a taxi? Have you
got your things there too? That is fine and dandy!'

Even his secretary, a young layman with the shy manners
of a young Englishman of good education, co-operated dis-

creetly in making the unfortunate stranger at home. Later on
René learnt that this young man had had much practice in
Eastern Canada, in helping to make the despised and rejected
welcome, for he had given his services to the House of Friendship night shelters. There he supervised nightly the housing
of a dozen or so bums. His parents were wealthy Montrealers.
He had been a Trappist: but in a year he had had to give it
up, because his health was unequal to the great rigours of
those vows. Now Father Moody used him as secretary. He
was active in their labour organization and lectured on social
problems. The Sacred Heart College Fathers co-operated with
American priests in Buffalo in various social activities.

O'Neill was the secretary's name. He was handsome,
sheepishly devout as well as competent, harmlessly sly. Rising
now from where he was working at an overloaded table, he
followed Father Moody, who had burst out of his enclosure,
rubbing his hands heartily, and exclaiming in vigorous
Canadian-Irish, 'So long as you're *here*, that's the principal
thing. The journey did not tire you too much I hope. I'm glad
you feel none the worse for it, you look fairly fit. Let us come
along to your apartment; I think you will be comfortable there.
I will get a cell ready for you. It won't take very long.' As
they entered the grand corridor (figures at the farther end of
it appeared quite diminutive), springing about a little Father
Moody shouted, 'Professor, where did you park your luggage?
. . . round there to the left, is it?' Father Moody and his
secretary swept up the luggage, and carried it, it seemed to
René, about half a mile, to the apartment, plushy and gilded,
set aside for visitors.

René's impression of these first days was that he was sinking down into the equivalent of a wonderful feather bed. It
was human wills which provided this overall sense of ineffable
comfort. Everywhere he was being bolstered and spared any
shock.

There was first an ordeal, however, from which he *might*
have issued not so cushily supported as all that if there had
been any hitch. The potential hitch was a dark, tall young
scrutinizing priest, named Father O'Shea. He and two other
priests, in the course of the first evening, filed into the

apartment, without explanation, headed by Father Moody, saying, 'I've brought you some visitors. I hope we are not disturbing you?'

Father O'Shea was in charge of the department of philosophy, which began and ended with St. Thomas Aquinas. He was the uncrowned King of the College, and made his views felt to such good effect that no one dared to do anything without his consent, this applying as much to the Father Superior as to the Registrar. The ultimate position of René in this institution would depend upon whether Father O'Shea liked him or not. So when this tall, slightly sinister-looking figure, with a long black cloak sailing out behind him, held at the neck by a spectacular silver clasp, entered the room, and fixed his dark eyes upon the visitor, the latter felt (although he had not been apprised of the true situation) that something of moment was about to occur. Of the other two priests, only one mattered; that was Father McAuliffe. He was the Librarian, and a great personal friend of the Registrar. The third priest was Father Lemoine, a French-Canadian priest who, for some reason, was a Maurician father. He was small, unlike the other two: and unlike their aggressive Irish faces his was gentle and self-effacing.

Well, the upshot of this examination was that Father O'Shea seemed rather to take to René, so there was no obstacle there to the benevolent designs of the Registrar.

René's mind was still so warped that no practical considerations could matter very much. He had informed no one at Momaco, for instance, where he was going, not even McKenzie. He just took his departure one fine morning, with the first instalment of his convalescent fees. Now, of course, it was entirely irresponsible to book himself up for another job. But he did not regard this place as a *job*: in any event, the fee would be so small that it could not be thought of in the same order of things as the University of Momaco, where the honorarium was larger than might be expected.

When a cell had been found for him, and he had been officially registered as an inmate, Father Moody discussed with him the question of doing something (a merely token activity) to regularize his residence at the College. Was he well enough yet to undertake any work, of however light a kind, the good Father wanted to know? Supposing he did nothing just yet, for a short while? That would be quite agreeable to them. But René declared that he was well enough to play some part in the life of the College. It actually never occurred to him that by accepting any fee, however small, he would be behaving in an extraordinary way, seeing that Momaco was handsomely supporting him as a convalescent professor. What Father Moody proposed was that, to begin with, he should give two lectures a week of a quite elementary kind. This would leave him free to do whatever he liked for the greater part of the week. René gladly consented to this arrangement, and with this went a fee so modest as not to prick his conscience into activity.

René's mental condition left much to be desired. Prior to the suicide of his wife, his personality had progressively acquired a toughness, a deadness which enabled him to proceed with his life along normal lines, though at a lower level, and only on condition of this kind of numbness. He was deadening and de-sensitizing himself, and considered that he was proof against any domestic assaults. At that time it would have required a very outstanding shock to de-anaesthetize him; but that shock would probably be fatal. The blow which was suddenly administered in the central police station, when he was confronted with his wife's mutilated body, was of such severity as to induce a completely new situation; but the sudden exposure of the profounder nervous tracts was a test of endurance beyond his powers. In the hospital the reason lay collapsed and on the verge of a conversion into an irrational entity. For some days it was uncertain what was going to happen, and whether he was going to issue from this internal conflict a man no longer sane, or a man still able to maintain himself in the company of the sane in a mentally precarious condition. It was the second of these alternatives which eventuated, and René went out of the hospital like a sleep-walker, able to go here and to go there, to converse rationally and to carry on with life, but still in a kind of frozen way, the *ultimate* issue not decided.

However, here he was, in an atmosphere very propitious

to a satisfactory outcome, surrounded by kindness, and removed from all likelihood of shock. He entered into pleasant social relations with those among whom he had come. He conducted himself normally, or almost normally. He would (infrequently) perhaps weep, but would smile and apologize. Soon he was on the best of terms with the ruling group.

His first evening at the Sacred Heart, then, he was visited by the three priests. On the second evening he was invited to join the select group of priests, described above, in the cell of Father McAuliffe. There the big Librarian dispensed a kind of supper of savouries and coffee. He stood before a gas-jet on which he cooked Welsh Rarebits, sausage items, eggs, sardines on toast, and such things. As he stood there with the smoke rising around his face, he conversed without looking up. Most nights Father Moody and Father O'Shea were present, and several other priests looked in as well sometimes.

It was a noisy, jovial scene, reminiscent of what one associates with, let us say, eighteenth-century undergraduate life—it was a kind of cross between that and the life of men in the North Lands of Canada. All taking part at this nightly gathering-place were bold and intimate, very comradely, Fathers. And the next day, when René was asked to go up and visit Father McAuliffe by himself, after a little talk the Librarian went across to where a short curtain hung in front of a recess, and pulling it back produced a bottle of gin and two glasses. 'Let us have a snort, what do you say?' And when René left, about an hour later, Father McAuliffe, as he was putting the gin back into the recess, remarked, 'Whenever you feel you would like a drink, just come along. I always have something here.'

So the atmosphere was of the most genial kind. These new companions were a little too vigorous for him as yet. He spent a good deal of time resting, but otherwise his habits differed in no way from those of the Fathers. He had his meals in the large refectory: he sat with the priests at a long table dominating the hall. There was a rapid grace, and then the twenty priests dropped quickly into their places, and set about devouring the food automatically and sometimes violently. About two hundred Seminarians sat at four or five tables in front of the long table, and during the meal a young cassocked priest-to-be read in a loud, harsh, expressionless voice some section of the Old Testament. This was a rather alarmingly noisy place for someone who was still a sick man, but the food was good.

So there he was, in the next thing to a Monastery, nursing his sick mind; the rest and peace of a negation of life (or of the dynamic order which was what life meant for him). This was as much a negation as the Hotel Blundell. It was his second withdrawal and suspension of the intellectual processes, the giving-up of being himself. Some weeks before Hester killed herself he had mailed the MSS. of his new book to the New York publisher by whom his last book had been taken. But he had forgotten that he had done this: it was just as though no book had been written at all. As he had not told anyone in Momaco where he was going, he would hear nothing about what was happening to his book. He had turned his back upon all that, upon the new start he had made at Momaco, and the book he had been so breathlessly writing; he was repeating the gesture by which he had given up his academic career in England. Only, the earlier of these two exits had for its rationale a great moral issue, and his second exit was not a martyrdom but a sacrifice, an emotional act of propitiation and to assuage a phantom.

In the first weeks here, Hester was constantly in his mind. But he was not so fundamentally changed that he was not ready to be amused. There were, almost weekly, cultural and social visitors to the College. Every month some well-known personality came to lecture, the lecture taking place in some cinema or hall in Niagara. There was always a good attendance, a number of people coming over from the United States. These lecturers spent the night in the visitors' suite. René insisted that his presence in the College was a circumstance as regards which a silence should be observed. But, although he did not attend the lectures, he was at times entertained by what he saw of these eminent personalities. Once, for instance, he was passing the visitors' suite, and the Irish poet, Padraic O'Flaherty, emerged from one of the doors ahead of him. The Father Superior and another priest were deep in conversation

a short distance away. As Padraic observed the dignitary, he
crossed himself, and greeted him. René had never seen crossing oneself employed as a salute. An oblate, who had just
arrived from Ireland, was informing the Superior of the object
of his visit. By affecting to look at a notice-board René was
able surreptitiously to observe what transpired. The poet
now drew level with the Father Superior, and crossed himself
again. Next the poet and the oblate greeted one another,
Padraic again crossing himself. This may have been because
of the enormous cross blotting out the stomach of the oblate,
suspended by a gold chain around his neck. Killarney was
where the young oblate came from, and his childish blue eyes
burst into a shy smile as his fellow-countryman addressed him.
Padraic involved the Father Superior in his boisterous but
dignified Irish mirth, and all three were laughing now. After
two minutes perhaps the poet moved away, crossing himself
as he left. Some further remark of the Superior's arrested him;
and, after delivering his jovial reply, he crossed himself again
as he turned away, the Superior adding his breast-cross to the
sum of lavish salutes. So these two Irishmen between them, the
poet, and the oblate with his terrific metal cross shining upon
his stomach, filled the corridor with an unusual atmosphere
of holiness. A German priest who had been staying at the
College for some weeks disapproved of the oblate, describing
the enormous cross hanging from his neck as 'exaggerated'.
He would certainly have disapproved of Padraic too, thought
René, but he realized that he himself was on the side of
Padraic, and smiled at this discovery.

It was during this void, this period of suspended life, that
he began to think of a conversion. The fact that his mother
had been a Catholic was a deterrent rather than otherwise, but
the void exposed him to irrelevant impulses, and he drifted
towards 'the old religion'. This was irrational, but he had
buried his reason in the tomb of his wife as an expression of
remorse, or so he once put it to himself. There was, of course,
a magnetism in the uniformity of the habits of these people.
When he would sit with Father O'Donnell, one of his new
friends, that good priest would stand up and shake himself,
exclaiming, 'Well now, I must go and settle my accounts

with Rome.' The time had come, in other words, to say his
office.

René felt attracted to this routine, of office, of pedagogy,
of office again, of farm-labour; for what he needed just then
was a discipline, and prayer was a technique which at last
he understood. Hester, with whom he communed continually
at present, was of the same order of things with God. God
was for all the priests and seminarians, all the other people
in this place, the same kind of being that Hester was for him,
having a similar obsessional reality. He had been introduced, through what had happened to him, into the world of
the devout. It was therefore quite easy, when he fell upon
his knees—for the first time since he had been a child—to
approach God as though to the manner born; to feel him as
a reality, of the same flesh and blood with Hester. There were
times when he went from one to the other, as a man visiting
a friend in a certain quarter of the town would say to himself, 'As old So and So lives hereabouts too, I think I will
look him up before I return.'

It was after he had been there a month that he asked if
he might go to Mass on Sunday. Father Moody's face was
irradiated with a smiling joy, and his forehead was almost a
tomato colour. 'Sure! Whoi not! I am so glad, Professor! Come
and fetch me on Sunday morning, we will go along to Mass
together.' The priest's eyes shone with so benign a light that
René flushed. This was certainly one of God's most authentic
officers. Without any enquiries at all as to why he wished to
do this, he began to go to Mass on Sundays.

He imagined God inhabiting a void, a nothingness, which
might be thought of as a cavern: his costume was that of a
Roman citizen of two thousand years ago. God was historic.
How he became aware of Him physically was after the manner
of his contacting Hester. He could see only a shadowy face,
which was vaguely ecstatic.

When he had said to himself that everyone in this College
was engaged in a communion (namely, with God) as he was
with Hester, that would only be true ideally. It was only
the Saints who communed with God as he did with Hester.
Naturally, it would be most improbable that any of these

13*

teaching priests or seminarians enjoyed any intense and obsessional communion with God similar to his own with his dead wife: the idea of God certainly ruled their lives, but He would hardly be more than an abstraction. And René did realize this, to some extent, and, without formulating it very much, he knew that he was nearer to God, at this period, than most of those around him.

About this time he paid frequent visits to the cell of Father O'Shea. Their conversation bore upon questions of Catholic teaching and a number of other kindred subjects, such as the technique of prayer. It was after a week or two, during which these visits had been continuous, that the priest unexpectedly asked him, 'Are you becoming a Catholic?' To this, after a moment's hesitation, René answered, 'Yes'.—'In that case,' Father O'Shea observed, 'you will require these.' And he handed him a half-dozen booklets.

René accepted the books. But he was never more explicit than that. All the priests ever knew about his intentions was his 'Yes' in reply to Father O'Shea's question. And it was not long after this that he began to experience a change of heart or a change of mind.

CHAPTER XXXIII

Return to the Normal

RENÉ'S change of mind, and the deep emotional shift, was a process not abrupt, but of so profoundly radical a kind that, from the first moment this movement set in, there was something in the nature of a revolution. It possibly began as a result of his lectures. These were elementary, but they did take him back to his normal way of thought: to things belonging to the sphere of reason, rather than to the spiritist degeneration which had ensued upon the suicide of Hester (which is not, of course, to say that his contacts with God were a 'degeneration', but what led to them was a degeneration for him, the springs of whose life lay far away from the extremes of mysticism). The reason began to assert itself once more—it was a rather queer sensation for him at first. He would, from time to time, find himself thinking about something pertaining to the world of the intellect, which had been so completely displaced by what he soon was to call 'Hesteria'. So gradually he recovered his mental health—with a strict limitation which did not, however, make any practical difference, only a profound modification. The 'frozenness', as it has been described, remained. All that occurred was that he came out of the highly artificial atmosphere he had adopted as a temporary sheath of cotton-wool, and attempted to force his invalid personality back into life again. These developments progressively weakened the clutch of the dead woman, and, as part of the same movement away from spiritual realities, the reality of God receded. He did not repudiate the latter, but merely ceased to experience it. This was a painful movement, away from 'Hesteria' back to the rational; for of course there must be pain in any movement away from something powerfully experienced over to something else violently contradicting it. By the beginning of his third month at the College he was for the first time thinking objectively of the suicide of his wife—and this

389

caused him the acutest discomfort. At first, this return to objectivity had the shock of a revelation. His old love for Hester and their comradely solidarity in the days of hardship, which had been the Hester of the hospital, and which had survived until now, struggled against the unmasking and debunking that had begun. But once the destructive analysis was under way nothing could arrest it.—Why had Hester killed herself? It had been, of course, the culmination of a long period during which, day in and day out, she had been attempting to move him from the position he had taken up. But it was for purely selfish reasons that she desired this return to England. It was not, as frequently she would assert, because of her concern for his career. That was the bunk. It was her private life, not his public life, that was the issue. It was simply because she wished to be near her mother, near Susan, and all her other friends—that was why she was trying to force him to return to England. Then a genuine hatred was there, almost as compelling as love for mother and friends. She did entertain the most vicious feelings where Canada was concerned; she was ferociously obsessed with the memory of the ostracism they had suffered for more than three years. Mr. Furber (who actually in his ghastly way had befriended them) she loathed, and refused to concede him any merit. No Canadian was capable of a good action. No doubt all this bitterness, and rancour, enduring for so long, had built up the state of mind which had made her capable, ultimately, of her furious act. All the circumstances, too, of the fire; incendiarism and murder, and the subsequent execution of the criminal, had done nothing to steady her mind.

But these considerations did not absolve her from the original charge of a destructive selfishness. For had she not placed her private wishes in competition with everything he desired? With insolence she demanded that he should act upon her counsels and not his own,

Her will did not prevail, in spite of long and violent struggling. But does someone kill himself, or herself, because their advice is not taken? Yes: at least Hester did. He now understood precisely why Hester had taken her life. It was with hatred that he brought his analysis to the point at which he declared, 'Hester's suicide was an act of insane coercion. My cold refusal to do what she wanted crazed her egoistic will. She was willing to die in order to force me off the path I had chosen. She probably thought, among other things, that her suicide would oblige me to give up my job at the University. She was acting vindictively.' Having arrived at this explicit condemnation of his dead wife—having denied her any of the usual motives for suicide: namely inability to support the pain of living, life having become an unbearable torture; having decided that her suicide was committed as an act of supreme coercion, and malign retribution, there was a question which had to be answered. He had not asked this directly up till then. Was Hester insane? He was obliged to answer that she must have been demented to do what she did: and had, therefore, not been responsible. In spite of this, Hester had revealed a character disfigured by an unlovely vanity, René told himself. Now he cast his horrified gaze back upon the *graffito* occupying the slab in the police mortuary. There was the severed head; but, in spite of the severance, self-sufficient; as though it could exist all by itself; and, as he stared in memory, with a hardly sane intensity, upon what had been so dear to him, severity melted, his recriminations dissolved, and he almost plunged back again into the 'Hesteria' he was abandoning. It was with a mad wrench that he dragged himself away from a new surrender. He all but sank back into the old love and comradeship. And now, as never before, his heart seemed about to break, as he fixed his eyes upon the two slender blood-darkened legs, so pathetically isolated, one behind the other, exhibits displayed in a police court case.— 'The severed legs of the deceased.'

He was striding up and down his cell as he was in travail with his new picture of his dead wife. At this point he banged himself down aggressively upon a chair. 'This sentiment that misleads,' he reproached himself. It was just the same with his Mother! We (men) have all these tender reactions about any women, but they (women) on their side do not entertain feelings of that sort about us. It is a one-way sentiment. All their life is spent in fooling us, in creating such feelings as these. To make themselves desirable, 'little', pathetic. They very well understand what a wealth of tenderness is associated with the sensation of pity. In most cases they are the *smaller* animal, sometimes only half the size of the male. This they put to wonderful advantage. They congratulate themselves when they hear themselves called 'little rabbit' or 'little squirrel' or some such diminutive; it signifies that they have succeeded. Then an unfailing *passivity* is a prettiness that goes with smallness. They ideally, in this ancient technique, are the passive little things to whom things are done. (The only women who have discarded this technique are the Americans, with a corresponding loss of something of vital use to the female. Had Hemingway (in *For Whom the Bell Tolls*) been putting his hero into a fleabag with an American woman, 'little rabbit' would not have been the endearment employed.) So René's mind whirled on. And when he looked at the *graffito* again (in his brightly-lit memory) he saw nothing but a masterpiece of illusionism. How uniquely useful it was that the head (the face) was intact. She had, even in death, whisked it out of the way, when something was about to smash or disfigure it, as she lay under the truck. That *must* survive intact, to pull the heartstrings. In the Momaco newspapers, in their account of the suicide, they had said that her head rolled away into the gutter, miraculously escaping destruction. Ah! thought René, she had steered it to safety, using the neck to give whatever impulse desired. He now regarded his *graffito* with the scorn which would be meted out to some unmasked impostor, more especially when the technique employed in the imposture had been designed to awaken pity and tenderness.

At this point he went to his suitcase and took from it Hester's letter, which had been delivered to him in the hospital. He examined it sentence by sentence. The text of it was as follows. *What can I say, René darling, except to ask your forgiveness. I loathe this country so much, where I can see you burying yourself. I cannot leave you physically—go away from you back to England. I can only go out of the world. Good-bye, my darling. Ess.*

When he had read this in the hospital, he had smiled tenderly as he saw the handwriting, but later on had burst into a hurricane of tears, beating his head up and down on the pillow. Now he violently crushed the letter in his hand, tore it into several pieces, flung it upon the floor, sprang up and stamped upon it. 'Quelle comédie! Quelle sale comédie!' And he spat down at the ruined sheets— 'Fumier!'

Immediately after this scene, nine weeks after his arrival in the College, he sent a note to McKenzie, upon College of the Sacred Heart paper; but asking him not to reveal his where-abouts. 'Soon I shall be back in Momaco,' he added. He enclosed a larger envelope, stamped and addressed, asking McKenzie to forward any letters which might have arrived for him. Five days later this large envelope returned, well swelled out with mail. There was a long letter from McKenzie, a couple of cheques from the University, several letters from the New York publisher, one accepting the work, and offering him generous terms, and the rest urging him to reply. There were other letters, of less urgency. He despatched telegrams at once to McKenzie, to Momaco University (Registrar), and to the U.S. publisher, accepting terms.

But this first striking triumph over 'Hesteria' was not as yet conclusive. A piteous and reproachful, Hester dogged him for a time, approaching him in moments when he was off his guard, or genially relaxed, having laid aside his new militancy; or even during Mass. There was one occasion when Hester won a distinct victory. He had gone to bed, after listening to the radio for two hours or more. Buffalo N.Y. was only a few miles away, and that was the station in to which he always tuned. 'Henry Aldridge', that splendid satire on the American schoolboy, was part of the programme. One of the things which had lightened the burden of their life at the Hotel Blundell had been precisely this radio-serial. As he lay on his bed, listening to the whining voice, full of a dry cunning, of Homer Brown; to the tremulous and querulous appeals of the hero; and to the ironic expostulation of Aldridge Senior, massively resigned at having given birth to such a son— absorbed in this wonderful entertainment, without realizing it, he had slipped back into the years of evenings passed in the Room, where Hester and he were enabled to forget the ghastly isolation and boredom of their lives. Nothing so much as the American radio, with all its wonderful gusto, the many-sidedness of its interests, provided the necessary anaesthesia. There was one moment at which he forgot where he was, and it was his impulse to turn to Hester, to share with her the joy of some quip of Schnozzle Durante. It was at that point that he realized what had been happening, and that he had allowed himself to be led into a past where the living Hester was unavoidably to be encountered. But *after* that, and quite consciously, he gave himself up to the retrospective enjoyment of the warm comfort of this shabby room in the Blundell Annexe, the zero weather outside, and the wonderful companionship of this woman he had shared so much with, and with whom he would soon coagulate in the pneumatic expanses of the Murphy bed. This was one of the pleasantest evenings he had spent at the College.

But next day he made up for this lapse. He took his cue from the happenings of the last evening, spent, in imagination, with Hester, culminating in the ardour of conjugal embraces. Here was a major factor in the things of value to the 'little rabbit', in her creation of a male tenderness of ludicrous sentimental intensity: the ecstasies of the marriage-bed. 'Well!' snorted René, he owed nothing to Hester in that connection. The lubricious little beast had got as much out of him as he had got out of her! (In using such expressions about her he was not so lost to all sense of justice as not to realize it was a striking case of pot calling the kettle black. And for that matter, his own abnormal addiction to the sports of Venus was something he never ceased to regret.) Did he owe her any more tenderness than she owed him on that score? Of course not! They were quits. A dog and a bitch were not sentimental about such things as that. Why should men and women be? Legitimate subjects for sentimental attachments, if there were any, were of a different kind; perhaps to do with offspring or matters relating to fellowship in man's destiny of a being condemned to death. Having unmasked the 'little rabbit', he proceeded, in detail, to debunk the claim of the woman that she is conferring some favour upon the male by going to bed with him. That of course is nonsense, for is it not her *duty* to do so, as it is man's duty also to play his part in nature's comedy? He is usually, it is true, quite ready to comply with nature's commands, since nature rewarded fulfilment of these functions with delights embodied in the nervous system. Where the snag exists is in the great disparity between the social and intellectual needs, and fundamental tastes, of the man and the woman: and the fact that they are supposed to cohabit. It is the cohabitation that is the trouble. This is so well understood by every mature man and woman as to be a commonplace, though of course it does not follow that they admit to this understanding. Finally, he looked at the suicide again. Was any pity due from him to this mutilated corpse? How pitiable almost any corpse is! But *this* was an aggressive corpse—it was death militant. *This* dead body was there with a purpose. It was designed to upset his applecart, violently to interfere with his life. It was a Japanese-like suicide, a form of vengeance. Suppose you are a Japanese, and, on arriving home one evening, you find a corpse on your doorstep. You recognize it as that of a man with a grievance. You know that this man has taken his life in order to injure you. If you were this Japanese, what would your attitude be towards the aggressive corpse? You could not be otherwise than extremely indignant. You would kick the body off your doorstep, spitting on it contemptuously. This imaginary drama from far Japan gave René great satisfaction. He decided that Hester dead was even less worthy of respect than Hester alive. Nor did he fail to review the sheer volume of sentimentality attracted by death. On all sides he found himself beset by false sentiment. He congratulated himself upon the good work he had done in reducing in his personal life these mounds of slush to reasonable proportions. Towards the end of this period he felt he had cleansed things to such an extent that he could end this particular activity. He had driven Hester out of his mind, in which she had dangerously intruded. So all that was overcome, and he could now once more proceed on his way.

But to start with he must say farewell to these wonderfully considerate young priests, who had done their best to help him, and allowed him to live among them almost as a fellow-priest. First, he visited Father O'Shea, with whom he had formed a friendly relationship. 'I regret that I am going to leave you,' he said.

'When?' asked the priest, looking at him calmly and appraisingly. 'You have been called away or something?' he asked lazily.

'Something,' René replied. Father O'Shea had no very strong missionary impulses. He had been a seminarian; but he had preferred not to enter the priesthood, he had gone into business instead. That is how he began. 'Life in an office, however,' he had explained to René, 'obliged me to become a lickspittle, to abase myself to such continuous servility that I gave it up and returned to my original idea of becoming a priest. In a primitive democracy such as we enjoy in our community life here at the College, it may not be an ideal type of existence for every kind of man, but at least one does not have to lick the shoes of half-a-dozen lousy power-addicts every morning, and offer one's bottom to be kicked.'

Canadian business life, like American business life, is of a somewhat Oriental type. The big shot haughtily isolates himself, and all the department-heads under him follow his example, exacting as much servility as it is possible to extract from a human being. It may be that Big Money is somewhat more democratic in the States at present; but in Canada these conditions still fearfully flourish. Father O'Shea's experience was in no way an unusual one. Just what Father O'Shea did *not* say was that his clothes were of the most expensive cloth —and although the deep black was obligatory, it was very becoming to Father O'Shea. Then he smuggled over from Buffalo numbers of excellent cigars. Economic worries were unknown to him—no income-tax, no rent, no keeping up with the Joneses. He was one of the priests who did a great deal of work over in Buffalo, where he would make his way in the College car with his small grip—which was never examined by the Customs officers, who were all Catholic to a man—Poles, or Wops, or Germans. So it seemed to René that this priest did not have so bad a life—especially in view of the fact that St. Thomas Aquinas was a study he greatly enjoyed. Lastly, he was an ambitious man, and would no doubt go to headquarters before very long, and might end as the head of the Order of St. Maurice.

The young priest, whose horizons were far wider than the walls of a Seminary, admired the worldly success of René, approved in his private mind of René's departure: for to stop much longer in this neck of the woods would have reduced René in his estimation. 'I didn't think you could stick it so long here,' he said, smiling.

'The peace here is terrific. You are so used to it that you fail to appreciate it,' René told him.

Father O'Shea stretched his arms out to their full length, as he said with a sleepy yawn, 'Gosh, I could do with a little less peace sometimes.'

As René was leaving the cell, Father O'Shea enquired, 'You said you were becoming a Catholic. You have not given up the idea, I hope?'

'Ah no,' said René. 'Quite soon, when my mind is entirely at peace, I shall be reading those books you gave me.' He looked up at the priest suddenly, with an expression which startled Father O'Shea. 'But there is no peace for me, I should tell you. I see a fiery mist wherever I direct my eyes. But the fire is not outside me, the fire is in my brain.'

Father O'Shea blinked. 'You had a bad break, René. You ought to see a physician.'

Father Moody, the enthusiast, the bright-eyed missionary, was disappointed, but he made no reference to this at all. He had cherished the hope that this well-known professor and author would move into the Roman communion within those four walls. But Professor Harding might return to the Sacred Heart, might he not? And he lavished his innocent flatteries upon the departing visitor. O'Neill, who shared the disappointment of the Registrar, shared it genteelly. The colourless but amiable Superior concealed his satisfaction that this prolonged visit was drawing to a close. An orthodox period for visitors (who did not usually dress in a cassock) was at most three days, not almost three long months.

It should perhaps be added that a couple of weeks after

René's departure a cheque was received by the Registrar for
a small sum representing the fees for lectures which René had
delivered during his stay at the College. So that possible indiscretion, retrospectively, was eliminated.

CHAPTER XXXIV

The Cemetery of Shells

BACK in Momaco; René found himself, as he put it, among bowed heads and muted voices. He was received as a man struck down, and, rumour had it, actually crazed with grief. He was looked at rather timidly, as though he might, unless handled very carefully, bite. He was obliged to improvise a technique, in order to cope with all this misunderstanding: for he regarded it as preferable not to say, 'My dear sir, you are mistaken: My wife was a selfish, scheming old bag, whose death placed me in a very awkward position.' Self-defensively he accepted the rule of a grief-stricken husband. They were capable of dismissing him from the University (at the instance of the wives of the members of the Board) if he showed himself otherwise than paralysed with uxorious sorrow. When someone came up to him and began offering him, in a choked voice, his heartfelt sympathy, René just answered with a muffled gasp and an hysterical squeeze of the hand. Sometimes his squeeze was so painfully compressive, though, and the noise he made in his throat was so fierce, that the would-be mourner would say afterwards, 'I think that man's mind has been turned by what he has gone through. He seizes one's hand like some wild animal.'

With McKenzie, whom he trusted like a brother, he was quite explicit. 'I am not heart-broken. I have no sensation of grief whatever. I have thought all that out, since I came out of the hospital. The fire at the Hotel Blundell, and still more the other things associated with the fire, left my wife a little mental. I did my best; she just set herself to obstruct everything, as if she were possessed. Her death was her last act of obstruction. Also it showed how deeply her reason had been affected.—We had got to such a pitch just before she threw herself under the truck that it seemed to be a matter of her life or mine, almost. For I understand a great many things

399

that she could not, and she wanted to drag me down into her backwater, and into modes of life from which I had rescued myself, into a decaying society, into the rotten old dreamlands of her youth. She clung to me like a drowning woman, and her suicide was her last effort to drag me under. So you see . . . but I must put on a mask of grief for these good Momacoans. It is a bore, but they would think me an awful brute if I did not do so.' This was quite a temperate, quite normal-sounding statement, and McKenzie accepted it as all there was to know about this sad affair. He never asked him-self whether René had not been associated with his wife in a neuropathic duet.

Meanwhile, with a feverish energy, René proceeded with the work of digging himself in with concrete and steel, so that no change of fortune could overtake him again. The successful 'young' historian of the old days in London was one man— buoyant, elastic, inventive, and fearless: the present man, professor of history at the University of Momaco, Dominion of Canada, was quite another. He no longer even believed in his theories of a new approach to History; that had almost become a racket; for him it had all frozen into a freak anti-historical museum, of which he was the Keeper, containing many libel-lous wax-works of famous kings and queens. He carried on mechanically with what the bright, rushing, idealistic mind of another man had begun. The man of former days had been replaced by a machine, which was a good imitation of the reality, which had superficially much of the charm, even the vivacity of the living model, but, when it came to one of the acid tests of authenticity, it would be recognized as an imposture.

If the personality is emptied of mother-love, emptied of wife-love, emptied of the illusions upon which sex-in-society depends, and finally emptied of the illusions upon which the will to create depends, then the personality becomes a shell. In René's case that daring and defiant act, the resignation of his professorship in 1939, had made imperative the acquisition of something massive to counterbalance the loss, else dis-equilibrium could not but ensue. But, reacting with bitterness to criticism, he began hurling overboard the conventional ballast, mother-love going first.

The process of radical revaluation, the process which was responsible for the revolutionary character of his work, that analysis, turned inwards (upon, for instance, such things as the intimate structure of domestic life), this furious analysis began disintegrating many relationships and attitudes which only an exceptionally creative spirit, under very favourable conditions, can afford to dispense with. Into this situation came world war, came also Canada, with all that means; came the three years in the Hotel Blundell—three mortal, barren, desolating years. A major hotel fire put a violent close to that period and so far nothing irretrievable had happened. The man who left England in the summer of 1939 was still there. If only latent, what was necessary for full vitality was intact. It was from that point onwards that either the personality had to reflower, as it were, or there must be degeneration. There was nothing that compelled degeneration—it was the bitter struggle that then began which led to it. The incipient dementia of his wife, and the pressure of its unreason upon him; another pressure from within, namely the pressure of his own will-to-success, of the most vulgar type, these pressures, both irrational and both touched with dementia, brought into being, as has been seen, something insanely militant, from which the finer inspirations of his intellect shrank, and with which his original self found it impossible to co-exist.

There was this too; whatever he might say, he had been deprived of his natural audience; it is not until he loses it that a man of letters, or of ideas, knows how much he depends upon the deep cultural soil in which he has grown, or upon that atmosphere and that climate of thought. His withdrawal from that into an outlandish culture-less world (as he, even more than Hester, felt it to be), the long obliterating years of the war; in the end, the necessity of accepting this tenth-rate alternative to what had been his backgrounds before his resignation—all of this deeply disillusioning situation had, first of all, impaired, and, a little later, injured irreparably his creative will. He was half-way through that process while he and McKenzie were working upon the foundations of his new enterprise. Such a process does not proceed illuminated by consciousness, where it may be watched, and where steps may

be taken, perhaps, to arrest it. So it was that one day consciousness asserted itself, and René discovered that he was
only a half-crazed replica of his former self. He did actually
perceive this for a moment, and then it was swallowed up by
other emotions; but the revelation, which had horrified him,
was not obliterated.

It was not, of course, at all as a wreck, or as a gutted shell
or as an empty hangover of himself, that he appeared to
himself or to anybody else. Naturally he continued to live as
if there had been no such tragic fracture of the personality.
There was still enough animal vitality in the shell, and enough
residue of ambitious intellectual potency to carry on 'brilliantly' with his professional duties, carefully to pilot himself
through the social shallows of Momaco (with enough, but just
enough, control not to explode, amorously or vituperatively,
and to wreck everything); to pass pleasant hours with the
McKenzies, to conduct his business efficiently with New York.
McKenzie was very attached to him, and though he could not
fail to notice an alteration he disregarded it: there were plenty
of things in the immediate past amply to account for quite a
lot of change if it made its appearance. McKenzie felt that the
new haunted look was only temporary.

René was tenacious of rules; there was no slackening in his
observance of the rules for the conduct of his life which he
occasionally formulated. He had laid it down that there must,
under no circumstances, be another marriage. Introducing
into his life a new factor, charged with all the potency of sex
and all its unpredictability, would not be in the interests of
security: and to the ideal of material security he was dedicated. He was surrounded by attractive, unmarried women,
and his temperament was at boiling point. So he found this
rule very irksome.

The loneliness he experienced at this period was almost
indescribable. To start with, it was now for the first time that
he comprehended what it meant to be an exile. On the one
hand, like his dead wife before him, he suffered from an
unceasing ache for the old condition of things, and for the
English scene; which, of course, he promptly pulverized with
the same arguments he had employed with Hester. This was

very unpleasant and very unexpected. On the other hand, his loneliness produced, temporarily, a quite violent antipathy to the Canadian. He had to make a rule about this: it was to the effect that he must never regard a Canadian as anything but a Briton disguised with an American accent, and an anti-British bias as big as a house. In any case, the vacuum left by the departed Hester was large, darksome and chilling. The temptation to provide himself with a human buffer against the environing cold (within and without) was at times painful. But, in the event, all he did for himself in that direction was to spend such time as he had to spare with a chocolate-eyed Peasoup, of course in another quarter of the city.

The fire in his brain, of which he had spoken to Father O'Shea, would sometimes kindle in the most startling fashion. He would be very near to bursting out of this cage he had constructed for himself, with a shriek of rage which would have frozen the blood of Momaco. He was probably prevented from doing this by a minor explosion when he was alone with McKenzie one evening, the latter's wife being on a motoring trip with the Rushforths. This came about quite suddenly.

'The success of your book has been tremendous,' McKenzie had remarked. 'I believe I am even more pleased about this than you are yourself.'

'I am perfectly sure you are,' René coldly sneered.

'Oh dear! Is *that* how you feel!' McKenzie looked embarrassed.

'Yes, I feel like that . . . very much like that,' René answered evenly, as if he were repeating something. 'The success . . . *the tremendous success,* of which you speak, does not make my heart beat faster. As a matter of fact, when I think of it, I feel a little sick.' He leapt to his feet. McKenzie could only see his face in profile, but it was pulled in all directions, he could see, as a result of some mental convulsion.

'No! I feel a tremendous nausea at my tremendous success. I am sick—I am terribly sick; and I am *bored*'—his voice became suddenly guttural. 'I am not bored, no, I am not bored, I am butchered.'

But when the French house-boy arrived to sweep away the empty coffee-cups, he shouted, 'Et toi! n'est-ce pas que tu es emmerdé par l'hospitalité du locataire! N'est-ce pas qu'il est emmerdeur!' Balancing the cups, the house-boy jazzed out of the room.

'B-o-r-e-d—never speak to me of boredom again. I'm split down the middle with dreary horror—I am squashed flat with the horrible weight of boredom! My body is in a torturer's press, the bones are being squeezed through the skin; my mind as well, it is in a malignant vice. It is not my body, it is my mind that is in the press.' He stared round at his friend. 'Yes, Ian, I am in a torture chamber, not in a yawning gallery. My book, my wonderful book! I hope my book bores everybody as much as I am . . . as much as I soon shall be . . . soon be . . . croaked with the stink of this man-hole.' He looked down with a bleak grin at McKenzie. 'Ian, cheer up! I killed a student yesterday who said "Aw, Professor, don't you ever want to yell, Professor?" '

McKenzie, very uneasy, produced a polite laugh. 'You were quite right to kill that student. I have been wanting to do so for some time. But, René, don't be silly about your book. It is a very fine book indeed . . .'

'Stop!' René panted in the bass-de profundis—an involuntary command. He dropped back upon the sofa, where he had been sitting, as if dropped by somebody who just now had violently snatched him up, as if a supernatural being had whipped him up into the standing position, forced his terror-struck 'Stop!' out of him: and now had dropped him back on to the sofa with a gravitational thud.

McKenzie was a sober man, not prone to feyness, but he experienced the presence of the supernatural. He seemed to intuit that poor René *had been dropped back*—that some power (and he felt an evil power) was responsible for the behaviour of the body of his friend, which had become an automaton. And he responded to the word 'Stop!' as he would to the command of a god. His tongue froze to his palate, he sat stock-still.

René had plunged his face into his hollow hands. 'That is too silly; that is all past,' came a hollow, precipitate whisper. 'Don't you understand?'

'I understand,' responded McKenzie, a little awestruck,

satisfying the categorical intervention of that by which René was possessed—that which had picked him up, and that which had thrown him down; at the same time replying tenderly to his friend's appeal.

After some minutes René removed his hands and turned his face towards the other. McKenzie was very shocked by the extraordinary alteration. The face now presented to him was haggard and despairing: it made him feel, somehow, that the face had just been vomiting, although of course it had not. Actually, that was what it was *about* to do; with a series of rapid spasmodic movements René simultaneously, and with surprising deftness, leant abruptly sideways to be sick, and yanked a handkerchief out of his pocket, and his hand flew with it to his mouth. A small quantity of vomit was in his handkerchief, which he folded and refolded, and poked away into the side pocket of his jacket.

'My brain is burning.' He began to speak stolidly and matter-of-factly, as if transmitting a piece of information about one of the organs of his body. 'I have had that sense of a hot devouring something inside my skull, and of a light as well, of a fire-coloured light, since that day I banged my head in the police morgue. You know, I told you how I fell.'

'Yes, I remember, René: you hurt yourself very badly.'

McKenzie looked grave and dejected. This was the first time anything of this kind had occurred between René and himself. But René grew calmer; at the same time, however, he became taciturn. In about ten minutes he took his leave.

This scene had revealed to McKenzie an inner situation of a severity which he had not, prior to this, so much as suspected. He maintained the strictest silence regarding what he had learnt, only informing his wife that René was not quite himself, but refusing to be explicit. There was one subject which, in future, in conversation with René, he was very careful to avoid, namely his friend's book.

The real depth of the chasm into which he had involuntarily been gazing, was not realized even yet by him. But he did understand that to mention his poor friend's latest work was the showdown. To speak of *that* meant that one had to think

of René as he had been, and as he now was—had to speak of
his decadence: of his *death*.

Not that McKenzie would have gone so far as to have
envisaged the extinction of his personality. He regarded this
condition as a neurotic phase, something that would pass. He
could not, naturally, appreciate the full—the massive, the
terrible—truth of the position. The fact was that René Harding
had stood up to the Gods, when he resigned his professorship in England. The Gods had struck him down. They had
humiliated him, made him a laughing-stock, cut him off from
all recovery; they had driven him into the wilderness. The
hotel fire gave him a chance of a second lease of life. He
seized it with a mad alacrity; he was not, he had not been,
killed—he had survived the first retaliatory blow—the expulsion, the ostracism. He was still *almost*, and up-to-a-point, his
original self, when he and McKenzie were scrutinizing the
philosophic foundations of his contemporary literary enterprise; though already he was being shaken by the unceasing
psychological pressure of the obsessed Hester. In fact, it had
been *then* that the suppression, the battening down, began:
he was obliged to push under and hold down the gathering
instability and hysteria. When the Gods struck the second
time there was, from the moment of the blow, and the days
spent in the white silence of the hospital, no chance that he
could survive, at all intact. You cannot kill a man twice, the
Gods cannot strike *twice* and the man survive.

The outburst at McKenzie's had not been a confession, but
was something like it; it was an unmasking of a most thorough
description. The act of doing this had been a shock to René, as
it had been a shock to McKenzie. When he came out of his fit
he made a resolution never to permit this to happen again. In
fact, he locked himself up twice as tight as he had been locked
up before.

The presence of all this molten material within did not
affect the impenetrability of the shell, nor did it interfere with
the insect-like activity with which he proceeded with the

concreting of his position of academic success and widely acclaimed authorship. He even managed to write some quite authentic-looking magazine articles, 'from the pen of the celebrated British historian, Professor René Harding'.

It was with unusual rapidity that the existence of so distinguished a man upon the North-American Continent was recognized. It was not more than a year or two after the scene just described in the McKenzie home that a great university in one of the eastern States of the U.S.A. offered him a professorship. With a kind of mechanical thrill of frigid delight he accepted it, after expressing his great regret at leaving them to the Governors and Chancellor of Momaco University. As to McKenzie, that was another matter. He was actually extremely distressed at this parting. Almost he was frightened at finding himself withdrawing from the warm personal contact of these friends. At one moment, this fear was so present to him that he felt he must not accept *yet* such an offer from the United States, but stick to Momaco. He was within an ace of sending a letter to the American University to say he had changed his mind. But he did not do so, and in a few months he was installed in a small, warm, wooden dwelling not far from the campus of this much more pretentious seat of learning, five hundred miles farther south; and the Faculty had no idea that it was a glacial shell of a man who had come to live among them, mainly because they were themselves unfilled with anything more than a little academic stuffing.

Date Due